Outskirts

Queer Experiences on the Fringe

Edited by

D'Lane R. Compton *and* Amy L. Stone

NEW YORK UNIVERSITY PRESS

New York

NEW YORK UNIVERSITY PRESS
New York www.nyupress.org

Library of Congress Cataloging-in-Publication Data
Names: Compton, D'Lane R. (D'Lane Rebecca), 1977– editor. | Stone, Amy L., editor.
Title: Outskirts : queer experiences on the fringe / edited by D'Lane R. Compton
and Amy L. Stone.
Description: New York : New York University Press, [2024] |
Includes bibliographical references and index.
Identifiers: LCCN 2023030012 (print) | LCCN 2023030013 (ebook) |
ISBN 9781479821488 (hardback ; alk. paper) | ISBN 9781479821501 (paperback ; alk. paper) |
ISBN 9781479821532 (ebook) | ISBN 9781479821549 (ebook other)
Subjects: LCSH: Gays—United States—Social conditions. | Sexual minorities—United
States—Social conditions.
Classification: LCC HQ76.3.U5 O9925 2024 (print) | LCC HQ76.3.U5 (ebook) |
DDC 306.76/60973—dc23/eng/20230902
LC record available at https://lccn.loc.gov/2023030012
LC ebook record available at https://lccn.loc.gov/2023030013

This book is printed on acid-free paper, and its binding materials are chosen for strength
and durability. We strive to use environmentally responsible suppliers and materials to the
greatest extent possible in publishing our books.

Manufactured in the United States of America

10 9 8 7 6 5 4 3 2 1

Also available as an ebook

For the Kids,

especially Benjamin, Maggie, Sierra, and Emily.

CONTENTS

Introduction

Theorizing from the Outskirts Enhances Sociology

AMY L. STONE AND D'LANE R. COMPTON

We, the editors, are gender non-conforming, queer white people doing queer work in Texas and the US South. Our locations, both physical and social, have strongly influenced our work. Neither of us has ever subscribed to the idea that there are places where queers do not belong. We use "queer" as a shorthand to understand the breadth of gender and sexual non-conformity, including transgender identities and the refusal and ambivalence around bounded identities. We also draw on the older meanings of queer that evoked odd or perplexing ways of being that deviate from norms and despoil understandings of norms about space, place, and identity. We have not lived in metropolitan centers of US lesbian, gay, bisexual, transgender, and queer (LGBTQ) life—major cities like Chicago, San Francisco, New York, and Los Angeles. Indeed, we are fascinated by the view from the outskirts of queer life, the places that are not at the center of typical academic inquiry into queer life, and what can be learned from these locations.

Our intention in this work is to examine the places, spaces, and identities that decenter queer cultural stereotypes and associations. Being queer and residing in Texas and the South gives us a particular view that challenges prior assumptions about LGBTQ life. There are three interrelated aspects of this work and experience: our sites of study being in less commonly studied locations; our topics of study—LGBTQ life in the US—being academically marginalized within sociology; and our own identities as researchers and academics being liminal. Each layer offers a different view of the outskirts of queerness. Currently, we, the editors, live and work outside the geographic centers of queer life, and working on the outskirts has benefited our careers. LGBTQ geographic centers, such as the Castro area of San Francisco, are generally seen to be necessary, productive, and useful for queer life, and these centers impact both everyday narratives and academic theories about the queer social world.

Growing up in rural Texas, it never occurred to Compton that cowboys could not be gay. In fact, the life of a cowboy seems quite aligned with queer life. Historically, cowboys were looked down upon as working-class or even an underclass. They were often unmarried and considered loners, outsiders, and outlaws. Indeed, as a child, Compton assumed the Wild West outlaws Butch and Sundance were life partners and more recently wondered if they were perhaps a poly throuple with their companion Etta Place. Bank robbers George Curry and Kid Curry Logan appeared to have a similar relationship (Kid even took Curry's name at some point). Macho outlaw Johnny Ringo killed himself after fellow outlaw Curly Bill died in a shootout. And the list goes on. Most of all, cowboys never seemed to want to stay with the girl. They were often portrayed in movies as leaving offers of a warm meal and warm bed of a wanting woman for sleeping on rocks or meeting up with their male friends, or simply riding off into the distance alone. Compton's transy straightboy identity rendered this choice incomprehensible. Overall, cowboy life was presented as void of women and in complete contradistinction of mainstream family life. Reminiscent of themes from *Brokeback Mountain*, the solitary life of cowboys seemed to be a precursor to the solitary life of being gay in a small town, and rurality was a great defense mechanism that allowed for autonomy and living life outside of the mainstream gaze. In small towns, people can know things without acknowledging them or talking about them. Growing up, Compton found these paradoxes normal and found people to be both complicated and predictable and just because something wasn't talked about didn't mean that it wasn't there.

Compton's first book project described where LGBTQ same-sex couples live, putting aside common assumptions about where LGBTQ live to look at the data. It focused on a demographic description of same-sex households and their locations, broadening understandings of LGBTQ geography (Baumle, Compton, and Poston, Jr 2009; Compton and Baumle 2012). They found same-sex households in 99% of American counties or parishes (Baumle et al. 2009). Compton's later work focuses on increasing and improving data and measures regarding sexual and gender minorities (Lagos and Compton 2021).

Stone's entry into queer life came through white dyke culture in un-usual places. They first learned about dyke culture at Girl Scout camp in the mountains of Southern California. There, in a remote camp on the edges of the Pacific Crest Trail, they learned lesbian feminist folk music songs by Cris Williamson and Ferron, songs taught to them by young white women with suspiciously short hair. They remember their first childhood crush on an adolescent counselor. The camp counselor held their hand when they were afraid while climbing into a narrow cave next to a waterfall, a situation that in retrospect seems hopelessly vaginal. As an evangelical teen, they won a creative writing contest at their high school for an essay regarding romantic feelings they had about their counselor who did not shave their legs and clearly had a girlfriend at camp. "I just really looked up to her, that's what the story was about," they told their friends. As they grew older, they discovered that only some young women want to spend their summers in the company of other women.

Their first lesbian bar experience was in Osaka, Japan, a tiny bar named Jellyfish that had fewer than ten barstools pressed with little standing room behind. They were one of three white patrons who regu-larly came and were almost always mistaken for their friend Andrea, who also was white with brown hair. They would sit up until all hours sharing stories in Japanese and English with other patrons, ignoring the young Japanese women who wanted to pet their hair and slide phone numbers on thin slips of paper into their hands. "Your hair reminds me of a doll I had as a child; it's so soft," these young women remarked, which felt uncomfortably like being chased for being young, white, and American. It was a strange sort of exoticization that felt connected to their grandfather's involvement in the occupation of Japan by Ameri-can forces after World War II. Their first feminist bookstore experience was in Northampton, Massachusetts; they had inadvertently attended a liberal arts college next to a small city that was referred to as a "lesbian mecca." They realized how lesbian-dominated the city was when they saw a white woman motorist shout "breeder!" at a white man jaywalk-ing. The bookstore was filled with women-centric materials that reso-nated with white cultural feminist culture, like the small bookcase next to the front door with lesbian and feminist-made pornography on VHS tape featuring curvy white women with armpit hair. In the Detroit enclave city of Hamtramck, they loved people watching at the working-class butch-femme bar, where raging fights would break out between butches with long mullets and a fierce right hook. The whiteness of the club was a testament to the stark segregation in the enclave, which had been carved out in the middle of Detroit. A Girl Scout camp, a lesbian bar, a feminist bookstore, a butch-femme bar in the suburbs of Detroit—all but one of these smaller spaces were predominantly white, all centered women who were attracted to other women, and yet none of these geographic locations dominate the public imaginary of where queer life supposedly takes place.

Stone's work has focused on how place matters in understanding LGBTQ life in the United States. Their dissertation investigated transgender inclusion in non-discrimination ordinances in small and medium-size cities in Michigan in the 1990s. They expanded the project into their first book, which reported on a national study of the ballot measures that often challenge these ordinances (Stone 2012). One of their most profound memories of conducting interviews was speaking to LGBTQ organizers in states like Montana, Nebraska, and Missouri, where most of the same-sex marriage bans were fought unsuccessfully. They developed their perspective further after moving to Texas for work and discovering its vibrant queer life. The queerest activity they ever indulged in San Antonio was to perform in femme drag on a stage in front of almost five thousand people, raising money for AIDS service organizations during a festival event called Cornyation, a mock debutante pageant during the city's annual festival. Their face was almost unidentifiable in makeup done by a Latina trans woman with a history in the local drag community. Stone went on to write two books on LGBTQ involvement in festival life in the South and Southwest (Stone 2017; 2022). This work focused on urban cultural forms like Mardi Gras krewes and festival organizations in the South and Southwest that have been overlooked by many scholars who have investigated queer life.

We have often engendered reactions from others as a result of studying queer life on the outskirts. Reactions to our work demonstrate how even academics carry restrictive (and biased) notions of where queer life is and where queers belong. At the beginning of Compton's career, post-presentation conversations were largely centered not on the actual paper they presented but around their experiences as an openly queer person living and working in Texas. Their experience challenged stereotypes and cultural assumptions about queer life and so piqued the curiosity of attendees. Popular images of Texas focus on its red-state qualities such as being rural, conservative, intolerant, and resistant to change, which is contrary to the image of an LGBTQ person who is stereotyped as liberal, urban, and progressive. A fellow academic in New York once curled their lip at Stone and said "Texas? I don't think Texas and gay go together." Stone just shrugged and noted that Texas housed the third largest queer population in the country in 2000 (Baumle, Compton, and Poston, Jr. 2009) and the fourth in 2020, dropping behind Florida ("Population Density of Same-Sex Couples: United States, The Williams Institute" 2022). To date, sociologists understudy queer life in the South, with only one in ten sociological studies on LGBTQ life examining queer people in the South or Southeast (Stone 2018). This focus is contrary to the actual location of LGBTQ life. And ideas about where queer life is shapes how, who, and where we study.

This edited collection is part of the growing momentum in sociological research that studies LGBTQ life and wants to push beyond commonly studied identities in the larger cities. Sociology lags behind geography, which has long since expanded its sense of place and sexuality (Brown-Saracino 2019). Fortunately, we have seen a recent increase in scholarly work on queer life driven by locations and settings that reflects the complexity of where LGBTQ people live in the United States. Like other scholars, the authors of these chapters emphasize place, space, and identity on the outskirts, suggesting that the outskirts are not only worth studying but should shape the center of sociological knowledge production. We believe the outskirts are not just a contrast for the center but hold important truths about how the social world works.

Pushing beyond the Great Cities and Metronormativity

Historically, most scholarly attention has focused on queer life in the city rather than the country, small cities, or suburbs. This focus on urban life also activates assumptions about metronormativity that queer people should move to a "place of tolerance" and away from their current home to come out and thrive (Halberstam 2005, 36–37). This metronormativity focuses on big cities as part of what anthropologist Kath Weston

(1995) refers to as the "gay imaginary." This "Get thee to a Big City" gay imaginary narrates an exodus from rural to urban areas as the way for gay and lesbian people in the United States to find community and freedom from surveillance. Even in Weston's classic piece on this imaginary, she argues that for many gay men and lesbians this image of the city as full of connection and freedom did not match reality. However, scholarship on queer life in the United States focuses disproportionately on urban life, particularly city life in New York, Chicago, Los Angeles, and San Francisco (Herring 2010; Stone 2018). Before the internet and social media transformed social research recruitment, these places were likely an easy way of meeting gay and lesbian research participants. Although there is increasing research on rural, suburban, and small-city queer life, these great cities still loom large in the LGBTQ imagination as places where queer life happens (Bain and Podmore 2021). Sociologists have disproportionately focused on these "great cities" (Stone 2018), even with an abundance of evidence that LGBTQ people live in every county in the United States and often intentionally move to the country or down south (Baumle and Compton 2015; Kazyak 2012).

Part of this metronormativity is an assumption that queer life in these big cities reflects some universal gay experience (Abraham 2011; Brown 2012; Herring 2010). Places like New York City are positioned as an imaginary homeland for LGBTQ people everywhere, a place where one moves to escape hostility and enjoy a fantasy of radicalism (Tongson 2011; Waugh 1996; Weston 1995). This metronormativity centers maleness and whiteness and feeds assumptions that the lives of white urban gay men are typical of LGBTQ people across the United States. The resident of these cities, the white cosmopolitan gay man, goes to places like gayborhoods, Pride Parades, and gay bars, where most of this great city gay life happens (Perez 2005, 171; Brown 2008).

However, this focus erases the complex experiences of people of color living in cities. While most studies of LGBTQ people of color also take place in these great cities, particularly Black and Latinx communities in New York City and Los Angeles (Asencio 2011; M. A. Hunter 2010; M. R. Moore 2015; M. Moore 2011; Muñoz-Laboy et al. 2009; Ocampo 2012; Thing 2010; Winder 2015; Acosta 2013), this work has not dethroned the white gay urban resident and can result in the commodification of Black and Brown bodies (Pérez 2015). For example, the canonical classic documentary *Paris Is Burning* about ball culture in Harlem simultaneously expanded understandings of New York gay life, was an exploitation of Black queer bodies by a white filmmaker, and was a powerful challenge to the dominant approach to studying queer life.

Many things are overlooked by focusing on the "great cities," even for the study of Black and Latinx urban life. For example, overwhelming attention to the great cities leads scholars to neglect majority-minority areas of the United States. Latinx-majority cities in the Southwest like San Antonio, El Paso, and Miami and Black-majority cities in the South and Midwest like Atlanta, Detroit, Cleveland, Flint, and Baton Rouge are often missing from the study of LGBTQ urban life. Some of the most methodologically and theoretically creative sociological work on LGBTQ communities of color expands beyond these great cities to study Mexican immigrant gay and bisexual men in San Diego (Carrillo 2018), ball culture in Detroit (Bailey 2013), gayborhoods in Washington, DC (Greene 2014), Asian gay men in Seattle (Han 2015), and intersections of gay Latino and Filipino identities in LA (Ocampo 2012). These studies do disproportionately focus on men.

There is value in studying all places where LGBTQ people live, including the great cities. However, sociological theories about LGBTQ life does not adequately advance if it relies on these prototypical cities for theorizing about how sexuality works. The conversation in this book demonstrates the contributions of scholarship on the outskirts to illuminate assumptions that were previously made and applied to the whole queer population based on work on white gay men and the great cities. Rather, demographic studies have demonstrated a very dynamic and diverse population (Compton, Baumle, and Poston 2009; Compton and Baumle 2012). Much as southern city life challenges existing sociological theories about race, urban forms, gentrification, and immigration in the city (Lloyd 2012), so does queer southern life (Rogers 2020).

One example of the value of studying the outskirts is analyzing the use of bars and public spaces, particularly in the southern United States (Mattson 2023). Consider: the dominance of the Stonewall Riots in the cultural imaginary means that scholars and students often imagine 1950s and 1960s gay bar life happening in the middle of the city in a bar run by members of the Mafia. Images of red brick, blacked-out windows, and seedy nightlife may follow. Conversely, when Stone was conducting research on queer history in San Antonio, Texas, senior members of the community described the most vibrant, permissive bars as happening outside the city limits in rural areas on the outskirts of town. These bars were often colloquially referred to as "the country" and were locations where queers could get away for the evening or weekend to play softball, do drag, swim in the swimming pool, and dance with each other (Stone 2017; Gohlke 2012). While there are multiple studies on gay bars and neighborhoods in the great cities, we do not have sufficient theory developed about the privacy and freedom that happens on the outskirts of the city limits. Further, the way queer people use public space may be more complex beyond these great cities. Scholars have affirmed that in LGBTQ vacation spots like Key West and Fire Island, there is abundant drag and camp (Newton 1996; Rupp and Taylor 2015). In *Queering the Redneck Riviera*, historian Jerry Watkins, III (2018) described the Emma Jones Society and their Independence Day festivities in the 1960s on the beaches of Pensacola, Florida, just across the causeway from Mobile. Their Independence Day party attracted thousands of sexually and racially diverse attendees to an event on the public beach that included camp and drag. In 1971, the event became a full-fledged convention instead of a public beach party, making it one of the largest gay-organized events in the country at the time (Watkins, III 2018, 123). The event combined patriotism, camp, and a push for visibility in the South. This event and its brazenness contradict popular understandings about queer life in the seventies and southern tolerance for queers. We ask, what happens when we theorize from the beach of Pensacola about queer life? Rather than seeing those gatherings as an anomaly, we may view them as a reflection of common experiences of public queer life, open spaces, and tourism. More broadly, theorizing about the beaches of Pensacola contributes to sociology by theorizing about people's relationship with the city, rurality, and tourism, along with the ways that communities are built and that people craft identities for themselves. These aspects of space and place influence identity formation and self-expression. An example is S. L. Crawley's (2008) autoethnography on how growing up in the subtropics directed their identity toward butchness rather than transness under the premise that it is hard to be trans in hot places. The outskirts are important in this way, as phenomena from the outskirts test and shape general sociological theories.

Centering the Outskirts

We envision the outskirts as the material, physical, and emotional space lingering on the edges of the center. The outskirts evoke the edges of the city, the liminal places in between, the identities that cannot be easily pigeonholed. The outskirts are not about one particular space or place but rather the relationship between spaces, places, and identities. There have been many metaphors used to describe the outskirts. These metaphors often center the body and the body's experience (March 2021) or have less rigid boundaries about spaces, places, and identities (Bain and Podmore 2021). Ideas about spaces and places blur lines between inside and outside, queer and straight, along with the past and the present (Bain and Podmore 2021; 1314; Ghaziani 2019).

The outskirts are a rich site for creating and developing new theories, identities, and possibilities. Inherently, they push back against the marginalization of these theories within the field of sociology. Understanding the margins led to theories of intersectionality (Atallah, Bacigalupe, and Repetto 2019; Crenshaw 1990). Kimberlé Crenshaw (1990) located the experiences of women of color who experience rape as at the margins of feminism and antiracism. The borderlands are a space for the marginalized, those like *la mestiza* who straddle two cultures (Anzaldúa 1987). Katie Acosta (2008) described the way immigrant, sexually nonconforming Latinas created their lives in the borderlands, a place between places. These places are invaluable for developing identity and consciousness.

The outskirts are also about different ways of moving through space, along with new ways of being. Some theories about queer space rely on the settler colonial ideals of occupying land and establishing it as one's territory, hence the emphasis on how white urban gay men have established gayborhoods and gay bars. Consequently, social scientists know more about the gayborhoods of Boystown in Chicago and the Castro in San Francisco than LGBTQ life in all the major metropolitan areas in Texas. An overemphasis on gayborhoods as spaces sometimes ignores coffee shops, house parties, piers, and other public spaces that are important for women, trans people, and people of color in the LGBTQ community (Adeyemi, Khubchandani, and Rivera-Servera 2021; Brown-Saracino 2019; Gieseking 2013; 2020; Lane 2015; Moore 2015).

Attending to the outskirts focuses on the ways that new marginal-izations are made through this territorial use of space. Karen Tongson (2011) in her work on the suburbs argues that spatial Others are created by this territorial use of space. Studies of gayborhoods increasingly em-phasize the ways that LGBTQ youth, trans people, and Black, Asian, and Latinx queer people are marginalized and policed within these spaces (Greene 2014; 2021; Han 2015; Nero 2005; Hunter 2015). Scholars have searched for alternative metaphors to understand the ways that LGBTQ people relate to space. These metaphors are often more attentive to the ways that trans, non-binary, and queer people of color have been pushed to the margins of space, moved into the outskirts (Greene 2021; Rosen-berg 2017; R. D. Rosenberg 2021).

John Howard's classic work on white and Black gay men in rural Mis-sissippi argued that *circulation* was a more apt metaphor than congre-gation for understanding gay life (Howard 2001). Other scholars have used metaphors of *constellations* to describe the ways queer women and trans people use space (Chisholm 2005; Gieseking 2020). This concept resists the idea that owning property and claiming territory is the way to liberation and instead examines the "mythical (imagined), calendri-cal (temporal), and navigational (wayfinding) qualities of lesbian-queer life" (Gieseking 2020, 3). The temporal use of space is featured in work on queer pop-ups (Stillwagon and Ghaziani 2019). Queer notions of time and space also challenge the way scholars address presence. Some queer literature on ghosts and haunting creates new ways of thinking about time. For example, scholars write about the "ghostly placemaking residues" in spaces by queer people of color (Bacchetta, El-Tayeb, and Haritaworn 2015, 775).

These outskirts become spaces for the proliferation of identities and ways of being (Bailey 2013). There is a broader attention to fluid-ity and complexity in relationships and identities. A growing body of work analyzes the way bisexual, non-binary, and polyamorous people resist binary identities. This resistance to binary identities navigates the attempts of people and institutions to foreclose fluidity in identities, a type of inequality that involves "the symbolic or material removal of fluid possibilities from sexual and gender experience and categori-zation" (Sumerau, Mathers, and Moon 2020, 205). Even heterosexual identites involve fluidity and complexity; bisexual sexual practices have been integrated into straight men's sexual identities, including "bud sex" between rural men with strong attachments to straight culture (Silva 2017).

These outskirts are also about new approaches to methods and how we learn about the world. Sociologists have produced three edited volumes on queer methods (Compton, Meadow, and Schilt 2018; Ghaziani and Brim 2019; Browne and Nash 2010) that expand the ways sociologists think about methodology. Queering methods sometimes means accepting the way autoethnography creates windows into queer life (Crawley and Willman 2018; Shange 2019). At other times, it means embracing the sexuality of life, using carnal ethnography or a pornographic imagination (Hoang 2018; Jones 2018).

Centering the outskirts is not just about being curious about the varied experiences of queer life in the outskirts, but also placing the idea of the outskirts at the center of theorizing and social inquiry. It is asking the question, *what happens when the outskirts become the center*? For example, what if theories about gay urban life were developed studying circulation more than congregation, house parties more than bars? What if sociological theories about queer life in the United States were developed centered around the southern queer experience?

As people who live in the South, this last question has given us much cause for thought. Stone considers it more deeply in their chapter on LGBTQ Mardi Gras. If southern queer life in the city were centered in sociological inquiry, we can imagine that Black queer experiences in urban, rural, and suburban places would be an integral part of the research on US queer life. There would likely be a broader acknowledgment of the diffuse impact of southern culture on life throughout the US (Hunter and Robinson 2018). Also, there would be a greater analysis of the impact of the automobile on queer life (Howard 2001; Watkins, III 2018). Historian E. Patrick Johnson (2011; 2018) locates Black queer life within the southern Black church, as a space that encouraged the gender expression of Black gay men, and also as a space for Black queer women to resist and seek more women-centered worship. Stone's new work finds that LGBTQ people are often visible participants in citywide festivals like Mardi Gras or Fiesta, and the oldest LGBTQ organizations in some towns are the Metropolitan Community Church and a Carnival krewe in the South (Stone 2022).

Over the past two decades, we have seen a surge in studies of both sexualities and sexual orientation. Within sociology, studies of LGBTQ life have become more accepted in the discipline and increasingly published in major sociology journals. This is a crucial moment to be critical of LGBTQ studies in sociology. Rather than theorizing from the center of queer life that disproportionately focuses on white gay men's identities and spaces in major cities, this book deeply considers the issues of place and placelessness in LGBTQ life, particularly the way the outskirts of places, spaces, identities, and institutions impact the way we understand sexualities. This work re-orients the sociological study of sexualities to address both the diversity and complexity, the bad and the good, of the queer experience in fringe or liminal spaces and places in addition to articulating how these studies contribute to the field of sociology. Particularly, we see this book as a much-needed and innovative contribution to sociological theory and methods of LGBTQ studies.

Theorizing from the Outskirts

We argue that theorizing from the outskirts is crucial for sociological theory. In general, queer scholarship is important for and to sociology. Indeed, Seidman (1996) argued that queer scholarship has a kind of elective affinity with the sociological enterprise. While contributions from scholarship on sexualities can be focused on specific populations, this scholarship also informs sociological understandings applicable to all social life. Work on sexualities is important for understanding queer life, but also for knowledge production in general. Work from diverse perspectives, minority perspectives, and from the outside or outskirt perspectives are important for challenging mainstream or standing theories. Work from the outskirts answers important sociological questions central to the field about place and space: how communities are built, how states are governed, how people are oppressed, how people counter oppression, the scale and scope of identity projects, and more.

However, sociological theorizing from the outskirts is taken less seriously at the moment for several reasons. First, the study of sexualities is a relatively recent subfield within sociology, far more recent than the study of gender, family life, work, or race. Due to this, sociologists do not know some basic things about LGBTQ lives; in fact, only during this past decade have sociologists felt confident in our estimations of how many LGBTQ people there are in the United States. Survey data on gender identities and sexual orientation is rarely collected or captured in nationally representative surveys. When a major survey like the Behavioral Risk Factor Surveillance Survey (BRFSS) asks questions about gender and sexual identity, there is an explosion of new knowledge about queer life. We have little to no representative or comparative data on the LGBTQ population or their behaviors and attitudes. A related problem is that some members of the LGBTQ community have been studied more than others. During the dramatic growth of lesbian and gay public life after World War II, white gay men had the easiest access to public space (d'Emilio 1983). The earliest research in sociology on queer life focused on the lives of urban white gay men and queer life in the great cities due to the ways this part of queer culture was most visible at the times. These subcultures and places for queer life are seen as more legitimate within sociology as they are supported by earlier research. The disproportionate focus on some people and places then shapes the body of knowledge on queer life dramatically.

Second, even with the rapid growth of scholarship on queer life, the sociology of sexualities has a history of being marginalized within the discipline. In the edited volume, *Other, Please Specify*, many sexualities scholars mention that they have been accused of doing "me-search" when they study subcultures within the LGBTQ community (Compton, Meadow, and Schilt 2018). Kristen Schilt identifies the "attempt to dismiss scholarship on group X as too 'fringe' to sociologically matter" as one of the "interactional and institutional strategies that push queer work to the sociological margins" (Schilt 2018, 39). As such, sexuality scholarship is often "dirty work"—academic knowledge often stigmatized institutionally through barriers to funding, publication, and promotion (Jones 2019; Irvine 2014). The marginalization of sociological research exploring the lives of bisexual and transgender people are a case in point (Mathers and Sumerau, this collection). By focusing on the size of groups/subcultures, sociology gatekeepers ignore the important questions being asked and answered by this research. The size of some LGBTQ communities or the supposed rarity of some sexual behaviors may be part of the argument against studying these things. However, such critiques are often rooted in bias or ignorance about the topic at hand and preconceived notions of what should be studied, and what is valued. Scholarship regarding queer lives has only within the last two decades inched slowly toward the center of sociology.

The marginalization of work on LGBTQ lives and sexuality within sociology then affects knowledge production and how theory is produced within the discipline. There are social aspects to science and knowledge production. Knowledge production is socially organized, institutionalized, and stratified. Whose work is seen as theoretically central has historically been contested in US sociology (Morris 2017). In "Theorizing from the Margins" (2022), Kimberly Kay Hoang elucidated who gets to be a theorist and what kind of theoretical work gets defined as theory. While Hoang's focus is critiquing Western-centric racial theory, these criticisms apply to queer scholarship as well. Marginal work often incorporates contrast, includes multiple truths, and is undertaken with undervalued qualitative methods (Hoang 2022). This work is challenging and is meant to challenge existing theories. Marginal work is often discounted or undervalued as theory and advancing theory, and instead viewed as advancing an empirical case. Similarly, sexual practices and identities are pigeonholed as descriptions of subcultural populations rather than sex being understood as a central part of the social world.

Sociology has always been a discipline that attracts outsiders and outliers, but there has been a continuing struggle on the role of the outskirts in theorizing. In 1972, Alexander Liazos (1972) pinpointed ideological biases in the study of deviance in sociology, what he termed the study of "nuts, sluts, and preverts," including the emphasis on what were then considered dramatic cases of deviance like sex work and juvenile delinquency. Theories about gender performance were based disproportionately on one case, the study of Agnes by Garfinkel (1967), a transgender woman who "passed" as an intersex woman to attain medical service and support. The "exemplary case" of Agnes "calls to our attention what is for us [cisgender people] otherwise hidden. . . . that's what Agnes is good for" (Schilt 2016, 288). Many sociological theories about identity are developed using liminal and deviant subjectivities at the center (e.g., Becker's 1953 study of marijuana users). Sociology has also swung in the opposite direction to fetishize generalizability and delegitimate the exemplary case (Love 2021). Studying the outskirts then becomes dismissed as a case study.

Yet, there are many benefits from scholarship that focus on the outskirts and diverse contexts. First, from an empirical standpoint, studying from the outskirts allows for a more critical and complete analysis. The outskirts challenge firmly held "truths" (or social facts). There is a tendency for people to ignore evidence that contradicts their beliefs, assumptions, and experiences. Commonly referred to as the black swan fallacy, this is the tendency to believe that things that have never been witnessed do not exist. For decades, many scientists believed that swans were white such that it was considered a "universal truth." This universal truth of the white swan was used as an example in deductive logic where their coloring (white) was a condition in defining them. However, one day black swans were discovered and falsified this universal truth.

Studying from the outskirts informs our understandings of the social world. These events are outliers (initially), yet they have a profound impact on our knowledge production. Most briefly, black swan phenomena are relative to knowledge and social locations. What is a black swan to some may be completely expected to others. Consider the stereotype that LGBTQ people are more likely to live in the city. In 2000, the US Census found that there were lesbian and gay households in 99.3% of all counties in the US (Smith and Gates 2001). This stereotype was hard to overcome and took almost three decades. Rather than being viewed as believable, the census data on lesbian and gay households was challenged, and its validity was questioned. The primary challenge was the concern that the findings were not valid because straight households were not answering accurately. Those completing the census forms must not understand what an "unmarried partner" is! This idea was further supported by the assertion that "unmarried partner" was a new category added to the relationship status question and therefore should be subject to further investigation. The question was first employed in 1990, ten years earlier, and found problematic and not usable in part due to methodological concerns. However, another reason for not using it was due to its unbelievability. The 2000 data led to more demographic studies and qualitative explorations. Here we see science working, albeit slowly. The 2010 data was employed cautiously and only until the 2020 Census data did census data become believable and accepted, or at least less challenged for its accuracy. It took thirty years of data, from 1990 to 2020 for the data to be accepted. This census data, however, had a powerful impact on what we know about the LGBTQ population. In this way, the liminal, the seemingly insignificant, and those who live on the outskirts transform worldviews. The outskirts unveil blind spots and new vantage points. Access and acceptance of census data on same-sex unmarried partners opened the door for a surge of literature and questions for LGBTQ studies scholars.

When sociologists ask, "What happens when we theorize from the margins?" we shed light on the general phenomenon and check our collective academic assumptions regarding the social world. This line of inquiry strengthens theory. We can make contributions by studying the exceptions and those left out.

Overview of Chapters

This book is organized across four sections—places, spaces, dislocations, and identities and relationships. While there is much overlap and crossover among places, spaces, and relationships, the editors largely grouped across fluid conceptualizations from the specific to the more abstract and from the more macro to micro, and back again.

Places

The first section of the book delves deeply into the thinking about LGBTQ life outside of the metronormative model, reaching into rural areas and suburbia, along with challenging the existing theories about queer urban social organizations like bars and social clubs. In the first two chapters, S. L. Crawley and Miriam Abelson critique the urban-rural binary and metronormative narratives about queer life. Crawley questions sociological understandings of place drawing on Florida as a both place and non-place, considering the methodological implications for suburban and highly mobile research sites. They theorize that Florida is not as much a place as a postmodern, late capitalist, twenty-first century "American" moment. Abelson also questions the center of LGBTQ life as urbanity and instead understands non-metropolitan queer and transgender lives as their own social worlds in rural locations. These chapters challenge the common narratives that contrast urban and rural LGBTQ life.

In the next two chapters, Greggor Mattson and Amy L. Stone illuminate different organizational forms in their understanding of queer life. Mattson examines outpost gay bars, the modal type of gay bar that is often an hour's drive from the next bar. Rather than theorizing about gay bar life based on big-city gayborhoods, Mattson reveals that the typical gay bar is multi-gendered, welcomes heterosexual patrons, features drag prominently, and has owners who are integrated into small-town life. Stone's chapter argues that we have ignored a social form in theorizing about queer urban life—the festival organization or Mardi Gras krewe. Yearly queer Mardi Gras krewes across the Gulf South hold parades, host balls, and make space for themselves within local urban cultures.

Spaces

The internet, the spa, the rodeo, the church, the festival. The spaces for queer life are complex and unpredictable. This section explores spaces that were not intentionally built for queer life but have been reappropriated to be part of queer life. In chapter 5, Spencer Garrison analyzes how the technological affordances of the Tumblr social media site shape the identity formation of trans and gender non-conforming youth. Online spaces like Tumblr become sites of identity exploration but also profound ambivalence. In chapter 6, Kendall Ota takes us into the world of Korean spas in the United States, a space definitely not made for queer men that is occupied and appropriated for queer sex. Ota examines the way Korean spas are made into queer liminal spaces as part of a romanticization of a return to the sexual margins for white gay men.

Dislocating Spaces and Places

Institutions form certain kinds of spaces, ones that historically have marginalized LGBTQ people. This section focuses on these institutional spaces with an emphasis on how they operate in the Southwest and southeastern parts of the United States. Chapter 7 illuminates how the university is often a predominantly white, heterosexist, cisnormative institution. TehQuin Forbes analyzes the nuances of institutional spaces at predominantly white institutions (PWIs) and historically Black colleges and universities (HBCUs) in the Southeast in order to understand the ways that these universities as institutional spaces are welcoming or not for Black queer students. In this research, the institution itself becomes a site for marginalization. Institutions like religion, schools, and child custody systems also discipline, punish, and otherwise subjugate LGBTQ youth, particularly poor Black and Brown LGBTQ youth. In their work on LGBTQ homelessness in Texas, Brandon Robinson theorizes that scholars must look beyond family rejection to understand the institutional roots of LGBTQ youth homelessness in chapter 8. Their work pushes sociologists to examine youth-serving institutions more closely as institutions that contribute to the punishment and marginalization of youth. In chapter 9, Jamie O'Quinn and Cayden Goldstein-Kral consider the ways that policing and city life restrict sex for adults experiencing homelessness. They push for moving beyond an individual framework of sexual rights for people experiencing homelessness and towards an intersectional understanding of sexual justice.

Identities and Relationships

The outskirts are not always a place or space. The outskirts of queerness include subjectivities, identities, and relationships. In this section, Terrell Winder uses the case of Black gay men's formation of their own racial and sexual identities to carve out new theory about sexuality, identity, race, and society in chapter 10. How Black gay men in Los Angeles elect to express their racial and sexual identity reveals that these young men share similar stigmatizing experiences yet also prioritize race and sexuality differently as individuals. Similarly, in chapter 11, Antonia Randolph analyzes hip hop as a space for queer intimacy as she expands the study of male sexual fluidity to include emotional friendships. Randolph analyzes the "platonic couple" of Guru and Solar, two Black hip-hop artists, for the ways this relationship challenges how sociology collapses the boundaries between sexual desire, sexual identity, and emotional attachment. Randolph centers emotional attachment in understanding the sexual fluidity of men and sexuality more generally. This expansive understanding of sexuality is also reflected in Megan Carroll's chapter in this collection on asexualities. In her analysis of the 2020 Asexual Community Survey, Carroll pairs quantitative data with theoretical advancements about sexuality, identity, community, and intersectionality.

Centering the Disciplinary Outskirts

The intention of this book is to center the outskirts in larger disciplinary conversations within sociology. This final section of chapters crafts specific interventions to the discipline of sociology that centers the margins. In chapter 13, Lain Mathers and J. E. Sumerau place the study of bisexuality in a more central position in contemporary sociology. Although bi+ people are the largest sexual minority statistically in the United States, sociological theory about bisexuality is woefully inadequate. Mathers and Sumerau illuminate the disciplinary gatekeeping, monosexism, and bi+ erasure that stymies work on bisexuality. This chapter centers the bi+ experience in understanding sexual identities and experiences in a monosexist world. Similarly, entire fields of theory have been formed without considering the role of queer sexuality. Theories about hookup cultures on college campuses, for example, almost exclusively examine the dynamics of men seeking women (and vice versa) although twenty percent of students today identify as non-heterosexual. In chapter 14, Lisa Wade and Janelle Pham use sexual field theory to understand the way queer hookups are constituted and marginalized within heterosexualized spaces on campus. Finally, in chapter 15, Mary Bernstein theorizes about power, sexuality, and social change. Bernstein argues that a multi-institutional power approach to studying social change helps sociologists understand the complex changes in sexuality.

REFERENCES

Abraham, Julie. 2011. "The Homosexuality of Cities." *The New Blackwell Companion to the City*, edited by Gary Bridge and Sophie Watson, 586–95. Malden, MA: Blackwell.

Acosta, Katie L. 2008. "Lesbianas in the Borderlands: Shifting Identities and Imagined Communities." *Gender & Society* 22 (5): 639–59.

Acosta, Katie L. 2013. *Amigas y Amantes: Sexually Nonconforming Latinas Negotiate Family*. New Brunswick: Rutgers University Press.

Adeyemi, Kemi, Kareem Khubchandani, and Ramon Rivera-Servera. 2021. *Queer Nightlife*. Ann Arbor: University of Michigan Press.

Asencio, Marysol. 2011. "'Locas,' Respect, and Masculinity: Gender Conformity in Migrant Puerto Rican Gay Masculinities." *Gender & Society* 25 (3): 335–54.

Atallah, Devin G., Gonzalo Bacigalupe, and Paula Repetto. 2019. "Centering at the Margins: Critical Community Resilience Praxis." *Journal of Humanistic Psychology*, January, 002216781882530. https://doi.org/10.1177/0022167818825305.

Bacchetta, Paola, Fatima El-Tayeb, and Jin Haritaworn. 2015. "Queer of Colour Formations and Translocal Spaces in Europe." *Environment and Planning D: Society and Space* 33 (5): 769–78.

Bailey, Marlon M. 2013. *Butch Queens Up in Pumps: Gender, Performance, and Ballroom Culture in Detroit*. Ann Arbor: University of Michigan Press.

Bain, Alison L. and Julie A. Podmore. 2021. "Placing LGBTQ+ Urban Activisms." *Urban Studies* 58 (7): 1305–26. https://doi.org/10.1177/0042098020986048.

Baumle, Amanda K. and D'Lane R. Compton. 2015. *Legalizing LGBT Families. Legalizing LGBT Families*. New York: New York University Press.

Baumle, Amanda K., D'Lane R. Compton, and Dudley L. Poston, Jr. 2009. *Same-Sex Partners: The Social Demography of Sexual Orientation*. Albany: SUNY Press.

Brown, Gavin. 2008. "Urban (Homo) Sexualities: Ordinary Cities and Ordinary Sexualities." *Geography Compass* 2 (4): 1215–31.

Brown, Gavin. 2012. "Homonormativity: A Metropolitan Concept That Denigrates 'Ordinary' Gay Lives." *Journal of Homosexuality* 59 (7): 1065–72.

Browne, Kath, and Catherine J. Nash. 2010. *Queer Methods and Methodologies: Intersecting Queer Theories and Social Science Research*. London: Taylor & Francis.

Brown-Saracino, Japonica. 2019. "Aligning Our Maps: A Call to Reconcile Distinct Visions of Literatures on Sexualities, Space, and Place." *City & Community* 18 (1): 37–43. https://doi.org/10.1111/cico.12378.

Carrillo, Héctor. 2018. *Pathways of Desire: The Sexual Migration of Mexican Gay Men*. Chicago: University of Chicago Press.

Chisholm, Dianne. 2005. *Queer Constellations: Subcultural Space in the Wake of the City*. Minneapolis: University of Minnesota Press.

Compton, D'Lane R. and Amanda K. Baumle. 2012. "Beyond the Castro: The Role of Demographics in the Selection of Gay and Lesbian Enclaves." *Journal of Homosexuality* 59 (10): 1327–55.

Compton, D'Lane R., Tey Meadow, and Kristen Schilt, eds. 2018. *Other, Please Specify: Queer Methods in Sociology*. Berkeley: University of California Press.

Crawley, S. L. 2008. "The Clothes Make the Trans: Region and Geography in Experiences of the Body." *Journal of Lesbian Studies* 12 (4): 365–79. https://doi.org/10.1080/10894160802278242.

Crawley, S. L. and Rebecca K. Willman. 2018. "Heteronormativity Made Me Lesbian: Femme, Butch and the Production of Sexual Embodiment Projects." *Sexualities* 21 (1–2): 156–73. https://doi.org/10.1177/1363460716677484.

Crenshaw, Kimberlé. 1991. "Mapping the Margins: Intersectionality, Identity Politics, and Violence against Women of Color." *Stanford Law Review* 43: 1241–99.

d'Emilio, John. 1998 [1983]. "Capitalism and Gay Identity." *Families in the US: Kinship and Domestic Politics*, edited by Karen V. Hansen and Anita Ilta Garey, 131–41. Philadelphia: Temple University Press.

Ghaziani, Amin. 2019. "Cultural Archipelagos: New Directions in the Study of Sexuality and Space." *City and Community* 18 (1): 4–22.

Ghaziani, Amin and Matt Brim, eds. 2019. *Imagining Queer Methods*. New York University Press.

Gieseking, Jen Jack. 2013. "Queering the Meaning of 'Neighbourhood': Reinterpreting the Lesbian-Queer Experience of Park Slope, Brooklyn, 1983–2008." In *Queer Presences and Absences*, edited by Yvette Taylor and Michelle Addison, 178–200. London: Palgrave Macmillan UK. https://doi.org/10.1057/9781137314352_10.

Gieseking, Jen Jack. 2020. *A Queer New York: Geographies of Lesbians, Dykes, and Queers*. New York: New York University Press.

Gohlke, Melissa Ann. 2012. "Out in the Alamo City: Revealing San Antonio's Gay and Lesbian Past, World War II to the 1990s." PhD diss., University of Texas at San Antonio.

Greene, Theodore. 2014. "Gay Neighborhoods and the Rights of the Vicarious Citizen." *City & Community* 13 (2): 99–118. https://doi.org/10.1111/cico.12059.

Greene, Theodore. 2021. "The Whiteness of Queer Urban Placemaking." *The Gayborhood: From Sexual Liberation to Cosmopolitan Spectacle*, edited by Christopher T. Conner and Daniel Okamura, 143–160. Lanham, MD: Lexington Books.

Halberstam, J. Jack. 2005. *In a Queer Time and Place: Transgender Bodies, Subcultural Lives*. New York: New York University Press.

Han, C. Winter. 2015. *Geisha of a Different Kind: Race and Sexuality in Gaysian America*. New York: New York University Press.

Herring, Scott. 2010. *Another Country: Queer Anti-Urbanism*. New York: New York University Press.

Hoang, Kimberly Kay. 2018. "Gendering Carnal Ethnography: A Queer Reception." In *Other, Please Specify: Queer Methods in Sociology*, edited by D'Lane R. Compton, Tey Meadow, and Kristen Schilt, 230–46. Berkeley: University of California Press.

Hoang, Kimberly Kay. 2022. "Theorizing from the Margins: A Tribute to Lewis and Rose Laub Coser." *Sociological Theory* (June). https://doi.org/10.1177/07352751221106199.

Howard, John. 2001. *Men Like That: A Southern Queer History*. Chicago: University of Chicago Press.

Hunter, Marcus Anthony. 2015. "All the Gayborhoods Are White." *Metropolitics*. 19 May. https://metropolitics.org.

Hunter, Marcus Anthony. 2010. "The Nightly Round: Space, Social Capital, and Urban Black Nightlife." *City & Community* 9 (2): 165–86.

Hunter, Marcus Anthony and Zandria Robinson. 2018. *Chocolate Cities: The Black Map of American Life*. Berkeley: University of California Press.

Irvine, Janice M. 2014. "Is Sexuality Research 'Dirty Work'? Institutionalized Stigma in the Production of Sexual Knowledge." *Sexualities* 17 (5–6): 632–56.

Johnson, E. Patrick. 2011. *Sweet Tea: Black Gay Men of the South*. Chapel Hill: University of North Carolina Press.

Johnson, E. Patrick. 2018. *Black. Queer. Southern. Women.: An Oral History*. Chapel Hill: University of North Carolina Press.

Jones, Angela. 2018. "Pornographics as Queer Method." *Other, Please Specify: Queer Methods in Sociology*, edited by D'Lane R. Compton, Tey Meadow, and Kristen Schilt, 95–108. Berkeley: University of California Press.

Jones, Angela. 2019. "Sex Is Not a Problem: The Erasure of Pleasure in Sexual Science Research." *Sexualities* 22 (4): 643–68.

Kazyak, Emily. 2012. "Midwest or Lesbian? Gender, Rurality, and Sexuality." *Gender & Society* 26 (6): 825–48.

Lagos, Danya and D'Lane R. Compton. 2021. "Evaluating the Use of a Two-Step Gender Identity Measure in the 2018 General Social Survey." *Demography* 58 (2): 763–72. https://doi.org/10.1215/00703370-8976151.

Lane, Nikki. 2015. "All the Lesbians Are White, All the Villages Are Gay, but Some of Us Are Brave: Intersectionality, Belonging, and Black Queer Women's Scene Space in Washington DC." In *Lesbian Geographies*, edited by Kath Browne and Eduarda Ferreira, 219–242. New York: Routledge.

Liazos, Alexander. 1972. "The Poverty of the Sociology of Deviance: Nuts, Sluts, and Preverts." *Social Problems* 20 (1): 103–20.

Lloyd, Richard. 2012. "Urbanization and the Southern United States." *Annual Review of Sociology* 38: 483–506.

Love, Heather. 2021. "Underdogs: Social Deviance and Queer Theory." Chicago, IL: University of Chicago Press.

March, Loren. 2021. "Queer and Trans* Geographies of Liminality: A Literature Review." *Progress in Human Geography* 45 (3): 455–71.

Mattson, Greggor. 2023. *Who Needs Gay Bars? Bar-Hopping through America's Endangered LGBTQ+ Places*. Stanford, CA: Redwood Press.

Moore, Mignon. 2011. *Invisible Families: Gay Identities, Relationships, and Motherhood among Black Women*. Berkeley: University of California Press.

Moore, Mignon R. 2015. "LGBT Populations in Studies of Urban Neighborhoods: Making the Invisible Visible." *City & Community* 14 (3): 245–48. https://doi.org/10.1111/cico.12127.

Morris, Aldon. 2017. *The Scholar Denied: W. E. B. Du Bois and the Birth of Modern Sociology*. Berkeley: University of California Press.

Muñoz-Laboy, Miguel, Carmen Juana Yon Leau, Veena Sriram, Hannah Jean Weinstein, Ernesto Vasquez del Aquila, and Richard Parker. 2009. "Bisexual Desire and Familism: Latino/a Bisexual Young Men and Women in New York City." *Culture, Health & Sexuality* 11 (3): 331–44. https://doi.org/10.1080/13691050802710634.

Nero, Charles I. 2005. "Why Are Gay Ghettoes White?" In *Black Queer Studies: A Critical Anthology*, edited by E. Patrick Johnson and Mae G. Henderson, 228–46. Durham, NC: Duke University Press.

Newton, Esther. 1996. "Dick (Less) Tracy and the Homecoming Queen: Lesbian Power and Representation in Gay Male Cherry Grove." In *Inventing Lesbian Cultures*, edited by Ellen Lewin, 161–93. Boston: Beacon Press.

Ocampo, Anthony C. 2012. "Making Masculinity: Negotiations of Gender Presentation among Latino Gay Men." *Latino Studies* 10 (4): 448–72.

Pérez, Hiram. 2005. "You Can Have My Brown Body and Eat It, Too!" *Social Text* 23 (3–4): 171–91. https://doi.org/10.1215/01642472-23-3-4_84-85-171.

Pérez, Hiram. 2015. *A Taste for Brown Bodies: Gay Modernity and Cosmopolitan Desire.* New York: New York University Press.

Rogers, Baker A. 2020. *Trans Men in the South: Becoming Men.* Lanham, MD: Lexington Books.

Rosenberg, Rae Daniel. 2017. "The Whiteness of Gay Urban Belonging: Criminalizing LGBTQ Youth of Color in Queer Spaces of Care." *Urban Geography* 38 (1): 137–48.

Rosenberg, Rae Daniel. 2021. "Negotiating Racialised (Un)Belonging: Black LGBTQ Resistance in Toronto's Gay Village." *Urban Studies*, 58 (7): 1397-1413. https://doi.org/10.1177/0042098020914857.

Rupp, Leila J. and Verta Taylor. 2015. *Drag Queens at the 801 Cabaret.* Chicago: University of Chicago Press.

Schilt, Kristen. 2016. "The Importance of Being Agnes." *Symbolic Interaction* 39 (2): 287–94. https://doi.org/10.1002/symb.231.

Schilt, Kristen. 2018. "The 'Not Sociology' Problem." In *Other, Please Specify: Queer Methods in Sociology*, edited by D'Lane R. Compton, Tey Meadow, and Kristen Schilt, 37–50. Berkeley: University of California Press.

Shange, Savannah. 2019. "Play Aunties and Dyke Bitches: Gender, Generation, and the Ethics of Black Queer Kinship." *Black Scholar* 49 (1): 40–54. https://doi.org/10.1080/00064246.2019.1548058.

Silva, Tony. 2017. "Bud-Sex: Constructing Normative Masculinity among Rural Straight Men That Have Sex with Men." *Gender & Society* 31 (1): 51–73.

Smith, David M. and Gary J. Gates. 2001. *Gay and Lesbian Families in the United States: Same-Sex Unmarried Partner Households. A Preliminary Analysis of 2000 United States Census Data.* Human Rights Campaign, 919 18th St. https://eric.ed.gov/?id=ED457285.

Stillwagon, Ryan, and Amin Ghaziani. 2019. "Queer Pop-Ups: A Cultural Innovation in Urban Life." *City & Community* 18 (3): 874–95.

Stone, Amy L. 2012. *Gay Rights at the Ballot Box.* Minneapolis: University of Minnesota Press.

Stone, Amy L. 2017. *Cornyation: San Antonio's Outrageous Fiesta Tradition.* San Antonio: Trinity University Press.

Stone, Amy L. 2018. "The Geography of Research on LGBTQ Life: Why Sociologists Should Study the South, Rural Queers, and Ordinary Cities." *Sociology Compass* 12 (11): e12638.

Stone, Amy L. 2022. *Queer Carnival: Festivals and Mardi Gras in the South.* New York: New York University Press.

Sumerau, J. E., Lain A. B. Mathers, and Dawne Moon. 2020. "Foreclosing Fluidity at the Intersection of Gender and Sexual Normativities." *Symbolic Interaction* 43 (2): 205–34. https://doi.org/10.1002/symb.431.

Thing, James. 2010. "Gay, Mexican and Immigrant: Intersecting Identities among Gay Men in Los Angeles." *Social Identities* 16 (6): 809–31.

Tongson, Karen. 2011. *Relocations*. New York: New York University Press.

Watkins, III, Jerry T. 2018. *Queering the Redneck Riviera: Sexuality and the Rise of Florida Tourism*. Gainesville: University Press of Florida.

Waugh, Thomas. 1996. *Hard to Imagine: Gay Male Eroticism in Photography and Film from Their Beginnings to Stonewall*. New York: Columbia University Press.

Weston, Kath. 1995. "Get Thee to a Big City: Sexual Imaginary and the Great Gay Migration." *GLQ: A Journal of Lesbian and Gay Studies* 2 (3): 253–77.

Winder, Terrell J. A. 2015. "'Shouting It Out': Religion and the Development of Black Gay Identities." *Qualitative Sociology* 38 (4): 375–94. https://doi.org/10.1007/s11133-015-9316-1.

PART I

Place

1

Florida as Postmodern Moment

Skirting the Urban/Rural Binary and Queering Generalizability

S. L. CRAWLEY

Everybody has a cousin in Miami.
—Jimmy Buffett

In 1972 when I was six, my parents divorced and, in 1974 when I was eight, they remarried each other, in the process moving from our familial, rural, Midwest place of origin (Indiana) to Florida. In the interim, my dad had relocated with his corporate job (IBM). Disrupting the nuclear family narrative by living in a chosen, non-familial place, my life story used to seem odd to me—as if I were atypical. More recently, I wonder if indeed that is so.

As a researcher and as a trans/butch lesbian from Florida, I have frequently felt *out of place* in academia. At a conference on butch identity a few years ago, I realized I was the only one not wearing all black—the queer, urban uniform. My tropical shirts made me a bit too bright and colorful. There is something different about the interactional rules in Florida—something less metropolitan, more subtropical. As a result, collecting data—both ethnographic and interview data—in Florida has brought moments of methodological reflection. Gender and sexualities studies focuses on discursive productions of identities, which are also implicitly about place and time. Wrestling with ethnographic and interview work in Florida has raised several questions about the veracity of traditional social science methods in this non-traditional place. What can be learned about methods by reflecting on Florida as a site of study?

In LGBTQ+ research, there has long existed an overriding myth that LGBTQ+ folks are rushing to a large metropolis to come out. Data from the American Community Survey on internal US migration patterns through Florida calls into question the singular narrative of migration from rural birth places to urban gay ghettos. Florida as a primarily suburban and highly mobile research site challenges common narratives about LGBTQ+ experience, binarized as either rural or urban. Further, a more historical and demographic reflection on suburban Florida as both place and non-place in the broader US context establishes that *Florida is not simply a place but the definitive postmodern, late capitalist, twenty-first century "American" moment.* That is to say, Florida is a little bit of *everyplace* while being exemplary of the experience of this moment in time for people far beyond the state borders.

Postmodern experiences of place as temporary and commodified (Massey 1994; Oswin 2019) are now a common part of everyday life in and through the US. These contemporary experiences challenge the limitations of both traditional ethnography, with its emphasis on idiosyncrasy, and positivist demographic methods, with their emphasis on generalizability. Recognition of the postmodern context of our lives should encourage social scientists to rethink traditional methods. In this chapter, I apply postmodernist insights into productions of discursive reality and its potential impacts on methodologies. I undertake three tasks: 1) reconceptualize LGBTQ+ experience in terms of suburban migration, not just the prototypically storied relocation from rural birthplace to urban gay ghetto; 2) demonstrate the importance of Florida (as place and non-place) as significant with regard to internal migration patterns in the US; and 3) rethink method such that we can focus, not on the idiosyncratic character of ethnographies of place or of the realist generalizability of quantification, but on the *relevance of narratives* in identity production among practical actors operating within the relations of ruling. In sum, this chapter calls for future LGBTQ+ work to focus on narrative and discursive identity production queering temporal and spatial relations—that, perhaps, data collected in Florida may have much broader *relevance* nationwide.

Suburbia and Twenty-First Century Mobility

Ethnography in sociology has a long held urban preference, such that the study itself is often called "urban ethnography." Such traditions can develop a sort of myopia wherein even working to "unbound" the method does not stray from "the metropolis" (e.g., Burawoy et al. 1991). Traditional ethnography has been critiqued for not sufficiently adding much beyond simply documenting local places (Hammersley 1992; Wacquant 2002). More recently, calls have been made to add theory back into ethnography (Puddephatt et al. 2009, 25), especially in ways that engage ourselves reflexively as researchers and that "challenge established wisdom." Elsewhere I have advocated for the reflexivity of autoethnographic work in grasping experience that cannot be gained by traditional ethnography or interviews (Crawley 2012). It is with this impulse that I consider qualitative data collection of LGBTQ+ worlds in an atypical place (Florida) and the claims that can be made with reflexive relationship to it.

By now, it goes without saying that sexualities affect geographies and vice versa (Abelson 2019, Browne, Lim, and Brown 2007; Crawley 2008; Knopp and Brown 2003; Massey 1994; Oswin 2019). A well-developed tradition of urban ethnography and history cataloguing LGBTQ+ "gayborhoods" across the US and around the globe has sufficiently produced knowledge of their existence on a scale too numerous to cite here. In "Get Thee to the Big City," Weston (1995) outlines the rural/urban migration narrative, noting how the narrative itself had become part of the discursive production of lesbian and gay subjectivity by the mid-1990s. Coining the term metronormativity, Halberstam (2005) confirms this point that LGBTQ+ cultures tend to foreground and assume urban queerness over other spatial preferences or possibilities. More recently, an emerging literature has attempted to counter this overarching narrative, interrogating assumptions that include whether gay ghettos are still relevant (Abelson, this collection; Ghaziani 2014; Mattson, this collection), whether the cataloging of "gayborhoods" in the sociological literature has tended to miss racial and ethnic dynamics always already involved in urban place-making (Carrillo 2019; Greene 2019), how class (Taylor 2008) and gender may be implicated in queer place-making (Brown-Saracino 2018; Brown-Saracino and Parker 2017; Forstie 2019). Studies specific to lesbians, bisexual, and queer (LBQ) women (Brown-Saracino 2018; Brown-Saracino and Parker 2017; Forstie 2019) note a gendered pattern wherein women chose "small cities" rather than the requisite metropolis.

Several authors have worked to problematize metronormativity by recording rural LGBTQ+ lives and refiguring what LGBTQ+ experience is like outside the big city (Gray, Johnson, and Gilley 2016; Whit-lock 2013). Pointing to the use of virtual media among queer youth in rural Kentucky, Gray (2009) asks her readers to abandon the notion that queer visibility and effective activism should be understood as centered in urban spaces. Similarly, Kazyak (2011) points out that rural performa-tivity and embodiment among Midwest lesbians cannot be assumed to look like their urban counterparts. Recognizing the pull to rural places to "escape the city," Soderling (2016) notes the experience of "queer time" changes markedly in sparsely populated, economically depressed places. Herring (2010, 35) seeks a distinctive "queer anti-urbanism" in asking:

> What would this lesbian and gay worlding begin to look like if we con-centrated on in-house productions that failed to adhere to metronor-mative stylistics, that voiced dissatisfactions from inside the confines of queer urbanized modernism?

Indeed. Desire for all things urban must be recognized as one nar-rative among others and the rural/urban distinction problematized as static and insufficiently binary (Tongson 2011). Brekhus (2003) reminds us that we have recorded few nostalgic or even painful narratives of the suburbs. We seem to have forgotten that suburbia—a configuration that defies boundaries (Tongson 2011)—exists. Shoring up the binary, au-thors that mention suburbia tend to link it to either the urban (as a space outside big cities) or the rural (as situated similarly against urban-ness) not as a specific kind of space in itself. In doing so, we are missing—or perhaps skirting[1]—a large proportion of LGBTQ+ experience. Interro-gating assumptions of a singular migration pattern involves questioning long standing narratives about gay urban subjectivity (Stone 2018) and corrects some previous myopias. The case of LGBTQ+ Puerto Ricans provides an interesting example.

In *Queer Ricans*, LaFountain-Stokes (2009) insists those coming out move to New York, Philadelphia, Chicago, and San Francisco—prototypical urban gay ghettos. However, the American Community Survey in 2012[2] shows 29% of all Puerto Ricans migrating to the US moved to Florida (21,638 of 74,400)—three times that of any other US destination (~7000 to Pennsylvania, ~7000 to New York, ~4000 to Texas, and ~4000 to Massachusetts) (2012 "international" migration dataset). Though my data are not specific to LGBTQ+ migrants, it would seem highly unlikely that the proportions of Puerto Rican migration would change by that order of magnitude only for LGBTQ+ folks. LaFountain-Stokes references Florida on only two pages of the book. This seems a clear instance of myopia organized by the queer migration narrative—an odd oversight given that migration in and out of Florida from Caribbean, Central American, and South American places of origin is not only common but perhaps might be expected given closer proximity and similar climates. (See for example, Peña's [2005] study of gay men settling in Miami after the Mariel boatlift from Cuba.) Pathways to Orlando, Tampa, and Miami, among other small cities fail to fit the narrative of the prototypical LGBTQ+ migration pattern.

Further, populated largely by small cities and suburban sprawl, Florida is *the most common* destination for state-to-state internal migration in the US, which I address further below. What might we learn about LGBTQ+ place-making if we were to focus on suburban experience? As I illuminate below, suburban mobility questions not only the LGBTQ+ rural/urban migration myth (Tongson 2011), but also sociology's methodological binary between realist demographic generalizability and interpretive, idiosyncratic study of urban places.

A Tale of Two Floridas

Exemplifying Harvey's (1993, 25) argument that "places, like space and time, are social constructs," Florida is as much a storied narrative as an actual place. Counter to common colloquial expectations, place is much more a relational process of social production than a historically specific "truth" of geography (Massey 1994). "In short, . . . places are never complete, finished or bounded but are always becoming—in process" (Cresswell 2002, 20). People all over the US and many parts of Europe, the Caribbean, and Central and South America participate in the production of Florida as a concept in addition to inhabiting—long- or short-term— the physical place. Existing in the popular cultural imaginary as much as on land, Florida has characteristics and a specific history of both a largely suburban place as well as a postmodern, narrative non-place.

Florida as a (Mostly) Suburban Place

Florida is primarily a suburban place with much rural landscape and a few metropolitan centers, though both rural and urban spaces in Florida are constantly being overtaken by the construction of suburban housing developments growing over the landscape like capillaries on steroids. My entire experience of home (Palm Beach County) is the disorientation of not recognizing what street corner I am at, given ever-present new developments of homes, condos, or strip malls.

For me, suburbia can be distinguished from urban environs, by definition, as places in which people mobilize almost entirely by driving cars (as opposed to accessing mass transit)—that is, suburbia is a place where cars are necessary to get around (see also Tongson 2011). Florida is overrun with cars, "settled" by tourists driving through to enjoy the weather—and this has never changed. Largely eschewing mass transit, automobiles are how we travel. Though Miami, Jacksonville, and Tampa each have a (relatively smallish) metropolitan downtown, even these "cities" are actually legally counties—several towns linked imperceptibly together governmentally and practically by suburban sprawl and superhighways. As such, even in the most dense, metropolitan places in Florida, one has the general feeling of ever-expanding suburbia.

Owing to the post-WWII economic boom combined with a lack of need for reconstruction as was the case in Europe and Japan, suburbs are a historical event of late industrial capitalism in the US (Beauregard 2006). In North America beginning in the late nineteenth century through the mid-twentieth-century economic boom, a significant preference for "home" came to be seen as a single-family, suburban dwelling with some yard or garden separating one's family from the neighbors (Kusenbach and Paulson 2013), especially among white and middle-class families who had the means and the mobility (Beauregard 2006). Suburbs have their own moral order—"transience, fragmentation, weak family and communal ties" (Baumgartner 1988). People moved to the suburbs rather than being from the suburbs, affecting one's way of life and experience of identity (Baumgartner 1988; Beauregard 2006; Kusenbach and Paulson 2013). While many racial and ethnic groups were moving north to escape southern racism in the great migrations north, migration to Florida was a big part of that historical expansion beyond the metropolis, albeit somewhat less storied. With a distinct history related to national and transnational dynamics, Florida has distinct characteristics of place-ness.

As a function of settler colonial expansion writ forward to today, *Florida is constantly re-colonizing.* Land is sold and re-sold to higher and higher bidders. It's a constant land grab from those who previously occupied it, putting ever more pressure on Native tribes, ethnic groups who settled in the nineteenth and twentieth centuries, and even working-class white migrants from the mid-twentieth century to hold less and less of the shifting sand. Even now, relatively few people are from here. In the early 1900s, the beachfront of South Florida and the Florida Keys were "settled" by Henry Flagler for seasonal tourism by the super-rich. First by boat, then later the construction of a railroad down the East Coast brought the first waves of wealthy, northern, white tourists seeking winter warmth, beginning the displacement the Seminole and Miccosukee Indian[3] tribes and escaped formerly enslaved people who had previously found refuge in the swampy, hot, mosquito-ridden, jungle-like natural scrub vegetation that made mobility over land difficult. Though port cities (Jacksonville, Miami, Key West, and Tampa) had long been on the overseas trade routes, the railroads and subsequent roadways eventually opened up Florida's mild winters to middle- and working-class ex-patriots from other states escaping the Great Depression. Sometimes people moved for jobs, like strike-busting maneuvers among the cigar-rolling industry in Ybor City in the 1930s (Mormino 2005), including my wife's grandparents. Returning from the spatial disruption of World War II in the 1940s, soldiers and sailors with only working-class prospects chose Florida, a dynamic that continues today with considerable military bases in Tampa, Jacksonville, Key West, and Pensacola—as well as the NASA facility on the "space coast." Post-WWII middle-class economic expansion lasted throughout the 1960s and later. Enabled by an expanding superhighway system nationally, working-class northerners drove here with little money—at least if one were to be working for a living, one could live a modest life in the sun. By the early 1970s, this was my family's actual story—a small suburban home for a factory line worker, a nurse, and two kids, two miles from the beach.

Exemplifying quintessential late capitalist, suburban mobility, *Florida is fluid.* At over 537,000 internal US migrants in 2012, Florida was *the most popular destination* for state-to-state migration, followed by Texas, California, Georgia, North Carolina, New York (from 2012 American Community Survey 1-Year Estimates of State-to-state migration). Seventy-five percent of people moving to Florida came from east of the Mississippi while 25% came from west of the Mississippi. Hence, much of the migration comes from the eastern US but not exclusively. At least 1,000 people from every state in 2012 (except North Dakota, Wyoming, and Nebraska) moved to Florida. Further, over 428,000 *people left Florida* and moved to (in order of highest concentration) Georgia, Texas, New York, North Carolina, and California, demonstrating that internal migration is regional and nationwide—not just short hops over the local border. Importantly, while internal migration pervasively affects broad swaths of the US population, Florida is the very pinnacle of this mobility.

Though the American Community Survey data do not show LGBTQ+ migration specifically, Doan's (2019) research, focusing on Tampa's Ybor City, shores up that LGBTQ+ migration was likely always more fluid and revolving than the rural-to-urban binary narrative suggests. Florida, especially South Beach, Ft. Lauderdale, and Key West (and now increasingly St. Petersburg), has long been a destination for LGBTQ+ folks even before it was such a widely popular mainstream destination (Mishoe and Perez 2009).

Subculturally, *Florida is a mirror*—the reflection of the entire eastern US. North Florida feels like the Deep South; central Florida is a common destination for Midwesterners; and South Florida feels more cosmopolitan with residents frequently hailing from the Northeast, especially New York and New Jersey, as well as the Caribbean and Central and South America. As Portes (1993) documents, ensuing waves of international migration, like the Cuban Mariel boatlifts among others, made Miami and South Florida into a vibrant place of international culture, though African American communities predating waves of international migration continue to be left behind economically and politically. Florida also reflects national trends. Since at least the 2000 presidential election, we have been a quintessential swing state in national politics—both reflecting and driving purple politics in a primarily red or blue country. Florida is national and global—often a temporary spot through which many people migrate rather than a singular place with one traditional culture.

Florida is for sale. With a tourism-based, service economy beginning about the second half of the twentieth century, in Florida we prostitute our land—real estate, beaches, weather, wildlife, etc. (Mormino 2005; Revels 2011). Florida has no state income tax because we keep selling pieces of ourselves to tourists, financing a piece of the sunshine by sales and ever-spiraling property taxes. Florida is middle-class cosmopolitanism—a recognition of consumerism and the class- and race-based dynamics of its history and present. Pointing to the undertheorized notion of class in sexual citizenship, Binnie and Skeggs (2004) note that the definition of "cosmopolitan" references forms of late capitalist consumption that both expand markets while sorting the privileged from those who are less so. Cosmopolitans are "seen as elite professionals in high-status occupations" who are "members of the transnational capitalist class" (42). Mansions dotting the entire coastline from Jacksonville to Miami closing off beach access for the world's super-rich, but for short, one-mile strips of city-owned beachfront, demonstrate this form of global cosmopolitanism. Constant mobility, the tourism- and real estate-based economy, and drivable access also have created a kind of middle-class version of cosmopolitanism in which middle-class and some working-class people can retire to Florida or live temporarily as "snowbirds" (typically US and Canadian citizens who live half the year in their northern homes but spend winter in Florida [Desrosiers-Lauzon 2011]). And as Binnie and Skeggs point out, market expansion and consumption necessarily dilute the authenticity of any place with "just another attempt at banal consumption by branding" (57)—impacting the subjectivities available in those places. In short, Florida is not just a place, it is also a non-place.

Florida as Non-Place

There is both an *authenticity* and an *inauthenticity* of place to Florida. The actual migration patterns through this place are not what LGBTQ+ expectations might have predicted. Similarly, notions about LGBTQ+ experience are simultaneously discursive and embodied in actuality. Florida "in the Popular Imagination" (Glassman 2009) exists as a place and a postmodern experience. Denzin (1991) summarizes postmodernism as both a moment in time (following WWII) and an experience of reality characterized by late industrialist, service economy with high technological advancement and ready communication. Citing Baudrillard's concept of hypperreality, he writes "Representations of the real have become stand-ins for actual, lived experience. . . . the real is now judged against its staged, cinematic-video counterpart" (x).

Using Disney as the defining example, Florida is the quintessential Baudrillardian simulacra. Baudrillard (1983) claimed that Disney is more real than the media-saturated consumerist hyperreality of everyday life that we perceive as real, in that, at least Disney represents itself as hyperreality. A virtual and physical space of short, commercially-mediated experiences, Florida has become a representation of "real" American life and an *actual part of many American's everyday lived experience*—at least for some portion of their lives. Giroux (1999) asserts that multinational corporations, especially Disney, now establish American cultural meanings for children and adults alike. *One can now live in an actual, suburban town (called Celebration, no less) on Disney property.*

Prior to Disney, there were always what are referred to locally as "the attractions"—Parrot Jungle, Cypress Gardens, Marineland, Sunken Gardens among many, many others (Huneycutt 2009). Thanks to Disney, Florida is now a permanent side show. *Florida is a non-place.* "Nonplaces are sites such as casinos, airports, theme-parks, shopping malls, supermarkets, museums, freeways, motels, and others," which "lacking history, identity, or tradition . . . promote the urgent and perpetual present" (Gottschalk and Salvaggio (2013, 6–7). Like other highly commercialized tourist destinations such as Las Vegas (Borchard 1998; Gottschalk 1995), Florida is awash with commercialized images, organizing texts, and affective experiences that emanate from mass media—which is to say, seemingly nowhere. The highly mediated experience has a temporal sense of placelessness—replicated over and over as the everpresent here and now.

Florida is US popular culture. Keith Olbermann declared Florida as "the weirdest of the 50 states" (Glassman 2009). Alligator wrestling, Burmese pythons, stand-your-ground laws, and political elections make us the jackass of states, giving late-night comedians more and more material to work with. "Florida Man" internet memes and US Presidents alike profane normalcy, in favor of bombastic pop culture hyperreality, replicated innumerably over social media. Florida has been the fodder of bad TV shows for decades, from *Miami Vice* to M^TV's *Spring Break* and *The Real World* to *SUV: Miami* to *Gator Boys*. Beaches and subtropical weather make pretty television; quirky residents make for comedy. Representations of "spring break" create instructions for actual experiences being enacted up and down the coasts—now seemingly year-round. Florida has become a narrative scene. Loseke's (2019) work on narrative sociology posits that social issues are commonly told as formula stories with events, types of characters, and scenes. "Stories are located in *scenes*, the particular settings in which story events unfold. Some stories . . . are scene driven. . . . scene almost always is critical because story *meanings* are scene dependent" (Loseke 2019, 5). The limitations of formula stories suggests also that there are stories that cannot be told (Loseke 2019). Florida as narrative may be part of the reason why the actual internal and transnational migration patterns through Florida do not overshadow the singular LGBTQ+ narrative that we must get to the big city. Continued focus on where one is "really" from, combined with the narrative of Florida as tourist destination—temporary place—overshadow the recognition of Florida's relevance in many US lives.

Florida as both a place and as non-place exemplifies the postmodern experience of late capitalism; indeed, perhaps Florida is *everyplace*. As such, *Florida is the quintessential postmodern American moment*. Every American seems to have a piece of it for a time. As suburbia, it is endlessly bought and sold as the American Dream. The technological moment of mobility, fast transportation, and ready communication make a piece of Florida, as space and as narrative, available to many in ever smaller periods of time. Florida has long been the retirement moment for many, though still not "home," which provides momentary visits by younger family members to "grandma and grandpa's place." Through seasonal winter homes, weekly time-share condos, weekend winter getaways, or an hour of M^TV's *Spring Break*, Florida is for sale in whatever increment one can afford.

Seeing contemporary life as part of the mobile society, Gottschalk and Salvaggio (2015, 30) note, "as passengers of the mobile society, we increasingly find ourselves circulating through non-places—sometimes by choice, sometimes against our will; sometimes for pleasure, sometimes by necessity." They add, "What happens in Vegas does not, in fact, stay in Vegas." Methodologists need to take note of these dynamics. Florida evades generalizability. Nonetheless, Florida as place and as discursive production is from and of a broader US and transnational moment. Studying Florida has *far greater relevance* than simply within Florida.

Queering Generalizability, Idiosyncratic Cases, Place and Time

What does constant mobility during our historic moment imply for research on LGBTQ+ issues and for sociologists more broadly? I offer four points.

First, *we must challenge common narratives about LGBTQ+ experience*, about migration to gay ghettos and more. The view of LGBTQ+ migration from rural outcasts to urban gay ghettos refuses to see broader, more circular and mobile patterns of migration in US history and at present—which also must encompass LGBTQ+ migrations (Tongson 2011). Perhaps the suburban migration experience is more pervasive than the previously perceived urban one. Narratives shape subjectivities, including what we cannot imagine (Loseke 2019). LGBTQ+ people would seem to be much more mobile than our narratives suggest.

LGBTQ+ identities rather famously resist generalizability, as these identities often seek fluidity and unboundedness, resist definition, and foreground personal voices. A basic queer critique of positivism is that LGBTQ+ people are not very countable and that we ought to turn our critical lens instead on the desire to count. Similarly, researchers of LGBTQ+ experience should be suspect of any purported phenomenon about LGBTQ+ people as an incontrovertible pattern. Second, a reflection on Florida as research site offers insight into much more than LGBTQ+ people; *Florida queers traditional notions of place*. Internal migration has become a common American experience over the second half of the twentieth century and beginning of the twenty-first. Everyone seems to have a cousin (or a grandparent or themselves for at least part of the time) in Miami. My lived experience is not so atypical. Importantly, it is not just that modernist LGBT people have become postmodernist queers in political life, but that the postmodern experience is now part of everyday life for many people in ways that distinctly affect non-urban, especially suburban life (Massey 1994). Knopp and Brown (2003, 409) ask us to question how spatiality itself might be queered by notions of diffusion—the "spread of phenomena through space and time"—as Florida seems to exemplify. The non-place-ness of suburban sprawl, the ever-recurring capitalist, colonial expansion of the land itself, and the high mobility of "internal" and "international" migration through Florida combined with the mythologizing of Florida as a pop culture narrative unsettle the actual place-ness of Florida, reflecting and producing this cultural moment up and down the eastern US, if not throughout the US and farther afield (to Europe? Canada? Central and South America?).

Owing to pervasive mobility and ready technology and communication, not only rich people but also many middle-class and some working-class people today access place as temporary or for moments in time. It is a rather common experience these days for many people in the US to be born somewhere, live temporarily in a place to receive education or training, then move again for a job or a relationship, or develop attachments to places that they visit temporarily but regularly—a vacation site or home of friends or family. Technologies of media, communication, and transportation allow for this temporary relationship to place. As fragmented as selves have become in late capitalism, perhaps many of us have, not place, but parts of places in us.

"Home" is now a much more mobile concept than our traditional concept of place (Kusenbach and Paulsen 2013; Massey 1994). Soukup (2012, 226) has challenged methodologists to embrace postmodern life by honoring its fleeting character and conceptualizing ethnography as "partial, subjective, and reflexive." Gottschalk and Salvaggio (2015) appeal to methodologists to recognize "the mobility turn"—"the powerful impact of mobility—the movement of people, objects, ideas, and information—in reshaping all levels of social life" (5). One cannot think of Florida as a local place without understanding its setting in a global context of interconnected relations—not just in terms of economics but in political ideology and pop-cultural practice.

Mobility is still class-based and racially linked, affecting the production of place as much as place affects its inhabitants (Oswin 2019). Lack of resources and connectivity leaves some less mobile and less connected than others. We need not forego a consideration of materiality by focusing on postmodern experiences of twenty-first-century worlding. Analysis of material conditions and their global connections need not cease when we consider mobility, though attention to mobility can extend our analysis of material relations by turning our focus to time.

Third, *postmodern technologies and mobility queer place and time.* As Soderling (2016) shows us, place queers time. Time in urban places feel much more rushed, whereas time in rural places alter material experience completely. Technology queers the lived experience of time. Place can now be momentary. Florida is the quintessential example that non-places are about this historical moment.

Realist methods such as demography and traditional ethnography implicitly trap "data" into finished moments of recent history. Metaphorically, they offer snapshots, if you will, rather than videos. Interpretive and postmodern epistemologies and methods have the advantage of looking processually—seeing lives and places as being in motion, as process. This necessitates a focus on time—both historically as Foucauldian queer theory has advocated, and phenomenologically as Gottschalk and Salvaggio note with the "mobility turn," highlighting the experience of time in places.[4] This is not a rebuke of realism and materiality, but a recognition that various epistemologies and methodologies can offer interesting insights. Elsewhere I have argued that there need not be a duel to the end over whose epistemology has it right, developing instead a concept of *relevance* (Crawley 2019). What can we come to know using various epistemological frames? If Florida is a moment and not a place, then we have to think of it as connected to other moments, not bounded or disconnected from other places. Experience as postmodern moments is more, not less connected, than as a series of disparate places.

Finally, neither nationally generalizable in the positivist methodological sense nor locally idiosyncratic in the inductive sense, Florida has a kind of *reverse generalizability*—a broader *relevance* to the entirety of the US rather than existing as simply a traditional place. Florida is more moment than place to many people in the US (and internationally) today, connecting it, not separating it, from other places. How, then, do researchers regard postmodern moments as evidence—that is, methodologically?

Recognition of the postmodern character of our lives need not raise fears of ethnography itself devolving into endless difference and fluid personal stories as some worry (Puddephatt et al. 2009). Challenges provided by postmodern[5] criticism can be fodder for honing our previously unquestioned assumptions, allowing researchers the analytic freedom to expand our methodological repertoire. Both the placeness—the connection to actual places and actual people all over the US—and the non-placeness—the popular cultural production of Florida as ahistorical narrative—should queer the methodological understanding of what it means to do data collection here. Not only is Florida not generalizable to elsewhere—neither is LGBTQ+ experience—but it is relevant and broadly connected to other experiences of place, time, and historical moment.

Ethnography has its roots in opposing a positivist, deductive epistemology of generalizability (Baszanger & Dodier 2004; Savin-Baden & Major 2013; Silverman 2004). Centering place as specific and local, ethnographers rather famously pursued their work inductively so as to counter grand, predictive theories of how humanity works (Silverman 2004). Still, ethnography as case study was also not typically intended to be fully idiosyncratic—of only one place. Inductive work compiled as several case studies over time were intended to give a picture of culture (Baszanger & Dodier 2004; Savin-Baden and Major 2013) or of some larger phenomenon being described—like the rural to urban narrative of LGBTQ+ place-making. Though not predictive or generalizable, ethnographies were still intended to tell us something of a phenomenon—if only about urbanization and the present historical moment. So what might qualitative research in Florida—a fluid, mobile, storied, place/non-place—tell us about methods in the early twenty-first century moment?

We might rethink method such that we can focus, not just on the idiosyncratic character of ethnographies of place or of the generalizability of quantification, but on the *relevance* of narratives in identity production among practical actors operating in circulating, connected patterns within the relations of ruling. Postmodern concepts offer a challenge to the strictures of traditional method. Florida is more historical and transnational process than place. It is difficult to use traditional methods in a non-traditional place. I offer the concept of relevance as a healthy reverse and reflexive challenge to methodological habits of mind that have bound us to immobility. Perhaps the atypical has become the typical, and there is a little bit of Florida in all of us.

NOTES

1 Colloquial usage of "skirting" means to get around something, whereas in British vernacular, it apparently means a border around something, as in baseboards. I believe either metaphor could apply to my usage here.

2 I have not provided "updated" data on Puerto Rico from the American Community Survey as of this writing for two reasons. My analysis of the data from 2012 more closely matches the moment in which La Fountain-Stokes published *Queer Ricans* (2009), supporting my claim that their claim about migration to big cities is myopic. Further, I expected that migration patterns between Florida and Puerto Rico may have changed following the cataclysmic events of Hurricanes Irma and Maria in 2017. A cursory review of the 2017 data shows very similar patterns, hence providing 2017 data would not change the argument.

3 I use the term Indian rather than Native American as the tribes themselves do. See https://tribe.miccosukee.com and https://www.semtribe.com/stof.

4 As Kusenbach and Brown-Saracino (2021) note, ethnography comes in many types and many authors are now working to incorporate time, mobility, and multi-sited work in ethnographies. Further, there is a long tradition of interpretive epistemology in some cultural ethnography.

5 I use the term postmodern here in the sense of questioning the incorrigible propositions of the modern (i.e., concreteness, certainty, fixed truths and realities, linear motion, especially as it implies progress), rather than in the sense of Denzin's (2009) "postmodern ethnography" calling researchers to "take sides," which I read as more political manifesto than postmodern method. While that may have its own values, my interest in the uses of postmodern thought involve critical reflection on epistemological and methodological strictures like the position of the researcher and criticism of abstract theory-building.

REFERENCES

Abelson, Miriam J. 2019. *Men in Place: Trans Masculinity, Race, and Sexuality in America*. Minneapolis: University of Minnesota Press.

Baszanger, Isabelle, and Nicolas Dodier. 2004. "Ethnography: Relating the Part to the Whole." In *Qualitative Research: Theory, Method and Practice, Second Edition*, edited by David Silverman, 9–34. London: Sage.

Baudrillard, Jean. 1983. *Simulations*. New York: Semiotext(e).

Baumgartner, M. P. 1988. *The Moral Order of a Suburb*. New York: Oxford University Press.

Beauregard, Robert A. 2006. *When America Became a Suburb*. Minneapolis: University of Minnesota Press.

Binnie, Jon and Beverley Skeggs. 2004. "Cosmopolitan Knowledge and the Production and Consumption of Sexualized Space: Manchester's Gay Village." *Sociological Review* 52 (1): 39–61.

Borchard, Kurt, 1998. "Between a Hard Rock and Postmodernism: Opening the Hard Rock Hotel and Casino." *Journal of Contemporary Ethnography* 27 (2): 242–69.

Brekhus, Wayne H. 2003. *Peacocks, Chameleons, Centaurs: Gay Suburbia and the Grammar of Social Identity*. Chicago: University of Chicago Press.

Browne, Kathe, Jason Lim, & Gavin Brown, eds. 2007. *Geographies of Sexualities*. Hampshire, England: Ashgate.

Brown-Saracino, Japonica. 2018. *How Places Make Us: Novel LBQ Identities in Four Small Cities*. Chicago: University of Chicago Press.

Brown-Saracino, Japonica and Jeffrey Nathaniel Parker. 2017. "'What Is Up with My Sisters? Where Are You?' The Origins and Consequences of Lesbian-Friendly Place Reputations for LBQ Migrants." *Sexualities* 20 (7): 835–74.

Burawoy, Michael, Alice Burton, Ann Arnett Ferguson, Kathrn J. Fox, Joshua Gamson, Nadine Gartrell, Leslie Hurst, Charles Kurzman, Leslie Salzinger, Josepha Schiffman, and Shiori Ui. 1991. *Ethnography Unbound: Power and Resistance in the Modern Metropolis*. Berkeley: University of California Press.

Carrillo, Héctor. 2019. "Cultural Archipelagos and Immigrants' Experiences." *City & Community* 18 (1): 44–48.

Crawley, S. L. 2008. "The Clothes Make the Trans: Region and Geography in Experiences of the Body." *Journal of Lesbian Studies* 12 (4): 365–79.

Crawley, S. L. 2012. "Autoethnography as Feminist Self-interview." In *The SAGE Handbook of Interview Research: The Complexity of the Craft, 2nd edition*, edited by J. A. Holstein, J. F. Gubrium, K. McKinney, and A. Marvasti, 143–60. Los Angeles: Sage.

Crawley, S. L. 2019. "Reality Disjunctures and Epistemological Encampment: Addressing Relevance in Constructionist Perspectives on Social Problems." *American Sociologist* 50 (2): 255–70.

Cresswell, Tim. 2002. "Introduction: Theorizing Place." In *Mobilizing Place, Placing Mobility: The Politics of Representation in a Globalized World*, edited by Tim Cresswell and Ginette Verstraete, 11–32. Leiden: Brill.

Denzin, Norman K. 1991. *Images of Postmodern Society: Social Theory and Contemporary Cinema*. London: Sage.

Denzin, Norman K. 2009. "Researching Alcoholics and Alcoholism in American Society." In *Ethnographies Revisited: Constructing Theory in the Field*, edited by Antony J. Puddephatt, William Shaffir, and Steven W. Kleinknecht, 152–68. London: Routledge.

Desrosiers-Lauzon, Godefroy. 2011. *Florida's Snowbirds: Spectacle, Mobility, and Community since 1945*. Montreal: McGill-Queen's University Press.

Doan, Petra L. 2019. "Cultural Archipelagos or Planetary Systems." *City & Community* 18(1): 30–36.

Forstie, Clare. 2019. "Theory Making from the Middle: Researching LGBTQ Communities in Small Cities." *City & Community*, online pre-publication. doi: 10.1111/cico.12446.

Ghaziani, Amin. 2014. *There Goes the Gayborhood?* Princeton: Princeton University Press.

Gieryn, Thomas F. 2000. "A Space for Place in Sociology." *Annual Review of Sociology* 26: 463–96.

Giroux, Henry A. 1999. *The Mouse That Roared: Disney and the End of Innocence*. Lanham, MD: Rowman & Littlefield.

Glassman, Steve, ed. 2009. *Florida in the Popular Imagination*. Jefferson, NC: MacFarland & Co.

Gottschalk, Simon. 1995. "Ethnographic Fragments in Postmodern Space." *Journal of Contemporary Ethnography* 24 (2): 195–228.

Gottschalk, Simon and Marko Salvaggio. 2015. "Stuck Inside of Mobile: Ethnography in Non-Places." *Journal of Contemporary Ethnography* 44(1): 3–33.

Gray, Mary L. 2009. *Out in the Country: Youth, Media, and Queer Visibility in Rural America*. New York: New York University Press.

Gray, Mary L., Colin R. Johnson, and Brian J. Gilley, eds. 2016. *Queering the Countryside: New Frontiers in Rural Queer Studies*. New York: New York University Press.

Greene, Theodore. 2019. "Queer Cultural Archipelagos are New to Us." *City & Community* 18 (1): 23–29.

Halberstam, J. Jack. 2005. *In a Queer Time and Place: Transgender Bodies, Subcultural Lives*. New York: New York University Press.

Hammersley, M. 1992. *What's Wrong with Ethnography?* New York: Routledge.

Harvey, David. 1993. "From Space to Place and Back Again: Reflections on the Condition of Postmodernity." In *Mapping the Futures*, edited by Jon Bird, Barry Curtis, Tim Putnam, and Lisa Tucker, 3–29. London: Routledge.

Herring, Scott. 2010. *Another Country: Queer Anti-Urbanism*. New York: New York University Press.

Huneycutt, Keith L. 2009. "Before the Mouse: From Glass-Bottom Boats to Gatorland." In *Florida in the Popular Imagination*, edited by Steve Glassman, 19–32. Jefferson, NC: MacFarland & Co.

Kazyak, Emily A. 2011. "Disrupting Cultural Selves: Constructing Gay and Lesbian Identities in Rural Locales." *Qualitative Sociology* 34: 561–81.

Knopp, Larry and Michael Brown. 2003. "Queer Diffusions." *Environment and Planning D: Society and Space* 21: 409–424.

Kusenbach, Margarethe and Japonica Brown-Saracino. 2021. "Urban Ethnography." In *Companion to Urban and Regional Studies*, edited by Anthony Orum, Serena Vicari, and Javier Ruiz-Tagle, 282–310. Hoboken, NJ: Wiley-Blackwell.

Kusenbach, Margarethe and Krista E. Paulson. 2013. *Home: International Perspectives on Culture, Identity, and Belonging*. Frankfurt am Main, Germany: PL Academic Research.

LaFountain-Stokes, Lawrence. 2009. *Queer Ricans: Cultures and Sexualities in the Diaspora*. Minneapolis: University of Minnesota.

Loseke, Donileen R. 2019. *Narrative Productions of Meanings*. Lanham, MD: Lexington Press.

Massey, Doreen. 1994. *Space, Place, and Gender*. Cambridge, UK: Polity Press.

Mishoe, Margaret and Michael Perez. 2009. "Where Being Gay Isn't a Drag." In *Florida in the Popular Imagination*, edited by Steve Glassman, 33–45. Jefferson, NC: MacFarland & Co.

Mormino, Gary R. 2005. *Land of Sunshine, State of Dreams: A Social History of Modern Florida*. Gainesville: University Press of Florida.

Oswin, Natalie. 2019. *Global City Futures: Desire and Development in Singapore*. Athens: University of Georgia Press.

Peña, Susana. 2005. "Visibility and Silence: Mariel and Cuban American Gay Male Experience and Representation." In *Queer Migrations: Sexuality, U.S. Citizenship, and Border Crossings*, edited by E. Luibheid and L. Cantu, Jr., 172–92. Minneapolis: University of Minnesota Press.

Portes, Alejandro. 1993. *City on the Edge—the Transformation of Miami*. Berkeley: University of California Press.

Puddephatt, Antony, William Shaffir and Steven Kleinknecht. 2009. "Introduction: Exercises in Reflexivity: Situating Theory in Practice." In *Ethnographies Revisited, Constructing Theory in the Field*, edited by A. J. Puddephatt, W. Shaffir and S. W. Kleinknecht, 1–34. London: Routledge.

Revels, Tracy J. 2011. *Sunshine Paradise: A History of Florida Tourism*. Gainesville: University Press of Florida.

Savin-Baden, Maggi, and Claire Howell Major. 2013. *Qualitative Research: The Essential Guide to Theory and Practice*. London: Routledge.

Silverman, David. 2004. "Who Cares about 'Experience'? Missing Issues in Qualitative Research." In *Qualitative Research: Theory, Method and Practice, Second Edition*, edited by David Silverman, 342–67. London: Sage.

Soderling, Stina. 2016. "Queer Rurality and the Materiality of Time" In *Queering the Countryside: New Frontiers in Rural Queer Studies*, edited by Mary L. Gray, Colin R. Johnson, and Brian J. Gilley, 333–48. New York: New York University Press.

Soukup, Charles. 2012. "The Postmodern Ethnographic Flaneur and the Study of Hyper-Mediated Everyday Life." *Journal of Contemporary Ethnography* 42(2): 226–54.

Stone, Amy L. 2018. "The Geography of Research on LGBTQ Life: Why Sociologists Should Study the South, Rural Queers, and Ordinary Cities." *Sociology Compass* 12:e12638.

Taylor, Yvette. 2008. "'That's Not Really My Scene': Working-Class Lesbians in (and Out of) Place." *Sexualities* 11(5): 523–46.

Tongson, Karen. 2011. *Relocations: Queer Suburban Imaginaries*. New York: New York University Press.

Wacquant, L. (2002) "Scrutinizing the Street: Poverty, Morality, and the Pitfalls of Urban Ethnography." *American Journal of Sociology* 107: 1468–532.

Weston, Kath. 1995. "Get Thee to the Big City: Sexual Imaginary and the Great Gay Migration." *GLQ* 2: 253–77.

Whitlock, Rea Ugena. 2013. *Queer South Rising: Voices of a Contested Place*. Charlotte, NC: Information Age Publishing.

2

Going to the Country

LGBTQ Rural Research as Queer Anti-Urbanism and Coalition

MIRIAM J. ABELSON

Where is the center of LGBTQ life? I have learned through conducting two research projects with rural LGBTQ people that while the city looms large in the minds of LGBTQ people, it is not always the end destination of sexual and gender freedom. Some LGBTQ people resist the urban pull, or do not feel it at all, in these rural spaces on the geographic edges. Sean, a trans man I interviewed who was living in the rural Midwest expressed this well when he said, "Why should I live in the city? Isn't the point that I should be able to do what I want?" This research has taught me that it is key that urban sexualities researchers recognize the dominant narratives of LGBTQ life we carry and that we should seek to understand non-metropolitan queer and trans lives on their own terms. Indeed, it is crucial for all sociologists to recognize these kinds of ingrained spatial narratives as we seek to carry out research and comprehend our social worlds.

In this chapter I will further unpack the urban-centered bias of research on LGBTQ life, describe my rural research projects, outline key findings, and discuss methodological insights and challenges from this work. These insights provide suggestions and strategies for sexualities researchers and other scholars interested in doing rural research. Recentering on rural spaces allows us to understand how both private and public LGBTQ life operates in different spatial registers. On the whole, I find that understanding the full scope of queer and trans life means traveling to the imagined and physical edges of what and where LGBTQ life is supposed to be.

This journey provides a greater understanding of both rural and urban life, as well as the connections between the two. I will illustrate that urban spaces are not necessarily more livable for all LGBTQ people. In fact, rural and other non-urban spaces can offer unique benefits to queer and trans people. Non-metropolitan LGBTQ life operates under its own logics and modes of organization that may not resemble urban practices. When researchers make urban assumptions about visibility, as one example, when studying rural communities, they may not only misrepresent those communities but also risk limiting practical aspects of their research, like recruitment. One may not actually find rural queer and trans people if they are only looking for a particular kind of visibility. Finally, urban and rural spaces, and other spaces in between, are highly interconnected in the twenty-first century. Engaging in research across those spaces opens possibilities for political solidarity between people who hold both shared and different marginalities, setting the ground for deeper understanding of one another and potential for coalitions across spatial difference.

Metronormativity and Queer Rural Research

Bobby, a white transgender man living in suburban Kentucky when I interviewed him, had grown up in a rural area in the deep South and identified as a lesbian in high school. He and his handful of queer friends dreamed of escaping the homophobia of their conservative community. Bobby explained, "When we get done with high school . . . like every gay teenager, 'We're gonna go to San Francisco! . . . We're going to the gay bay; we're getting the hell out of here.' you know?" Bobby and his friends' hopes and dreams mirrored a popular narrative of migration central to queer and transgender life.

San Francisco has long loomed large for many queer people as an "imagined homeland" to which individuals could travel from left-behind rural areas and become LGBTQ people and part of a sexual community (Weston 1998, 49). As Bobby and his friends demonstrated, the "great gay imaginary" at the center of this rural-to-urban migration narrative is still foundational to accounts of LGBTQ identities and communities in the United States in the twenty-first century. This sexual and gender imaginary relies on a metronormative narrative that in order to live a full queer life one must move from the homophobic and transphobic country to the open and accepting city, especially "great" cities like San Francisco (Halberstam 2005).

Yet, despite the pull of this migration narrative and the violence and harassment he reported experiencing in his small town, Bobby did not move right after high school. When he finally made it to San Francisco while working as a long-haul trucker he found something unexpected:

> And then I actually saw it [San Francisco] and that was too much . . . Drove by it in a big truck. That was enough to see. No way, shape, form, fashion. It all sounds good and looks good on TV, but wow. That's a big place. [laughter] Too stressful. Uh, it just looked stressful. Just driving by the Interstate, going, "Wow!" you know. No, no, no. I have problems walking around [his current small city]. I get turned around downtown here. I couldn't imagine bein' somewhere like that.

The great gay imaginary shaped Bobby and his friends' desires for a more open life, but the reality of the crowded hectic urban space was not appealing. In fact, Bobby only moved away from his hometown in his early twenties to live with his girlfriend in a small Kentucky city. With his transition a few years before and the recent breakup of that relationship, Bobby was planning to move to a nearby rural area at the time I interviewed him. He thought that area would allow him to live the rural lifestyle that he desired and fit in like any other guy.

In contrast to Bobby, I grew up in the San Francisco Bay Area. I could see the Golden Gate Bridge, when it was not shrouded in fog, from the windows of my middle and high school. As a teenager I came to understand myself as a queer along with some of my friends in the small cities on the east side of the Bay. Once I got my driver's license at sixteen, I would load my friends into the family station wagon and, unbeknownst to my parents, follow that same sexual imaginary by driving twenty minutes into San Francisco to hang out in the Castro, the central gay neighborhood. Too young to go to bars and not yet in possession of fake IDs, we went to coffee shops and just walked around soaking it all in. Unlike Bobby, I loved the hustle of the city and the anonymity of being lost in the crowd. Some of my friends left for college, but most returned, and I stayed until moving to Oregon for graduate school in my late twenties. It's not that we did not experience the occasional harassment or threat of violence—I certainly did as one of a few out queer kids at our high school—but we imagined it would have been so much worse elsewhere outside of our relatively ideal queer place.

Despite my own experiences growing up at the edge of the supposed gay mecca, I have come to recognize that the drive across the San Francisco Bay as a teenager did not bring me to a full knowledge of queer life. It was my travels across the Southeast and Midwest where I met people like Bobby or, more recently, to the rural inland Northwest where I truly understood the limits of my own urban-centered perspective. I learned that Bobby's story is not as unique as the ubiquitous migration narrative would suggest. Instead, my research with rural LGBTQ people made clear that queer and transgender life not only exists outside of urban spaces but does so on its own terms. Some LGBTQ people fare better in rural areas where everyday ways of life and more specific local ways of expressing their identities (or not) align with who they see themselves to be. In what follows, I briefly share some of my own insights about LGBTQ rural research and then offer suggestions on how such efforts can work toward coalition building across liminal positions for sexualities scholars and sociologists more broadly. Recentering our lens on sexualities and genders in rural communities broadens our knowledge, but more importantly offers a model to rethink our social and political aims.

Doing Rural LGBTQ Research

The reflections in this chapter come from two different studies that included interviews with LGBTQ people who currently lived or had lived in rural spaces. For the first project I interviewed sixty-six transgender men living in the US West, Southeast, and Midwest, mostly in person, from 2009–2013. About twenty percent of the men lived in rural places at the time of their interview and others had previously lived in or spent significant time in rural areas. These interviews focused on trans men's everyday lives as men and the resulting analysis demonstrated how the spaces and places they moved through in their everyday lives deeply shaped their experiences of gender, sexuality, and race (Abelson 2019).

The second project came from a larger ongoing collaborative study of LGBTQ people's coming-of-age experiences in the Pacific Northwest of the United States. I conducted eighteen in-depth interviews with rural queer and transgender people, age 16–60, in the inland Northwest, focusing on Eastern Oregon and Eastern Washington. I completed the interviews mostly in person in 2017–2018. For these rural interviews I included questions about current experiences living in rural spaces that are far from large cities such as Seattle or Portland. As of early 2023, I am doing additional rural interviews in the inland Northwest, including Idaho, for a project focused on rural LGBTQ people living amidst particularly divisive local and national political rhetoric in the region.

These projects build on the insights of others examining rural queer and trans life. As in ethnographies and interview studies by Arlene Stein (2001), Mary Gray (2009), Emily Kazyak (2012), I have found that rural queer and transgender people survive and sometimes thrive living in rural spaces where they create lives in line with where they live as opposed to taking on urban styles and cultures (See also Bell and Valentine 1995; Woodell, Kazyak, and Compton 2015). Scholarship that is critical of metronormativity illustrates that common understandings of LGBTQ identities rely on a binary opposition between urban and rural, or at least urban and elsewhere (Tongson and Herring 2019). In this setup, the rural is framed as backward, traditional, and repressive in opposition to urban spaces as enlightened, modern, and accepting (Gray 2009; Halberstam 2005; Herring 2010).

The queer urban-to-rural migration narrative at the center of metronormativity mirrors the racialized and colonial narratives of global migration where queer people must move from impoverished, overly traditional, and repressive countries in the Global South to live full lives as modern gay subjects in the Global North (Grewal and Kaplan 2001). At both regional and global levels these narratives ignore the constant movement between and increasing interconnection of rural and urban spaces in general and specifically relative to queer life (Mattson, this collection; Lichter and Ziliak 2017). Further, the urban/rural binary ignores the particulars of suburban queer life (Crawley, this collection; Tongson 2011).

In contrast to the dominant narrative, my research has shown that some rural queer and transgender people can find tolerance and even acceptance in rural communities through making claims to sameness and belonging. In my work with rural trans men, I found that whiteness and performing rural working-class masculinities are the ground for inclusion in predominantly white rural communities (Abelson 2016). My ongoing work in the rural inland Northwest shows further evidence of how key claims to rural community belonging are directly tied to Western settler colonialism and racist violence. These claims of community belonging are often premised on family connections to white settlement. The experiences of rural people of color also illustrate that whiteness can be key to belonging in predominantly white rural spaces.

Across the two projects, I have found a number of unexpected migrations from places like San Francisco to small towns in Tennessee or Eastern Oregon. Upsetting the imagined metronormative trajectory, rural locales can allow trans men to be recognized solely as men and offer other ways for LGBTQ people to blend into their communities. I have encountered stories of long-term HIV survivors and others who cannot afford rapidly gentrifying and expensive cities migrating to small conservative towns in the Northwest. These migration stories illustrate that sometimes it is urban rather than rural spaces where it is impossible to sustain a queer or trans person's life. Like many other rural people, LGBTQ people often have to travel out of their areas to access medical care or education, or even to find romantic and sexual partners, but these are temporary visits, lasting a few hours or a few years, and they often return to rural life. Thus, queer and trans people are part of the flow of larger patterns of urban and rural migration and interconnections between these spaces that undoes the binary opposition of urban and rural.

While the literature documenting rural queer life and expanding the metronormative critique has existed for quite some time, I still frequently meet with both disbelief and fascination when I describe my research with rural queer and transgender people to coastal urban dwellers. Most often they question whether I would find anyone to interview or whether they'll be too scared to actually talk to me. This work is not only possible but, for an urban sexualities scholar like myself, rural research is a chance at building relationships and engaging with other LGBTQ people who find themselves in physically liminal spaces on the outside of urban-centered queer life.

I have come to see my work with rural and other non-urban queer and transgender people as an attempt to foster what Maria Lugones (2006) described as deep coalition with other liminal people where interviewing becomes an act of complex communication. Engaging across spatial locations in this case has potential as a practice of critical queer anti-urbanism, which does not necessarily reject urban queerness but acknowledges that it is just one possible way of queer life (Herring 2010). Traveling to rural communities and connecting with other LGBTQ people there has given me a more complete picture of what it can mean to be queer and trans. Each step of the research process provided new information, but conducting the interviews themselves provided opportunity for deeper connection and laid the ground for complex communication. In my experience, engaging in queer-anti urbanism has had political implications for fostering coalition across spaces, as well as practical implications for successfully completing research projects. I hope that in sharing these experiences, other sexualities researchers and sociologists will find both inspiration and advice in how to reexamine their own urban-centered approaches.

Finding Rural LGBTQ Sites

For both projects, my main method of recruitment across urban, rural, and suburban spaces has been to persistently send hundreds of cold emails into the abyss. I used internet searches to find local, statewide, and regional organizations, listservs or other online groups, and in-person gathering places that were directly or tangentially LGBTQ-related. In both projects, I started by contacting local support groups, sending flyers to be posted at community institutions, and contacting people I knew in the region. I found interview subjects through personal contacts, postings to online communities or email lists, and fliers posted at community centers and medical clinics. I do not have an exact estimate of the proportion of responses I received, but it was very few compared to the flood of messages I sent out. In all those efforts, I sought to strike a balance between being comprehensive and persistent but not annoying.

Fruitful virtual recruitment sites, particularly in the internet age, shift across time and are specific to place. In the West, South, and Midwest various email listservs, Yahoo Groups, and Google Groups were the most successful means of connecting with potential participants, though many were defunct a few years later. In the inland Northwest, private Facebook groups have been most effective for these purposes, though they are difficult to find. These groups offer a space for organizing and social support for LGBTQ people in rural areas, as well as a tenuous but perhaps necessary link for individuals without any connections to larger LGBTQ communities, sometimes called lone wolves. If we step outside a metronormative framework, these more hidden sites of organizing do not suggest that rural LGBTQ groups are backwards but rather, as Carly Thomsen (2021) argued, that they do not necessarily rely on visibility as a central political principle.

In the project with trans men, this small and often hard to find population posed particular recruitment challenges. These interviews took place before the increased media attention and expansion of everyday knowledge of transgender people in recent years, which felt unimaginable when I conducted the interviews in the West and South in 2009–2010. When recruiting trans men in the rural Midwest the classifieds website Craigslist was useful for finding participants.[1] I posted in the volunteer section of the site for each of the midwestern states I planned to visit. Through this site I found less visible members of the population, such as one interviewee who reported he had never met another transgender person, but also community leaders, like one that managed a local transgender email list. I tried Craigslist again in Oregon and Washington in 2017 but did not find any additional respondents through the site. I attribute this partially to regional differences in use and the site's declining popularity overall, especially amidst recent changes to the site due to the anti-sex trafficking federal law known as FOSTA (Lingel 2020).

In the inland Northwest I found some youth participants through Gay/Straight Alliances at local high schools, but it was initially difficult to identify other LGBTQ groups or organizations. I learned that rural queer and trans groups and service providers tend to use organizational frames that provide cover for their explicit LGBTQ work. For example, in my early internet searches in the inland Northwest, I found a number of PFLAG (Parents and Friends of Lesbians and Gays) groups. Some of these groups aligned with the mission of PFLAG as an organization that serves families and allies of LGBTQ people, yet others were run by and directly served LGBTQ people themselves. In these cases, PFLAG, as a straight and cisgender-oriented space, operated as a cover that made the group and its LGBTQ members less of a target for harassment.

Social services organizations, like disability or anti-violence services, also worked as LGBTQ organizing sites in rural spaces. The multicultural center of a local college was an effective site for recruiting people of color but also white queer and trans people. Spaces that focus on a single axis of identity, such as race or disability, should attend to their queer and transgender constituents, but in these cases they also acted as cover for serving a broader range of LGBTQ people. In seeking moments of cover and space to come together, LGBTQ people were not necessarily hiding; instead they creatively used an existing rural space with less regard for the metronormative politics of visibility. Recruiting in sites like these is a useful strategy for forming diverse samples of LGBTQ people in non-rural spaces as well.

These more hidden organizing tactics do not mean that every rural queer and trans person faces danger for belonging to an explicit LGBTQ group. Instead, the groups allow members to join who are more vulnerable to potential threats in rural spaces, where one is enmeshed in interdependent rural relationships with communities and neighbors and cannot fall into crowds of urban anonymity. The limitation with this kind of cover is that others in the community might not know that the resource is available. For example, a young trans woman in the rural Northwest described her sense of loneliness and isolation because she did not think there were any other trans people in the area. Yet, she lived near a town with an active PFLAG group consisting mostly of trans people. She knew of the PFLAG group but not that it was actually chock-full of trans people until I told her. There is potential in these kinds of circumstances for reciprocity and substantive solidarity when researchers act as a resource and share local knowledge that they have gained from other community members.

In sum, recruitment methods need to be as varied as the organizational strategies and tactics of each community. Recruitment in these spaces is severely limited if it relies on urban logics of visibility or the assumption that all rural LGBTQ organizing across different locations and times will use the same structure or tactics. Rural ingenuity will persist, and it is up to the researcher to equally persist in identifying and seeking individuals and organizations within those varied terrains. This approach offers insights for sociologists in different spaces to recognize how questioning the dominant spatial logics that shape their perspectives can lead to more diverse samples.

Gatekeepers

Regional and local leaders, as well as online group administrators, acted as gatekeepers, points of contact who often determine access to a group, organization, or community. Working collaboratively with local gate-keepers allowed me to recruit rural LGBTQ people who may have been difficult or impossible to contact without insider knowledge. These gate-keepers, who are sometimes self-appointed and in other instances an officially acknowledged leader of the group or community, are a key resource for rural LGBTQ individuals to control their own privacy while participating in some form of collective LGBTQ life. Gatekeepers keep LGBTQ identities confidential and maintain the safer spaces of both in-person and online communities. In doing so, they attempt to protect community members from job discrimination, family loss, and other potential forms of harassment and violence.

Gatekeeping can also serve to protect community members from violence perpetuated by researchers themselves, though gatekeeper attempts at protection also have negative effects. There is a long history in Western social science of the representational violence of misconstruing how respondents and communities see themselves. This dynamic is clear in exploitative relations between researched and researcher in gender and sexualities research, especially with transgender populations (Hale n.d.; Schilt and Lagos 2017). Gatekeepers face a tension between potential abuse that makes them want to limit access and a desire for the proliferation of research that takes rural people's voices seriously. All gatekeepers seemed to have their community's best interest at heart, but some also spoke about their communities in paternalistic ways. I found myself wondering at times what kinds of protection the community needed most, if any, and how the gatekeeper role also provided a sense of importance for the individual, in addition to the power of shaping representation. Once I made contact with other community members, it was clear that some gatekeepers did not represent all constituencies equally well.

To satisfy gatekeepers in email exchanges and sometimes lengthy phone calls, it was vital to show that that I had both good intentions and enough knowledge of LGBTQ people to not treat community members as a spectacle or object of curiosity. Having some community knowledge, regardless of the researcher's identity, is invaluable when doing ethical research. Yet, even if an initial interaction with a gatekeeper seemed to go well, I did not know how they would present my work to their community. In one instance, after what felt like a positive email exchange, a moderator posted my call for participants to a group for trans men in a way that casted some doubt as to whether I could be trusted. Luckily, a couple of trans men I knew on the list posted in response vouching for my credibility and let me know what happened. Without my own connections in that community, the moderator's post might have limited my recruitment efforts. Therefore, additional work beyond interacting with a single gatekeeper can be crucial to build trust with potential participants.

Taking a collaborative approach to conversations with gatekeepers and research participants throughout all of my research projects has been invaluable. This effort is not just a tactic to solve recruitment issues or to form a more representative sample (generalizability is not really a goal of this kind of qualitative research) but to deepen my knowledge and foster coalition with other LGBTQ people. Maria Lugones (2006) argues that shared liminality, such as being LGBTQ, does not automatically create solidarity or understanding between people, since we are often implicated in one another's subjugation through our differences. In order to foster the potential for coalition, Lugones calls for moving toward deep understanding of each other's positions and a thorough reckoning of these differences through complex communication. I have come to see my work with rural and other non-urban queer and transgender people as an attempt to foster this kind of exchange with other liminal people. Interviewing and other moments in the research process work toward solidarity through understanding and addressing the issues that matter to participants and gatekeepers, not just fulfilling my own research aims.

Overall, I believe that it was coming into each place as educated but open that allowed gatekeepers and participants to give me some trust and set the possibility for complex communication. For example, in my project with trans men I was already well aware of transgender identities and issues from scholarly literature and being in close community with trans people. I highlighted that my work focused on trans men as men rather than a search for the origins of a trans identity or some kind of Transgender 101. While I valued participants' expertise, they did not have to waste their time educating me on basic information that had already been extensively covered by other researchers. In my rural research in both projects, participants expressed appreciation that I was producing work about rural LGBTQ people since they saw few representations of themselves. This is an example of how engaging in a shared project of critical queer anti-urbanism that moves away from a focus on urban queer life (Herring 2010) extends reciprocity and encourages participation in research. Both my genuine interest in people's lives and the knowledge I came into the interview with helped me find participants and establish rapport. In all, most people I interacted with were helpful and willing, even if reasonably suspicious at first. I found that deeper engagement as a researcher through seeking out opportunities for complex communication broadened the range of individuals who wanted to participate.

Who Was Likely to Participate?

Through these different methods of recruitment and gaining access from gatekeepers across both projects, I encountered a number of different motivations for individuals to agree to participate. These motivations highlight additional reciprocal possibilities in conducting rural LGBTQ research. A gift card or cash incentive was reason enough for some individuals to participate, especially young people and those with few economic resources. For others, a personal recommendation encouraged them to volunteer, and for many it was a chance to further their own goals.

Local activists and organizers were frequently eager participants who provided valuable insights about issues in their area. At the same time, activists were conscious about representing their community in ways that aligned with their political goals. A group that I named "contributors" overlapped with activists in that they were motivated to participate to increase general and scholarly understanding of LGBTQ rural people, or they felt their stories were particularly meaningful. Activists shared some of these characteristics or aims, but the contributors tended to focus on sharing their life as it was, rather than a particular narrative in line with explicit political goals.

The other unique group of interviewees in these rural projects were the "lonely wolves" who were isolated from other LGBTQ people and sought connection through the interview. Most lonely wolves had not found community in their local areas and lived their daily lives with few people knowing about their LGBTQ identity except for their partners and perhaps some family members. Some of the trans men in particular had chosen to blend into their communities and not be seen as transgender due to the salience of their own identities as "just men" or to maintain their safety. The most heart-wrenching stories came from these lonely wolves. For example, one trans man in the Southeast told me with tears in the corners of his eyes how he had not seen his young son in over a year, because his ex-wife had cut off contact due to his transition. Another trans man who lived rurally had lost the only local trans man friend he had made in his rural area to suicide a few months before the interview and was looking for space to process that profound loss. These lonely wolves reported that they were grateful that doing the interview gave them a chance to talk to someone who understood LGBTQ issues. While some of these moments departed from my own expectations of the interview setting, for lonely wolves, activists, and contributors alike these were opportunities where I could reciprocate interviewees' participation by providing brief moments of support or a platform for their activist or personal goals.

Outsiders in Rural Communities

When research and politics constantly center urban spaces, especially in light of queer metronormativity, rural people can feel left out and even resentful. In Oregon and Washington urban areas like Portland or Seattle dominate the politics and culture of the state, leaving the vast stretches of less densely populated areas with a sense that their priorities are unmet. In the inland Northwest I encountered multiple stories of frustrations with outsiders who would pledge their commitments to supporting rural organizing work and then not follow through. Several interviewees noted a lack of willingness from urban dwellers to visit rural areas paired with an expectation that rural dwellers should make the trip to visit cities. Rural people are used to traveling to urbanized areas to fulfill some social and material needs, such as expanded retail options and specialized healthcare. Yet they expressed frustration that the burden of travel for political work or research participation should once again fall to them, as if somehow the trip between the city and the country is longer or more difficult for urban rather than rural residents. This dynamic compounds the isolation that rural people experience, particularly in winter months when travel is more difficult in remote areas.

Keeping up these connections and attempting to push against these typical urban/rural asymmetries is not just a matter of conducting ethical research, though it is that too, but is important as a larger project of queer liberation through critical queer anti-urbanism and building coalitions in difficult times across spaces. As a researcher I am still trying to figure out how to follow through on those commitments. In the inland Northwest, I found myself saying time and again that I did not want to be one of those people who comes out from Portland and then disappears. Yet, a combination of factors such as research funding, family crises, and COVID-19 have made it difficult to keep up travel and connection. Despite these difficulties, I have found great value in traveling to conduct interviews and continue to engage in the ways I can.

Traveling long distances to conduct interviews shows a commitment to interviewees and gives the researcher a better sense of place, but presents its own challenges. It can be difficult to find public places to meet for interviews in rural areas, where there are fewer of the ubiquitous chain coffee shops I use in urban and suburban places. If there is a local coffee shop or restaurant, the interviewee might be particularly worried that someone they know could overhear our conversation. However, many rural LGBTQ residents do not care about being interviewed in a public space, because they say that everyone knows everyone else's business anyway. Conducting interviews in a participant's homes or office, taking safety into account, or private rooms at local libraries might be a better option.

Time also presents challenges with traveling to conduct research. It is often difficult to reschedule interviews that participants cancel at the last minute if one is only in an area for a short time. I have also found myself testing my own endurance by conducting one interview and then immediately driving several hours to meet another participant. While traveling to conduct interviews can test a researcher's stamina and resources, it can provide a deeper sense of place, invaluable when writing about space and place, and a chance for connection across spatial locales. Even without doing in-depth ethnographic observation, a short visit to the place can give the researcher a taste for everyday life and add important context to interviewees' stories.

Video communication technologies have their limits but make it possible for researchers to speak face-to-face with research participants hundreds or thousands of miles away. Indeed, during much of the COVID-19 pandemic, distance technologies have been the only way to conduct interviews safely. Yet, video conferencing sessions can have glitches and delays that make the flow of an in-person interview difficult to reproduce. Phone interviews can also be valuable but, like a video feed, can shift how interviewer and interviewee perceive emotion and the tone of questions and responses. Rural residents in general tend to have less access to high-speed internet and are less likely to have smart phones, or adequate cell reception, than their urban and suburban counterparts (Perrin 2019), which limit the use of these technologies and are likely to affect communication quality.

For urban researchers seeking to learn from and build alliances with rural people, it is crucial to avoid replicating existing urban and rural power dynamics. Traveling to conduct some or all of the interviews for a project on LGBTQ rural communities forces the researcher to limit the geographic scope of their work, but that may help avoid a continued reliance on scattered geographic samples in LGBTQ research and better attend to particularities of place. Research that has a broad geographic focus or uses distance technologies can have meaningful insights and be more practical with limited resources, but we must pay attention to how they reproduce existing divides and limit our understanding. Sociological research that does not attend to this kind of spatial specificity, within and beyond sexualities research, risks missing key characteristics that shape social life.

Creating connection and the ground for solidarity between urban and rural people, whether LGBTQ or not, through complex communication is particularly important since the urban/rural divide is currently central to political polarization in the US and beyond. Continuing to pit urban and rural against one another through framing the rural as backward and urban as elitist will only deepen these divides. Complex communication can highlight a deep understanding of both the actual textures of everyday lives across spaces and overlapping economic and political interests. Those overlaps are important sites of coalition, people working together for shared aims across differences, for political organizing on diverse issues such as environmental protection. Relationship and understanding also create the potential to act in solidarity for one another across spaces. Meaningful coalition between LGBTQ people and across these spaces offers a model for a politics that shift political polarization and forge new paths for political alliance in particularly fraught times. It adds hope for political solidarity beyond many kinds of differences.

Moving Forward

I hope the insights I gained from doing research with rural LGBTQ people will provide both motivation and practical strategies for other sociologists to engage in work across the political and social divides of the urban-rural continuum. Decentering the urban and considering a wider range of spaces is crucial in this moment for sociologists across subfields. Whether studying LGBTQ populations or not, sociologists need to attend to how imagined rural/urban divides or specific features of place shape their approaches to research, as well as the dynamics of inequality or social problems that they seek to understand. When doing research work with populations that seem to be hidden or less visible, the researcher must examine how their approach to recruitment employs normative perspectives, such as metronormativity, that make it difficult to see those on the edges of our spatial and social worlds. Sociologists studying rural areas should continue to attend to differences of race, sexuality, and gender in rural communities and spaces. Difference in rural scale or population size is key to understanding rural communities more broadly and the specific roles that LGBTQ+ and Indigenous and other people of color play in rural spaces. For sociologists more broadly, understanding the lives of those who seem most marginal and out of place in rural places helps us to comprehend the deeper texture and dynamics of rural community life. Rural queer and trans people are not an aberration; rather, their lives elucidate the deeper dynamics of community inclusion and especially the nexus of race, gender, and sexuality outside of urban spaces.

Where is the center of LGBTQ life? Like my own journeys across the San Francisco Bay, and through the rural South, Midwest, and Northwest, understanding the full range of LGBTQ subjectivity means going far beyond the urban enclaves that still loom large in metronormative narratives. If we want to understand the scope of LGBTQ life but also build coalitions to change the conditions under which LGBTQ people and others are marginalized, we need to practice critical queer anti-urbanism. Traveling to the spaces that are liminal, in the sense of being on the far reaches or outside of the urban spaces that are often centered in our queer imaginaries, allows an opportunity to seek out complex communication with other liminal beings. For scholars doing work across the intersections of sexuality, gender, race and other aspects of difference, an awareness of how our spatial perspectives shape our research creates both more effective methods, especially with less visible populations, and forms the ground for coalitions across spaces.

NOTE

1 Emily Kazyak suggested using Craigslist to me based on her own recruitment of gays and lesbians in the Midwest.

REFERENCES

Abelson, Miriam J. 2016. "'You Aren't from around Here': Race, Masculinity, and Rural Transgender Men." *Gender, Place & Culture* 23 (11): 1535–46.

Abelson, Miriam J. 2019. *Men in Place: Trans Masculinity, Race, and Sexuality in America*. Minneapolis: University of Minnesota Press.

Bell, David and Gill Valentine. 1995. "Queer Country: Rural Lesbian and Gay Lives." *Journal of Rural Studies* 11 (2): 113–22.

Gray, Mary L. 2009. *Out in the Country: Youth, Media, and Queer Visibility in Rural America*. New York: New York University Press.

Grewal, Inderpal and Caren Kaplan. 2001. "Global Identities: Theorizing Transnational Studies of Sexuality." *GLQ: A Journal of Lesbian and Gay Studies* 7 (4): 663–79.

Halberstam, J. Jack. 2005. *In a Queer Time and Place: Transgender Bodies, Subcultural Lives*. New York: New York University Press.

Hale, Jacob C. n.d. "Suggested Rules for Non-Transsexuals Writing about Transsexuals, Transsexuality, Transsexualism, or Trans-." http://sandystone.com/hale.rules.html.

Herring, Scott. 2010. *Another Country: Queer Anti-Urbanism*. New York: New York University Press.

Kazyak, Emily. 2012. "Midwest or Lesbian? Gender, Rurality, and Sexuality." *Gender & Society* 26 (6): 828–48.

Lichter, Daniel T. and James P. Ziliak. 2017. "The Rural-Urban Interface: New Patterns of Spatial Interdependence and Inequality in America." *Annals of the American Academy of Political and Social Science* 672 (1): 6–25. https://doi.org/10.1177/0002716217714180.

Lingel, Jessa. 2020. *An Internet for the People: The Politics and Promise of Craigslist.* Princeton, NJ: Princeton University Press.

Lugones, María. 2006. "On Complex Communication." *Hypatia* 21 (3): 75–85.

Mattson, Greggor. "Outposts: Centering Lone Gay Bars of the American Interior." In *Outskirts.*

Perrin, Andrew. 2019, May 31. "Digital Gap between Rural and Nonrural America Persists." *Pew Research Center* (blog). www.pewresearch.org.

Schilt, Kristen and Danya Lagos. 2017. "The Development of Transgender Studies in Sociology." *Annual Review of Sociology* 43 (1): 425–43.

Stein, Arlene. 2001. *The Stranger Next Door: The Story of a Small Community's Battle over Sex, Faith, and Civil Rights.* Boston: Beacon Press.

Thomsen, Carly Ann. 2021. *Visibility Interrupted: Rural Queer Life and the Politics of Unbecoming.* Minneapolis: University of Minnesota Press.

Tongson, Karen. 2011. *Relocations: Queer Suburban Imaginaries.* New York: New York University Press.

Tongson, Karen and Scott Herring. 2019. "The Sexual Imaginarium." *GLQ: A Journal of Lesbian and Gay Studies* 25 (1): 51–56. https://doi.org/10.1215/10642684-7275292.

Weston, Kath. 1998. *Long Slow Burn: Sexuality and Social Science.* New York: Routledge.

Woodell, Brandi, Emily Kazyak, and D'Lane R. Compton. 2015. "Reconciling LGB and Christian Identities in the Rural South." *Social Sciences* 4 (3): 859–78.

3

Outposts

Centering Lone Gay Bars of the American Interior

GREGGOR MATTSON

June 29, 2017. Gun Barrel City, Texas.

Red Garlow did not live to see the gay bar that now bears his name. There was already one gay bar in Gun Barrel City, Texas, but "it smelt bad and it was seedy. He just didn't like it, so the plan was to be the opposite of what that bar was," explained his partner, Michael Slingerland, to me and my research assistant Tory Sparks. "Garlow," as he was known, fell ill with cancer before his "grandiose ideas" could be realized. Michael cared for Red for two-and-a-half years until he passed, "and then I opened up the bar he wanted to open," in 2010, and called it Garlow's. From the outside, the bar looks like the plumbing warehouse it used to be, marked by a sign sporting the bar's logo with its signature rainbow swirl and the tagline, "where friends become family." Inside, murals depict silhouettes of classic Hollywood: top-hatted dancers are framed by unspooled film reels, the effect interrupted by small wooden signs. One reads "Drink til he's cute," another "Pony Express: Young, Wiry Boys Wanted," and "Not everyone can be the queen: someone needs to stand and applaud when I enter the room." Above the door to the patio one simply reads: "Red."

Today, Garlow's is the only gay bar in Gun Barrel City Texas, a town of 5,672 people a little over an hour southeast of Dallas, so named because its main drag is as straight as a gun's barrel. It may sound like an Old West frontier town, but it was incorporated in 1969 on the banks of the recently built Cedar Creek Lake, a reservoir to quench Fort Worth's thirst and supply recreation for the booming Dallas-Fort Worth Metroplex. It's the only gay bar in Henderson County (pop. 75,532), a deep-red county in a red state: at least 77% of every precinct voted for Trump in 2016. It lies on the urban-rural interface (Lichter and Brown 2011) where poor country folk and modest small-town dwellers rub elbows with wealthy weekending urbanites.

Not only is Garlow's the only gay bar in Henderson County, it's also the only one in any of the eight counties that border it. Gun Barrel City may be only a one-hour's drive from the big city gayborhood of Oak Lawn in Dallas, but for most folks in these other counties, Garlow's is the closest gay bar by more than an hour's drive. It's just a gay bar in a small town in one of the reddest counties of a red state, one whose very existence challenges much of what we think we know about gay bars or LGBTQ life in the interior of the United States.

Studying Outpost Gay Bars

Gun Barrel City's gay bar may seem like an oddity or outlier, but it's not alone. As the celebrated documentary *Small Town Gay Bar* revealed, they're just part of everyday life in much of the American interior (Ingram 2006). Indeed, there are more municipalities (93) with a lone gay bar than the total number of gay bars in San Francisco, Los Angeles, and Chicago *combined* (Mattson 2020). Scholarship too often ignores the places where the majority of LGBTQ people live, including the South, Appalachia, rural areas, suburbs, and ordinary cities (see Stone 2018; Forstie 2020; and the Introduction to this book). Understanding gay bars as an institution, and the LGBTQ life they foster, means understanding gay bars beyond the gayborhoods in which we stereotypically find them, and considering their manifestations in the places where most LGBTQ people live.

Existing studies of gay bars paint a fairly consistent picture of them. As I have summarized elsewhere, they depict businesses that are "dominated by men, are racially segregated, face unwelcome invasions of straight people, are harbingers of gentrification, and only a small subset feature drag performance" (Mattson 2020, 81). Such findings generalize from outliers—the big-city gayborhood (Brown 2008)—a critique that some have called metronormative (Halberstam 2005). Four gayborhoods in particular garner much of the attention—New York, Chicago, Los Angeles, and San Francisco—metropolitan areas that comprise less than 15% of the US population. In the gay neighborhoods and gay bar districts of these cities (Mattson 2015), bars can subdivide to serve niche LGBTQ subcultures. Keith Orr, one of the co-owners of "/aut/ bar" in Ann Arbor, Michigan, explained to me his plans to realize "what we envisioned as a modern-day gay bar. Not just a men's bar, or a lesbian bar, or a suit bar, or a leather bar. Big cities have those, they have a huge community and can subdivide like that. We're just a little town and this is the gathering place for everybody." To understand gay bars as an institution—and to understand LGBTQ life the way it is lived by the majority of Americans—we need to understand gay bars in their diverse geographical manifestations.

To understand gay bars beyond gayborhoods, I visited what I call outposts—gay bars that are more than an hour's drive from another one (or forty minutes in New England). This was part of a larger project for which I interviewed more than 120 gay bar owners and managers in thirty-eight states between 2016 and 2021 about the state of their business, their challenges and successes, changes in their patronage, and their plans for the future. Owners and managers are best placed to notice recent changes in LGBTQ leisure patterns yet have been heretofore an untapped resource for understanding one of the most iconic of LGBTQ places. Not all of these visits garnered both interviews and fieldnotes, and not all interviews were in outposts, but my research design of month-long multi-thousand-mile road trips allowed me to visit fifty-six outposts in thirty states.

I identified outpost bars using the Damron Guide, a printed travel directory of LGBTQ businesses and organizations that was published annually between 1964 and 2017, and again in 2019. It is the longest-running and only national source of consistent, LGBTQ+ placemaking records (Knopp and Brown 2021). Listings were suggested by users and confirmed by Guide editorial staff, making it an example of crowdsourcing that differs from the algorithmic kind that we're used to with contemporary online business directories. I supplemented these legacy printed records with two of these internet business listing services, Yelp and Google Business. Average driving distances were computed using Google Maps.

I contacted bars by phone and email but found the most reliable way to get a response was through Facebook. Many bars did not respond to requests for interviews; others were closed at the time I visited, contradicting the hours of operation listed on their own social media sites and popular consumer websites. Many bars had disconnected phones or websites with copyrights indicating their most recent updates were more than five years ago. My interviews are thus, at best, a convenience sample of outpost bars—convenience being defined relative to the four road trips of more than 7,500 miles to visit places that were, by research design, geographically distant from each other.

These gay bars may seem remote to outsiders—they are rarely accessible by reliable public transportation, the nearest international airport may be more than 90 minutes away, and there is unlikely to be a PhD-granting institution with inquisitive researchers nearby. But for locals, driving ninety minutes to go out may not be that big of a deal, and the miles between the bar and your hometown, family, and coworkers may be welcome. And outpost bars are tied to national LGBTQ culture through YouTube videos and TikToks and smartphone apps, the travels of their patrons, the migrations of drag queens, queer content on television, and the perhaps-universal desire to be around like-minded people.

The task of understanding gay bars takes on an urgent cast in light of their widespread closures. Between 2007 and 2019, for example, business listings suggest that perhaps as many as 36.6% of gay bars closed (Mattson 2019). Some bars are especially at risk of closure, including those that serve women, people of color, and men into radical sexual practices—these bars close at much greater rates than bars that serve only gay men or that serve men and women together. And coastal handwringing about gay bars seems to be justified: controlling for population change and the decline of straight bars too, gay bars are more resilient in ordinary cities than the "great cities" of the coasts (Spicer and Mattson 2021). It may be that the resiliency of small-town gay bars is due to the relative gay-unfriendliness of their regions, and thus LGBTQ+ people must flock together for support. But it also possible that the lower cost of living, and the lower cost of doing business, means that bars that are only one source of income are more sustainable outside the great cities.

I learned that these outpost bars bear many similarities to each other: they have long, deliberately embraced straight patronage; they are gender-integrated; almost all feature drag performances; they reflect the diversity of their regions; and they are tied to their owners' ties to rural and/or small-city life and the leisure activities and family relation-ships that can be fostered there (Forstie 2020; Mattson 2020). For all the similarities of outpost bars, their fortunes varied as widely as did their regional economics. For every gay bar owner who said smartphone apps like Grindr had decimated business, there were others who use social media to great effect. For every owner who blamed Millennials for abandoning gay bars, there was another who bemoaned the older crowd for staying home. And for every gay bar squeezed by economic redevelopment, there were more squeezed by local economic collapses, the changing landscape of marijuana legalization, regional population decline, or an inability to serve new populations who demand equal-ity for transgender and gender nonconforming patrons. Gay bars aren't closing everywhere, and they aren't closing for the same reasons. They are changing in surprising ways that serve old audiences and cultivate new ones in ways that are different than big-city gayborhood bars, as Garlow's demonstrates.

"Local Faggot Makes Good"

Michael assesses Gun Barrel City with a businessman's gimlet eye. The town has 5,600 people and nine bars, and of the residents "half drink and half don't, so you're fighting for everybody's entertainment dollar and to struggle to get enough people to get in here to pay your damn bills." Michael explained that the later evenings attracted a mix of gay and straight younger patrons, all of whom socialize in mixed-orientation groups: "The kids go out to the other bars but they come back because they know their gay friends are here. The straight younger ones, they all went to school together, they're friends together, whether you were gay or straight isn't an issue." To facilitate this mixing, Michael employs security that allows him to admit eighteen-year-olds, one of only two bars in town that bothers with the cost and trouble. By offering safety and unique entertainment, Garlow's is a place for gay people and their childhood friends even when childhood was something that ended only last year.

Although other gay bar owners blame social media for the decline of gay bars, Michael uses them to keep tabs on his customers' whereabouts. "You see it on Facebook how many are going to hit Garlow's, how many will be here all night, and how many will hit another place during the night." Social media lets people socialize online, but also lets them alert each other—and Michael—about where they're meeting in the physical world, and why. As Michael answered, in response to my question about why own a gay bar in the age of Grindr and gay marriage, "You have to have a conjugating place, and this here is the conjugating place for all the locals."

Garlow's may be an outpost of LGBTQ culture in a small town in a rural county, but it is intimately connected to the Metroplex. Michael explained to me that "on the weekends we have a good Dallas crowd. A lot of Dallas people, they have houses out on the lake so they come in on Saturday and Sunday after they've been on the lake. Our Friday and Saturday night crowd is 70% Dallas and 30% local." Weekdays sees a local crowd, one that is a mix of gay and straight people.

Garlow's is part of this local LGBTQ community but isn't the entirety of it. Michael estimates that the town is 30–35% gay, making it perhaps a modest, lesser-known Texas variety of the gay resort towns like Fire Island, New York, Key West, Florida, or Provincetown, Massachusetts (Newton 1995; Rupp and Taylor 2003; Brown-Saracino 2010). "The [straight] shopkeepers, they don't mind it because we pay well so they shut up!" Michael admits that the weekend crowd doesn't have so many lesbians, but this isn't true during weekdays: "we get a lot of lesbians, the locals. The Dallas lesbians, they don't own houses out here like the men do." Gender thus plays a role in who are weekenders and who are weekday residents.

Michael describes how the bar partners with the church among other organizations to organize charity events that draw people into Garlow's: "The gay church, they're having a big fundraiser and plus there's a golf tournament. They come in here for drag." Named Celebration on the Lake, the congregation meets in the neighboring town of Mabank. Their website cheekily proclaims, "God loves you and there's nothing you can do about it." Straight people come for other charity events, especially the bar's fundraisers for organizations like Toys for Tots: "We do a food drive for the food pantry, and we join forces with the American Legion. I was a veteran—I was in the Army—so I know a lot of them, and they come over here too." Michael Slingerland may be gay, but it's not the entirety of him. Garlow's may be a gay bar, but it's also deeply embedded in its small-town Texas community even as it maintains its gay-resort ties to the big city nearby.

Like all small-city gay bars, straight people are a significant portion of patrons, and are drawn to the bar in part by the safety it offers, which had been provided long before the Pulse nightclub shooting in Orlando put all gay bars on high alert. As Michael explains, "On a steady night you can see two guys kissing, two gals kissing, and a guy and a gal. It's an everybody, no-drama bar. We haven't had a fight in years, we don't have any troubles from anybody. It's got the good, laid-back vibe when you walk in." He explains why: "We're the only bar with a doorman, so you can feel all right by yourself and see what's going on in a gay bar."

Originally, this security was put in place to comply with regulations allowing eighteen-year-olds to be in Garlow's. This hassle and expense means most bars don't take the trouble, but having an eighteen-and-up door policy was important to Michael, both from a moral sense and a business sense: "That's your next customer base." He continued: "We nurtured the young crowd. Coming here because they won't get chastised or be made fun of or be put down or bullied, so when they become of age they came here. Why would you go to [another bar in town], which is a redneck bar? This is the only bar they *should* go to!" When I asked whether the underage patrons spend enough to make it worth the bar's while, Michael replies with the long-term perspective of a successful businessman: "The old crowd may have money, the young crowd not so much, but they will *eventually* have money, they will be the old crowd someday. That's just business." The fact that the bar is now one of the most popular for straight kids in town? "You have to adapt: you're in a small town," he told me.

In contrast to the previous gay bar, Michael told us that it was his bar's classier environment that drew this younger, straighter crowd from the beginning. "First it was the little girls who wanted to get away from their boys in the big pickups, and they weren't going to be seen in a queer bar! But then they realized if they wanted to see their girls they'd best get over it! So now all the young kids come in and nobody gives a shit anymore." Part of not being "seedy and crummy" is banning smoking on the weekends, even though Michael himself smokes in the bar during the week. Contradicting the pop journalism that blames Millennials for all ills, Michael explains: "A lot of the younger people don't smoke—well, they probably smoke dope but they don't smoke cigarettes—they don't do the things the older crowd does. My boyfriend has three daughters and none of them smoke and never have smoked, but he does because he's older." Summarizing his approval both of the young crowd's integrated socializing and their healthy living, he measures Garlow's present against its past: "It's a better crowd, but it's because the kids are better."

Michael was one of several gay bar owners I interviewed who praised younger patrons, but he reports some disadvantages to a bar that attracts the "kids" who "dance their asses off." "My friends don't come in here because it is loud, but the young people are here spending money. Yes, it's too loud on Saturday night! I don't even stay in my own damn bar! It's too crowded and you can't get a goddamn drink," so he hired manager Glen Robison "to deal with all that." Describing the calm afternoon during which we were speaking, Michael noted, "I like it when it's quiet, when I can watch sports and not offend everyone, but on Saturday nights I found myself getting pissed off because it was noisy and crowded so I gave it to Glen and let Glen run it." He concluded with sound management advice: "Know when you're good at something and know when you're not and just get the fuck over it."

In addition to the drag shows, the bar has a series of weekly events. The Thursday that Tory and I visited was going to be poker night—Texas hold 'em, naturally—"and there won't be a gay person here," laughed Michael. "And the queers will come in later and the queers will be over here," he swept his hand across the bar, "and the straights will be over there," he gestured to the pool tables. The bar also books local talent. "We have a guitar player that is very popular locally, a good-looking kid, not gay, who plays the guitar like ringing a bell." With evident pride, Michael reports that "the mayor's been in lots of times." Of hosting events that feature and attract straight people, Michael claims: "If you didn't do that, we wouldn't have survived. When we opened up in 2010 it's like there was no water in the lake, we were on the Obama economy." To my raised eyebrows at his attribution of blame for the Great Recession to the just-elected president, Michael explained: "It's a very food-stamp-oriented town. It's very different when nobody has a job and nobody has any money." The regional economy may have improved with the national one—perhaps despite that president's best efforts—but that may be because GBC is one of those "paradises" where the rural poor, getting-by small-town folks, and the urban land speculators rub shoulders, at least on the weekends (Sherman 2021).

Michael is well-known in town, and this was part of his marketing strategy for Garlow's. "I'm on the City Council, I'm on the Economic Development Council, I'm on the Zoning Council. I know everyone in this town. I thought, if I got involved in politics, everyone would know who the hell we were. And they do." Becoming a civic fixture bemuses him, because it stands in stark contrast to his childhood and young adulthood: "I'm more popular than in my entire life!" Growing up, he describes himself as getting bullied until he went to college to "get out of that damn town. Now that I opened up this bar, Christ! Everybody knows me but I don't know anybody! I've got 6,000 friends on Facebook but I couldn't tell you much about any one of them." While Michael clearly enjoys this turn of events, it's also good for business: "You have to keep the name out there, the name Garlow's has got to be out there all the time. I go to many city council events, and so when I'm getting my picture took I always say, 'Local faggot makes good!'"

Inspired by another city councilor who invited the council to meet in their place of business, Michael conducts city business at Garlow's as well. "When I'm on committee meetings I won't have them at City Hall. I make them come in here! And everybody likes to smoke and drink and so we do the committee work here, so the city of Gun Barrel is sitting in the gay bar." As he summarizes, "I'm a name brand at 67. Well, how about that!"

Like every small-city gay bar I've visited, drag shows are a big draw. On the day we visited, manager Glen Robison was in a rush to drive to Dallas to pick up Onyx, a performer for that Saturday's show. "All of them have drama dripping the fuck off them," Michael said good-naturedly as Glen hurried away. Hosting out-of-town drag queens brings in patrons, but also incurs expenses. "Anytime we bring in outside talent we put them in a hotel room, we get a deal with the La Quinta so we give them rooms. Not their own room mind you, we stack them in there like cord wood, but we have six rooms reserved every Saturday night for drag queens." Few small-city gay bars have such a large visiting roster, but few of them are as close to a major drag talent center as small-town "GBC" is to Dallas, home to the Davenport dynasty familiar to fans of *RuPaul's Drag Race*.

Patrons also come for Garlow's expansive patio. From the road, the bar is an unassuming metal shed, but the wood-fenced yard features tropical plants, a fountain, Greek statues, and pub games including a beer pong table and cornhole boards branded with Garlow's logo and trademark rainbow swirl. "In a small town you invent shit to do. It's not Dallas, you don't have everything at your disposal," he explains. Michael's staff developed an elaborate, life-sized board game they call "Bario Party," a real-life tribute to Nintendo's Mario Brothers franchise. Concrete paving stones are painted with familiar mushrooms and stars, with multicolored toilet plungers to mark players' progression along the path. "On your back patio we have adult Mario with stepping stones. You roll a big dice and land on the right square and get a free drink, and you go around the board. Candace came up with that game. You invent things to do, you invent reasons to get people in here." Some of these events are for escaping real life, and some are for addressing its problems.

Garlow's is a significant source of charity in town, as are many gay bars (Mattson 2023; Rupp and Taylor 2003). "This bar gave $57,000 to charity last year—that's more than most families make around here. Anyone who knows us knows we're the number one charity bar in the county. Toys For Tots, ASPCA [American Society for the Protection of Cruelty to Animals], the [Social Services] Resource Center . . . we do shows so they can give money to help people with their rent or for their electric, they help take care of people." On the wall near the bar is a brass plaque honoring Michael and Red with the 2008 Citizen's Achievement Award. As Michael reported a recent benefit for the Volunteer Fire Department to buy hoses, I interrupted him: "Are you telling me your volunteer fire department has gay hoses?" He laughed, "I don't know about that, but they sure as hell bought them with my damn gay beer!"

Michael continued, describing how the bar facilitates the charity of others year-round more than giving of its own resources. Describing a $12,000 haul for Toys for Tots that allowed them to buy thirty-seven bicycles in a town of under 6,000 people, he describes how the bar donates the stage and the drag queens donate the venue. "We didn't give away a fucking nickel. The people of this town came in here and starting tipping the queens so everybody in this town did, they didn't consciously know that they gave away $57,000. That brings the whole town together, to help a charity." If Garlow's is a "conjugating place for all the locals," this is in no small part because Michael has local concerns and has embedded his bar in them.

For Michael, this charity work honors Red Garlow's life, is the right thing to do, and is perhaps a necessity for the success of any bar, gay or straight, in small-town Texas: "That's how we became a household name, because we became the number-one charity in the world. When you do that in a small community you get to be very well-known, very quick." Michael described Garlow as the source of the couple's charity giving, which continues after his death: "Nobody needs to know that, but that's how all this charity got started." Michael finished with a flourish: "Ta daa! That, as that man says, is 'the rest of the story.'" That man being quoted is right-wing radio host Paul Harvey who railed against homosexuality during his half-century radio career, and who might be rolling in his grave to be quoted by a "local faggot made good."

Small-town life suits Michael, and he wouldn't have opened a gay bar anyplace else. "Being a rural bar has its advantages. If you want to be going to a gay bar, well, we're the pick of the litter! If they ever open up some chain gay bar they'd better buy me out because they'll put me out of business in a month." He knows many of the bar owners in the Metroplex and does not envy them. "I would hate to have to compete in Dallas with all the major bars for their entertainment dollars. There's a lot of people in Dallas but I would hate to be a chickenshit little bar, getting only the scraps from when the others are full."

Michael grew up in small-town life, and measures the quality of his current living against his childhood in a town of 1,500 people with twenty-eight people in his graduating class. "If you were gay everybody knew it, and it was terrible. I didn't go to a gay bar until I was twenty-one because I was scared to death someone would see me, but it doesn't dawn on you then that the stark raving terror of being found out is the most terrible part. I had a friend of mine that hung himself because he was gay. He couldn't quite get over it." He attributes the changes to the youths who congregate in his bar on weekend nights: "Nowadays it's a lot better because the kids have *made* it a lot better. We made it better together, maybe. Being gay now is not a stigma, and people are lot more forgiving and easier on gays I guess, so it's a lot better than it was when I was growing up."

Looking around the bar, he summarizes his later-in-life turn of events. "There's no money in gay bars. You have to really like this or really like queers. It's a tough job. I wouldn't wish this fucker on anybody." But he clearly loves the place. "It's got the good, laid-back vibe when you walk in. That was Garlow. I know that Garlow is in here, and I know that he's in Heaven, and I knew when I opened this that I wouldn't fail because he's watching."

Centering a Sociology of LGBTQ Life in the Interior

Michael's story complicates conventional sociological wisdom about the decline of gay bars and defies many of its simple oppositions. He opened a successful one, in an unlikely place, just as news stories announced that gay bars were failing during the "Obama economy" of the Great Recession (e.g., Thomas 2011). Garlow's may seem to be in a rural hamlet, but like Provincetown, Massachusetts, or Guerneville, California, it is intimately tied via patrons and performers to a metropolitan gay neighborhood, albeit Oak Lawn in Dallas, Texas, and not some more-famous coastal city. Garlow's is a bar that has embraced straight patrons from the beginning without experiencing them as invaders, and embraces the Millennials blamed for "ruining" other markets. And while smartphones and social media are blamed for causing gay bars to close, Michael Slingerland uses them to track his patrons and advertise his successful establishment.

His is an exceptional story, too, to be sure—no other bar owner I interviewed was as much a fixture of local politics as he was, and most small-city gay bars aren't as close to a gayborhood. Certainly, few big-city gay bar owners could (or would) express right-leaning critiques of Barack Obama, and Michael's embeddedness in local politics serves his economic interests even as it integrates his gay bar into Gun Barrel City's civic life.

But increasingly other small-city gay bar owners *are* interviewed in local newspapers or serve on local chambers of commerce, integrated and not sidelined in their communities. And like Michael, many other gay bar owners don't depend on nightlife as their sole source of income, evidence that gay bars aren't exactly moneymakers and that owners are prioritizing something other than return on investment for their troubles. They are, as I call them, "not-quite-for-profit" enterprises (Mattson 2023).

Embedded in the stories sociologists tell about gay bar closures are some stark assumptions that don't hold up to scrutiny. Online and face-to-face aren't zero-sum opposites—we use Facebook to plan lunches and political protests, for example, and the places we've visited in real life trail after us in email notifications tied to our credit card use. The gentrification blamed for the rising rents of big-city clubs is only a dream for struggling manufacturing towns or the depopulating farm regions of the interior. The idea that "any bar is a gay bar" now is suspect given the uneven geography of LGBTQ acceptance, whether in Indiana or Mississippi, but especially in the less gay-friendly neighborhoods of our gay-friendliest metropolises. And LGBTQ acceptance may be as much of a business opportunity as a threat, as onetime gay-only spaces can attract straight people to their drag shows and cabarets (Rupp and Taylor 2003), just as straight people were key supporters of LGBTQ through the first half of the twentieth century (Heap 2010; Paulson and Simpson 1996).

True, the gay bars in big-city gayborhoods are most definitely squeezed by runaway rent increases, "invasions" of disruptive straight people, smartphone apps that offer an endless parade of hot profiles, and most non-gay bars feel gay-friendly enough (see Ghaziani 2015; Orne 2017). But these enclaves also have regional gay press to advertise every closure to their nationally known mainstream newspapers; we don't ever get national press about the goings-on in gay neighborhoods in Oklahoma City or Milwaukee or Baltimore, much less the majority of cities in which there's no gay neighborhood or gay press. Smartphone cruising apps maybe be wonderlands for some in the big city, but in rural areas they either display people who are twenty-five miles away as the crow flies but 100 by road, or a "virtual wasteland of blank 'discreet' profiles" (Mustain 2019).

The metronormative critique that research overgeneralizes from urban LGBTQ lifeways is well-placed but can erase the back-and-forth movement of LGBTQ people from the country to the city to the country and back again (Annes and Redlin 2012; see also Abelson in this collection). And these need not be migrations to the coastal "great cities" so often studied (see Crawley this collection). For example, Mary Gray (2009) writes of her interlocutors that:

> these youth can (and regularly do) travel to gay enclaves in Louisville [Kentucky], Lexington, and Nashville [Tennessee]. But they cannot pro-

duce in their rural daily lives the sustained infrastructure of visibility that defines urban LGBT communities. Instead, they travel to each other's houses and caravan roundtrip to a larger city with a gay bar.

Other researchers similarly find that LGBTQ lives in "ordinary" cities and rural areas are similarly not in opposition to big cities or LGBTQ culture centers, but in "slippery" concert with them (Myrdahl 2013; McGlynn 2018). And cosmopolitan critiques about proper queer politics and lifestyles can erase the lives of "ordinary," "rural," and "small-city" LGBTQ lives (Annes and Redlin 2012; Brown 2012; Brown-Saracino 2017). What seem to be queer rural or smalltown lives are not necessarily anti-urban, and must be studied in their interrelationships and interfaces among geographies, and not in strict binary oppositions, or on terms set by big-city LGBTQ+ politicos or queer theorists.

In vast swaths of the country, it was in the region's only gay bar that I could find the only all-gender restroom, a bulletin board with public advertisements for LGBTQ groups and businesses, fundraisers for gender confirmation surgeries or queer cancer treatments, or a place to see real live LGBTQ people on demand. These may be old hat in Chicago's Boystown but they're not in Boise, and I'm skeptical that they're regular features of straight bars that are gay friendly even in San Francisco. In places without feminist bookstores or LGBTQ centers, the gay bar galvanizes activism, plans local pride celebrations, and brings a cosmopolitan flair to the region, including for gay-friendly straight folks (Mattson and Sparks 2018). Gay bars may seem banal in big cities, but they can be lifesavers in regions where they are the only public LGBTQ+ address.

In places with more than one gay bar, the racism of one owner or sudden closure of a business means the community has other places to go and other institutions other than bars. In places with an outpost and no other institutions of LGBTQ life like high school gay-straight alliances or PFLAG chapters (see Abelson, this collection), the entire community may depend on the foibles and fortunes of one individual business owner. These outpost bars seem unaffected by big-city ills like gentrification, but they are prone to closure due to regional economic busts, population declines, the failing health of owners, and the fragility of LGBTQ businesses in regions where there are few other entrepreneurs with means.

LGBTQ culture takes place in gay bars, and queer connections can be forged there, although the online world means that they're not the only spaces for culture and connection anymore, and the presence of alcohol means that they are spaces that have always excluded many LGBTQ people. These suggest that stories that exclude outpost bars can't capture the nation's diversity, the uneven geography of its LGBTQ acceptance, or the variety of LGBTQ lives forged in the American interior. Gay bars may be closing but they aren't disappearing, and the experiences of outpost bars like Garlow's demonstrate the surprises that can be discovered when what seems fringe is made center.

ACKNOWLEDGMENTS

Thanks to Patrick O'Connor for reading an early version and Phillip Fucella, Libby Murphy, and Lisa Stampnitzky for later ones. For more on Garlow's and other outpost bars, see my 2023 book with Redwood Press, *Who Needs Gay Bars? Bar-Hopping through America's Endangered LGBTQ+ Places*.

REFERENCES

Annes, Alexis and Meredith Redlin. 2012. "Coming Out and Coming Back: Rural Gay Migration and the City." *Journal of Rural Studies* 28 (1): 56–68. doi: 10.1016/j.jrurstud.2011.08.005.

Brown, Gavin. 2008. "Urban (Homo)Sexualities: Ordinary Cities and Ordinary Sexualities." *Geography Compass* 2 (4): 1215–31. doi: 10.1111/j.1749-8198.2008.00127.x.

Brown, Gavin. 2012. "Homonormativity: A Metropolitan Concept That Denigrates 'Ordinary' Gay Lives." *Journal of Homosexuality* 59 (7): 1065–72.

Brown-Saracino, Japonica. 2010. *A Neighborhood That Never Changes: Gentrification, Social Preservation, and the Search for Authenticity*. Chicago: University of Chicago Press.

Brown-Saracino, Japonica. 2017. *How Places Make Us: Novel LBQ Identities in Four Small Cities*. Chicago: University of Chicago Press.

Forstie, Clare. 2020. "Theory Making from the Middle: Researching LGBTQ Communities in Small Cities." *City & Community* 19 (1): 153–68.

Ghaziani, Amin. 2015. *There Goes the Gayborhood?* Princeton, NJ: Princeton University Press.

Gray, Mary L. 2009. *Out in the Country: Youth, Media, and Queer Visibility in Rural America*. New York: New York University Press.

Halberstam, J. Jack. 2005. *In a Queer Time and Place: Transgender Bodies, Subcultural Lives*. New York: New York University Press.

Heap, Chad. 2010. *Slumming: Sexual and Racial Encounters in American Nightlife*. Chicago: University of Chicago Press.

Ingram, Malcolm. 2006. *Small Town Gay Bar*. Red Bank, NJ: View Askew Productions.

Knopp, Larry, and Michael Brown. 2021. "Travel Guides, Urban Spatial Imaginaries and LGBTQ+ Activism: The Case of Damron Guides." *Urban Studies* 58 (7): 1380–96. doi: 10.1177/0042098020913457.

Lichter, Daniel T. and David L. Brown. 2011. "Rural America in an Urban Society: Changing Spatial and Social Boundaries." *Annual Review of Sociology* 37: 565–92.

Mattson, Greggor. 2015. "Bar Districts as Subcultural Amenities." *City, Culture and Society* 6 (1): 1–8.

Mattson, Greggor. 2019. "Are Gay Bars Closing? Using Business Listings to Infer Rates of Gay Bar Closure in the United States, 1977–2019." *Socius* 5. doi: 10.1177/2378023119894832.

Mattson, Greggor. 2020. "Small-City Gay Bars, Big-City Urbanism." *City & Community* 19 (1): 76–97. doi: 10.1111/cico.12443.

Mattson, Greggor. 2023. *Who Needs Gay Bars? Bar-Hopping through America's Endangered LGBTQ+ Places*. Stanford, CA: Redwood Press.

Mattson, Greggor and Tory Sparks. 2018. "'We Have a Gay Bar Here.' You Don't Need a Coast to Be Cosmopolitan." In *Red State Blues: Stories from Midwestern Life on the Left*, 109–14. Cleveland: Belt Publishing.

McGlynn, Nick. 2018. "Slippery Geographies of the Urban and the Rural: Public Sector LGBT Equalities Work in the Shadow of the 'Gay Capital.'" *Journal of Rural Studies* 57:65–77. doi: 10.1016/j.jrurstud.2017.10.008.

Mustain, Kyle. 2019. "The New Glory Hole." *Slate*, June 27.

Myrdahl, Tiffany Muller. 2013. "Ordinary (Small) Cities and LGBQ Lives." *ACME: An International Journal for Critical Geographies* 12 (2): 279–304.

Newton, Esther. 1995. *Cherry Grove Fire Island: Sixty Years in America's First Gay and Lesbian Town*. Boston: Beacon Press.

Orne, Jason. 2017. *Boystown: Sex and Community in Chicago*. Chicago: University of Chicago Press.

Paulson, Don, and Roger Simpson. 1996. *An Evening at the Garden of Allah: A Gay Cabaret in Seattle*. New York: Columbia University Press.

Rupp, Leila J. and Verta Taylor. 2003. *Drag Queens at the 801 Cabaret*. Chicago: University of Chicago Press.

Sherman, Jennifer. 2021. *Dividing Paradise: Rural Inequality and the Diminishing American Dream*. Berkeley: University of California Press.

Spicer, Jason and Greggor Mattson. 2021. "Towards a Holistic Queer Geography: Changing Spatial Distributions and Relationships among LGBTQ+ Households and Businesses." *American Sociological Association Annual Meeting*. Virtual.

Stone, Amy L. 2018. "The Geography of Research on LGBTQ Life: Why Sociologists Should Study the South, Rural Queers, and Ordinary Cities." *Sociology Compass* 12 (11): e12638. doi: 10.1111/soc4.12638.

Thomas, June. 2011. "The Gay Bar: Is It Dying?" *Slate*. Retrieved March 23, 2016 (www.slate.com).

4

Festival Krewes

Rethinking the Southern Urban Queer Experience

AMY L. STONE

When I went to my first gay Mardi Gras ball in Baton Rouge, Louisiana, there were over one thousand people attending, guests clad in tuxedos or floor-length ballgowns of all ages, genders, races, and sexualities enjoying the spectacular costumes and drag of the all-men's Krewe of Apollo. The Krewe of Apollo Baton Rouge was a gay-run, predominantly white festival organization (or krewe), one of many such groups throughout the Gulf South. These krewes are private clubs of twenty to forty people who hosted annual balls during Carnival season. I was impressed by the size and scale of the ball, the way it was introduced by the mayor of Baton Rouge, and the positive regard expressed by family and friends who attended for the men who put on the event. I was completely blown away that my second Mardi Gras ball, the Order of Osiris in Mobile, Alabama, was almost twice the size of the Krewe of Apollo. The gender-diverse group of forty krewe members elaborately decorated the Mobile Convention Center and had almost two thousand guests in attendance. In both Baton Rouge and Mobile, the two oldest LGBTQ social organizations in each city were these krewes and the local Metropolitan Community Church (MCC), all of which were founded in the early 1980s. The last Mardi Gras ball I attended at the end of five years of fieldwork on southern urban festivals was the Mystic Womyn of Color ball in Mobile. This ball was the smallest, attended almost exclusively by around three hundred Black lesbian and queer women who traveled from all over the South and Midwest to create Black lesbian community together for a long weekend.

The more I researched these festival organizations, the more I realized that they are an important part of urban life in the Gulf South, the area along the coastline of the Gulf of Mexico. Mardi Gras, also known as the Carnival season, is part of the social, political, and cultural structures of urban life in the Gulf South. Mardi Gras is organized by private festival organizations—krewes, mystic societies, or social aid and pleasure clubs—that host events and parades. In the LGBTQ community, krewes are often the oldest LGBTQ organizations in town and play an important role in visibility, community building, and developing a sense of belonging in the city.

Although there is a literature on ballroom culture and a history of cross-dressing balls in the Northern US (Bailey 2013; Stryker 2008; Chauncey 1994; Joseph 2020), there are few academic accounts of these Mardi Gras balls and their importance in LGBTQ life (Smith 2017; Stone 2022; 2019; Machado 2023). Indeed, there is little sociological research on southern urban queer life, much less festival life. I argue here that these festival organizations are an overlooked but important part of urban queer life. I contend that research on urban queer life has missed out on a regional form of urban organization—the festival organization.

I think festival organizations have been overlooked by scholars due to the marginalization of queer urban southern experiences, along with misunderstandings about festivals and Mardi Gras. Below, I evaluate these reasons why the LGBTQ festival organization has been ignored. Then, I consider the ways that LGBTQ Mardi Gras krewes are an enduring urban organization that provide visibility, cultivate cultural citizenship for LGBTQ urban residents, and connect LGBTQ people with regional or city traditions and placemaking. Overall, I encourage scholars to center the queer South in their scholarship on what it means be LGBTQ in the city.

Marginalization of Southern Queer Urban Experiences

Sociologists do not center the experiences of southern urban queers in the study of LGBTQ life in the United States. Theorizing about gay urban life began with a focus on northern and coastal great cities, a bias that persisted through the first twenty years of sociological work on sexualities (Stone 2018). A few classic studies—Manuel Castells's (1983) study of a gay urban enclave in San Francisco, George Chauncey's (1994) history of gay men in New York—center the gay bar and neighborhood as an integral part of the LGBTQ urban experience. The emphasis on these organizational forms depends on theories about gay territoriality of space developed through work like d'Emilio's theory on capitalism and gay community development (d'Emilio 1983).

This omission is a result of neglect within sociology of the urban South generally and the queer urban South specifically. Sociologists know surprisingly little about southern urban life. Sociologists often frame northern urban life as representative of all US urban life, including the framing of Chicago as the classic American city, which renders the impact of regional culture on northern cities invisible (Garner 2018). Conversely, the ways that southern cities have taken shape and form are often ignored or considered anomalous (Lloyd 2012). Urban ethnography has neglected the southern city, suggesting that "few scholars recognize Southern cities as real 'American' cities" (Rushing 2009, 11). The absence of major southern metropolitan areas like Dallas, Houston, Washington, DC, Miami, and Atlanta from discourse about the great American cities is a case in point.

Sociology misses out on key parts of urban life by neglecting the southern city. This neglect belies the importance of southern culture for Black urban life across the United States (Hunter and Robinson 2018) and importance of work on Black culture and community in the urban South (Robinson 2014; Lacy 2004). Southern city life challenges existing sociological theories about race, urban forms, gentrification, and immigration in the city due to the way southern cities grew later compared to some of their northern counterparts (Lloyd 2012; Yonto and Thill 2020). The Sun Belt cities of the United States—a region of urban development that spans between Southern California to the southeastern coast of the United States—are some of the fastest-growing cities in the country with the most dramatic development taking place since World War II (Bernard and Rice 2014; Shermer 2013; Hollander 2011). These cities are just as important as work on Northern cities, in terms of understanding urban life.

Startlingly little is known about southern queer urban life, given that over a third of LGBTQ people in the United States live in the South (Stone 2018). The scholarship on southern queer urban life was set back for decades based on understandings that southern life was incompatible with queerness (D. J. Smith 1997). Seeing the South as having a specialized hostility to LGBTQ life is connected to a broader history of distancing from the South (Ward, Bone, and Link 2015) and treating the South as an "internal other" to contrast the overcivilized East and progressive West Coast (Jansson 2003; Griffin 2006; Lassiter and Crespino 2009; McPherson 2003). In this, the South becomes an "easy repository for all that is backward and hurtful in the United States" (Dews and Law 2001, 3). According to historian Donna Jo Smith, "America has long projected its 'Queer Other' onto the South" (D. J. Smith 1997, 278). This Othering leads to ignoring the ways that the South is full of multiplicities (Eaves 2017) and southern culture and traditions create unique spaces for queer life (Stone 2022). Scholar E. Patrick Johnson asserts that "the South is *always already queer*" (Johnson 2011, 5).

The earliest books about southern queer life focused on rurality, such as historian John Howard's (2001) classic, *Men Like That*, about same-sex desire among men in Mississippi. A growing body of work studies LGBTQ experiences in the South more generally, including sociological work on transgender life in the South (Abelson 2019; Baker and Kelly 2016; Rogers 2020; 2021). Sociologists who study the LGBTQ+ southern experience, like J. Sumerau and Baker Rogers, are growing in number. They build on an interdisciplinary body of work in the study of southern gay vacation towns like Eureka Springs, Pensacola, and Key West (Rupp and Taylor 2015; Thompson 2010; Watkins, III 2018) and gayborhoods in southern cities like New Orleans, Baton Rouge, Tampa, and Atlanta (Doan 2019; Nero 2005; Kanai and Kenttamaa-Squires 2015; Greene 2021; Stone 2021). The growth of this literature on the queer South pulls this scholarship out of the margins and closer to the center. Still, there is almost no sociological attention to Mardi Gras, a major festival season in the Gulf South.

Misunderstandings about Festivals

This lack of attention to the urban South includes surprisingly little sociological research on Mardi Gras or Carnival, apart from some work on tourism, moral holidays, and disrobing rituals in the French Quarter of New Orleans (Shrum and Kilburn 1996; Gotham 2005; Redmon 2003; Gotham 2007). I think it is easy to not take festivals seriously, dismissing them as temporary moral holidays or moments of fun that have little impact on life the rest of the year. Most work on festivals is conducted in the humanities. When I tell fellow sociologists that I have conducted work on festivals, they often respond with referencing the one or two theoretical texts on the carnivalesque from the humanities, typically work by Mikhail Bakhtin on popular humor or Peter Stallybrass and Allon White's book on early European festivals (Bakhtin 1984; Stallybrass and White 1986). Sometimes they've read anthropological work by Victor Turner on ritual (Turner, Abrahams, and Harris 2017).

Sociologists may be familiar with the term "carnivalesque," a political tradition of mocking the powerful during rituals and festivals. In academic presentations I often describe this as the "peasant as king, marching through the town with a meatball on a fork as a scepter." That's a long-winded metaphor, but most of these theories about festivals focus on early European peasants and their relationship with royalty and the elite. There's a huge debate within the study of festivals about whether carnivalesque practices are a legitimate, sustained challenge to power dynamics, but mostly this literature frames festival time as a special time or "time out of time" that does not impact power dynamics the rest of the year (Falassi 1987). Festivals are romanticized but also trivialized as something inconsequential.

I draw more on studies of Mardi Gras in colonized or postcolonial spaces that deeply challenge the scholarly separation of Carnival time from existing social inequalities and antagonisms (Aching 2010; Riggio 2004; Guss 2001; Picard and Robinson 2006). Carnival is not separate from everyday life; it is deeply embedded in all the other social processes in the city (Gotham 2005). Festivals can be a time when people push back against elites and make space in the city for marginalized community members.

Thinking of festival time as distinctly different from the rest of the time ignores the ways that festival organizations operate throughout the year and the ways that festivals strengthen and create social networks all year round. Gulf South urban culture is deeply shaped by Mardi Gras. In his book *Lords of Misrule*, journalist James Gill describes Mardi Gras in New Orleans as providing "year-round obsessions for many people" and observes that "much of the city's social intercourse centers on krewe get-togethers and the endless planning for the next parade" (Gill 1997, 4). The rituals that occur year-round to prepare for Carnival are just as important as the events themselves. For people who live in these southern cities, there is a porousness between regular time and Carnival time, "forcefully interwoven with daily life" (Lohman 1999).

In my book *Queer Carnival*, I argue that these citywide festivals are an important form of substantive citizenship or cultural citizenship. Evelyn Nakano Glenn (2011) describes this substantive citizenship as one that centers place-based and face-to-face interactions in making citizenship. Belonging in the city and feeling acknowledged for one's unique cultural contributions to the annual festival are both important parts of cultural citizenship. Marginalized groups are often not recognized for their contributions to society. Scholars like Nancy Fraser have long argued inequality comes not just from the unequal distribution of resources like money but also through differences in recognition (Fraser 2000; Ong 1996; Rosaldo 1994; Stevenson 2007). This recognition is about acknowledging the personal dignity in individuals and their place in society, what Margaret Somers refers to as "a moral equal treated by the same standards and values and due the same level of respect and dignity as all other members" (Somers 2008, 6). Michèle Lamont (2018) asserts that one issue faced by marginalized groups in society is a *recognition gap*, that the positive social worth of a group is unacknowledged and unrecognized by others. This recognition gap is multilayered, from the interpersonal to the institutional level. In my work, I argue that Mardi Gras can play a role in filling this recognition gap for LGBTQ people.

How Mardi Gras Works

There are some common misconceptions about what Mardi Gras is or how it works. When I tell students, friends, or colleagues that I study Mardi Gras, they describe Mardi Gras as a long weekend of thousands of half-naked college students in the New Orleans French Quarter engaging in unrestricted debauchery. One of the most iconic aspects of the New Orleans French Quarter Mardi Gras is a ritual around "boobs for beads" in which women raise their shirts to get parade beads thrown at them. However, throughout most of the Gulf South, Mardi Gras is a family-oriented festival. While the term Mardi Gras refers to the day before Lent starts, the Carnival season runs for one to two months, a season of private balls for mostly adults and public parades for everyone.

Carnival is celebrated not just in New Orleans but throughout the Gulf South, from Galveston, Texas, to Pensacola, Florida. Almost all parades and balls are run by private social clubs or secret societies. These festival organizations are called krewes, mystic societies, or social aid and pleasure clubs.

American Mardi Gras is run by festival organizations that operate throughout the year and are often highly visible in Gulf South cities. There are some subtle differences between these festival organizations; social aid and pleasure clubs emerged in the Black community of New Orleans and are oriented toward benevolent aid and community support; krewes are clubs that are modeled after organizations like secretive Masonic societies; and some krewes are mystic societies with secret group membership (Kinser 1990). Krewes are similar to American fraternities and sororities in that the groups tend to be single-sex, racially homogenous groups of people who are from a similar class background (Kinser 1990). One becomes a member through being voted into the group, and the most elite krewes may only take family members of existing krewe members.

Many krewes are actively, purposefully segregated by race. The oldest krewes are white, upper-class businessmen who proactively safeguard their organizations and events from racial integration; in New Orleans, these elite, segregated krewes "have played a big part in perpetuating the myth that the South sustained a great civilization until it was destroyed by Yankee vandals" (Gill 1997, 280). In New Orleans, legal attempts to racially integrate parading krewes were met with strong opposition and limited success (Gill 1997). A strong Black Carnival tradition in cities like New Orleans and Mobile includes the debut of Black debutantes, operating as a "parallel structure" to white Carnival events (Dawkins 2004).

The largest, richest krewes have club houses, recruit hundreds of members, and host huge parades with floats they have made themselves. The smallest krewes are groups of a dozen people who have access to a flatbed trailer, a truck big enough to tow it, and their imagination. These smallest krewes often parade in the "people's parades," huge community parades that only require a small entry fee for a float and are composed of many krewes. Krewe members parade, throwing beads, stuffed animals, light-up toys, and sweets to eager parade attendees, many of whom are children. Second-line parades are walking parades with high participant involvement and expressive movement that are a historical response from the Black community to a history of racial segregation in parading in New Orleans and other cities (Lohman 1999).

Not all krewes parade. However, almost all big krewes host a ball or other major private gathering during Carnival season. Masque balls are typically elaborate, costumed affairs that require formal attire for guests, all of whom are invited through krewe member social networks. These krewes host elaborate balls for their family, friends, and neighbors; occasionally, the public can buy tickets to these events. All these balls include refreshments, decorations, music, and tableaus or "call outs" of acting, dancing, or displays put on by the krewe members that are related to the theme of the event that year. Each krewe typically crowns their own royalty at their ball, comprised of devoted members who have contributed to the group. In high-status krewes, these balls are used to debut the teenage daughters of krewe members, one of whom is selected to be the krewe queen for that year.

For adults living in the Gulf South, these exclusive balls are an important component of the Carnival season. Scholars rarely study Carnival balls, as they are more challenging to access, and they are mostly studied historically rather than ethnographically (Atkins 2017). The omission of these events from understanding urban festivals means that scholars focus disproportionately on public drunkenness and celebrations rather than on events that involve status intensification, such as balls. Yet, the private Carnival balls of LGBTQ krewes are important events in the annual social calendar of many Gulf South cities.

Studying LGBTQ Krewes as Part of Centering the Southern Queer Experience

I think that LGBTQ Carnival organizations are important for sociologists to analyze as an enduring social organization that provides consistent, annual opportunities for LGBTQ visibility. LGBTQ people have a long history of being involved in Carnival activities. In the 1950s, scholar Munro Edmonson (1956) observed a high incidence of cross-dressing masquerade on the streets of New Orleans and portrayals of fairies and Greek gods by participants. White gay men have organized gay krewes since the 1950s and 1960s in cities throughout the Gulf South

(Carey 2006; H. P. Smith 2017). These early attempts at organizing were not without opposition; early krewes faced police raids and bomb threats (H. P. Smith 2017; Stone 2022). In the documentary *Sons of Tennessee Williams*, about the history of predominantly white gay Carnival krewes in New Orleans, several older white gay men wax nostalgic about how in the 1950s and 1960s, the only time cross-dressing in public was not policed in the city was during Carnival season. Since World War II, there has been increasing visibility for LGBTQ people during urban Carnival events. In the 1980s, krewe organizing began to be racially integrated and include women.

Krewes run by LGBTQ people are extremely common in Gulf South cities like Pensacola, Mobile, Baton Rouge, New Orleans, and Lafayette. In 2022, there were at least twenty LGBTQ-run krewes in six different cities in the Gulf South. In each of these cities, hundreds of LGBTQ people consistently participate in putting together festival events and thousands of additional LGBTQ people and their heterosexual friends and family attend these events. Many of the existing krewes today put on elaborate balls annually and (at times) parade during Mardi Gras. Sometimes these krewes are associated with one another. The Mystic Krewe of Apollo, for example, was founded in New Orleans in 1969 and has a history of krewes in Lafayette, New Orleans, Baton Rouge, Birmingham, Houston, and Shreveport.

The race and gender composition of these krewes varies. Krewes in the cities of Baton Rouge, Lafayette, and New Orleans are typically men-only krewes, whereas in the cities of Mobile and Pensacola there is a long history of multi-gender "all inclusive" krewes for LGBTQ people that are open to people of any gender or sexuality. I have only found three krewes explicitly for lesbian, bisexual, and queer (LBQ) women in all the Gulf South: the Mystic Womyn of Color in Mobile, which was active in the 2010s, and the Krewe of Ishtar in New Orleans and Daughters of Gaia in Mobile, both of which were active only in the 1980s. There is also a long history of LBQ women being involved in women's krewes, some of which are known to be more lesbian-friendly than others.

Despite the stark racial segregation of Carnival krewes, in which many white krewes continue to not only restrict membership but who can attend the ball based on race, there is a long history of racially inclusive LGBTQ krewes in the Gulf South, particularly in Mobile. Krewes organized by LGBTQ people in the Gulf South have historically been open to Black participants and guests but are predominantly white organizations. A few krewes are organized exclusively by Black LGBTQ participants (Stone 2022). Mwindo in New Orleans is a krewe for Black men, and Mystic Womyn of Color in Mobile is organized by Black women.

These festival organizations play an important role in southern city life throughout the year. Much of the literature on festivals stresses the temporary nature of festivals, but the organizations that run festivals often have long histories and are active throughout the year. These organizations host fundraisers, social events, and other events, along with being featured in the newspaper, Pride Parades, and other public events. These organizations have both longevity and importance in many cities. In the southern cities of New Orleans, Mobile, Lafayette, and Baton Rouge, the oldest LGBTQ organizations are typically Carnival krewes and Metropolitan Community Church (MCC) churches. In Mobile, Cornerstone MCC and the Order of Osiris are the two oldest continuously existing LGBTQ organizations in the city, both being founded in the early 1980s. Similarly, in Baton Rouge, the Mystic Krewe of Apollo Baton Rouge and the Baton Rouge MCC were formed in 1980 and 1983, respectively. In both cities, other organizations had been founded earlier but did not persist. Both krewes and churches have longevity. These krewes often have longstanding professional connections to large venues like convention centers, high profiles in the city as fundraisers for HIV/AIDS, and a physical presence on the street during festival events and other events throughout the year (Stone 2022).

LGBTQ Citizenship During Festivals

One of the central claims in my book *Queer Carnival* (Stone 2022) is that these festival balls and parades run by LGBTQ krewes are part of cultural citizenship for LGBTQ people in southern cities. Festivals such as Mardi Gras are understood as an important part of city life and perhaps characteristic of the city itself. In this way, festivals are part of how a sense of place is made in the city (Cobb 2016; Davis 2016; Wynn 2015). How LGBTQ people fit into city festival life depends on how they relate to the cultural traditions of the festival and city in question, how they are positioned in relation to other festival participants, and their demographics. But festival participation can be a rich site for LGBTQ participants to be valued for their cultural differences and find a sense of belonging in the city.

LGBTQ krewes get a lot of public recognition during Mardi Gras, with city residents publicly praising the fabulousness of their balls and desiring tickets to them. Often mayors, school superintendents, and other public officials attend. LGBTQ contributions to the festivals are frequently featured in museum exhibits or in public accounts of the festival history. In Mobile, the Order of Osiris has a track record for being voted as the Best Mardi Gras Ball through the Lagniappe Readers' Choice Awards. LGBTQ contributions to Mardi Gras are considered overwhelmingly positive.

As I show in my book *Queer Carnival*, LGBTQ festival participation gains the most recognition when it fits within the traditions of local urban culture. Festival traditions are one part of how cities are socially and culturally made. Gerald Suttles (1984, 283) astutely describes some of these urban traditions as the durability and "cumulative texture of local urban culture," stressing the importance of "sentiments and symbols" in the creation of this local culture. In my multi-site ethnographic study of festival life, some festival traditions were considered distinct to each city and its local culture. LGBTQ people are often considered at odds with tradition, yet in my study LGBTQ people engage meaningfully with local traditions that are important to them. And this engagement enhances their sense of belonging in the city. Some of these festival traditions overlap well with LGBTQ culture. For example, one white lesbian interviewee in Mobile, Alabama, told me that, "Mobile is a party town anyway, so if you put on a good party, everybody respects you for it." And, indeed, some LGBTQ people can put on a good party. But urban festivals are also an opportunity for LGBTQ people to grapple with their feelings about belonging and contributing to cultural traditions—everything from religious ritual to segregated events. This often involved resisting these cultural traditions, including a longstanding opposition to racial segregation during Mardi Gras.

Rethinking Queer Urban Life

Studying queer life in the urban South pushes back against classic works on LGBTQ urban life that reflect white gay urban life in major metropolitan cities like New York, San Francisco, and Chicago. In this chapter, I argue that our understanding of queer urban life would be different if it centered on southern rather than northern cities. If instead of being treated like an internal other, what would happen if the queer South were central to theorizing about LGBTQ urban life in the United States? The urban South is a rich and complex site for queer life that has its own organizations, customs, and possibilities within local urban culture. Centering queer life in the urban South illuminates new, potentially important ways of moving through urban life for LGBTQ people.

LGBTQ festival life is an important component of the cultural citizenship of queer people in the urban South. Krewes as a form of queer urban organization contributes to understanding how queer people make life for themselves in the city. I think krewes fit within the model of constellations proposed by geographer Jen Jack Gieseking by creating a production of space that is less territorial and more "mythical (imagined), calendrical (temporal), and navigational (wayfinding)" (Gieseking 2020, 3), a production of space that should be centered more in the study of LGBTQ life in the United States.

This chapter opens up questions about what else sociologists might be missing in their study of the queer urban South. It is an invitation to think more broadly about the important elements of queer urban life: what organizations might be important, what questions we should ask about queer life, and what happens when we center the South.

REFERENCES

Abelson, Miriam J. 2019. *Men in Place: Trans Masculinity, Race, and Sexuality in America*. Minneapolis: University of Minnesota Press.

Aching, Gerard. 2010. "Carnival Time versus Modern Social Life: A False Distinction." *Social Identities* 16 (4): 415–25. https://doi.org/10.1080/13504630.2010.497699.

Atkins, Jennifer. 2017. *New Orleans Carnival Balls: The Secret Side of Mardi Gras, 1870–1920*. Baton Rouge: Louisiana State University Press.

Bailey, Marlon M. 2013. *Butch Queens Up in Pumps: Gender, Performance, and Ballroom Culture in Detroit*. Ann Arbor: University of Michigan Press.

Baker, Ashley A. and Kimberly Kelly. 2016. "Live Like a King, Y'All: Gender Negotiation and the Performance of Masculinity among Southern Drag Kings." *Sexualities* 19 (1–2): 46–63.

Bakhtin, Mikhail. 1984. *Rabelais and His World*. Bloomington: Indiana University Press.

Bernard, Richard M. and Bradley R. Rice. 2014. *Sunbelt Cities: Politics and Growth since World War II*. Austin: University of Texas Press.

Carey, Albert. 2006. "New Orleans Mardi Gras Krewes." *Glbtq: An Encyclopedia of Gay, Lesbian, Bisexual, Transgender and Queer Culture*. Accessed July 24, 2023 (www.glbtq.com).

Castells, Manuel. 1983. *The City and the Grassroots: A Cross-Cultural Theory of Urban Social Movements*. Berkeley: University of California Press.

Chauncey, George. 1994. *Gay New York: Gender, Urban Culture, and the Makings of the Gay Male World, 1890–1940*. New York: Basic Books.

Cobb, Maggie C. 2016. "'For a While They Live a Few Feet Off the Ground': Place and Cultural Performance at the Walnut Valley Festival." *Journal of Contemporary Ethnography* 45 (4): 367–95. https://doi.org/10.1177/0891241614568192.

Davis, Andrew. 2016. "Experiential Places or Places of Experience? Place Identity and Place Attachment as Mechanisms for Creating Festival Environment." *Tourism Management* 55: 49–61.

Dawkins, Marvin P. 2004. "Race Relations and the Sport of Golf: The African American Golf Legacy." *Western Journal of Black Studies* 28 (1): 327.

Dews, Carlos Lee Barney and Carolyn Leste Law. 2001. *Out in the South*. Philadelphia: Temple University Press.

Doan, Petra L. 2019. "Cultural Archipelagos or Planetary Systems." *City & Community* 18 (1): 30–36.

Eaves, Latoya E. 2017. "Black Geographic Possibilities: On a Queer Black South." *Southeastern Geographer* 57 (1): 80–95.

Edmonson, Munro S. 1956. "Carnival in New Orleans." *Caribbean Quarterly* 4 (3–4): 233–45.

d'Emilio, John. 1983. "Capitalism and Gay Identity." *Families in the US: Kinship and Domestic Politics*, 131–41.

Falassi, Alessandro. 1987. *Time out of Time: Essays on the Festival*. Albuquerque: University of New Mexico Press.

Fraser, Nancy. 2000. "Rethinking Recognition." *New Left Review* 3: 107.

Garner, Betsie. 2018. "The Distinctive South and the Invisible North: Why Urban Ethnography Needs Regional Sociology." *Sociology Compass* 12 (6): e12589.

Gieseking, Jen Jack. 2020. *A Queer New York: Geographies of Lesbians, Dykes, and Queers*. New York: New York University Press.

Gill, James. 1997. *Lords of Misrule: Mardi Gras and the Politics of Race in New Orleans*. Jackson: University Press of Mississippi.

Glenn, Evelyn Nakano. 2011. "Constructing Citizenship: Exclusion, Subordination, and Resistance." *American Sociological Review* 76 (1): 1–24. https://doi.org/10.1177/0003122411398443.

Gotham, Kevin Fox. 2005. "Theorizing Urban Spectacles." *City* 9 (2): 225–46.

Gotham, Kevin Fox. 2007. *Authentic New Orleans: Tourism, Culture, and Race in the Big Easy*. New York: New York University Press. https://doi.org/10.18574/nyu/9780814733073.001.0001.

Greene, Theodore. 2021. "The Whiteness of Queer Urban Placemaking." *The Gayborhood: From Sexual Liberation to Cosmopolitan Spectacle*, edited by Christopher T. Conner and Daniel Okamura, 143–60. Lanham, MD: Lexington Books.

Griffin, Larry J. 2006. "The American South and the Self." *Southern Cultures* 12 (3): 6–28.

Guss, David M. 2001. *The Festive State: Race, Ethnicity, and Nationalism as Cultural Performance*. Berkeley: University of California Press.

Hollander, Justin B. 2011. *Sunburnt Cities: The Great Recession, Depopulation and Urban Planning in the American Sunbelt*. Oxon, UK: Routledge.

Howard, John. 2001. *Men Like That: A Southern Queer History*. Chicago: University of Chicago Press.

Hunter, Marcus Anthony and Zandria Robinson. 2018. *Chocolate Cities: The Black Map of American Life*. Berkeley: University of California Press.

Jansson, David R. 2003. "Internal Orientalism in America: W. J. Cash's *The Mind of the South* and the Spatial Construction of American National Identity." *Political Geography* 22 (3): 293–316.

Johnson, E. Patrick. 2011. *Sweet Tea: Black Gay Men of the South*. Chapel Hill: University of North Carolina Press.

Joseph, Channing Gerard. 2020, Jan. 31. "The First Drag Queen Was a Former Slave." *Nation*. www.thenation.com.

Kanai, Juan Miguel and Kai Kenttamaa-Squires. 2015. "Remaking South Beach: Metropolitan Gayborhood Trajectories under Homonormative Entrepreneurialism." *Urban Geography* 36 (3): 385–402.

Kinser, Samuel. 1990. *Carnival, American Style: Mardi Gras at New Orleans and Mobile*. Chicago: University of Chicago Press.

Lacy, Karyn R. 2004. "Black Spaces, Black Places: Strategic Assimilation and Identity Construction in Middle-Class Suburbia." *Ethnic and Racial Studies* 27 (6): 908–30.

Lamont, Michèle. 2018. "Addressing Recognition Gaps: Destigmatization and the Reduction of Inequality." *American Sociological Review* 83 (3): 419–44.

Lassiter, Matthew D. and Joseph Crespino. 2009. *The Myth of Southern Exceptionalism*. Oxford: Oxford University Press.

Lloyd, Richard. 2012. "Urbanization and the Southern United States." *Annual Review of Sociology* 38: 483–506.

Lohman, Jon. 1999. "'It Can't Rain Every Day': The Year-Round Experience of Carnival." *Western Folklore* 58 (3/4): 279–98. https://doi.org/10.2307/1500462.

Machado, Isabel. 2023. *Carnival in Alabama: Marked Bodies and Invented Traditions in Mobile*. Jackson: University Press of Mississippi.

McPherson, Tara. 2003. *Reconstructing Dixie: Race, Gender, and Nostalgia in the Imagined South*. Durham, NC: Duke University Press.

Nero, Charles I. 2005. "Why Are Gay Ghettoes White?" In *Black Queer Studies*, 228–46. Durham, NC: Duke University Press.

Ong, Aihwa. 1996. "Cultural Citizenship as Subject-Making: Immigrants Negotiate Racial and Cultural Boundaries in the United States [and Comments and Reply]." *Current Anthropology* 37 (5): 737–62. https://doi.org/10.1086/204560.

Picard, David and Mike Robinson. 2006. "Remaking Worlds: Festivals, Tourism and Change." *Festivals, Tourism and Social Change: Remaking Worlds*, edited by David Picard and Mike Robinson, 1–31. Clevedon, UK: Channel View Publications.

Redmon, Davis. 2003. "Examining Low Self-Control Theory at Mardi Gras: Critiquing the General Theory of Crime within the Framework of Normative Deviance." *Deviant Behavior* 24 (4): 373–92.

Riggio, Milla Cozart. 2004. *Carnival: Culture in Action—The Trinidad Experience*. Routledge.

Robinson, Zandria F. 2014. *This Ain't Chicago: Race, Class, and Regional Identity in the Post-Soul South*. Chapel Hill: University of North Carolina Press.

Rogers, Baker A. 2020. *Trans Men in the South: Becoming Men*. Lanham, MD: Lexington Books.

Rogers, Baker A. 2021. *King of Hearts: Drag Kings in the American South*. New Brunswick, NJ: Rutgers University Press.

Rosaldo, Renato. 1994. "Cultural Citizenship and Educational Democracy." *Cultural Anthropology* 9 (3): 402–11.

Rupp, Leila J. and Verta Taylor. 2015. *Drag Queens at the 801 Cabaret*. Chicago: University of Chicago Press.

Rushing, Wanda. 2009. *Memphis and the Paradox of Place: Globalization in the American South*. Chapel Hill: University of North Carolina Press.

Shermer, Elizabeth Tandy. 2013. *Sunbelt Capitalism: Phoenix and the Transformation of American Politics*. Philadelphia: University of Pennsylvania Press.

Shrum, Wesley and John Kilburn. 1996. "Ritual Disrobement at Mardi Gras: Ceremonial Exchange and Moral Order." *Social Forces* 75 (2): 423–58.

Smith, Donna Jo. 1997. "Queering the South: Constructions of Southern/Queer Identity." *Carryin' On in the Lesbian and Gay South*, edited by John Howard, 370–85. New York: New York University, 1997.

Smith, Howard Philips. 2017. *Unveiling the Muse: The Lost History of Gay Carnival in New Orleans*. Jackson: University Press of Mississippi.

Somers, Margaret. 2008. *Genealogies of Citizenship: Knowledge, Markets, and the Right to Have Rights*. Cambridge: Cambridge University Press.

Stallybrass, Peter and Allon White. 1986. *The Politics and Poetics of Transgression*. Ithaca, NY: Cornell University Press.

Stevenson, Nick. 2007. "Cultural Citizenship." *The Blackwell Encyclopedia of Sociology*, 1–4.

Stone, Amy L. 2018. "The Geography of Research on LGBTQ Life: Why Sociologists Should Study the South, Rural Queers, and Ordinary Cities." *Sociology Compass* 12 (11): e12638.

Stone, Amy L. 2019. "'You Out-Gayed the Gays': Gay Aesthetic Power and Lesbian, Bisexual, and Queer Women in LGBTQ Spaces." *Journal of Lesbian Studies*, 1–12.

Stone, Amy L. 2021. "Wearing Pink in Fairy Town: The Heterosexualization of the Spanish Town Neighborhood and Carnival Parade in Baton Rouge." *The Life and Afterlife of Gay Neighborhoods: Renaissance and Resurgence*, 139–58.

Stone, Amy L. 2022. *Queer Carnival: Festivals and Mardi Gras in the South*. New York: New York University Press.

Stryker, Susan. 2008. "Transgender History, Homonormativity, and Disciplinarity." *Radical History Review* 2008 (100): 145–57. https://doi.org/10.1215/01636545-2007-026.

Suttles, Gerald D. 1984. "The Cumulative Texture of Local Urban Culture." *American Journal of Sociology* 90 (2): 283–304. https://doi.org/10.1086/228080.

Thompson, Brock. 2010. *The Un-Natural State: Arkansas and the Queer South*. Fayetteville: University of Arkansas Press.

Turner, Victor, Roger D. Abrahams, and Alfred Harris. 2017. *The Ritual Process: Structure and Anti-Structure*. New York: Routledge.

Ward, Brian, Martyn Bone, and William Link. 2015. "Preface: Understanding the South." *Creating and Consuming the American South*, ix–x. Gainesville: University Press of Florida.

Watkins, III, Jerry T. 2018. *Queering the Redneck Riviera: Sexuality and the Rise of Florida Tourism*. Gainesville: University Press of Florida.

Wynn, Jonathan R. 2015. *Music/City: American Festivals and Placemaking in Austin, Nashville, and Newport*. Chicago: University of Chicago Press.

Yonto, Daniel and Jean-Claude Thill. 2020. "Gentrification in the US New South: Evidence from Two Types of African American Communities in Charlotte." *Cities* 97: 102475.

PART II

Space

5

Tumblr as "Heaven," Tumblr as "Hell"

How Platform Architecture Informs Identity Challenge for Trans and Non-Binary Tumblr Users

SPENCER GARRISON

CAMERON (22, THEY/THEM): There's a phrase that we use called 'being online' . . . like, when someone is like, 'oh, she's so online.' It's [when] somebody is just very, you know—they won't shut up about the internet . . . [And I think] trans people inherently being very 'online' people, a lot of the time, is because it's kind of in our heritage . . . [it's] our home.

Like Haraway's cyborgs (1985), today's trans and non-binary (TNB+) young people are well accustomed to life in the machine. In an era that has witnessed both the erosion of queer public spaces (Mattson, this collection; Cavalcante 2019; Ghaziani 2014) and the dissolution of safe, unsupervised public spaces for youth (boyd 2014), the internet has been celebrated as a locus of community for queer and trans young people worldwide (Fox and Ralston 2016). By providing young people with community spaces that promote information and resource-sharing, that facilitate connections with like-minded others, and that afford them some measure of privacy from hostile peers and parents, the internet enables queer and trans youth to explore identity under conditions that feel empowering, accessible, and safe (Cavalcante 2019; Fox and Ralston 2016; Oakley 2016; Renninger 2015; Cooper and Dzara 2010).

While social media use for *all* young adults has increased in recent years (McInroy et al. 2018), trans and non-binary (TNB+) youth are arguably the *most* active online, outpacing even other cohorts of youth under the LGBTQ+ umbrella. As I embarked upon my own interviews with

TNB+ teens and college students, nearly forty percent (38.9%) of my participants reported that they spent *at least* eight hours a day consuming social media content (the equivalent of a shift at a full-time job); more than a fifth (21.7%) invested more than 12 hours. As participant Presley (25, they/them) joked, "my entire life is basically online." The allure is high. Although trans people have leveraged the internet for as long as the internet has been publicly accessible (Dame-Griff 2022; Giardina 2019), today's digital landscape affords possibilities that would have been unfathomable even twenty years ago. Today's TNB+ youth regulate others' access to information about their identities on a post-by-post basis, tailoring privacy settings to suit different cohorts of peers. They explore new forms of embodiment, aided by digital tools (like Snapchat filters) that can transform their appearances, and supported by a community of others that can offer real-time feedback on their presentation. They comb through archives of information on TNB+ identities that span across decades—a process afforded by the internet's limitless memory and streamlined by the advent of user-generated hashtags. They communicate with other TNB+ people in an ever-expanding variety of modalities (synchronously and asynchronously; on public message boards, or one-on-one; pseudonymously, or "in person," via teleconference). Inaccessible (or unknown) to the public, hidden in plain sight or secured behind gauntlets of screening questions, the virtual communities they populate are positioned at "the margins"—yet, for TNB+ youth, they form the internet's bloody, beating heart.

In recent years, the micro-blogging platform Tumblr has been hailed as a particular locus of community for TNB+ young people. Earlier this year—and following years of much-trumpeted news proclaiming Tumblr's decline (Feldman 2018; Graham 2018; Swisher 2019; Nguyen 2021)—Tumblr executives came forth to pronounce Tumblr "the queerest place on the Internet" (Cohen 2021). Much beloved (and also highly contentious), the platform has been enshrined as a "cultural institution" (Richard 2018) among TNB+ youth: a place that has "normalized queerness and social justice" (Sarappo 2018) and that "takes pride in being a home for LGBTQ people" (Strapagiel 2021). As Emma Madden (2020) recently described it:

> If you came out as non-binary in the 2010s, some meathead probably told you that you 'spend too much time on Tumblr.' If this offended you,

you'd likely be called a 'snowflake' . . . [and] your newfound sense of self would have been derided as some Internet-created phenomenon you, and other young people like you, were using to get attention. But if you could have shown these Chads the state of the world at the end of the 2010s, they would have eaten their words . . . [for] there's no doubt that the microblogging site helped facilitate non-binary's transition from an online, underground identity to a mainstream one with offline consequences.

Having come of age as a Millennial trans man—someone who came out in college in the late aughts, and started HRT in 2015—I was well-acquainted with Tumblr myself. As I'd grappled with my own coming out process, I'd benefited *hugely* from the resources shared on Tumblr. Moreover, I understood that Tumblr was known as a *repository* for this kind of information—that it was seen as a place where trans people "hung out." But I'd heard through friends that Tumblr could also be a contentious place, where "drama" reigned supreme, and I cringed at the stereotypes of Tumblr users I heard circulating online. Ultimately, I was too anxious even to create an account, preferring to source my Tumblr content secondhand (generally, through screenshots circulated on more "mainstream" platforms).

As I set out to interview TNB+ young people about their own experiences with social media, I encountered echoes of this same ambivalence. Many—70% of my sample—were Tumblr users, and several spoke positively of the role that Tumblr had played in their lives. Cameron (22, they/them), for instance, broke into peals of laughter as I introduced the topic of Tumblr, crowing, "Tumblr *made* me trans!" For other participants, however, this enthusiasm was tempered by skepticism—or even outright apprehension. As Avery (22, they/them) explained, "Tumblr is, like, anarchy . . . the 'queer utopia' [idea] is more wishful thinking." Ramona (20, they/he) was more candid, joking, "I call it the Hell Site . . . in terms of [my] mental health, I would say [that] Tumblr is definitely one of the most unsafe places for me. But in terms of my identity, it's one of the safest." Participant Crystal (19, she/her), who described herself as "afraid" of Tumblr, lowered her voice to a whisper—even though we were alone—as she said, "some people on Tumblr really fucking scare me." Why did so many of these dedicated Tumblr users also claim to "hate" or to "fear" it? What can our reactions to Tumblr teach us about how *space* and *digital architecture*—even in "peripheral" or "marginal" online communities—organize community dynamics?

In this chapter, I argue that the *very same set of features* that TNB+ Tumblr users cite as most attractive and empowering have *also* given rise to a climate on Tumblr where identity-based conflicts pervade, inhibiting coalition-building between TNB+ people (and introducing new risks to users' self-confidence and mental health). Tumblr's unique features and affordances—in particular, its identity-based community building, its separation from existing social networks, its emphasis on *labels* as a core arbiter of identity, and its unique post and tagging structures—offer valuable new tools for exploring and articulating identity; and yet, these tools also produce and maintain a climate of identity *challenge* on Tumblr that can dissuade users from full participation.

Methods

I use semi-structured interviews with forty-six TNB+ young people (ages 18–25) to explore users' perceptions of Tumblr as a safe (or unsafe) space for exploring gender identity. Data presented here are drawn from a larger project (Garrison 2022) examining TNB+ social media use. Twenty-two respondents were interviewed twice , for a total dataset of sixty-eight interview sessions. A demographic overview of the sample—along with a more comprehensive account of the project's recruitment protocol and methodology—can be found in Garrison (2022, 28–47).

Each of the forty-six participants completed a pre-interview screening questionnaire on Qualtrics, where they described their online activity and provided information about their identities and peer networks. In addition to the interview(s), each participant was subsequently followed on social media (across *all* of their preferred platforms—including, but not limited to, Tumblr) for a minimum period of six months. Throughout this observational period, I maintained a regular log of participants' activities across their favored platforms, developing a portfolio of their content for us to analyze together in follow-up interview sessions.

Owing to the geographic dispersal of participants, interviews were conducted remotely using the videoconferencing program BlueJeans. When technological constraints impeded the use of BlueJeans, a telephone interview was substituted (n = 18). Interview sessions lasted from fifty to 200 minutes, with a mean length of 115 minutes. All data for the project—screenshots from social media, Qualtrics data, and interview transcripts—were compiled and analyzed using the QDA software program Dedoose. As themes emerged and further questions arose, I occasionally emailed participants to seek clarification on their responses. I also offered each participant a copy of their interview transcript, providing an additional opportunity to amend or extend the answers provided.

Tumblr as "Heaven," Tumblr as "Hell"

Though undisputedly a form of "social media," Tumblr differs in many ways from platforms like Facebook or Twitter. Tumblr users can't access rosters of each other's followers, and they generally don't create "profile" pages. Instead, Tumblr is a living archive; it acts as both a space for short-form blogging, and a repository of curated digital artifacts. It allows users to post written work, photos, or videos that they've created, or to share external links to content hosted elsewhere online. It also affords "re-blogging"—the recirculation (and amplification) of content generated by other users. Part support group, part commonplace book, and part journal, Tumblr helps to connect young TNB+ people while also affording them the option to retain their *privacy*, exploring presentation of self in a space secure from others' prying eyes.

For these reasons, Tumblr has been characterized as a powerful site of identity formation for TNB+ youth. Fink and Miller (2014) argue that the last decade ushered in a "trans Tumblr renaissance"—an interval of time where trans users flocked *en masse* to Tumblr, constructing a quasi-utopian community there (affirming not only of TNB+ people, but also of intersex people, asexual people [Renninger 2015], and members of other marginalized groups). Tumblr's unique affordances—described by Jacobsen et al. (2021) as "world-building capacities"—render it a space which actively facilitates identity exploration (Haimson et al. 2021; Cavalcante 2019; Oakley 2016), the coining of new gender and sexual identity labels (Cover 2019; Schudson and van Anders 2019; Dame 2016), and the rapid collation of information about queer and trans identities (Jacobsen et al. 2021; Haimson et al. 2021). Characterizations of Tumblr as a trans-affirming space are so pervasive that some scholars have argued for Tumblr's labeling as a fundamentally "trans technology"—a platform that actively "support[s] trans experiences by enabling users . . . to embody (in a digital space) identities that would eventually become material," and which "enable[s] non-normative, fluid, non-linear, and multiple identity presentations, making it [Tumblr] queer" (Haimson et al. 2021).

Many of my participants provisionally supported this assessment, agreeing that they had celebrated Tumblr as a place to connect with other trans people and to learn about TNB+ identities. Yet, many of these same participants also understood Tumblr to be a source of toxicity and antagonism, where conflicts over participants' rights to membership were daily (and inescapable) events. As Cosmo (25, it/they) described, in their experience, this "discourse" around legitimacy sometimes seemed so relentless that it served to push users away:

> I ended up moving away from Tumblr . . . because as wonderful as it was, as helpful as it was over the years, the whole, uh—the whole sort of culture . . . the toxic social habits—I realized I had peaked on how much help I could get from the site, and it was starting to affect me negatively. There was pressure to be seen as "enough" . . . like, "Well, if you don't try hard enough to present as your gender, then you're not valid."

Identity challenges like these—concerns about whether specific community members are valid, legitimate, or "enough" to merit belonging—are endemic to identity-based movements, and the appearance of such challenges on Tumblr is not a surprise. When group membership is predicated upon one's claim to a given identity label, it is unsurprising that group members feel a pressure to defend their identity claims. However, while these kinds of interpersonal dynamics are assuredly pervasive, it is important not to lose sight of such dynamics as an *artifact of space and context*—that is, as a product of the *setting*, as much as of the interactants within it. The "particularities of place" (Abelson, this collection) are instrumental in shaping interaction, and this is no less so when spaces are organized virtually. How have Tumblr's unique architecture and affordances helped to shape the climate that TNB+ users confront on the platform—and, in turn, to inform users' perceptions (both of other TNB+ young people, and of themselves)?

In this section, I argue that the *same features* that have rendered Tumblr a "safe space" to explore TNB+ identity have also contributed to shaping (A) a proliferation of *new* and *increasingly specific* neo-identity labels, and (B) a propensity for *identity policing* on Tumblr, which in turn have worked to (C) shape community dynamics that can inhibit users' engagement. In the following sections, I examine four of the features participants highlighted as making Tumblr uniquely TNB+-affirming, and assess the roles these features have played in shaping community engagement on Tumblr (for better, and for worse).

Anonymity and Separation from Existing Networks

One feature that provides support for the identity projects of TNB+ youth is Tumblr's *separation from existing networks*. While platforms like Facebook and Instagram are imbricated by their shared ownership—such that indicating preferences on one platform will change the content and recommendations displayed on the other—Tumblr stands alone. Where Facebook and Twitter users identify one another through existing social ties or institutional affiliations (e.g., public ties to a workplace), the only "real-world" signifier available to identify Tumblr users is their email address. Thus, many Tumblr users—particularly those who create "throw-away" email accounts to host their profiles—can navigate Tumblr under conditions of relative anonymity.

Tumblr's architecture circumvents what boyd (2010) and Cho (2018) have critiqued as the "public-by-default setting" of more mainstream social media platforms. Cho (2018), for instance, finds that queer youth of color often favor Tumblr over Facebook to express intimate thoughts or feelings, highlighting Facebook's design bias toward "default publicness." While Tumblr as a platform is not fully anonymous—and indeed, may even be considered *less* private than Facebook, which offers tools for restricting a post's visibility and target audience that Tumblr does not—users in this sample suggested that family members and work colleagues were less likely to use Tumblr, making the space feel less vulnerable than platforms where connections to known others were predictable and expected. As Lee (25, they/them) explained, "[Tumblr] was kind of, like, the more 'private' social media platform . . . it was kind of 'underground' . . . I could post all this stuff that, like, I didn't actually want people to 'know.'" Cameron (22, they/them) echoed, "You don't have to necessarily represent yourself in an 'authentic' way . . . and, you know, you can go on Tumblr and make trans friends without your mom knowing."

While social media platforms are generally framed as a vehicle for connection, my participants affirmed that the promise of *isolation* online can feel just as rewarding—particularly for those who strain under the weight of "context collapse" (boyd 2014). Participant Fern (22, they/them) described the disconnection Tumblr offered as a source of relief, explaining, "A lot of times, [Tumblr] felt like I was just kind of shouting into the void. [But] it honestly helped . . . I think it was more about, like, seeing other people's posts [and stories] than about getting feedback on mine." In this sense, Tumblr is powerful for TNB+ users not only in that it affords community connection, but also in the sense that it affords space to be *alone* and reflect (Haimson et al. 2021).

Tumblr as Identity-Based SMS

While "bond-based" communities (like Facebook) draw users together using their existing social ties—and, thereafter, may highlight content or recommend connections *based* on those ties—"identity-based" communities (like Tumblr) anchor user connections around shared identities or interests (Resnick et al. 2011). Users seek out new content primarily through keyword-based searches: a feature that encourages users to think carefully about the labels and descriptors most likely to yield a return. As users "like" or reblog others' posts, Tumblr's algorithm links the user to existing clusters of content which have been tagged in similar ways. Through this algorithm, users can visualize whether their own interpretations of keywords or identity labels harmonize with those of other users, helping to assess whether they "belong" to specific communities (Seko and Lewis 2018).

Tumblr's "searchability" is especially helpful for populations that may encounter difficulty accessing information about their identities using more conventional search tools. Many participants disclosed how their initial efforts to search for information on trans identities turned up results that were less than desirable—sometimes, even frightening. Charlotte (22, she/her), for instance, recalled her first efforts to learn about trans identities online as quite traumatic:

I was looking on [Google], and I searched 'guy turns into girl,' because that was really the only way I knew how to phrase it . . . and I got some stuff about [this person] who got sent to prison—like, a men's prison—and so they cut open their scrotum and, like, dumped their testicles into the toilet, so that they could go to the women's prison . . . [and] I thought, 'wow, that's really gross and perverted' . . . [so] I thought [thinking of myself as a woman] was something to be really grossed out and ashamed of.

Turning to platforms like Tumblr for *targeted* information on trans identities can circumvent some of these risks. As participant Ramona (22, they/them) summarized, "You can get good information out of Google, but you have to really take a while . . . [and it sometimes] pops up with, like, fetish porn sites . . . [so] to be talking about specifically trans stuff, you have to go into an established community, and try to make your way into that." Tumblr's architecture makes it easy to identify and access these kinds of "established" communities—even without disclosing one's identity to the participants within. However, since connections on Tumblr are recommended based on established interests and content preferences, *establishing interests and preferences* is key to making Tumblr effective as a community-building tool. It's here that Tumblr's *post structure*—the tools it offers to collate, consume, and recirculate information related to TNB+ identities—takes on an instrumental role.

Hashtagging, Reblogging, and Post Structure

On Tumblr, users curate "streams" of content to share with the world, composed of a bricolage of text, images, and other found objects. In this sense, the activities that users participate in on Tumblr facilitate *creation* more than they facilitate direct *connection* (Haimson et al. 2021; Dame 2016). Tumblr blogs can be "followed"—and subsequently accessed in full—by anyone that encounters them, with no need for a mutually acknowledged relationship (Jacobsen et al. 2021). By "following" users that post content related to TNB+ identities, users can access massive repositories of information without ever approaching the curators directly.

In addition, the fact that Tumblr privileges *posts* rather than *comments* in algorithmically organizing a user's content feed can make Tumblr feel "safer" than some other platforms. While comments that users add to posts can be seen and tracked, they are not displayed to audiences automatically (as on, for instance, Facebook). This additional layer of concealment helps to deter would-be trolls from frequenting Tumblr to "spam" users with transphobic commentary; these comments reach fewer eyeballs than they do on platforms like Facebook, where the increased visibility of comments (and the amplification spurred by this visibility) can render trolling more rewarding.

Of course, to *access* these repositories, users must familiarize themselves with the *language* that group members use to describe themselves. Users that post under the tag #transsexual, for instance, may conceptualize their identities quite differently from users that post under the tag #trans. In an analysis of Tumblr tagging as ontological practice, Dame (2016) explains that tagging is an act of *enmeshment*, situating pieces of content in relational context. As users tag things, they link their content and commentary to larger, collective narratives. As Dame (2016, 31) describes, "tagging" in this context is as much an act of self-declaration as of information management: "[Users'] tags are their ontological stake: I am identifying myself and my self-narrative as trans, to be recognizable to you in this moment." The stakes of these ontological claims are high—and made *higher*, again as an effect of Tumblr's architecture, where choosing the *inappropriate* tag can open a user to the vulnerability of identity challenge (or—just as damaging—render them algorithmically invisible).

Knowledge of in-group nomenclature can facilitate connection with others, but it also serves a parallel function: namely, bolstering users' *own* identity claims. By labeling their content with community-specific metadata, users both underscore their claim to community membership, and increase the likelihood that their content will be discovered by others that *share* their experiences (Zappavigna 2014). Users acquaint themselves with group-specific terminology not only to engage other group members, but to help *themselves* articulate and define their identities.

Decentralization of the Body

Finally, it is important to consider that Tumblr's interface *decenters the physical body* in user interactions. Tumblr users have a great deal of control over the information others can access about their bodies: they can post visual content selectively, or refrain from posting images altogether. Many TNB+ people find this decentralization of the body as an identity marker to be deeply empowering. Participant Milo (21, he/they), for example, explained that "it's easy [online], because no one hears your voice or sees your face first . . . so it's very easy to establish yourself as the gender that you are, rather than the gender that others perceive you to be." Marcel (22, he/they) emphasized this in his interview, also, asserting that "I don't want to be, like, defined by my appearance—and being able to, like, be freed of my physical body [online] is liberating, in a sense."

However, this decentralization of the body can also have unintended consequences for community access (Garrison 2022, 128–155). In many digitally mediated contexts, presenting a particular kind of embodied gender *performance* is often treated as less important than clearly stating one's gender *descriptor* of choice. When the body is decentered, label-based and narrative-driven accounts of gender come to take center stage. Platforms like Tumblr center a user's preferred *labels* as core signifiers of identity, and place these labels at the center of the site's architecture. Unfortunately, as labels become increasingly critical to the project of defining the self, *conflict* over these labels and their usage also tends to increase (and to users' detriment).

Understanding Identity Policing and Identity Challenge on Tumblr

My interviewees described Tumblr as a space where challenges surrounding identity claims were a daily occurrence. Sophia (23, she/her) complained:

> You have people [on Tumblr] who are, like, grabbing at non-issues to make them issues . . . it's like everybody got obsessed with the minutiae of identity politics, and forgot about general class consciousness . . . [and] trans people, like, dealing with the shithole of the world together—and, like, decided to start fighting with people constantly. That's what it feels like.

That conflict over labels prevails on Tumblr is unsurprising: such challenges are common to identity-based movements, as members struggle to define community boundaries (Gamson 1995) and jockey for access to shared resources. As Tumblr serves as a crucible for the foundation of new identity terms (and for the deconstruction of older ones), it is sensible that bounding these labels would be a core concern (Garrison 2022). Indeed, many of the conflicts that participants pointed to as anchors of Tumblr community "discourse" are repackaged iterations of longer-standing tensions, threaded throughout LGBTQ history. For example, one repeated argument concerned which community members should be empowered to use the word "lesbian." As Jayde (24, she/her) explained, "there's the whole, like, 'can bisexual women call themselves lesbian' [thing] . . . [it feels] like, you know, [an] 'is cereal a soup or a salad' argument—and I think that's what makes it so powerful, is [that] nobody can really answer it conclusively and, like, end it." This concern over how to bound the term "lesbian," of course, is an outgrowth of feminist organizing throughout the 1960s and '70s, and the debates that prevailed in these spaces around bisexuality's challenge to lesbian separatist politics (Rust 1995). Another frequent debate surrounds whether people with ace-spectrum identities should be allowed to call themselves "queer"—an echo of debates surrounding whether "kinky" heterosexuals (Savage 2019) or those that practice polyamory (Barrett 2020) should be considered queer.

Perhaps the example *par excellence* of these tensions on Tumblr has been the "truscum"-versus-"tucute" debates: that is, discourse about whether (and to what extent) body-based dysphoria should be considered prerequisite to claiming trans identity. So-called "truscum" or "transmedicalists"—both terms originally coined on Tumblr (Wijnants 2013)—assert that body dysphoria *defines* trans experience, and that those who claim transness in the absence of body dysphoria confuse the symptoms of other mental illnesses (e.g., personality disorders) for the desire to transition. Those in the "tucute" corner—so named because some on Tumblr have joked, tongue-in-cheek, that they're "too cute to be cis" (@cabinet-dude 2018)—advocate for an *expansion* of the trans identity label to include those that don't experience body-based (or, for that matter, any) dysphoria. Participants reported that the debate between these two camps could feel all-consuming on Tumblr. Conflict between these two groups is what motivated participant Cosmo (25, it/they) to abandon the platform altogether:

> There was this whole thing that started up—I think in, like, 2015, 2016—where, uh, "truscum" or "transmeds" started being a thing, and the whole big debate over "you absolutely have to have dysphoria to be trans," "non-binary people don't exist," all of that. And so I experienced a lot of hate, a lot of trolling, from this little essentialist, extremist group on Tumblr . . . it was a wild experience. [And so] I ended up moving away from Tumblr . . . I started using it less and less.

Again, these kinds of identity conflicts are endemic to work within identity-based movements; to the extent that they enable agitation for change, we might even consider them productive (see, e.g., Risman 2018). However, what I suggest here is that the affordances of Tumblr as a platform have both rendered these challenges *more frequent* and amplified the *consequences* for those targeted. The ongoing imperative to justify one's claim to these identity labels foments a climate of inter-community harassment that leaves some would-be participants—myself included—hesitant to engage.

Because Tumblr is disconnected from many users' existing networks, it would be easy to dismiss these kinds of conflicts as irrelevant hair-splitting. Indeed, several of my own participants—frustrated by the frequency with which these kinds of debates seemed to arise online—derided these kinds of conflicts as insignificant. Participant Sebastian (20, they/them) bemoaned:

> . . . There's a lot of LGBT discourse that, like, can only occur on social media, right? Like . . . well, all of the bi/pan discourse, and . . . the *worst* one is "can a trans man identify as a lesbian?" That's another one that I—who cares? Like, *who cares?* At the end of the day, like—people are being murdered! . . . But we continue to engage *fully* in these, like, *absurd* conversations that, like, will probably never have any practical application.

Within the context of Tumblr, however, these conversations carry *profound* implications. When the "real" identities of users are unknown, group members develop a sense of paranoia about whether others "really are" who (or what) they purport to be. Coupled with this tension is the reality that Tumblr draws users together around shared identity labels—a focus with the potential to intensify users' attention to in-group and out-group boundaries. Perceiving "other" groups as threatening can intensify a user's allegiance to their "in-group" (Hogg and Terry 2000), and in online spaces, "out-groups" and potential antagonists can seem numerous and difficult to fight. Although being prominently *visible* online can certainly heighten perceptions of an out-group as a threat, insidiously, a group's perceived *invisibility* can too: when potential antagonists cannot be reliably counted, anxious users may tend to perceive many where there are in fact few, fearing unknown infiltrators that may be "lurking" in the void. Members are aware that anonymity breeds violence—if interlopers *should* breach the gates, harassment and antagonism are likely to follow. (Additional discussion of my own respondents' experiences with such harassment—including a more detailed analysis of the *sequelae* of such attacks, both for individual users and for Tumblr's TNB+ networks more generally—can be found in Garrison 2022, 190–253).

The climate of surveillance that emerges under such conditions demands users' *hypervigilance*: it requires that they be diligent in evaluating others' identity claims (and, thus, ensures that they *also* carefully monitor their own). As Sebastian (20, they/them) described:

Hypervigilance [means], like, "language is the most important thing." It's not about intent. It's not about meaning. It's *just* about language . . . [and] just policing everybody, constantly . . . [but] I *would* say that the main reason why I think words are so important in trans and queer spaces [is] because words are often the only thing that trans people have . . . [and] I think a lot of people just don't feel secure in themselves enough to not be terrified of losing their words.

Hypervigilance around label use helps to keep the community *closed* to outsiders (and, thus, "safer" for those that use it). By making it easy for platform users to *view* the label-based claims that users are making (and to see immediately which of these claims appear inconsistent, or which seem to "stick out"), Tumblr's post structure and tagging features enhance this process. Dame (2016) asserts that by participating in content tagging, Tumblr users forge a "folksonomy" of terms that—while initially empowering—can reify language use and further incentivize boundary policing:

> Limited vocabulary ultimately prompts user debate over tag definition. Given the deep importance of ontological security to trans self-narrative, users react strongly to contestations over meaning. Without a structuring apparatus to maintain social norms, users implemented horizontal discipline to resolve the embedded uncertainty around tag definition. (Dame 2016, 35)

By reviewing the content pool tagged with a particular label, Tumblr users develop a top-down perspective on how language in the community is being used, assessing how the discourse around a particular label has unfolded. When potential label appropriators are identified, Tumblr's "reblog" feature can amplify the reach and the effects of the identity challenges leveled at them. As Danny (24, he/him) argued, Tumblr's anonymity makes it easy for those mobilized to "pile on" to these kinds of challenges, without fear of retribution:

> The format of, like, Tumblr itself, like—the, um, ability to reblog things, and to add stuff on, and the fact that, like, is visible to everyone on those posts, so anybody can see anyone that has pinned that on. Um—I think that, and the ability of people to ask anonymous messages, and stir shit up in that way, without having to reveal yourself, or whatever . . . both those things contribute to that very much.

Thus, each of the core features highlighted in the preceding section as a source of *empowerment* for TNB+ users may *also* operate to produce a climate of harassment and identity policing that can place users at risk. Decentralization of the body on Tumblr centers participants' focus on *labels* as a core identity attribute; the fact that Tumblr is an identity-based SMS makes it even more important to choose and present a clear identity label. These affordances operate *together* to draw TNB+ users into community and to facilitate the sharing of identity-specific resources, but they *also* serve to heighten users' investment in *defending* identity labels, and in keeping the Tumblr community safe from interlopers.

Tumblr's anonymity—an asset to TNB+ young people still exploring their identities—serves here to motivate *suspicion*, and that suspicion motivates boundary-policing. Established group members may attempt to defend the sanctity of the space by pushing back against newcomers, questioning their intentions in ways that can undercut some TNB+ users' access to the same spaces established to protect them.

The Future, By Design: UX Research at "The Margins"

Tumblr has been framed as a contradictory space, both fraught with risk and ripe with promise. In this chapter, I have argued that spaces like Tumblr—in many cases, selected by TNB+ young people *because* of the things these platforms do to protect users' privacy, enable connections with other trans people, and facilitate self-expression—are *also* spaces that can foster a greater propensity for identity challenge. Fear that other users might challenge their identity claims may reinforce TNB+ young people's insecurity about their identities (ironically, motivating further self-doubt and self-policing). This conflict over labels both contributes to users' anxiety about whether they are "trans enough" to participate in trans spaces on Tumblr, and contributes to perceptions of Tumblr itself as a hostile space, discouraging some would-be users from ever engaging. Just as Tumblr's affordances introduce new strategies of action for TNB+ youth, they also generate new vulnerabilities.

In service of this book's broader call to action, I close with three reflections on how this study of "the margins" contributes to the more general sociological enterprise. For one, this research contributes to theorizing on identity-based social movements, and how digital environments shape movement mobilization. While many have explored the utility of social media for social movements, there remains uncertainty regarding the *function* of these spaces, and the precise nature of their impacts (Khazraee and Novak 2018). Specifically, much remains unknown about whether social media platforms serve to *motivate* collective action, or to break users into factions that *inhibit* collective action. Conflicts over group boundaries are common to all identity-based movements (Gamson 1995), but studying Tumblr as a *context* for these encounters enables us to observe how the organization of social media platforms themselves can temper or exacerbate such conflicts. If social media is to help mobilize and extend identity movements, it is critical for sociologists to interrogate the structural characteristics that facilitate or inhibit such mobilization. Elaborating the dualistic nature of some of these attributes constitutes an important first step in this direction.

Secondly, this work makes important contributions to our understanding of social media platform design. TNB+ young people are a rapidly growing population, and they comprise a significant share of today's SMS user base (especially given that they tend to be disproportionately *heavy* users, in terms of hours invested online). While UX[1] researchers have historically framed TNB+ people as "edge cases"—users whose experiences are considered "extreme," and aren't treated as fundamental in anchoring platform design—the rising prominence of TNB+ people renders this framing unsustainable. As Mike Monteiro eloquently summarizes:

> When you decide who you're designing for, you're making an implicit statement about who you're *not* designing for . . . Facebook now claims to have two billion users. 1% of two billion people, which most products would consider an "edge case," is twenty million people. *Those* are the people at the margins. These are the trans people who get caught on the edges of "real names" projects . . . They are not edge cases. They are human beings, and we owe them our best work. (Monteiro 2019)

My findings suggest that the features and affordances that render online spaces compelling for TNB+ young people are often *identical* to the features and affordances that precipitate harassment and exclusion for TNB+ users: a critical insight for UX design. The fundamental "duality" of these impacts suggests that even as we strive to design with trans users in mind, these efforts can yield unintended consequences. Social media companies would benefit from integrating TNB+ young people more intentionally into the platform design process—both by attending to their desires and experiences through qualitative UX research, and by *employing* TNB+ designers and community leaders to aid in data collection and analysis, in an effort to anticipate these issues and further mitigate their potential for harm.

This project also contributes to our understanding of how these technologies shape the day-to-day social experience of TNB+ users—

especially given that these experiences have such profound potential to influence peer relationships and users' self-esteem. LGBTQ+ youth—and trans youth in particular (James et al. 2016)—are a population disproportionately vulnerable to depression and anxiety, disordered eating and other body-image issues, self-harm, and suicidal ideation. Understanding how the online spaces where young adults spend much of their time might contribute to these outcomes will enable mentors, teachers, and other support figures to more effectively intervene and address the needs of those navigating (or at risk of) these issues. In addition, this research helps us to assess the ways in which the affordances of different platforms may contribute to the risk of identity challenge that users face more generally (as well as the form that these challenges take). As the internet continues to be regarded as a sanctuary for many marginalized identity groups (TNB+ youth included), it is crucial for us to determine the conditions that make some online spaces more (or less) likely to deliver upon that promise than others—for the benefit of all youth, and of all genders, traversing the vast ether of the Web.

NOTE

1 "UX" (short for "user experience") research is a branch of inquiry that leverages direct consumer insights to intervene upon or improve the design of a product (often digital).

REFERENCES

@cabinet-dude [Tumblr handle]. 2018. "Tucutes: Know Your Damn Roots." Retrieved on November 24, 2021 (https://terflies.tumblr.com/post/175928048376/tucutes-know-your-damn-roots).

Barrett, Kim. 2020. "Does Polyamory Fall under the LGBT+ Umbrella?" *Medium*, January 24. Retrieved on November 23, 2021 (https://medium.com).

boyd, danah. 2010. "Social Network Sites as Networked Publics: Affordances, Dynamics, and Implications." In *A Networked Self: Identity, Community, and Culture on Social Network Sites*, edited by Zizi Papacharissi, 39–58. New York: Routledge.

boyd, danah. 2014. *It's Complicated: The Social Lives of Networked Teens*. New Haven, CT: Yale University Press.

Cavalcante, Andre. 2019. "Tumbling into Queer Utopias and Vortexes: Experiences of LGBTQ Social Media Users on Tumblr." *Journal of Homosexuality* 66 (12): 1715–35.

Cho, Alexander. 2018. "Default Publicness: Queer Youth of Color, Social Media, and Being Outed by the Machine." *New Media and Society* 20 (9): 3183–200.

Cohen, David. 2021. "Tumblr Stakes Its Claim as the Queerest Place on the Internet." Adweek, May 5. Retrieved on November 20, 2021 (www.adweek.com).

Cooper, Margaret and Kristina Dzara. 2010. "The Facebook Revolution: LGBT Identity and Activism." In *LGBT Identity and Online New Media*, edited by Christopher Pullen and Margaret Cooper, 100–112. New York: Routledge.

Cover, Rob. 2019. "The Proliferation of Gender and Sexual Identities, Categories, and Labels Among Young People: Emergent Taxonomies." In *Youth, Sexuality, and Sexual Citizenship*, edited by Peter Aggleton, Rob Cover, Deana Leahy, Daniel Marshall, and Mary Lou Rasmussen, 278–90. New York: Routledge.

Dame, Avery. 2016. "Making a Name for Yourself: Tagging as Transgender Ontological Practice on Tumblr." *Critical Studies in Media Communication* 33 (1): 23–37.

Dame-Griff, Avery. 2022. *The Two Revolutions: A History of the Transgender Internet*. New York: New York University Press.

Feldman, Brian. 2018, December 4. "Tumblr's Most Evergreen Meme Has Always Been Its Own Death." *New York Magazine*. Retrieved on November 20, 2021 (https://nymag.com).

Fink, Marty and Quinn Miller. 2014. "Trans Media Moments: Tumblr, 2011–2013." *Television and New Media* 15 (7): 611–626.

Fox, Jesse and Rachel Ralston. 2016. "Queer Identity Online: Informal Learning and Teaching Experiences of LGBTQ Individuals on Social Media." *Computers in Human Behavior* 65: 635–42.

Gamson, Joshua. 1995. "Must Identity Movements Self Destruct? A Queer Dilemma." *Social Problems* 42 (3): 390–407.

Garrison, Spencer. 2022. "'Trans Enough' for Tumblr? Gender Accountability and Identity Challenge in Online Communities for Trans and Non-Binary Youth." PhD diss., University of Michigan.

Ghaziani, Amin. 2014. *There Goes the Gayborhood?* Princeton, NJ: Princeton University Press.

Giardina, Henry. 2019. "An Oral History of the Early Trans Internet." Gizmodo, July 9. Retrieved on November 5, 2021 (https://gizmodo.com).

Graham, Nathalie. 2018. "Tumblr Is Dead." The Stranger, December 17. Retrieved on November 20, 2021 (www.thestranger.com).

Haimson, Oliver L., Avery Dame-Griff, Elias Capello, and Zahari Richter. 2021. "Tumblr Was a Trans Technology: The Meaning, Importance, History, and Future of Trans Technologies." *Feminist Media Studies* 21 (3): 345–61.

Hogg, Michael A. and Deborah J. Terry. 2000. "Social Identity and Self-Categorization Processes in Organizational Contexts." *Academy of Management Review* 25 (1): 121–40.

Jacobsen, Kai, Aaron Devor, and Edwin Hodge. 2021. "Who Counts as Trans? A Critical Discourse Analysis of Trans Tumblr Posts." *Journal of Communication Inquiry* [preprint]: https://doi.org/10.1177/01968599211040835

James, Sandy E., Jody L. Herman, Susan Rankin, Mara Keisling, Lisa Mottet, and Ma'ayan Anafi. 2016. "The Report of the 2015 U.S. Transgender Survey." National Center for Transgender Equality. Retrieved on October 25, 2021 (https://transequality.org).

Khazraee, Emad and Alison N. Novak. 2018. "Digitally Mediated Protest: Social Media Affordances for Collective Identity Construction." *Social Media and Society* 4 (1): 1–14.

Madden, Emma. 2020. "How Tumblr Created Space for Nonbinary Communities to Thrive." Nylon, March 5. Retrieved on October 28, 2021 (www.nylon.com).

McInroy, Lauren and Faye Mishna. 2017 "Cyberbullying on Online Gaming Platforms for Children and Youth." *Child and Adolescent Social Work Journal* 34 (2): 597–607.

Monteiro, Mike. 2019. *Ruined by Design: How Designers Destroyed the World, and What They Can Do to Fix It.* San Francisco: Mule Books.

Nguyen, Jennimai. 2021. "Tumblr Died a Slow and Painful Death. Here's How TikTok Can Avoid the Same Fate." Mashable, February 2. Retrieved on November 20, 2021 (https://mashable.com).

Oakley, Abigail. 2016. "Disturbing Hegemonic Discourse: Nonbinary Gender and Sexual Orientation Labeling on Tumblr." *Social Media + Society* 2 (3): 1–12.

Renninger, Bryce J. 2015. "'Where I Can Be Myself . . . Where I Can Speak My Mind': Networked Counterpublics in a Polymedia Environment." *New Media and Society* 17 (9): 1513–529.

Resnick, Paul, Robert E. Kraut, and Sara Kiesler. 2011. *Building Successful Online Communities: Evidence-Based Social Design.* Cambridge, MA: MIT Press.

Richard, Doug. 2018. "Take Another Look at Tumblr." *Medium*, February 21. Retrieved on October 28, 2021 (https://medium.com).

Risman, Barbara. 2018. *Where the Millennials Will Take Us: A New Generation Wrestles with the Gender Structure.* New York: Oxford University Press.

Rust, Paula C. 1995. *Bisexuality and the Challenge to Lesbian Politics: Sex, Loyalty, and Revolution.* New York: New York University Press.

Sarappo, Emma. 2018, December 13. "How Tumblr Taught Social Justice to a Generation of Teenagers." Pacific Standard. Retrieved on October 27, 2021 (https://psmag.com).

Savage, Dan. 2019, June 25. "Are Straight Kinksters Queer? And Does Kink Belong at Pride?" The Stranger. Retrieved on November 21, 2021 (www.thestranger.com).

Schudson, Zach and Sari van Anders. 2019. "'You Have to Coin New Things': Sexual and Gender Identity Discourses in Asexual, Queer, and/or Trans Young People's Networked Counterpublics." *Psychology and Sexuality* 10 (4): 354–68.

Seko, Yukari and Stephen P. Lewis. 2018. "The Self—Harmed, Visualized, and Reblogged: Remaking of Self-Injury Narratives on Tumblr." *New Media and Society* 20 (1): 180–98.

Strapagiel, Lauren. 2021. "Tumblr Says It's the Queerest Social Media Platform, But Can It Hold on to That?" *BuzzFeed News*, May 4. Retrieved on October 27, 2021 (www.buzzfeednews.com).

Swisher, Kara. 2019. "Who Killed Tumblr? We All Did." *New York Times*, August 14. Retrieved on November 20, 2021 (www.nytimes.com).

Wijnants, Alexander. 2013. "Social Media and the Politicization versus Medicalization of Trans People." *Synaesthesia: Communication Across Cultures* 1 (4): 60–87.

Zappavigna, Michele. 2014. "Enacting Identity in Microblogging through Ambient Affiliation." *Discourse and Communication* 8 (2): 209–228.

6

"I'm Just Not Interested in a Bathhouse . . ."

Korean Spas as Queer Liminal Spaces

KENDALL OTA

> Part of the gay world taking shape in the streets was highly
> visible to outsiders, but even more of it was invisible . . . gay
> men had to contend with the threat of vigilante anti-gay vio-
> lence as well as with police. In response to this challenge, gay
> men devised a variety of tactics that allowed them to move
> freely about the city, to appropriate for themselves spaces
> that were not marked as gay, and to construct a gay city in
> the midst of, yet invisible to, the dominant city.
> —George Chauncey, *Gay New York*

A great deal of scholarship examining queer sexual communities starts
with investigating their emergence as sanctuary spaces, providing refuge
for queer folks from the institutionalized violence of a heteronormative society. Indeed, the organization of space along the lines of "moral"
sexual citizenship collectively served to accomplish heterosexuality as
natural, normal, and benign, relegating sexual "others" to segregated,
clandestine space (e.g., Hubbard 2001; Valentine 1993; d'Emilio 1983).
Research in this vein has documented that against the backdrop of
discrimination, gay identity and community were mobilized and collectively established within these spatial borderlands.

While acknowledging the past effectiveness of gay space in inculcating a sense of safety for queer folks, recent work questions their
enduring function and relevance in the contemporary "post-gay" era
(Ghaziani 2011; Seidman 2002). Interrogating how queer spaces are becoming increasingly absorbed by neoliberalism, some express concern
with whether gay communities have become divorced from the radical

queerness that characterized its political beginnings (Rushbrook 2002; Collins 2004; Ward 2003). In particular, the exaltation of middle-class aspirations and the intensive focus on heteronormative conventions of intimacy contribute to the formation of a respectably queer subject and the concomitant obstruction of non-normative public sexual cultures (Berlant and Warner 1998; Warner 1999; Weiss 2008). Symbols of "undesirable" sexual expression such as porn cinemas, sex shops, and gay bathhouses compromise assimilation politics such that these spaces are cast as immoral aberrations within an otherwise "respectable" gay culture (Sanders-McDonagh et al. 2016; Weiss 2008). Perhaps originally radical sites of social inclusion, contemporary gay consumption spaces rearticulate moral difference, thus "[trading] queer sexual connection for legal equality" (Orne 2017, 4).

Within this context, a schism is forged between spaces that produce either a valorized queer authenticity or a reductive gay conformity. In this chapter, I interrogate this dichotomy by analyzing a liminal space between the gay mainstream and the radically queer. I examine Korean spas as occupying such a space, one that is neither fully queer nor straight, private nor public; where men's bodies connect in the fulfillment of same-sex desire as they navigate an institution strictly *not* built for them. If in the passage opening this chapter, however, Chauncey identified the prevalence of outright hostility and state violence as necessitating the formation of a latent queer landscape, these coercive forces are perhaps less prevalent for gay men today and/or they take on radically different forms. In this chapter, I critically examine such social formations.

Utilizing public comments collected from an online forum, this chapter analyzes the motivations for this refashioning of space where, in a world of forceful declarations and colorful celebrations of "PRIDE," these same tactics of the past take on a different significance. In this case, they represent some of what queer culture lost as a direct result of what was gained. As a result, these comments represent the transforming landscape of sexual identity and inequality (i.e., Bridges 2014; Ward 2015).

I find that rather than strategies of survival, *some gay men romanticize a return to the margins*. In reimagining Korean spas as spaces for sexual adventure, these men desire and eroticize those same structures of surveillance and discretion that characterize a more punitive past. In contradistinction to gay bathhouses which are unquestionably sexual in nature, cruising the family-friendly environment of Korean spas provides the erotic veneer of ambiguity, necessitates extreme discretion, and involves a bit of risk. By extending conversations of queer spaces beyond the discrete bars, bathhouses, and gayborhoods, I develop our understanding of the diversity of queer experiences, illustrating both the challenges and vast opportunities of queer world building in the contemporary "post-gay" era.

I first turn to a discussion of a process I refer to as the "eroticization of discretion" (Ota 2021), highlighting various discursive tactics these men rely on to position Korean spas as distinct and desirable sexual venues, particularly when compared to gay bathhouses. By highlighting the particular sexual utility of Korean spas, these men locate the pleasurable potentialities of queer connection within these liminal spaces. Korean spas thus provide a foothold for us to examine the complex relationship that some gay men have with increased visibility and acceptance in the mainstream.

I then highlight Asian men's experiences as sexual actors in these spaces who, by virtue of being simultaneously invisible and hypervisible, face a unique double bind limiting their participation. While the Korean spa exists as a kind of sexual playground for non-Asians, Asian men experience exclusion reminiscent of their marginalization in gay communities writ large. The chapter concludes with a methodological consideration of the unique challenges associated with studying experiences at the margins.

Constructing Difference: Korean Spas vs. Gay Bathhouses

Pulling open the heavy glass door, you enter a small, dimly lit steam room where three men sit in silence. Thick clouds of hot mist climb the tiled walls, obscuring the ceiling light and carrying the faint aroma of eucalyptus. As your eyes adjust to your surroundings, you see they are fully naked. Each of them is sitting on top of a small washcloth with hands clasped loosely but strategically, barely covering their bodies. Stepping forward into the space, you notice eyes curiously and cautiously trained over you as you find a clearing in the corner of the room.

Through the wisps of steam, you sit and carefully evaluate the other occupants, wondering who else here is playing the same game.

After a few moments of acclimating to the heat, the stillness of the room is interrupted by one of the men moving his hands. In doing so, he reveals himself, adjusting his body before quickly returning to his former position. This prompts the other men to follow suit as they too begin to adjust themselves in the same swift, practiced gesture. You remember briefly those curious signs posted throughout: "THIS IS A FAMILY ENVIRONMENT. ANY OBSCENE OR INAPPROPRIATE BE-HAVIOR WILL NOT BE TOLERATED. WE WILL CALL POLICE."

From just outside the room you hear men conversing in Korean followed by friendly, raucous laughter. As the door to the steam room swings open, a pair of naked, middle-aged Korean men step confidently forward into the space, releasing a long and guttural sigh before firmly planting themselves in the nearest available seats. Previously curious eyes are now concentrated on the slick, wet floor. The game is over . . . for now. As quickly as the newcomers entered, one by one the other inhabitants collect themselves and exit the room, walking out of foggy obscurity and towards the open showers that line the outside wall.

As businesses open to the general public, Korean spas are a contested space involving the mixing of various intentions on the part of their diverse clientele. These "family-friendly" establishments are ubiquitous in Korea and are becoming increasingly common in cities throughout the US with a developed Korean immigrant community, including Los Angeles and Orange County, California. For an entrance fee of $15–$30, one can access this public bathhouse environment with some of the bigger spas providing designated lounge areas, dark rooms lined with sleeping mats to catch a quick nap, and restaurants offering traditional Korean cuisine. Often experienced in the company of close friends and family members, a day at the Korean spa is thus imagined as a wholesome outing associated with cleansing, relaxation, and socializing.

Relaxing alongside straight men enjoying the spa, however, some men cruise the space in search of potential sexual encounters. While this certainly includes Asian men, Korean spas have become a racially diverse sexual marketplace for those seeking same sex partners. Despite stern warnings from signs condemning "inappropriate" sexual behavior, at times even threatening police action, these men continue to use these spaces for hooking up. Though the landscape of Korean spas in southern CA is diverse, men's same-sex cruising occurs in both co-ed and men's-only establishments, with different spas offering slightly divergent experiences. For instance, based on factors such as gender composition, location, cost of entrance, and architecture of the space, some spas become more amenable to cruising than others. Underlying these experiences, however, is the assumed heteronormativity of the environment. Cruising the Korean spa thus involves navigating a liminal terrain where seemingly innocent gestures are potentially loaded with sexual meaning. Utilizing the same "tactics" Chauncey (1994) described twenty-five years earlier, the interactional and interpretive strategies these men use to gauge interest allows for the Korean spa to exist as a liminal space, both a heteronormative cultural institution and actively queer sexual field.

Men on the public forum I analyze, which exists as a platform for people to interact with one another regarding their specific Korean spa plans or past experiences, describe the process of negotiating their private play in a semi-public space as the unique draw of these environments. This delicate "cruising game" requires you to identify other players while navigating a liminal sexual space. Consider the following comment of this person's spa preferences:

> I do like going to Paradise spa.[1] It's real small in size, not the nicest place really, but the guys are diverse in ethnicity . . . And like myself, most are looking to fool around a bit in the steam room and sauna. No hard core stuff, just showing off, hj and bjs. I had a bj today in the steam room from an older slim Asian man with a nice twink body. Had to hurry a bit as others were in and out. But it makes it fun.

As this person notes, the "fun" of cruising in these spaces is contending with the ambiguity required by the spa's heteronormative context. For this man, the fact that sexual encounters in Korean spas are fleeting and difficult to maneuver creates an exciting challenge. Acting discreetly as to not draw negative attention is thus established as an erotic act providing a unique and thrilling form of sexual pleasure, a process I call the "eroticization of discretion" (Ota 2021). While Korean spa sex is limited by structures of surveillance that police its emergence within this space, it is this disruptive potential that makes the spa a uniquely desirable sexual locale.

Identifying the eroticization of discretion, many men looking for same-sex encounters regularly discuss the Korean spa environment as being qualitatively different than the outright, unapologetic sexuality characterizing gay bathhouses. The following comments begin to highlight this distinction:

> I don't go to bathhouses often, I get a very seedy feel from there most of the time, Like everyone is ready to be penetrated unprotected from everyone . . . At Korean spas I feel play is a bit more light/less extreme and the thought that guys in there are not supposed to go there to specifically play makes it more mysterious/hot.

> Not everyone is at a Korean Spa to get off. Most guys who go to Korean Spas are voyuers [sic]. It's fun to be nude with lots of other men of all types . . . But huge circle jerks or open sex when not everybody is playing is not cool. Again it's not a sex club and you could get thrown out of the spa or arrested. Be careful or you will shut these places down which will ruin it for all the gay men like me who know how to be discreet.

Unlike Korean spas, sex clubs and gay bathhouses are private, membership-based commercial establishments where sex is expected and forthright. At a gay bathhouse, where "everyone is ready to be penetrated from everyone," there is little room to hide your intentions. At Korean spas, however, it is in navigating this uncertainty, where sexual exploration is a clear violation of the normative context of the space, that these men embrace and collectively construct the eroticization of discretion. While "open sex" and "huge circle jerks" would be acceptable in a bathhouse, it is the illegality of negotiating this play within the spa that makes sex here "more mysterious/hot."

These comments demonstrate that gay bathhouses occupy a particular place in the contemporary queer imaginary for some same-sex seeking men. In "The Social World of the Baths," Chauncey (1994) writes, "As a sexual arena, the baths had distinct advantages over some of the other venues used by gay men, such as parks and washrooms. Perhaps most important, they were *safer*" (219, emphasis mine). Gay bathhouses were spaces on the fringe of society where men could congregate in relative security in an environment made exclusively by and for them. Fostering a sense of place-based community, the baths served various functions for a multitude of men including those "highly integrated into the larger gay world" (ibid.) as well as those infrequent or temporary visitors looking for anonymous, low-stakes sexual encounters. In comparison to Korean spas, however, gay bathhouses take on a different association for the men in this study:

> When I've been there [Korean spa], I've participated in discreet play a couple times . . . But we're just talking some jo and oral. The thing is, there are guys who want the chance for some man-to-man fun, but who have their reasons for not wanting to be seen going into a known gay bathhouse. I would assume a number of Asian men fall into that group, as well as others . . . I go [to Korean spas] for relaxation, but if I meet someone like-minded and there's the chance, I'll enjoy some discreet fun.

The necessity of discretion as the organizing logic for Korean spa cruising, while erotic, also protects against the implication of seeking sexual activity in the way that a bathhouse environment suggests. Evident from this comment is that for some men, the ambiguity provided by Korean spas allows one to explore same-sex desires outside of the more clearly defined gay bathhouses where pressure to engage is perhaps more prevalent. Others comment similarly on the sexual utility of Korean spas:

> I have found Daegu Spa to be far more bathhouse-like than Whitney. But I have since found Saints Spa & Sauna—and love it! Much more low key, less cruisy but occassional [sic] fun in the sleeping room, much cleaner and newer. It is a much more tame experience that I personally like better.

> At Saints Spa & Sauna right now and there's a couple hot guys. Jerked off with 2 a couple of times. No hard core action which is why I like coming here, there's always some action going on with good looking guys but nothing to [sic] crazy.

That is, spas foster a more "tame experience" where the expectation of "hardcore action" is necessarily thwarted given that the clientele certainly includes men not interested in such activity. As a liminal space, Korean spas provide an alternative, both for those who eroticize and thus seek to reclaim those systems of surveillance policing the emergence of queer sex and for others who find discomfort in the explicit sexuality characterizing the gay bathhouse scene. Korean spas are thus cast as spaces of experimentation, transgression, and ultimately, of cultivating queer desire.

Increasing normalization of queer subjectivities has been cause for both celebration and concern. Support for same-sex marriage in the US has risen over the years along with increasingly rich queer media representations. At the same time, long-standing gay bars and clubs continue to close along with queer folks being gentrified out of historically gay communities (Ghaziani 2014). In her work examining the social changes brought about by digital hookup/dating apps, Jody Ahlm (2017) describes the emergence of a "respectable promiscuity" where Grindr users negotiate their stigmatized sexual practices in a time when queerness is threatened by continual dilution. Ahlm finds that despite the potential of Grindr to reinvigorate transgressive modes of queer sexual connection in public space, the contemporary sociopolitical context limits these horizons of queer imagining such that sex is typically arranged in the privacy of one's home.

While acknowledging the limits of a respectability politic, I also locate new opportunities and potential where the dissolving of collective queer worlds simultaneously constructs the conditions for queer utopian visioning. Forgoing the gay bathhouse experience, some men refashion Korean spas as sites of subaltern queer sexual connection, thus signaling a shift in the types of interactions valued by some same-sex seeking men. While there is perhaps a certain level of safety afforded in scrolling through Grindr or cruising the gay bathhouse, the eroticization of discretion inherent to the Korean spa environment demonstrates the desire for some men in creating alternative spaces of opposition hidden and away from the gay mainstream. Through fleeting moments of sexual connection, these men contest and reimagine otherwise heteronormative institutions in service of queer sexual pleasure. Thus, identifying the eroticization of discretion in these locales helps us understand them as unique environments allowing for some men to recapture those experiences on the fringe, where danger and surveillance are repurposed as sexual thrill and are thus actively sought and curated.

At the same time, given the rich and storied history of gay men's cruising, I do not mean to suggest that Korean spas offer something never before created by queer communities. Indeed, tearooms, cottages, and gym locker rooms are long established institutions inviting the continued refashioning of these spaces by same-sex seeking men (e.g., Humphreys 1970; Tewksbury 2008; Troiden 1974). However, given the rapidly changing sociocultural and political landscape in the US around queer sexualities, Korean spas provide a foothold to examine the contemporary meanings and significance of these practices. By moving conversations beyond these locales, we open the door to explore new liminalities where the struggle for queer subversion endures.

What about (Gay)sian Men?

While the cruising practices of same-sex seeking men have long received substantial scholarly attention, it is the racial specificity of the Korean spa compared with other sex spaces which presents unique dynamics for men cruising this space. Having already discussed these ethnic businesses as cultivating a "family-friendly" environment and the subsequent necessity of discretion, cruising the Korean spa setting involves the back-and-forth of subtle hinting and playful flirting between knowing and willing participants. As such, Asian men occupy a particularly curious position, where the interpretation of their intentions is necessarily convoluted given the spa's identity as an Asian cultural institution. Consider the following commenter's musing of his favorite spa:

> Renewed You Spa & Sauna was my fav spa for a while . . . I liked the atmosphere of "mostly straight Asians" guys and just a few of "us." But a couple months back I noticed the chubby attendant was popping his head into the sleeping area off the lockers every few minutes it seemed, then on my next visit the lights were on . . . So apparently some of "us" weren't discreet enough and there were complaints.

Reflecting on the changes to his favorite spa brought about by some less than prudent spa-goers, this comment reveals some of the complex racial dynamics at play when cruising these spaces. By drawing a clear boundary between the "mostly straight Asians" and the few of "us" cruising the spa, this man underscores a common framework for interpreting Asian men's presence in these spaces as presumably straight and thus enjoying the spa for its manifest purpose. Given the association of Asian men with the cultural context of the space, they are often immediately overlooked as potential sexual partners, and rather, are cast as extensions of those systems of surveillance seeking to curb such behavior. The following comment also speaks to this dynamic:

> Was at my favorite local spa yesterday around 2–4 . . . I have had some action there, and did yesterday too. This was different because before I played with some of the Latino clientele, and yesterday I finally got together with a nice Asian guy. I was beginning to think the Asian clientele were mostly straight or just too shy/respectful to play. In fact, a different Asian guy was visibly arousing himself at the showers, which is kind of wild at this spa because the place is so compact and open.

In documenting the unexpected yet seemingly long-awaited moment of playing with an Asian man at a Korean spa, this comment demonstrates that the ambiguity of cruising in Korean spas is particularly exacerbated when interacting with Asian men who may be uninterested or even hostile towards such activities. As such, Asian men cruising the spa are tasked with the additional challenge of contending with this assumption when communicating sexual interest to others. In this case, the commenter above describes an instance in which he observes another Asian man abandon discretion and engage in an unexpectedly overt sexual display. The following exchange speaks to the complicated dynamics involved in Asian men's cruising experiences:

> COMMENTER 1: Star Sauna seems to be pretty quiet. But based on the past 2 times I went, there seemed to be a lot of cruising whenever . . . Korean guys weren't around. Has that been others' experiences too, or was it just my luck?
> COMMENTER 2: That is always the case. Part of the reason I think guys walk out on any and all Asians is because they think they work there. I have literally had to say "I don't work here" to guys.

COMMENTER 3: If you have a particular look, people may assume you may be a straight Korean/Asian and not want to take a chance on offending the "traditional" Korean spa cliente [sic]. Long story short, it's probably not that people don't want to play because you're Asian, unless you weren't going to a K-spa, but a KKK-spa.

As these comments, and many others like them demonstrate, while non-Asian clientele can flirt with the ambiguity of their presence in a Korean spa, this opportunity is less available to Asian men who are more readily subsumed as part of the heteronormative landscape. Presumed racial identity becomes a prism through which sexual intent is assessed, often at the expense of Asian men's participation. In an effort to make these advances more readily interpretable, some Asian men resort to more "wild" and "visible" demonstrations, thus separating themselves from the more "traditional" Asian clientele.

Violating the script of discrete cruising however is not without consequence, as such displays are met with universal chastising from the part of other spa-goers, especially the more tactful cruisers. For example:

I have seen many, and I do mean "many" asian guys just get downright creepy . . . They are the ones that walk by rooms and stare into the rooms looking for guys. Fuckin creepy as hell! I have watched two older asian men squeeze in between me and a twenty something white guy just so they can stare at him. Extremely awkward, not to mention the sheer intrusion on his personal space. So sorry but from what I have seen (a lot of) asian guys are almost stalker creepy.

Singling out Asian men in particular, this commenter identifies patterns of behavior that, in their lack of subtlety, are deemed inappropriate for the Korean spa environment. While others are quick to suggest that the attribution of "creep" status is not solely a racial categorization, instead emphasizing the label as primarily behavioral, it is perhaps no surprise that some Asian men experience this tendency as sexual racism. Indeed, the construction of Asian American men in general as emasculated and undersexualized (Chua and Fujino 1999; Eng 2001) extends to the particular experiences of gay Asian men who report discrimination, fetishization, and exclusion in gay sexual fields (e.g., Han 2007; Han and

Choi 2018; Poon and Ho 2008; Robinson 2015). Due to the centrality of whiteness as the organizing logic for gay erotic worlds, Asian men are often relegated to the outskirts of these queer spaces (Han 2021). Others express similar concerns regarding the prevalence of anti-Asian sentiments in their Korean spa excursions:

> COMMENTER 1: What do I do if I'm not a hung Asian? Or tattooed? . . . Like others, I do find guys who get up and leave immediately when I sit down. But sometimes they stay and allow me to sit close . . . I guess I just don't want to get my hand swatted away (I would feel even more rejected and embarrassed) or contribute to the Asian creeper stereotype. I guess I'm one of those guys who just sits around. But as they say, no risk, no reward.
>
> COMMENTER 2: It's definitely a "damned if you do, damned if you don't" situation for those who us who are unceremoniously pushed into the "fats, fems, old or asian" boxes. If we don't make a move . . . we don't get attention. If we do make a move, we get accused of being "creeps."

Identifying a dichotomy in which Asian men are either passively ignored by virtue of their association with the cultural context of Korean spas or actively rejected for making their advances more overt and thus undesirable, these comments highlight a paradoxical situation for Asian men seeking to cruise these spaces. Caught between being labeled as "Asian creeper" or "traditional clientele," some Asian men report experiencing a kind of sexual racism that bars them from participating in the sexual landscape of the spa. That is, despite Korean spas being Asian establishments, Asian men continue to experience a marginalization reminiscent of that in the larger gay community. In fact, it is this specificity itself that lends to this predicament where Asian men are made both invisible as potential sexual partners and hyper-visible as an assumed traditional spa goer.

Work examining gay Asian men's experiences of sexual racism highlights the marginalization and stereotyping of this diverse group. Han (2021) finds that gay men of color are constricted by the durability of racialized images in gay sexual marketplaces due to the centrality of whiteness in gay communities writ large. That is, the sexual dynamics of individual erotic worlds exist within a larger social system where structural factors like race ultimately organize sexual desirability. Put simply, "Sexual fields are not isolated arenas" (ibid., 35; Green 2014). Following this research, I find that an examination of Korean spa dynamics demonstrates the durability and transportability of racialized logics and inequality. While non-Asian men can reimagine the Korean spa as a kind of sexual playground organized by the eroticization of discretion, Asian men are often not afforded the same options. Being simultaneously invisible and hyper-visible, gay Asian men operate in a liminal space ultimately leading to their exclusion, even in spaces where we might expect otherwise. Korean spas thus become a space of queer transgression, experimentation, and of actualizing desire, but for whom?

I turn finally to a brief discussion of the methodological and ethical challenges of studying queer liminal spaces.

Studying Liminality: A Methodological Discussion of Korean Spas

Many of the methodological challenges in the sociology of sexualities are not entirely unique when compared with inquiries into other areas of social life. However, given the potentially fraught and sensitive nature of our studies, work in this area is doubly challenging in having to contend with both institutional and disciplinary boundaries around often already stigmatized topics. As a result, work on sexualities is situated as uniquely vulnerable to violations of ethical guidelines. For example, in investigating often private practices and identities, researchers of sexuality are tasked with (re)negotiating physical and emotional boundaries between themselves and their subjects in ways that are perhaps more salient than for other scholars. Thus, sexuality researchers are often put in the position where their own sexual identities and performances are being similarly interpreted and examined. Winder makes note of this in his chapter (this collection) discussing how his positionality as a Black gay scholar allowed access to his interviewees by virtue of them occupying a similar social location. Due to these shared identity aspects, Winder identifies both a deeper sense of trust with his respondents and responsibility for their stories.

In my own research, this dynamic presents unique challenges as the Korean spa environment, having already discussed these as ambiguously sexual spaces, also necessitates a certain level of exposure of one's body. In this way, the body itself becomes a kind of ethnographic "research tool" requiring constant reflexivity of its interpretation and as a "contested site of knowledge production" (Bain and Nash 2006). This process is further convoluted by my identities as a gay Asian/Korean American man whose own fraught journey with sexuality was gainfully informed by existing in these spaces. In fact, Andrew Ahn's film *Spa Night* (2016) about a young Korean American man exploring his sexuality through this hidden erotic world reflects the internal struggles involved in these self-reflective processes. Furthermore, as previously explained, the intersection of these identities suggests particular interpretations of my body and presence in the spa. Occupying these insider/outsider positionalities simultaneously results in a set of tensions wherein my own corporeality and desires are themselves also subject to the research process—both participant observer and observing participant. Given these challenges, I began this project by electing to forgo the collection of ethnographic data in favor of the online dialogue that I include in this chapter. The anonymity afforded by online engagement allows for a unique view of the complex social dynamics present in Korean spas while also inviting further conceptualization into the role of research in liminal sexual spaces.

Many of the men in this study are intentional in their efforts to curate a kind of marginality for their sexual practices in an increasingly "post-gay" society. That is, the element of surveillance in Korean spas as structuring sexual opportunity between men allows for uniquely desirable sexual scenarios where acting with discretion is cast as erotic. In this instance, the return to underground, liminal spaces reproduces the thrill of sexual transgression for men seeking experiences "on the fringe." Given the subversive nature of these encounters and efforts to preserve clandestine sexual experience in these spaces, as both a researcher and insider to this community, I am tasked with protecting the longevity of these businesses and, of course, the men engaging in these practices. At the same time however, identifying or illuminating these stories inherently jeopardizes the function of these spaces for these men, representing a critical concern for researchers examining liminalities. That is, for those staking their claim on the outskirts of the "charmed circle" (Rubin 1984), the research process is already a precarious enterprise. The anonymous nature of online interactions usefully minimizes this consideration; however, scholars doing this work must recognize the delicate balance of risk and opportunity of learning with and from those on the fringes.

The research described in this chapter is the first step in what I hope is a larger trajectory examining the consequences of a simultaneous push towards queer radicalization and pull for LGBTQ normalization as a particularly affecting dynamic for the meanings of same-sex seeking men's sexual practices. For the men in this study, developing ways of turning an otherwise heteronormative institution into a queer sexual landscape demonstrates transgression and subversion in the face of contemporary respectability politics. Thus, this research extends larger sociological conversations concerned with interrogating assimilationist modes of equality and inclusion while also revealing the ways in which stigmatized communities continue to inculcate resistance at the margins. If queerness necessitates taking a stand against normative structures, then a model which seeks to eliminate difference and subsume it as part of the mainstream must be reevaluated. That is, the trend towards liberalizing social attitudes and inclusive diversity discourse should invite challenge as it often conceals convoluted processes and structures of inequality.

Indeed, sociological work invested in upsetting modern forms of inequality highlights the adaptive nature of hegemonic systems of power. This scholarship considers how increasing challenges to institutionalized inequality in the US has shifted the expression of these prejudices, often in ways that obscure enduring power dynamics. From the emergence of a "colorblind" ideology in "post-race" America (Bonilla-Silva 2015), acts of "performative progressiveness" in an era of "post-gay" politics (Brodyn and Ghaziani 2018), and the "hybrid-masculinities" of the "New Man" (Bridges and Pascoe 2014; Diefendorf and Bridges 2020), these works suggest continued attention to the transformation of social inequalities in the face of "crisis tendencies" (Connell 1995).

Building on this body of scholarship, my work here demonstrates how interlocking systems of power can be simultaneously deconstructed and fortified. By examining the dynamics of race, space, and sexuality in the case of Korean spas, I analyze how these men challenge increasing visibility and respectability politics by inculcating liminal experience at the margins. At the same time, harmful racialized discourses are (re)deployed in ways that undermine this resistance. While these men refashion Korean spas into a liminal space of sexual transgression, these actions also rely on the co-optation of an Asian ethnic institution, wherein, perhaps ironically, Asian men are remarginalized. The queer occupation of Korean spas is thus liberating for some while constraining for others. The local specificity of this project then contributes to a larger understanding on the limits of neoliberal conceptions of equality and how disenfranchised communities develop strategies to deal with these changes.

Furthermore, I draw attention to the necessity of interrogating these strategies of resistance to ensure that intersecting structures of inequality are accounted for in ways that are legitimizing and empowering for all on the fringes of society. In this way, my discussion of Korean spas is perhaps better understood as not a niche analysis of a fringe space, but of capturing a historical moment in motion (see Crawley, this collection). Through highlighting the strategies that some gay men develop as a response to the changing landscape of queerness, the Korean spa becomes more than an idiosyncratic space, but rather, as Crawley suggests, a process in a greater timeline of queer cultural production. By shifting the domain of focus in this way, my discussion of Korean spas becomes less about the spa itself, and more of a critical moment in the greater struggle towards racial and sexual equality.

NOTE

1 Pseudonyms are used to protect the identities of both these businesses and participants.

REFERENCES

Ahlm, Jody. 2017. "Respectable Promiscuity: Digital Cruising in an Era of Queer Liberalism." *Sexualities* 20 (3): 364–79.

Ahn, Andrew, director. 2016. *Spa Night*. Nonetheless Productions and Extraordinary Renditions. 1 hr., 36 min. https://www.youtube.com/watch?v=xWgZpqMeDOM.

Bain, Alison L. and Catherine J. Nash. 2006. "Undressing the Researcher: Feminism, Embodiment and Sexuality at a Queer Bathhouse Event." *Area* 38 (1): 99–106.

Berlant, Lauren and Michael Warner. 1998. "Sex in Public." *Critical Inquiry* 24 (2): 547–66.

Bonilla-Silva, Eduardo. 2015. "The Structure of Racism in Color-Blind, 'Post-Racial' America." *American Behavioral Scientist* 59 (11): 1358–76.

Bridges, Tristan. 2014. "A Very 'Gay' Straight? Hybrid Masculinities, Sexual Aesthetics, and the Changing Relationship between Masculinity and Homophobia." *Gender and Society* 28 (1): 58–82.

Bridges, Tristan and C. J. Pascoe. 2014. "Hybrid Masculinities: New Directions in the Sociology of Men and Masculinities." *Sociology Compass* 8/3: 246–58.

Brodyn, Adriana and Amin Ghaziani. 2018. "Performative Progressiveness: Accounting for New Forms of Inequality in the Gayborhood." *City & Community* 17 (2): 307–329.

Chauncey, George. 1994. *Gay New York: Gender, Urban Culture, and the Making of the Gay Male World, 1890–1940*. New York: Basic Books.

Chua, Peter and Diane Fujino. 1999. "Negotiating Asian-American Masculinities: Attitudes and Gender Expectations." *Journal of Men's Studies* 7 (3): 391–413.

Collins, Alan. 2004. "Sexual Dissidence, Enterprise and Assimilation: Bedfellows in Urban Regression." *Urban Studies* 41 (9): 1789–806.

Connell, Raewyn. 1995. *Masculinities*. Stanford, CA: Stanford University Press.

D'Emilio, John. 1983. *Sexual Politics, Sexual Communities: The Making of a Homosexual Minority in the United States, 1940–1970*. Chicago: University of Chicago Press.

Diefendorf, Sarah and Tristan Bridges. 2020. "On the Enduring Relationship Between Masculinity and Homophobia." *Sexualities* 23 (7): 1299–1309.

Eng, David. 2001. *Racial Castration: Managing Masculinity in Asian America*. Durham, NC: Duke University Press.

Ghaziani, Amin. 2011. "Post-Gay Collective Identity Construction." *Social Problems* 58 (1): 99–125.

Ghaziani, Amin. 2014. *There Goes the Gayborhood?* Princeton, NJ: Princeton University Press.

Green, Adam Isaiah, ed. 2014. *Sexual Fields: Towards a Sociology of Collective Sexual Life*. Chicago: University of Chicago Press.

Han, C. Winter. 2007. "They Don't Want to Cruise Your Type: Gay Men of Color and the Racial Politics of Exclusion." *Social Identities* 13 (1): 51–67.

Han, C. Winter. 2015. *Geisha of a Different Kind: Race and Sexuality in Gaysian America*. New York: New York University Press.

Han, C. Winter. 2021. *Racial Erotics: Gay Men of Color, Sexual Racism, and the Politics of Desire*. Seattle: University of Washington Press.

Han, C. Winter and Kyung-Hee Choi. 2018. "Very Few People Say 'No Whites': Gay Men of Color and the Racial Politics of Desire." *Sociological Spectrum* 38 (3): 145–61.

Hubbard, Phil. 2001. "Sex Zones: Intimacy, Citizenship and Public Space." *Sexualities* 4 (1): 51–71.

Humphreys, Laud. 1970. *Tearoom Trade: A Study of Homosexual Encounters in Public Places*. Chicago: Aldine Pub. Co.

Ota, Kendall. 2021. "Queer Heterotopias in 'Straight(ish)' Spaces: The Case of Korean Spas," *Sexualities* 24 (8): 1019–40.

Orne, Jason. 2017. *Boystown: Sex and Community in Chicago*. Chicago: University of Chicago Press.

Poon, Maurice Kwong-Lai and Peter Trung-Thu Ho. 2008. "Negotiating Social Stigma among Gay Asian Men: Gay Men at the Start of the 21st Century." *Sexualities* 11 (1–2): 245–68.

Robinson, Brandon Andrew. 2015. "'Personal Preference' as the New Racism: Gay Desire and Racial Cleansing in Cyberspace." *Sociology of Race & Ethnicity* 1 (2): 317–30.

Rubin, Gayle. 1984. "Thinking Sex: Notes for a Radical Theory of the Politics of Sexuality." In *Pleasure and Danger: Exploring Female Sexuality*, edited by C. Vance, 267–319. New York: Routledge and Kegan Paul.

Rushbrook, Dereka. 2002. "Cities, Queer Space, and the Cosmopolitan Tourist." *GLQ: A Journal of Lesbian and Gay Studies* 8 (1–2): 183–206.

Sanders-Mcdonagh, Erin, Magali Peyrefitte, and Matt Ryalls. 2016. "Sanitising the City: Exploring Hegemonic Gentrification in London's Soho." *Sociological Research Online* 21 (3): 1–6.

Seidman, Steven. 2002. *Beyond the Closet: The Transformation of Gay and Lesbian Life*. New York: Routledge.

Tewksbury, Richard. 2008. "Finding Erotic Oases: Locating the Sites of Men's Same-Sex Anonymous Sexual Encounters." *Journal of Homosexuality* 55 (1): 1–19.

Troiden, Richard. 1974. "Homosexual Encounters in a Highway Rest Stop." In *Sexual Deviance and Sexual Deviants*, edited by E. Goode and R. Troiden, 211–28. New York: William Morrow.

Valentine, Gill. 1993. "(Hetero)sexing Space: Lesbian Perceptions and Experiences of Everyday Spaces." *Environment & Planning D: Society & Space* 11: 395–413.

Ward, Jane. 2003. "Producing 'Pride' in West Hollywood: Queer Cultural Capital for Queers with Cultural Capital." *Sexualities* 6 (1): 65–94.

Ward, Jane. 2015. *Not Gay: Sex between Straight White Men*. New York: New York University Press.

Warner, Michael. 1999. *The Trouble with Normal: Sex, Politics, and the Ethics of Queer Life*. Cambridge, MA: Harvard University Press.

Weiss, Margot. 2008. "Gay Shame and BDSM Pride: Neoliberalism, Privacy, and Sexual Politics." *Radical History Review* 100: 87–101.

PART III

Dislocating Spaces and Places

7

Expecting versus Experiencing

*Queer Black College Students and Discrimination
at Black and White Universities*

TEHQUIN D. FORBES

The US university campus largely remains an exclusionary place. It is a microcosm of, product of, and enabler of what bell hooks (hooks 1984) has called the white supremacist capitalist patriarchy. Minoritized students face discrimination in campus organizations (e.g., Silver 2020), in classrooms (e.g., Allen 1992; Forbes 2022; Johnson et al. 2021), and in returns on investment of their college degrees (e.g., Jackson and Reynolds 2013) compared to their in-group counterparts. One could argue, and evidence would support, that the institution of higher education and its university and college organizations are sites for the reproduction of social inequality, mimicking processes of marginalization that occur in society writ large.

Black students know all too well that college is an exclusionary place. For decades, they have faced issues related to accessing higher education (Allen and Jewell 2002; Clewell and Anderson 1995). Once at college, the ones attending predominantly white institutions have reported facing discrimination and racism on campus (Eschmann 2020; Feagin, Vera, and Imani 1996; Fisher and Hartmann 1995). After college, they have seen that their debts are higher (Jackson and Reynolds 2013) and their degrees are not as lucrative (Gould, Mokhiber, and Wolfe 2018; Wilson and Rodgers, III 2016). A notable exception to these rules includes Black students who attend historically Black colleges and universities. There, they enjoy the advantages of being members of the racial majority, which include items such as better grades and closer relationships with faculty members (Allen 1987).

However, queer Black students are *space invaders* (Puwar 2004) at both predominantly white institutions (PWIs) and historically Black colleges/universities (HBCUs). At PWIs, queer Black students find themselves marginalized based on queerness and Blackness. At HBCUs, Blackness is not a hindrance, but queerness is arguably a more prominent mark against students—relative to their counterparts at PWIs—because of the conservatism and respectability of HBCU culture (Mobley and Johnson 2019; Njoku, Butler, and Beatty 2017). These expected differences in severity of Black and queer inclusion mean that although queer Black students on both sorts of campus find themselves on the fringes of student life, they likely experience and understand their shared social location differently based on space.

In this chapter, I discuss respondents' expectations about Black and white universities prior to arriving on campus before reporting how students meet bigotry on both campuses. Critically, I analyze and compare higher education from two distinct racial standpoints—the white and Black campuses—to highlight how the overall racist and heterosexist structure of higher education leaves queer Black students disadvantaged to white and straight peers. I find that students faced racism and queerphobia to varying degrees at both campuses, ranging from name-calling to threat of physical violence. Despite what promises of inclusion the organization made, queer Black students either largely did not fit in, as was the case at the PWI, or could only fit in if they were willing to minimize their queer identities, as was the case at the HBCU. I argue that both Black and white spaces have failed to account for the unique social position of Black queers, and this conceptual finding demands that organizations rethink how diversity and inclusion efforts currently change, or fail to change, the material circumstances of some of their most minoritized members.

Data and Methods

The primary data for this project are twenty-six semi-structured, in-depth interviews with current queer Black college students or very recent graduates (sixteen from a PWI, ten from an HBCU) living in a mid-sized city in the southeastern US. As Stone points out earlier in chapter 4, sociology has much to gain in understanding how race and geography influence gender and sexuality through studying the South. To this end, I recruited participants using a variety of sampling approaches, including snowball sampling, emailing listserv pushes, visiting target population student groups, recruitment announcements made from my professional Twitter account (@Soc_Forbes), and recruitment flyers on college campuses. Students currently enrolled at either of my recruitment sites were eligible to participate in the study if they met two basic conditions: (1) they self-identify as African, African American, Afro-Caribbean, Afro-Latinx, Biracial or Multiracial Black, or otherwise Black; and (2) they self-identify as lesbian, gay, bisexual, transgender, queer, or otherwise nonheterosexual. My final sample included four nonbinary students, 13 students identifying as women or female, and nine identifying as men or male.

When analyzing my interview data, I employed an inductive and flexible coding method following the guidelines set out by Deterding and Waters (2021). I conducted two to three interviews before transcribing them all and then coding the transcripts using index codes derived from my interview schedules. Next, I went through my indexed sections and read them closely, performing analytic coding to identify emerging themes in the data. I repeated this process until I reached an adequate level of information power (Malterud, Siersma, and Guassora 2016), at which point I ended data collection.

The research site city has a storied history of anti-Black resentment and of LGBTQ+ erasure. While the university campuses can be called generally liberal, they are situated in a locale that is culturally conservative. For example, despite regularly "going blue" during general elections, the city lacks a gayborhood or thriving gay nightlife scene and hosts one of the most racially segregated school districts in its state. In light of the setting, queer Black respondents proved to be a hard-to-sample population. To shore up my analysis, I also drew on field observation, informal conversations, and campus climate survey findings from both universities as data sources.

In data collection efforts, I have noted strengths and limitations in my recruitment strategies. The strengths thus far have overwhelmingly been related to my shared queer and Black social location with respondents. I have leaned into this sense of communality and found it helpful for building quick, deep rapport with members of this marginalized and less visible group (Moore 2018). For example, on several occasions, respondents have cried during their interviews with me when discussing their experiences as queer Black students. I find it hard to believe they would as frequently show such vulnerability during interviews with someone straight and/or non-Black. At the same time, I note that as a cisgender man it is likely that there are some things my trans and gender minority (e.g., women, nonbinary) respondents might not share with me or, if they do share, I interpret differently than might someone who is also a gender minority. I try to hedge these limitations, however, by asking for clarification about things I am unsure of during interviews, especially as it relates to gender.

Although being Black and queer helped me build rapport with my respondents, I found it was sometimes an additional obstacle to building trust with my respondents from the HBCU. I did not highlight the fact that I had never attended an HBCU, but my then-institutional affiliation plastered on informed consent documents made clear that I attended a PWI. Njoku and colleagues (2017) speak of the *race secrets* that HBCU attendees keep so as not to contribute to the poor public perceptions of Black people. Even though I share Blackness with my respondents, I acknowledge that they may keep secrets from me, too, as a Black person affiliated with a PWI. For example, one respondent shared a long anecdote with me in response to my question, "How could the HBCU support you better as a gay student?" Their answer was tied to an incident of student death on campus. However, after they finished, they asked me to pause the recorder and strike everything they had just said from the record; they did not want it shared in any official write-up of my findings. I respected their wishes but noted that in this and future instances with HBCU students my outsider status would likely hinder me from accessing some important information about their time at the HBCU as queer Black students.

Findings

Pre-College Expectations of White and Black Campuses

Before ever stepping foot on their respective campuses, my respondents had already formed preconceived notions of what their college campuses might be like. Despite some evidence that Black students who choose to attend HBCUs are not that different demographically from their peers who choose to attend PWIs (Freeman and Thomas 2002), extant research suggests that these expectations about different kinds of campus environments matter for where students go and how they experience college once they arrive.

Current literature finds that Black students decide whether to attend an HBCU or PWI based on their interpretations of their time in high school. Whereas predominantly Black high school backgrounds and connections lead some to desire predominantly Black college campuses (Freeman 1999; Freeman and Thomas 2002; Johnson 2017; Johnson 2019), others seek seemingly more diverse university settings in attending predominantly white ones (Freeman 1999; Holland 2020). While a dearth of research examines the decision-making processes of queer Black students, some work done with gay Black male student populations finds that identity salience plays a part—those who identify more with their Black identity tend to enroll at HBCUs and those who identify more with their gay identity tend to enroll at PWIs (Squire and Mobley 2015).

Corroborating previous findings, I found that students at the HBCU reported seeking Black cultural connections and becoming part of Black educational legacies. Lamar put it succinctly when he said, "I knew I wanted to go to an HBCU, not only for the experience but because it's an HBCU." Students demonstrated strong convictions regarding their desire and choice to attend an HBCU. Lisa Raye's response when asked why she chose to attend an HBCU is typical of the HBCU participants:

> I just knew I wanted to go to HBCU. I wanted to be around more people that looked like me going to college so I could say, "Well, if they're doing it, I can do it." And also just the culture around HBCUs—it's just an experience that I don't think I would have gotten if I went to a PWI.

Students noted that they wished to enjoy the benefits of being surrounded by Black peers. For several of them, this desire began well before their senior year of high school. Many respondents shared an unyielding commitment to receiving an HBCU education and experience—and a few shared their commitment to the HBCU in particular. Lamar recalled how "proud" he was of being accepted to the HBCU after applying in

August and not receiving acceptance until he came off a waitlist in May. Deshaun applied repeatedly until his application materials were strong enough to gain admission:

> I wanted to come to this school since I was in sixth grade. And I wanted to join the band since I was a freshman in high school. This school, it was just a dream for me, honestly. I still personally can't believe that I'm here. I'm getting ready to go into my sophomore year. I worked way too hard to get into this school. Way too hard. After being denied five times, I worked my butt off to get into this school. Going to another school wasn't an option for me. It was this school that I'm like, "I'm going to graduate from here."

It was clear that students attending the HBCU held their institution in high regard not just for its educational pedigree, but because of its great symbolic meaning to them as Black students. Because it was a place celebrating Black people, Black scholarship, and even Black arts (e.g., the marching band), respondents made plans to attend the HBCU and worked hard to achieve that goal. The expectation was clear: That being at the HBCU was the place to be for young, bright Black people. In focusing so heavily on their racial identities during their decision-making, respondents who attended the HBCU apparently did not account for their queerness in formulating their expectations of the HBCU. They either gave it no consideration or figured queerness would have a negligible impact on their experiences once at a Black campus.

In stark contrast to the dedication that many students attending the HBCU felt toward their HBCU, virtually no students attending the PWI expressed a similar sentiment toward their PWI. None shared stories of applying several times until they were admitted, and none shared that they had dreamt of attending the PWI before—or after, for that matter—beginning the college application process. Two respondents, Albert and Lex, did share that they had grown a sense of attachment to the PWI once on campus. Albert said for him it was the memories he had made during his years in college that made him feel close to the institution, and Lex said for her it was the relationships she had forged with professors. However, they were outliers. The remainder of queer Black students attending the PWI that I interviewed made clear they did not feel such connection. Usually, they chalked it up to the PWI not being a space for them as Black students. Instead, they noted the ways they felt othered by peers, instructors, and seemingly the organization itself for being Black and queer. Trans and nonbinary respondents also noted how the space was not inclusive of their queerness, which incorporated gender identity and expression. Zami's response when asked if they felt connected to the PWI is illustrative: "Outside of [my home] department, no. It's really white, and it feels very straight and those are in direct opposition to my identity. I don't really spend a lot of time on campus." Here, I believe Zami is including gender, as well as sexual orientation, in their understanding of *straight*, highlighting how gender identity beyond the binary is also made to not fit in on campus.

The expectations and preconceived notions that my respondents from the PWI had of HBCUs largely made the HBCU a non-option for them. Whereas students attending the HBCU had not factored queerness into their college decision process, students attending the PWI did. Daniel said:

> I think growing up in a predominantly white community caused me to, um . . . I've never held resentment toward being Black. I just felt like that space [HBCU] wasn't for me, maybe because of my queer identity. And feeling like I'm maybe too much of an outsider in that space.

Similarly, Mercedes said that being lesbian, punk, and into screamo music made her reconsider applying to an HBCU:

> I actually considered the HBCU, but I almost felt like an Oreo a little bit, and I was like, "Do I really think that I'm gonna fit into a school like that?" And when I say "like that" I mean a school where the majority is a Black population. I have known Black people who are very judgmental about people because they are different. I think I was afraid of that judgement, and that's why I didn't end up applying to an HBCU, because I felt like at least the white people are okay with weirdness, so maybe I'll fit in more there.

The PWI respondents drew on mainstream stereotypes of Black spaces and Black cultures as queerphobic to explain why they did not consider HBCUs as places for them, even though their current institution was by their own admission also not a place for them because of their Blackness and, to a lesser extent, their queerness. Additionally, I note that respondents' ties to whiteness influence their beliefs about Black culture. For example, in the above excerpt, Daniel attributes his background in "predominantly white community" as a reason for his feeling like an "outsider" in Black space(s). However, taking lessons from Smith and Moore's (2002) findings, I posit that it could also be the case that a background in whiteness has readied Daniel for more of the same at the PWI, even if that should include racial isolation, violence, and/or tokenism as consequence for being part of the Black minority on a white campus.

Meeting Bigotry on Both Campuses

Despite what they expected to find or not find at either the PWI or the HBCU, respondents met bigotry at both campuses. The instances of anti-Blackness and anti-queerness respondents recounted spanned the psychological, interactional, and institutional realms. Moreover, I found that students at the PWI interpreted such racist and queerphobic events differently than their the HBCU peers.

At the PWI, students faced racism as well as queerphobia. (I use *queerphobia* as a more inclusive alternative to *homophobia* to mirror the violence inherit in the term racism, which I feel *heterosexism* fails to capture.) Typically, respondents described passive racism and queerphobia which made them feel othered and reminded them they were outsiders at their mostly straight, mostly white PWI. Julissa's story about a faculty-administered survey reflects this:

> I was in an education course and they were doing a survey, and the way they formulated a question to be queer friendly—it was really bad and it came off wrong. I know what their intentions were, but little things like not knowing terminology really feels problematic to me, especially when we have resources on campus where you can go to learn about things like that. It feels kind of disrespectful, but it also feels like the work of the majority being played out.

Julissa felt "disrespect" as a queer person on campus, even as she acknowledged the good intentions of attempted queer inclusivity. This

example highlights the pervasiveness of queerphobia in higher education and is analogous to the pervasiveness of racism in higher education,
too, as students shared such interactions with strangers, friends, staff,
faculty, and seemingly the institution itself. Although less frequently
shared, these incidents included some extremely violent acts as well.
For example, Taylor recalled going for an evening run down a popular
campus road when a white man called them "nigger" from a passing
truck, and Albert shared that men threw a glass bottle at him and his
boyfriend—again, from a passing truck—and shouted "Faggots!" as they
walked down a street near sorority row. To varying severity levels, queer
Black students at the PWI were made to feel as though they did not
belong there.

Respondents at the PWI readily articulated the ways they were minoritized on campus for being Black and queer. The language they used
to describe this phenomenon indicates that the institution afforded
them a toolkit to discuss oppression and privilege even as they faced
marginalization at that site. Primarily, they drew on theories of intersectionality to make sense of their college experiences. For example, Zami
discussed the inclusivity shortcomings of Black spaces and queer spaces
for them as a nonbinary student:

> Oh, brother. I feel like you get to choose between being around Black
> people or being around queer people, and the two don't really intersect
> that often. It kind of sucks. A lot of times when I'm in Black spaces, it's
> very gendered and not always understanding of, like, homosexuality
> and queerness. But then a lot of the queer people I hang out with, espe-
> cially on campus, are a lot of queer white people who, even when they
> try, they're just . . . They don't get it, so that's kind of difficult to navigate
> sometimes.

Of course, it is not the case that there are no queer students who are
Black and no Black students who are queer. Instead, Zami points out
that, due to their minoritized status and proportionally small share of
campus demographics, queer Black people can expect to be the sexual
and gender minorities among Black students on campus as well as racial
minorities among queer students on campus. This fact has consequences
for their sense of belonging on campus. For instance, Lex talked about

how she felt the LGBTQ+ student group at the PWI failed to appeal to her as a gay Black woman:

> I think for a lot of people in the LGBTQ+ student group, being gay is their end all be all, their most poignant identity. But for me, it's not just being gay, and it's not just being Black. It's being a Black gay woman. All of those experiences together really shaped how I view the world, and I feel like in the student group that wasn't reflected. I guess the best example I could give is I had a couple friends who I had talked to about my Blackness and how that infused with my gayness. That just seemed to go over their heads. I think in those spaces it goes over peoples' heads because a lot of times, we forget that there are not *just* gay people in the gay community.

Although my study is primarily an analysis of race and queerness, it is evident that students' experiences are also heavily shaped by class and gender. It is likely that other queer Black people without a college education—more specifically, without an education from a well-funded public PWI—would not use the same terminology or make the same connections between the personal and political as Zami and Lex do. Moreover, both Zami and Lex explicitly discuss how simultaneously being Black, being queer, and being gender minorities has made them feel left out at the PWI. Their interpretation of their experiences is in stark contrast to that of a cisgender man like Albert, who said he felt connected to the university despite experiencing something as potentially traumatizing as being called a gay slur while threatened with bodily harm. Overall, these respondents found the campus climate to be unaccepting or ambivalent toward them.

Unexpectedly, I found that the PWI students' expectations of what race would mean for their time at a PWI were not as robust as their expectations of what queerness would mean had they attended an HBCU. Although they met both racism and queerphobia, the PWI respondents seemed to have little to no expectations about what being Black at a PWI would mean for them before they arrived on campus. For instance, after Daniel talked about the woes of being a Black student leader and activist at the PWI, I asked him if he had anticipated having these issues at a PWI. "Oh, no," he said. "I came to the PWI because I fell in love with the campus and I felt like students' voices would be heard and uplifted." Yadiel, a student from the Dominican Republic who did not know that an HBCU was an option available to him, stated, "I didn't expect to have any racist or colorist shit happen to me at the PWI." Oson, a mixed-race Black student, explained they "didn't have any expectations about the racial climate" before arriving at the PWI because they "came into [their] Blackness in college." As I show below, this is in stark contrast to the HBCU students who had developed some more nuanced understanding of their Blackness much earlier than college, as evidenced by their express desires to attend Black universities.

As far as HBCU students were concerned, I found that although they also faced othering based on queerness and, to a lesser extent, African American ethnocentrism, they did not articulate the experiences as well as their PWI counterparts. Indeed, through my analysis I argue that while students at the PWI focused on all the ways they stood out, students at the HBCU focused on the ways they fit in—despite mounting evidence to the contrary.

I found anti-queerness at the HBCU on all levels, just as I had at the PWI. For example, I procured the final report of the HBCU campus climate survey and learned that one-third of the survey's total respondents reported hearing derogatory jokes made about the LGBTQ+ community. The survey itself proved to be a queerphobic instrument as it made space for trans denial via its language choice: the self-reported gender question included an option that read "There are only 2 genders," which was chosen by exactly one individual. When I visited the HBCU myself to discover what resources it made available to its queer students, I located a hard-to-find support center tucked away in the corner of an old services building with the assistance of my respondent Yadiel. The center was staffed by only one professional staff member (who was assisted by a student intern). The staff member shared in an unrecorded conversation that they were supposed to be an interim hire for the position because they were already employed by the college in another role and the last center head had quit suddenly. They noted that university administration had made clear to them that staffing the support center was their secondary job duty and all other responsibilities of their primary title took priority over the center and its constituents. Eventually, the university said that due to funding complications, there was no timeline on when a permanent replacement for the role could be hired, but the center head job and support for queer students were to remain secondary indefinitely. This lack of institutional support and funding for queer students and their specific resources is yet another component of a larger, systemic issue with heterosexism. In addition, students I spoke with made clear they had also witnessed or encountered individual-level discrimination at the HBCU in peer and faculty interactions. For example, Lamar shared the time he was called a slur:

> Recently I was leaving my on-campus apartment to go to a crossing party for one of my friends. I was wearing these shorts and they were shorter than usual. So, I was walking out and there was a gang of straight dudes at the exit. I remember I walked past them, and I paused my music on purpose because I felt like they were gonna say something, and I heard one of them say, "Dang, look at that faggot." I was going to say something but there were too many of them and I didn't want to get into a fight.

In line with other studies of HBCUs (Harper and Gasman 2008; Literte and Hodge 2012; Mobley and Johnson 2019; Njoku, Butler, and Beatty 2017), queerphobia and conservatism were found to be thriving at the HBCU at micro and macro levels.

In addition to queerphobia, I found evidence of ethnicity-based discrimination at the HBCU as well. One expects that Black students would confront anti-Black racism at predominantly white universities but attending an HBCU should reasonably protect against that negative experience. However, this was not the full story. Although the definitions and boundaries of Black and Blackness are always changing, it is widely held that HBCUs were founded on the premise of the advance of African Americans. Three respondents who attended the HBCU identified as Afro-Latinas, and they shared that they often felt dismissed as "not Black enough" because of their Latinidad. For example, when asked if she felt people treated her differently on campus because of her race, Dascha said, "I definitely think so," and began a conversation about ethnicity, saying, "I'm an African American studies major, so I'm in most classes with mostly Black people. I try to bring conversations about the experiences of Afro-Latinas into the conversation because it's such a huge world demographically, but I feel like African Americans, people who may not be Hispanic, don't want to talk about." She continued:

> I feel like walking into the room and knowing that I'm the only Hispanic person happens every single day at Midsouth's campus, which sort of drives me to make more conversations in my classrooms. I feel like that part of the conversation is definitely valid and to ignore that there's so many Afro-Latinas in the community of Blackness and write them off as not being Black enough or not being Black at all is just unfair because Hispanics definitely consider us Black, without a doubt.

While the anti-Black threads that run through the HBCU appear different than those seen at the PWI, they are there regardless. In this case, one interpretation is that xenophobia meets anti-Blackness to narrow the scope of what it means to be authentically Black rather than allowing Blackness itself to be diverse and multicultural. Because of a commitment to African American advancement, which is inherent in the respectability politics that HBCUs were founded on (Njoku, Butler, and Beatty 2017), non-African American Black students can feel othered as well, even if phenotypically they are part of the racial majority at their institution.

A major difference I found between respondents was that the HBCU students were much more likely than the PWI students to call their university's campus climate accepting. Whereas queer Black students at the PWI had readily discussed the ways they felt othered by their mostly white, mostly straight institution, students at the HBCU seemed to overlook discrimination and affirm the institution as a welcoming place. When it came to the campus climate for queer students, there was a gendered split in opinion. Men were much more likely than women to paint the climate for sexual and gender minorities in a positive light. For example, although Lamar described incidents such as being called a slur, when asked to describe the campus climate for queer students at the HBCU, he said, "Accepting. A good amount of the men on campus are a part of the LGBT community, so I really feel like people don't really care on campus." Xavier shared that he had witnessed conversations about "the gay agenda" take place online using the hashtag #Midsouth-StateTwitter. When I asked him whether he believed this led to people treating him differently on campus for being a homosexual student, he said, "I don't think so. Everyone's pretty cool. Everyone pretty much minds their business." Despite facing individual-level queerphobic violence, Lamar called his institution "accepting." Xavier interpreted tolerant apathy—or straight people minding their business—to mean that his peers were "pretty cool" with queer students on campus. From these examples, I draw that male respondents attending the HBCU had low expectations of what life for queer students would be like in university, and in the absence of physical violence they deem the campus to be mostly accepting of them.

Women more readily highlighted the HBCU's shortcoming in this regard. For example, Dascha responded, "I don't think it's as accepting as it could be," when asked to describe the campus's climate for LGBTQ+ students before citing a dearth of queer resources on campus. Krystal, mentioning discussions she had seen online at #MidsouthStateTwitter about opinions on raising LGBTQ+ children, said, "There's definitely a problem with homophobia on campus. I mean, where are you gonna go and not find homophobia on campus?" Evidence of this gendered split in the perception of the HBCU's queer campus climate supports previous findings that relatively more privileged students seem to hold weaker expectations of the support offered by non-queer people (Forbes and Ueno 2020). In the case of the HBCU, where most students are indeed Black, I saw that men held weaker expectations of would-be allies than women did.

Unlike their peers at the PWI, the students of the HBCU could rally behind their shared racial identity and the legacy of the HBCU to affirm the institution as a welcoming, accepting place. Despite evidence of queerphobia and sparse instances of ethnocentrism, each the HBCU student expressed a connection to their school that hardly anyone attending the PWI expressed. An illustrative example comes from Dascha. Earlier, I presented excerpts from our conversation together that demonstrated she experienced both ethnocentrism and a less-than-accepting LGBTQ+ campus climate at the HBCU. However, based on race alone, she found outstanding pride in her college. When I asked if she felt connected to the HBCU, she pointed to herself and reminded me she was wearing a school sweatshirt: "I have a deep sense of pride for the fact that I go to an HBCU. I'm proud to take part in it and I'm proud to be in a place where Black education is celebrated." By making Blackness the center of the solar system around which other factors like gender and sexuality revolved, students at the HBCU were able to name a respect and adoration they held for their school that their counterparts at the PWI simply could not. In other words, for the HBCU respondents, being Black students at a Black university served as a kind of buffer against perceived and experienced discriminations against queerness that did not substantially diminish the relationship they had to their school. Conversely, with no shared racial identity between the school and themselves, the PWI respondents' perceived and experienced discriminations against queerness were just yet another reason why they typically felt alienated on campus.

However, not all students were willing to assimilate. In few special cases, my data revealed that when the structure failed them, respondents might forge new paths. For example, one student who was initially enrolled at the HBCU transferred to the PWI to complete her degree after deciding that a sense of racial solidarity could not make up for a lack of educational resources relative to the better-funded white campus. In other instances, two PWI students spent considerable time traveling to the HBCU, establishing friendships and socializing there to compensate for the lack of racial solidarity they found at their home institution. In these special cases, I note that the onus is seemingly placed on individuals to fill their own needs—not on the universities to meet the needs of all its students.

Conclusion

As space invaders on campus, queer Black college students must forge their own spaces. But that's easier said than done. Higher education, as I reported, is unkind toward both queer students and Black students. I found that at the intersection of queerness and Blackness students were either forced to feel excluded or burdened to find community, even at the expense of their full selves.

My study demonstrates that despite formulating expectations of how they would be included at their chosen universities, my respondents faced exclusion upon arriving at campus. At the PWI, queer Black students find themselves othered on the bases of Blackness and queerness.

They face discrimination on campus that leaves them skeptical of their peers, their faculty, and their administrators. At the HBCU, queer Black students primarily find themselves othered based on queerness. I found that they get to enjoy the benefits of attending an HBCU and being part of the racial majority if they are willing to mute their queer identities in the name of respectability. Even after witnessing or experiencing first-hand queerphobia, they are still likely to call their school an inclusive and accepting place—and it very well might be for those who are willing to assimilate.

The campus is an interesting site to focus on because it is uniquely poised to reveal the capacity for even "inclusive" spaces to perpetuate inequalities. Despite all the efforts of the organization—or perhaps due to the efforts of the organization, depending on how you look at it—queer Black students found themselves on the outskirts of life on campus. In a later chapter of this book, Winder discusses how his sample of Black gay men respondents often found themselves "too Black for queer space, and too queer for Black space," including in school. Higher education, a site which caters to whiteness, heterosexuality, and gender conformity, left the overwhelming majority of my respondents feeling as though there was no place for them to be Black and queer in college. Those who could not prioritize one identity over the other were left on the outs, a space reserved for only the most marginalized.

The structure of higher education does not lend itself toward including Black people or queer people. This reality leaves queer Black students at a remarkable disadvantage in any case. Even on a Black campus, respondents met violence and discrimination from peers, administrators, and seemingly the institution itself if they could not or would not conform to standards of heterosexuality and racialized respectability politics. Ultimately, my findings challenge the current state of higher education for minoritized students. Because higher education itself is racist and heterosexist, it has not yet grappled with how to most effectively include Black queers. An investigation of any other US institution—family, criminal justice, employment—would likely reveal a similarly dire reality.

Moving forward, I propose that we begin rethinking what it means to be inclusive of difference in organizations and in society. As my research shows, it is not enough to simply admit queer Black students to college—when left on their own to oppose violent systems of oppression and the norms of wherever they find themselves, more students than not will lose the fight. To fully bring these students to center, policies and organizational changes must support their inclusion and advancement. Some suggestions include making student organizations that cater to their population more visible on campus, especially through funding support; mandating diversity education for all college faculty, staff, and students so that the campus population has a baseline understanding of why everyone should be invested in such equity work; and seeing the faculty who are the biggest advocates of this group, who often also find themselves marginalized in academia, through to tenure so that they might be more influential advocates for their students.

REFERENCES

Allen, Walter R. 1992. "The Color of Success: African-American College Student Outcomes at Predominantly White and Historically Black Public Colleges and Universities." *Harvard Educational Review* 62 (1): 26–45. https://doi.org/10.17763/haer.62.1.wv5627665007v701.

Allen, Walter R. 1987. "Black Colleges vs. White Colleges." *Change: The Magazine of Higher Learning* 19 (3): 28–34. https://doi.org/10.1080/00091383.1987.9939144.

Allen, Walter R. and Joseph O. Jewell. 2002. "A Backward Glance Forward: Past, Present and Future Perspectives on Historically Black Colleges and Universities." *Review of Higher Education* 25 (3): 241–61. https://doi.org/10.1353/rhe.2002.0007.

Chica, Christina Marie. 2019. "Queer Integrative Marginalization: LGBTQ Student Integration Strategies at an Elite University." *Socius: Sociological Research for a Dynamic World* 5 (January): 237802311983959. https://doi.org/10.1177/2378023119839590.

Clewell, Beatriz Chu, and Bernice Taylor Anderson. 1995. "African Americans in Higher Education: An Issue of Access." *Humboldt Journal of Social Relations* 21 (2): 55–79.

Deterding, Nicole M. and Mary C. Waters. 2021. "Flexible Coding of In-Depth Interviews: A Twenty-First-Century Approach." *Sociological Methods & Research* 50 (2): 708–739. https://doi.org/10.1177/0049124118799377.

Eschmann, Rob. 2020. "Unmasking Racism: Students of Color and Expressions of Racism in Online Spaces." *Social Problems* 67 (3): 418–36. https://doi.org/10.1093/socpro/spz026.

Feagin, Joe R., Hernan Vera, and Nikitah Imani. 1996. *The Agony of Education: Black Students at White Colleges and Universities*. New York: Routledge.

Fisher, Bradley J. and David J. Hartmann. 1995. "The Impact of Race on the Social Experience of College Students at a Predominantly White University." *Journal of Black Studies* 26 (2): 117–33. https://doi.org/10.1177/002193479502600202.

Forbes, TehQuin D. 2022. "Queer-Free Majors? LGBTQ+ College Students' Accounts of Chilly and Warm Academic Disciplines." *Journal of LGBT Youth* 19 (3): 330–49. https://doi.org/10.1080/19361653.2020.1813673.

Forbes, TehQuin D. and Koji Ueno. 2020. "Post-Gay, Political, and Pieced Together: Queer Expectations of Straight Allies." *Sociological Perspectives* 63 (1): 159–76. https://doi.org/10.1177/0731121419885353.

Freeman, Kassie. 1999. "HBCUs or PWIs? African American High School Students' Consideration of Higher Education Institution Types." *Review of Higher Education* 23 (1): 91–106.

Freeman, Kassie and Gail E. Thomas. 2002. "Black Colleges and College Choice: Characteristics of Students Who Choose HBCUs." *Review of Higher Education* 25 (3): 349–58. https://doi.org/10.1353/rhe.2002.0011.

Gould, Elise, Zane Mokhiber, and Julia Wolfe. 2018. "Class of 2018: College Edition." Washington DC: Economic Policy Institute.

Harper, Shaun R., and Marybeth Gasman. 2008. "Consequences of Conservatism: Black Male Undergraduates and the Politics of Historically Black Colleges and Universities." *Journal of Negro Education* 4 (77): 336–51.

Holland, Megan M. 2020. "Black Students' College Preferences: The Role of the White Racial Frame in Perpetuating Integration." *Sociological Perspectives* 63 (4): 552–70. https://doi.org/10.1177/0731121419895023.

hooks, bell. 1984. *Feminist Theory: From Margin to Center.* Boston: South End Press.

Jackson, Brandon A., and John R. Reynolds. 2013. "The Price of Opportunity: Race, Student Loan Debt, and College Achievement." *Sociological Inquiry* 83 (3): 335–68. https://doi.org/10.1111/soin.12012.

Johnson, Jennifer M. 2017. "Choosing HBCUs: Why African Americans Choose HBCUs in the Twenty-First Century." In *Black Colleges across the Diaspora: Global Perspectives on Race and Stratification in Postsecondary Education*, edited by M. Christopher Brown and T. Elon Dancy, 151–69. Bingley, UK: Emerald Publishing Limited. https://doi.org/10.1108/S1479-358X20160000014008.

Johnson, Jennifer M. 2019. "Pride or Prejudice? Motivations for Choosing Black Colleges." *Journal of Student Affairs Research and Practice* 56 (4): 409–22. https://doi.org/10.1080/19496591.2019.1614936.

Johnson, Kirk A, Willa M. Johnson, James M. Thomas, and John J. Green. 2021. "Mapping Microaggressions on a Southern University Campus: Where Are the Safe Spaces for Vulnerable Students?" *Social Problems* 68 (1): 1–18. https://doi.org/10.1093/socpro/spz055.

Literte, Patricia E., and Candice Hodge. 2012. "Sisterhood and Sexuality: Attitudes about Homosexuality among Members of Historically Black Sororities." *Journal of African American Studies* 16 (4): 674–99. https://doi.org/10.1007/s12111-011-9201-2.

Malterud, Kirsti, Volkert Dirk Siersma, and Ann Dorrit Guassora. 2016. "Sample Size in Qualitative Interview Studies: Guided by Information Power." *Qualitative Health Research* 26 (13): 1753–60. https://doi.org/10.1177/1049732315617444.

Mobley, Steve D. and Jennifer M. Johnson. 2019. "'No Pumps Allowed': The 'Problem' with Gender Expression and the Morehouse College 'Appropriate Attire Policy.'" *Journal of Homosexuality* 66 (7): 867–95. https://doi.org/10.1080/00918369.2018.148 6063.

Moore, Mignon R. 2018. "Challenges, Triumphs, and Praxis: Collecting Qualitative Data on Less Visible and Marginalized Populations." In *Other, Please Specify: Queer Methods in Sociology*, edited by D'Lane R. Compton, Tey Meadow, and Kristen Schilt, 169–84. Berkeley: University of California Press.

Njoku, Nadrea, Malika Butler, and Cameron C. Beatty. 2017. "Reimagining the Historically Black College and University (HBCU) Environment: Exposing Race Secrets and the Binding Chains of Respectability and Othermothering." *International Journal of Qualitative Studies in Education* 30 (8): 783–99. https://doi.org/10.1080/0 9518398.2017.1350297.

Puwar, Nirmal. 2004. *Space Invaders: Race, Gender, and Bodies out of Place*. New York: Berg.

Silver, Blake R. 2020. *The Cost of Inclusion: How Student Conformity Leads to Inequality on College Campuses*. Chicago: University of Chicago Press.

Smith, Sandra S. and Mignon R. Moore. 2002. "Expectations of Campus Racial Climate and Social Adjustment among African American College Students." In *African American Education: Race, Community, Inequality, and Achievement*, 2:93–118. Bingley, UK: Emerald Publishing Limited. https://doi.org/10.1016/ S1479-358X(02)80012-2.

Squire, Dian D., and Steve D. Mobley. 2015. "Negotiating Race and Sexual Orientation in the College Choice Process of Black Gay Males." *Urban Review* 47 (3): 466–91. https://psycnet.apa.org/doi/10.1007/s11256-014-0316-3.

Wilson, Valerie, and William M. Rodgers, III. 2016. "Black-White Wage Gaps Expand with Rising Wage Inequality." Washington DC: Economic Policy Institute.

8

Bad Queers

The Institutional Production of LGBTQ Youth Homelessness

BRANDON ANDREW ROBINSON

One in ten youth, ages eighteen to twenty-five years old, experience homelessness in the United States each year (Morton et al. 2018). Disproportionately, lesbian, gay, bisexual, transgender, and queer (LGBTQ) youth comprise around 40 percent of the US youth homelessness population, despite comprising 5 to 8 percent of the overall US youth population (Ray 2006; Durso and Gates 2012). Service providers who work with LGBTQ youth experiencing homelessness indicate that 68 percent of the youth ran away or their families kicked them out because of the youth's sexuality and/or gender identity (Durso and Gates 2012). Family rejection is often understood as *the* cause of LGBTQ youth homelessness.

In conducting eighteen months of ethnographic fieldwork and forty in-depth interviews with LGBTQ youth experiencing homelessness, I move beyond this family rejection narrative to examine how religion, schools, and state child custody systems contribute to the perceived pathways into homelessness for LGBTQ youth experiencing homelessness. Specifically, I document how the youth, especially the Black and Brown youth, said that institutional actors disciplined and punished their gendered behaviors and non-heterosexuality. These processes occurred through gender policing the youth's expansive expressions of gender. These gender policing processes intersected, as well, with the racial profiling of Black and Brown youth's gendered behaviors (Mogul, Ritchie, and Whitlock 2011). Building on sociologist Ann Ferguson's (2000) concept of "bad boys"—how school authorities see Black boys as inherently criminal and more harshly punish young Black boys' behaviors compared to white boys' behaviors—I contend that the policing and punishment of LGBTQ youth's behaviors creates *bad queers*. These disciplining processes produce certain LGBTQ youth—mainly, poor Black and Brown LGBTQ youth—as inferior, as criminals, as bad queers. Some youth in this study said they resisted these disciplining processes by going to live on the streets. Other youth said these punishing practices pushed them into jails and into homelessness.

Importantly, this chapter moves the narrative of LGBTQ youth homelessness away from family rejection to focus in on how other institutions also contribute to the youth's perceived pathways into homelessness. As LGBTQ youth experiencing homelessness come from backgrounds of poverty and mostly from families of color, this shift is important in not placing the burden of LGBTQ youth homelessness on already marginalized families (Robinson 2018b; 2018c; 2020). Likewise, this chapter challenges the notion of a pipeline or single pathway into homelessness for LGBTQ youth experiencing homelessness. Instead, I show how multiple institutions interconnect to discipline, punish, and subjugate poor LGBTQ youth, especially poor Black and Brown LGBTQ youth.

In doing so, this chapter calls on sociologists to rethink institutions, particularly youth-serving institutions. I ask, what do the margins tell us about youth-serving institutions? By turning to the outskirts of queer life and by asking questions from the margins of homelessness, this chapter sheds light on the general phenomenon of what youth-serving institutions do and checks our collective academic assumptions regarding the purpose of these institutions (Stone and Compton, this collection). In centering poor Black and Brown LGBTQ youth experiencing homelessness, this chapter urges sociologists to understand how institutions—that we often take for granted as important to the social fabric of society—contribute to the punishment and marginalization of multiply marginalized youth. I show how these institutions are complicit in contributing to LGBTQ youth homelessness and how dominant institutions often cannot serve youth who occupy multiply marginalized social locations. I also conclude by pushing sexualities scholars to continue to move beyond studying sexual identity to capture the complex, intersecting processes of sexuality, gender, race, and embodiment. These findings help us to work toward addressing LGBTQ youth homelessness.

Bad Queers

In *Bad Boys*, Ferguson (2000) documents how school rules, policies, and practices uphold the racial hierarchy and marginalize Black boys. Specifically, Ferguson examines the differential treatment of white boys' and Black boys' behaviors. When teachers and administrators see white boys acting out, they see this behavior as "boys will be boys" play. However, when teachers and administrators see Black boys acting out, they see this behavior as inherently criminal. Teachers and administrators punish Black boys through acts such as sending them to detention or the "punishing room." These labeling practices and uses of punishment create "bad boys," pushing Black boys out of schools and setting Black boys up to be in contact with carceral systems.

I build on Ferguson's work to examine how institutional rules, policies, and practices discipline and punish LGBTQ youth's behaviors, particularly their gendered behaviors and expressions of sexuality that challenge the gender binary and heteronormativity. I show how gender and sexuality intersect with race and class to create not only bad boys but for some LGBTQ youth of color to create bad queers. The concept of bad queers is an extension of bad boys that shows how upholding heteronormativity and the gender binary and policing gender, sexuality, and race turns some bad boys into bad queers as well as also turning other LGBTQ youth of color, including lesbian youth and trans youth of color, into bad queers as well.

Specifically, I document how religion, schools, and state child custody systems create *bad queers* through their punishment of poor Black or Brown LGBTQ youth's expansive expressions of gender and non-heterosexuality. Like bad boys, bad queers are classed and racialized in specific ways. These punishing and disciplinary practices monitor the gendered and sexual behaviors of poor Black and Brown LGBTQ youth. Because of how racial and class inequalities link to racial profiling, surveillance, and punishment, poor Black and Brown LGBTQ youth may disproportionately bear the brunt of these institutional disciplinary processes and gender policing practices. These practices work to legitimate white heterosexual cisgender youth as the right way to be in the world. This study shows, then, how the production of bad queers affects poor Black and Brown LGBTQ youth in ways that render them disposable and how these disciplinary practices uphold the white racial hierarchy, heteronormativity, and the gender binary. For the youth in this study, these institutional disciplinary processes shaped their perceived pathways into jails and homelessness.

Studying LGBTQ Youth Homelessness

This study is a multi-site ethnography on LGBTQ youth homelessness. From January 2015 to June 2016, I conducted the study primarily at two organizations that provide services to youth experiencing homelessness in central Texas. A great deal of research on LGBTQ youth homelessness, especially work that focuses on pathways into homelessness, is quantitative. Statistical surveys, however, often limit people to marking their one cause of homelessness from a list of categories presented to them, eclipsing the structural, interpersonal, and individual factors that converge to lead particular people to experience homelessness (Wright 2009 [1989]). Therefore, a qualitative study can provide a more nuanced examination of perceived pathways into homelessness in capturing the meanings the youth assign to understanding why they are experiencing homelessness and how processes into homelessness are more complicated than a single pathway.

For the study, I volunteered weekly at a youth homelessness drop-in center in Austin, Texas, and at a LGBTQ youth homelessness shelter in San Antonio, Texas. I conducted over 700 hours of fieldwork. Fieldwork at both sites involved getting to know the people in the social settings, their daily routines, developing relations with the people, and observing them (Emerson, Fretz, and Shaw 2011). As soon as I left the field each day, I took fieldnotes of my observations and experiences of being at the field site for that day.

I also conducted forty in-depth interviews with LGBTQ youth experiencing homelessness. I recruited most youth through the two field sites, though four youth came from a transitional living program associated with the Austin field site, and two youth came from a children's shelter in Austin licensed by Child Protective Services. Youth knew I was a researcher, and the youth whom I interviewed voluntarily agreed. I informed them about all processes of consent.

At the end of each interview, I asked the youth their demographic data. One youth was seventeen, two were twenty-five, and the rest were between eighteen and twenty-four. Thirty of the forty identified as youth of color. Ten youth identified as non-Hispanic white, ten identified as Black, fourteen identified as Hispanic and/or Latina/o, three identified as white Hispanic, one identified as Black Hispanic, one identified as Black, Mexican, and white, and one identified as mixed. Six youth identified as lesbians, eight (youth who identified as transgender) identified as heterosexual, ten identified as gay, twelve identified as bisexual, two identified as pansexual, one identified as "kind of everything," and one identified as "attracted to transgender women." One youth identified as a non-binary trans guy, one identified as a trans man, two identified as gender fluid, seven identified as transgender women, fourteen identified as men, and fifteen identified as women. I describe their gender, sexual, and racial/ethnic identities using the language they used to identify themselves. I have changed all names to keep confidentiality.

Notably, accessing LGBTQ youth experiencing homelessness is difficult, as they are often seen as a "hard-to-reach" population. I decided to go through organizations that work with LGBTQ youth experiencing homelessness as my way to meet and make contact with them. I also volunteered with these organizations for six months before beginning the interview portion of this study. Getting to know the youth before conducting formal interviews seemed to help in building rapport. Not all LGBTQ youth experiencing homelessness, though, access services. This methodological approach of using organizations to access this population misses LGBTQ youth experiencing homelessness who do not access services or who are not in contact with organizations. Nonetheless, this approach allowed me to spend time with the youth and get to know them, which helped in having meaningful interviews.

Recruitment for the interview portion of the study varied based on the field site. In Austin, one concern that the staff and I shared involved not "outing" anyone who wanted to participate. To address this concern, I conducted a survey with all youth at the drop-in center who expressed interest in taking the survey. Under the demographic section, if a youth marked transgender man, transgender woman, or wrote in another gender identity that did not include the specific category of cisgender man or woman, I told them about the interview portion of the study. Likewise, if a youth marked gay, lesbian, bisexual, queer, or wrote in another sexual identity that did not include heterosexual, I told them about the interview portion of the study. Everyone who filled out the survey got a bus pass from the drop-in center. Every LGBTQ youth in Austin who did the interview got a $10 gift card to Walmart, which the director of street outreach got Walmart to donate. In San Antonio, everyone staying at the shelter identified as LGBTQ. All youth knew me as a person conducting a study with LGBTQ youth experiencing homelessness. I interviewed every youth who stayed at the shelter for longer than two weeks. The director gave youth gift cards to restaurants such as Subway for doing the interview.

In collecting the interview data, I digitally audio-recorded all interviews. The interviews lasted around an hour. The interviews covered four major topics: the youth's perceived pathways into homelessness, the present needs of the youth, their strengths, and their everyday experiences. The findings presented in this chapter derive primarily from the qualitative data based on in-depth interviews about the youth's perceived pathways into homelessness. Moving beyond the narrative of family rejection, I focus in on the youth's discussions of how disciplinary practices within religious organizations, schools, and state child custody systems shaped the youth's perceived pathways into homelessness.

Religion

Andres, a twenty-three-year-old gay Hispanic youth, talked to me about his sexuality, his experiences with religion growing up, and his initial wariness to access services at the Austin drop-in center where I met him. "I grew up in a really religious community. And so, I did a pray the gay away for about six months," he explained. Sitting in a staff office room together, Andres continued, "With this pray the gay away—at the end of it—I almost felt like I hurt [my family] even more. Because I was letting them to believe that there was a hope. I myself was convincing myself that there was a hope out of like wanting to satisfy other people and having their love still." In connecting these past experiences with religion to his initial hesitation of accessing services at the drop-in center, Andres detailed, "'Cause it's a church, one. So, you think it's going to be weird. It's going to be what you always experienced at churches. But it wasn't at all, 'cause [the drop-in center] was not really affiliated with [the church that the drop-in center was located in]."

In *Pray the Gay Away*, sociologist Bernadette Barton (2012) shows how religious messages push LGBTQ people into a "toxic closet." In this toxic closet, LGBTQ people often experience shame and other emotional and physiological consequences because of hiding one's sexuality and/or gender identity. LGBTQ people also learn to not express themselves nor see themselves as equal to heterosexual people and people who identify with their assigned gender at birth. These religious messages teach LGBTQ people that they are inferior. This labeling of LGBTQ youth as inferior shapes some youth such as Andres to try to change their sexuality through entering what he called a "pray the gay away" program. Trying to change, though, generated more emotional turmoil in Andres's life.

Furthermore, these experiences with religion made Andres wary of accessing the drop-in center—because of its location in a church—and of accessing other religiously affiliated services in Austin. As the welfare state has been slashed and reduced through the neoliberal restructuring of society, faith-based charity organizations have become one of the largest institutions to now assist and help the poor (Adams 2013). Like non-profits, churches and religiously affiliated services become part of the "shadow state"—a third sector based on volunteer work that focuses on changing and fixing the individual but not on advocating for systemic change (Wolch 1990; Gilmore 2017). Individual giving, donations, and doing volunteer work—not mass mobilization—become ways to alleviate and address issues facing LGBTQ people, including poverty and homelessness (Gilmore 2017; Beam 2018). However, churches and other religiously affiliated services becoming a main part of the "shadow state" can have dire consequences for LGBTQ youth who may have experienced pain, rejection, and trauma from religious people and/or religious messages for their gender and/or sexuality. Andres overcame this hesitation. But some LGBTQ youth may not or cannot be able to perform that labor of reaching out to religiously affiliated services. As many services are religiously affiliated, these negative experiences with religion make accessing services difficult for some people experiencing homelessness.

Andres's good friend Jasper, a twenty-three-year-old mixed-race homosexual, discussed with me the policing of his gender and sexuality at a Christian-based recovery program that a judge sent him to instead of to jail. "You have to go to like classes and groups with them—like Bible study, and church, and CR, which is celebrate recovery," Jasper explained. Talking with me in the choir room at the drop-in center, Jasper continued with an imitation of what people taught him at the recovery program. "There's one true God," he exclaimed. "And what's his name? Jesus Christ! If you don't find him, you're not going to stay sober."

Jasper also discussed how staff at this Christian program policed his gender and sexuality. He stated, "The main issue was—one day, I went back to work. And they were like, 'What is this in [your] locker?' And it was a sweater, and part of the sleeves were laced. And they were like, 'You can't have this. It's a woman's shirt.'" He continued, "And I had some unisex cologne. And they were like, 'This is a woman perfume.' And that's what made me mad the most. I was like how ignorant. It's a scent. The only thing that makes it for men or women is the label." He went on, "And two weeks down the road, it happened again. And it just made me mad." He explained, "'Cause I had a scarf. And they called me down. And they were like, 'What's this?' And I was like, 'It's a scarf.' And this guy was like, 'No, it's not.' And I was like, 'Yeah, it's a scarf.' He was like, 'Jasper, this is what women wear to the beach.' And I was like, 'A sarong?' I was so angry." Jasper said that staff members punished him for these perceived gender transgressions. "They wrote me up. They put me on restriction," he recounted. "And I wasn't allowed to leave for a month unless I had an appointment. And those write-ups, you get four of them, and they can kick you out." Jasper linked part of this gender policing to his sexuality. "They know I'm gay. And I feel like they purposely—whether or not it was on purpose or not—in their mind, that was something they were looking for." A few weeks after I interviewed Jasper, service providers at the Austin drop-in center petitioned the court to get Jasper out of this program and into another program before staff suspended him, which would have been a violation of his probation orders.

As Black and Brown people are more likely to be caught up in carceral systems—because of racial inequality and racial profiling—the policing of Jasper's Brown body could have shaped his arrest and a judge sending him to this program. Furthermore, staff members at this Christian program policed Jasper's gender attire, which Jasper linked to the staff knowing that he is gay. Jasper even said that this gender policing led to staff putting him on restriction and almost expelling him—a potential violation of his court order. This gender policing furthered the punishment of being sent to this court-mandated program and could have also sent Jasper back to jail for violating probation if he did not have the drop-in center to help him get out of the program.

Religion, then, is part of producing bad queers. Certain religious messages label LGBTQ people as an abomination and as sinners and instill in LGBTQ people the idea that they are inferior. Negative religious messages about LGBTQ people work to produce LGBTQ people as different, as bad, as less than. Youth may even internalize these negative messages and try to change their gender and sexuality. These negative experiences with religion detrimentally affect LGBTQ youth experiencing homelessness, as they may be less likely to access faith-based religious services, which comprise most services helping the poor today. Religion infuses into other institutions as well such as the family and court-mandated programs to continue to punish LGBTQ youth and remind them that they are not equal to heterosexual cisgender people. These negative messages and punishing practices push some poor Black and Brown LGBTQ youth into jails and to the streets.

Schools

The production of bad queers doesn't just happen in and through the institution of religion. Nor is this production just related to punishing and policing gay boys of color. Transgender women of color discussed having their gender and sexuality policed and punished within youth-serving institutions such as schools. In talking one day on a bench outside of the LGBTQ shelter, Naomi, an eighteen-year-old bisexual transgender Latina, told me that her mom pulled her out of school her freshman year after Naomi got into a fight because of bullying. She explained, "I got into a fight with some girl for calling me a tranny. And just like the guys when I'd walk down the hallway would be like, 'Where's her dick at?' And it was just—it wasn't fun." In telling how the school policies marked Naomi as different, she went on, "When I was in dance class, I had to change all the way across campus. It was a big-ass high school, and I had to change—and the girls just had to go in the restroom right there and change. It bothered me 'cause that was at the same time when I would tuck and all that, and it was so painful just to do that."

As LGBTQ youth challenge the dominant relations of gender and sexuality, bullying is a common experience of school life to try to control and discipline them. This bullying is often through gender policing, as this type of bullying can be about re-inscribing the gender binary as the dominant mode of gender relations within society (Payne and Smith 2013). As people often monitor Black and Brown youth's behaviors more than white youth's behaviors, peers may target, bully, and gender police LGBTQ youth of color more as well. Naomi experienced peers calling her "tranny" and asking objectifying questions about her body to discipline and subjugate her for being transgender. These discriminatory experiences are also maintained on the institutional level. For instance, schools often have a "hidden curriculum," wherein schools uphold the dominant relations of gender and sexuality through disciplinary practices, the school curriculum, student-teacher relationships, and school events (Pascoe 2007). By making Naomi change separately and far away from everyone else, the school marked and punished Naomi for being transgender. In this way, schools make heteronormativity and the gender binary part of the hidden curriculum, which can further legitimize the bullying and violence that LGBTQ young people experience. Naomi resisted and fought back. This fighting back, though, can have consequences, as Naomi's mom removed Naomi from school, which could set Naomi up to have an even more precarious future if she does not finish her education (Travers 2018).

Another consequence for fighting back against bullying is that youth said that school authorities sent them to alternative educational institutions. "I got into fights here and there," Camila, a twenty-two-year-old heterosexual transgender Hispanic woman, explained to me, as she was lying in her bed at the LGBTQ shelter. "I got put into an alternative school when I was in—I was fourteen. And I got kicked out of alternative school for fighting. And then I got put into boot camp. So, I don't know—a little further punishment than the alternative schools." When I inquired why she was fighting, Camila replied, "Just people making comments about my sexuality."

Julian, a twenty-two-year-old gay Hispanic youth who I met at the drop-in center in Austin, also discussed fighting in school and linked fighting with going to jail. "I beat the hell out of people at school. I was fighting all the time," he explained. When I asked why he was fighting all the time, Julian replied, "The people who are homophobic are dicks.

And so, I just kicked their ass and got on with it. That's why I went to jail my first time was for assault."

In a telling example of bullying and fighting, Arthur, a twenty-five-year-old Black gay man whom I met at the LGBTQ shelter, told me, "I used to want to kill myself because people use to call me fag, gay, this and this and that. Look at you with your faggot ass—stuff like that. It would make me depressed." One day, Arthur fought back. He said, "I went to jail because I kicked this boy [at school] in the face with steel-toed boots on." In explaining to me why, Arthur continued, "He called me a *puta* and stuff like that. And then he was like you fucking faggot. And I just hit him." Arthur went to jail for the charge of an "assault with bodily injury." The other person dropped the charges. Arthur dropped out of school.

Camila's, Julian's, and Arthur's experiences with punishment showcase the expansion of carceral systems into schools. School administrators suspend or expel youth for violating school policies. These suspensions and expulsions push youth into jails and other carceral systems (Mitchum and Moodie-Mills 2014). These policies also disproportionately criminalize Black and Brown students and/or students with disabilities (Beadle 2012). These policies may also be affecting LGBTQ youth, especially LGBTQ youth of color. A recent national study has documented that LGB youth, particularly gender expansive girls, are up to three times more likely to experience disciplinary treatment at schools compared to their non-LGB counterparts (Himmelstein and Brückner 2011). When LGBTQ youth fight back against bullying, school authorities may blame and punish LGBTQ youth for their own victimization. School authorities presume that LGBTQ youth who try to protect themselves are guilty. These authorities also fail to recognize how gender policing and anti-LGBTQ discrimination shape experiences of bullies targeting LGBTQ people and why LGBTQ youth fight back. This dismissal of and/ or failure to understand the structural causes of bullying and the subsequent punishment of LGBTQ youth who fight back push some LGBTQ youth, especially LGBTQ youth of color, out of schools (Mitchum and Moodie-Mills 2014; Snapp et al. 2015).

These experiences of bullying mark the LGBTQ youth in this study as different and inferior. Youth fought back. School authorities, though, punished the youth, including suspending and expelling the youth and sending some youth to jail. Indeed, school authorities may overly punish, discipline, and criminalize Black and Brown LGBTQ youth, such as Camila, Julian, and Arthur. Intersecting being gender expansive, LGBTQ, poor, and Black or Brown, this bullying along with school disciplinary practices produces bad queers. This production of bad queers shapes why some LGBTQ youth may go to jail and to the streets.

State Child Custody

Many young people in this study ran away from state child custody systems or left the system when they turned eighteen years of age. Sitting on a couch at the LGBTQ shelter, Adelpha, an eighteen-year-old heterosexual white, Black, and Mexican transgender woman, discussed with me her experiences in Child Protective Services (CPS) and why she ran away. She began, "They locked me up in a RTC [residential treatment center] for six months in the middle of nowhere. And it's basically like this boot camp for CPS kids. And they treat—literally, it is worse than prison." While eating her dinner, Adelpha went on to discuss how CPS staff policed her gender expression. She stated, "I started wearing makeup and dressing really feminine [at the RTC]. And they were like— they would come up to me—and they were like, 'You need to stop that. This isn't Dallas.'" She continued, "They would make me take off my makeup. And then, I was trying to grow out my hair there. And they were just like, somebody would be there every day—well, not every day, but I think it was every month—to cut hair, 'cause everybody had like a buzz cut. I was like, 'No, I'm not cutting my hair.'"

Adelpha's description of RTCs as being like jails was prominent during this study. Treating young people as criminals can set them up to view themselves as dangerous and to see no alternative paths in their future lives except going to jail (Ferguson 2000). Adelpha said that the RTC staff members also policed her gender expression through acts such as making her remove her makeup and trying to cut her hair. According to Adelpha, RTC staff associated expansive expressions of gender with cities—Dallas. This conflation that only people in cities can be gender expansive did not respect Adelpha's needs and erased the fact that LGBTQ people, and specifically gender expansive people, exist everywhere. This policing of Adelpha's gender expression furthered the punishment of already being locked up at the RTC.

To further capture the youth's descriptions of state child custody systems and their policing of expansive expressions of gender and nonheterosexuality, I turn to Xander, who was residing at a CPS licensed shelter when I interviewed him. Xander was a nineteen-year-old Black gay youth, and he explained to me his experiences in CPS. He stated, "Things were sort of complicated being in my previous placement. And I sort of lost it for a second. And then, I was put on a thirty-day notice, which is sort of like an eviction notice. They are kicking you out." When I asked what happened, Xander replied, "I stabbed a dude. I'm not going to lie. He was throwing caramel in my hair. My hair is one of my trigger points." Xander said he stabbed the other person "in the balls with my [hair] pick." Before this incident though, Xander was already having problems at this previous placement. He detailed, "I was gay. They didn't want anyone around me. I wasn't allowed to be with the boys. And obviously, I wasn't allowed to be with the girls." This segregation generated feelings of difference. "I felt like a zoo animal put on the stage around those kids," he recalled. "Just 'cause I was the only gay dude. 'What's it like being gay? Are you a male or female?'"

The policing of Xander's gender, sexuality, and race shaped his experiences in state child custody systems. Xander said that staff segregated him from everyone. This segregation and isolation may be a way to protect LGBTQ youth, but for Xander, this segregation marked him as different. Gender segregation can try to produce transgender and gender expansive people as objects of scrutiny—as "zoo animals"—through labeling and marking them for challenging the gender binary (Robinson 2018a; 2020). This gender segregation—in upholding the gender binary—can also normalize bullying people who challenge the gender binary. Indeed, Xander said that other youth would bully him and question his sexuality and gender identity. Xander even said that one youth threw caramel in his hair. Hair has a significant political and personal meaning to Black people and communities, especially within a US context that degrades and derides Black hair. This attack on Xander's hair could be an attack on his racial identity. As Xander mentioned, his hair is a trigger point. Xander resisted this bullying and fought back. But his punishment for his resistance was eviction from this CPS placement. Staff members further punished Xander by moving him to different placements. These punishing processes furthered Xander's experiences of marginalization and instability.

State child custody systems rely on other institutions (e.g., RTCs), processes (e.g., eviction), and institutional housing arrangements (e.g., gender segregation) to assist in controlling and punishing the youth and their gender and sexuality. These systems continue the production of bad queers, by criminalizing LGBTQ youth—mainly, poor Black and Brown LGBTQ youth—and evicting them and pushing them into jails and/or to the streets. In Texas, there are not even any explicit CPS policies to protect or respect LGBTQ children and youth. Instead, state child custody systems produce LGBTQ youth as inferior and different.

Bad Queers and Addressing LGBTQ Youth Homelessness

This chapter introduced the concept of *bad queers* to put forth an analysis on the institutional punishment and disciplining of LGBTQ youth—especially poor Black and Brown LGBTQ youth—and how these processes produced the LGBTQ youth as inferior and disposable. By turning to the outskirts of homelessness, this chapter shows how youth-serving institutions impact the sexualities of deeply marginalized LGBTQ youth through policing and punishing them. Religious systems, educational systems, and state child custody systems punish, discipline, and criminalize expansive expressions of gender and non-heterosexuality. These surveillance practices and punishing processes mainly target Black and Brown people and bodies. Specifically, institutional actors discipline and police Black and Brown youth's gendered behaviors and sexuality that challenge the gender binary and heteronormativity. This punishment and production of bad queers—through teaching LGBTQ youth that they are inferior, sinners, different, and less than—push some poor Black and Brown LGBTQ youth to the streets and to jails. This finding challenges the family rejection narrative as *the* pathway into homelessness for LGBTQ youth experiencing homelessness. Other institutions are involved as well, showcasing the reality that there is not a single pathway into homelessness. We need more nuanced solutions than just educating unaccepting families if we want to address LGBTQ youth homelessness.

Importantly, this study pushes sociologists to see how disciplining processes intersect. Ferguson's (2000) work focuses on race and its intersection with masculinity. This study builds on Ferguson to show how discipline works to police race, class, gender, *and* sexuality and to constitute poor Black and Brown LGBTQ youth as bad queers. Indeed, for the youth in this study, these punishing processes happen simultaneously. Sociologists can see, then, how disciplining processes intersect to target multiply marginalized people. The language we often use to describe disciplining and policing processes (such as racial profiling and gender policing) fails to capture the intersectional component of these punishing practices. The concept of bad queers helps us to get at a deeper understanding of these intersectional processes, though we need new language to capture these complex disciplining, profiling, and policing processes.

Another solution that this study highlights is the need to sociologically rethink institutions and how they serve youth. Part of the problem is that dominant institutions often do not meet the needs of people who experience intersecting marginalized social locations (Crenshaw 1991; Abramovich and Shelton 2017; Robinson 2018a, 2020). Indeed, the point of legal scholar Kimberlé Crenshaw (1989) coining the term "intersectionality" was to show how an institution—the law—could not account for the multiply marginalized locations of women of color. Therefore, dominant youth-serving institutions often cannot help and support multiply marginalized children and youth. Instead, institutions and institutional actors police and punish marginalized youth for not upholding the dominant relations of power. Dominant institutions may not even want to serve marginalized youth, whereby the purpose of these institutions can be to discipline and punish youth who deviate from the dominant modes of relation in society. And as Forbes (this book) even shows, these processes can extend into other institutions, including higher education, to continue to other and minoritize Black queer people and make them feel as if they do not belong. In turn, these institutions become an extension of carceral systems—of punishing, disciplining, and pushing certain marginalized children and youth to jails, to the streets, and into disposability.

In response, we need to take action today to change current institutions to make life more bearable for marginalized youth, but we also need a bigger vision of creating new institutions that center the needs and experiences of marginalized youth. Actions that can be implemented today can include items such as ending the gender segregation of school bathrooms and of state child custody housing arrangements. We can also expand social safety nets and move away from religious-based social services. The point is that there are many actions we can take today to change youth-serving institutions to make life better for LGBTQ youth. These actions need to be youth-centered and youth-driven, and these actions need to focus on the respect and dignity of the youth, while also working to provide them stability.

As a broader political agenda, we also need new institutions and to perhaps abolish the current ones. We need to imagine new ways to provide education outside of schools and to help marginalized youth that do not involve the state taking custody of the child. As the carceral state has extended into youth-serving institutions, abolishing carceral systems and ending the practice of sending youth to jails and other carceral institutions needs to be part of this work as well. Importantly, centering the voices of LGBTQ youth experiencing homelessness needs to be at the heart of this new political vision. We need immediate youth-driven goals that we can implement today while we also work toward abolishing institutions and building new institutions and worlds that serve the most marginalized youth among us.

Moving forward, this study shows the need to continue to examine LGBTQ youth and their lives beyond just the notion of identity. That is, sexuality scholars need to not only focus on sexuality and sexual identity in their examination of LGBTQ people, but they also need to examine how embodiment shapes these experiences. Indeed, people already imbue sexual meaning onto gendered, racialized, and classed bodies. Therefore, sexuality scholars need to continue to examine embodiment and not just identity to get at the nuanced processes around sexuality and sexual meanings today. Moreover, poverty and homelessness scholars need to understand how homelessness and institutions that serve poor people and people experiencing homelessness shape sexualities, including access to sex (Robinson 2020; O'Quinn and Goldstein-Kral, this collection). We also need novel methodological approaches to studying LGBTQ youth outside of Gay–Straight Alliances, health centers, drop-in centers, and other organizations. LGBTQ youth exist elsewhere, and we are missing many of these youth. These new approaches will help in not only enriching LGBTQ scholarship but also help in improving LGBTQ people's lives, including the lives of LGBTQ youth experiencing homelessness. In the end, immediate action, broader political visions and work, and better scholarship can all help in making the world a better and more just place for all LGBTQ youth and in ending the production of bad queers.

REFERENCES

Abramovich, Alex and Jama Shelton. 2017. *Where Am I Going to Go? Intersectional Approaches to Ending LGBTQ2S Youth Homelessness in Canada & the U.S.* Toronto: Canadian Observatory on Homelessness Press.

Adams, Vincanne. 2013. *Markets of Sorrow, Labors of Faith.* Durham, NC: Duke University Press.

Barton, Bernadette. 2012. *Pray the Gay Away: The Extraordinary Lives of Bible Belt Gays.* New York: New York University Press.

Beadle, Amanda Peterson. 2012, March 6. "Report: Minority Students Face More Disciplinary Actions in Public Schools." ThinkProgress. https://thinkprogress.org.

Beam, Myrl. 2018. *Gay, Inc.* Minneapolis: University of Minnesota Press.

Crenshaw, Kimberlé. 1989. "Demarginalizing the Intersection of Race and Sex: A Black Feminist Critique of Antidiscrimination Doctrine, Feminist Theory and Antiracist Politics." *University of Chicago Legal Forum* 1: 139–167.

Crenshaw, Kimberlé. 1991. "Mapping the Margins: Intersectionality, Identity Politics, and Violence against Women of Color." *Stanford Law Review* 43 (6): 1241–1299.

Durso, Laura E. and Gary J. Gates. 2012. *Serving Our Youth: Findings from a National Survey of Services Providers Working with Lesbian, Gay, Bisexual and Transgender Youth Who Are Homeless or at Risk of Becoming Homeless.* Los Angeles: The Williams Institute.

Emerson, Robert M., Rachel I. Fretz, and Linda L. Shaw. 2001. *Writing Ethnographic Fieldnotes*, 2nd edition. Chicago: University of Chicago Press.

Ferguson, Ann Arnett. 2000. *Bad Boys: Public Schools in the Making of Black Masculinity.* Ann Arbor: University of Michigan Press.

Gilmore, Ruth Wilson. 2017. "In the Shadow of the Shadow State." In *The Revolution Will Not Be Funded*, edited by INCITE! Durham: Duke University Press.

Himmelstein, Kathryn E. and Hannah Brückner. 2011. "Criminal-Justice and School Sanctions Against Nonheterosexual Youth: A National Longitudinal Study." *Pediatrics* 127 (1): 49–57.

Mitchum, Preston and Aisha C. Moodie-Mills. 2014. *Beyond Bullying: How Hostile School Climate Perpetuates the School-to-Prison Pipeline for LGBTQ Youth.* Washington, DC: Center for American Progress.

Mogul, Joey L., Andrea J. Ritchie, and Kay Whitlock. 2011. *Queer (In)Justice: The Criminalization of LGBT People in the United States.* Boston: Beacon Press.

Morton, Matthew H., Amy Dworsky, Jennifer L. Matjasko, Susanna R. Curry, David Schlueter, Raúl Chávez, and Anne F. Farrell. 2018. "Prevalence and Correlates of Youth Homelessness in the United States." *Journal of Adolescent Health* 62: 14–21.

Pascoe, C. J. 2007. *Dude, You're a Fag: Masculinity and Sexuality in High School*. Berkeley: University of California Press.

Payne, Elizabethe and Melissa Smith. 2013. "LGBTQ Kids, School Safety, and Missing the Big Picture: How the Dominant Bullying Discourse Prevents School Professionals from Thinking about Systematic Marginalization or . . . Why We Need to Rethink LGBTQ Bullying." *QED: A Journal in GLBTQ Worldmaking* 1: 1–36.

Ray, Nicholas. 2006. *An Epidemic of Homelessness: Lesbian, Gay, Bisexual, and Transgender Youth*. Washington, DC: National Gay and Lesbian Task Force Policy Institute.

Robinson, Brandon Andrew. 2018a. "Child Welfare Systems and LGBTQ Youth Homelessness: Gender Segregation, Instability, and Intersectionality." *Child Welfare* 96 (2): 29–45.

Robinson, Brandon Andrew. 2018b. "Conditional Families and Lesbian, Gay, Bisexual, Transgender, and Queer Youth Homelessness: Gender, Sexuality, Family Instability, and Rejection." *Journal of Marriage & Family* 80 (2): 383–96.

Robinson, Brandon Andrew. 2018c. "'I Want to Be Happy in Life': Success, Failure, and Addressing LGBTQ Youth Homelessness." *The Unfinished Queer Agenda after Marriage Equality*, edited by Angela Jones, Joseph DeFilippis, and Michael W. Yarbrough, 117–129. New York: Routledge.

Robinson, Brandon Andrew. 2020. *Coming Out to the Streets: LGBTQ Youth Experiencing Homelessness*. Berkeley: University of California Press.

Snapp, Shannon D., Jennifer M. Hoenig, Amanda Fields, and Stephen T. Russell. 2015. "Messy, Butch, and Queer: LGBTQ Youth and the School-to-Prison Pipeline." *Journal of Adolescent Research* 30 (1): 57–82.

Travers, Ann. 2018. *The Trans Generation: How Trans Kids (and Their Parents) are Creating a Gender Revolution*. New York: New York University Press.

Wolch, Jennifer R. 1990. *The Shadow State: Government and Voluntary Sector in Transition*. Foundation Center.

Wright, James D. 2009 [1989]. *Address Unknown: The Homeless in America*. New Brunswick: Aldine Transaction.

9

Sex on the Streets and in the Margins

Homelessness, Sexual Citizenship, and Justice

JAMIE O'QUINN AND CAYDEN GOLDSTEIN-KRAL

Despite the fact that all individuals' sexual lives are subjected to state regulation, both formally through social policy and informally through regulatory institutions (Foucault 1990), there exists a common narrative that people's sexual lives can and should be kept "private." People experiencing homelessness[1] are granted no such privilege, as their daily interactions exist primarily in public. In the United States, there exists no accessible space for people experiencing homelessness to legally have sex. Sex outdoors, in cars, and in public buildings (including shelters) is illegal due to public indecency laws. Private areas that allow people to have sex outside of houses—for example, motels and hotels, bathhouses, theaters, and sex clubs—cost money to enter, rendering them largely inaccessible to people experiencing homelessness. While people experiencing homelessness do still have sex, institutional and legal restrictions require difficult tradeoffs, such as spending limited savings on a motel or using a "lookout" to have sex on the streets. People should not have to make constrained choices such as these.

Unlike other sexual rights movements, such as movements for LGBTQ rights or for reproductive rights, sexual rights for people experiencing homelessness have yet to receive broad social attention. In this chapter, we explore how a rights-based perspective of sexuality, or a perspective that focuses on proving that a particular group is entitled to certain sexual practices or behaviors, lends itself to quick gains for some people at the expense of those at the margins. We explore three justice frameworks: the legal "justice" system,[2] reproductive justice, and intimate justice, applying each framework to an understanding of sexual citizenship for people experiencing homelessness. We find that, in contrast to a rights-based perspective, a framework of justice lends itself to policy that aids everyone, including those who face multiple marginalities as is often the case for people experiencing homelessness. With implications beyond homelessness, we contend that the stratification of access to legal sex is a queer issue of sexual citizenship and sexual justice.

Here, and throughout the chapter, we use the term "queer" not to refer to people's sexual identities, but rather to refer to sexualities that contest, depart from, or remain marginalized by heteronormativity (Cohen 1997). In the United States, social life is structured by heteronormativity, a system that facilitates sex that is monogamous, procreative, white, upper-class, and straight at the expense of nonmonogamous, not procreative, non-white, lower class, and not straight sex (Rubin 1984; Warner 1991). We understand these nonnormative sexualities as occupying a liminal and marginalized status that is uniquely queer. While people experiencing homelessness, especially youth, disproportionately identify as lesbian, gay, bisexual, transgender, and/or queer (LGBTQ) (Durso and Gates 2012; Robinson, this collection), this discussion of "queer" in terms of identity is beyond the scope of this chapter. Instead, we understand sex among people experiencing homelessness as queer because it contests the privatized nature of sexuality, the ties between sexuality and consumption, and the racialized and classed projects that underpin the construction of sexual deviance and acceptability. In sum, sex between people experiencing homelessness is sex on the margins.

Homelessness and Sexuality Research

The current literature on homelessness and sex is indicative of its marginalized status. With notable exceptions (Liebow 1995; Rayburn and Corzine 2010), research on homelessness and sex largely focuses on survival sex, sexually transmitted infections, and sexual coercion (see, for example, Fletcher, Kisler, and Reback 2014; Tyler 2009; and Walls and Bell 2011). This research does the important and necessary work of delineating the potential harm associated with sex and generating policy recommendations to aid those who face structural vulnerabilities. However, the trend of studying poverty through a lens of "risk" may also lend itself to interventions that increase surveillance and regulation for economically marginalized individuals (Ray and Tillman 2018). This surveillance can paradoxically make life more difficult—and indeed riskier—for people experiencing homelessness.

This risk discourse mirrors public concerns over homelessness and sex, which constructs sex between people experiencing homelessness as a social problem rather than an issue of social justice. Public discussions about sex among people who are experiencing homelessness tend to center issues such as sex work, survival sex, and sex trafficking (Candid 2013; Ortiz 2015), rather than the dignity and humanity of people without homes. These concerns are deeply racialized, since the people experiencing homelessness in the United States are disproportionately people of color. According to a national, ten-day point-in-time survey, in which volunteers counted the number of people experiencing homelessness living on the streets and in shelters, Black people represent the highest proportion of people experiencing homelessness in the United States, followed by white and Hispanic people (HUD 2018).[3] Thus, we aim to offer an intersectional, queer, and structural investigation of the social conditions under which people experiencing homelessness are denied sexual citizenship.

"Sexual citizenship" refers to how legal recognition and belonging is constructed through the validation and exclusion of sexual identities, rights, and practices (Richardson 2000). People from marginalized groups are often seen as undeserving of sexual rights. Historically, these people have included LGBTQ individuals (Canaday 2011; Evans 1993; Richardson 2000; Ryan-Flood 2009), people of color (Mann 2013; Roberts 2017), sex workers (Sabsay 2013), people with disabilities (Shildrick 2013), and especially those people who face multiple marginalities (Collins 2008; Robinson, this collection). A fight for sexual citizenship often relies on rights discourse such as the right to *private* sexual acts or the right to *public* recognition of non-heterosexual identities through participation in normative institutions such as marriage and capitalism. People experiencing homelessness, who have limited access to private spaces or consumerism, are left out of these rights-based political efforts. Thus, when the LGBTQ movement made rights-based claims to sexual citizenship by bolstering heteronormative "hierarchies of property and propriety" (Berlant and Warner 1998, 548), this rights-based claim to privacy further situated people experiencing homelessness as outside the borders of citizenship.

Sexual citizenship is often framed as an issue of individual rights rather than collective justice (Richardson 2017). Through this framework, the achievement of sexual rights for one group of marginalized people impedes the development of sexual rights for others who occupy different precarious positions. Such a relationship, wherein change for one group comes at the expense of another, allows for larger systems of inequality to remain intact. A justice-based framework, by contrast, prompts us to consider the marginalities that many different groups face (Rudrappa 2015) and to focus our interrogations on the systems of oppression that prescribe sexual citizenship.

In this chapter, we begin a conversation on homelessness and sexual citizenship in the United States, moving beyond an individual framework of sexual rights for people experiencing homelessness and towards an intersectional understanding of sexual justice. To do so, we explore homelessness and sex through three distinct justice frameworks. First, we discuss how the acquisition of sexual rights through the legal "justice" system secured some sexual acts within the private sphere, barring people experiencing homelessness from sexual citizenship. We next delve into the concept of reproductive justice to understand how a denial of sexual citizenship to people experiencing homelessness mirrors broader efforts to restrict the reproductive capacities of low-income people of color. From there, we draw on an intimate justice framework to investigate how structures of inequality shape experiences of sexual pleasure and violence for people experiencing homelessness. We end with considerations for studying homelessness and sex. Here, we call for further sociological research that highlights systems of gendered racism and racialized sexism to work towards sexual justice for everyone, including those on the margins.

Homelessness and the Legal "Justice" System

Political efforts by LGBTQ activists to secure sexual citizenship through the legal "justice" system have revolved around two rights-based movements: 1) the decriminalization of private sexual acts, and 2) the legal recognition of public sexual identities—both strategies that ignore sexual citizenship for people experiencing homelessness. Jessica Fields (2004) describes how the political efforts to decriminalize queer sex in private and privilege privatized notions of sex through same-sex marriage neglect the sexual experiences of queer youth, who do not have access to sexual privacy. People experiencing homelessness are often infantilized, especially by housing and shelter service providers (Hoffman and Coffey 2019; Robinson 2020; Stevenson 2013). Like youth, people experiencing homelessness are considered undeserving of access to sex, which is secured through privacy, and thus largely do not benefit from these political efforts either. A justice-oriented framework, by contrast, prompts us to advocate for the social conditions that promote sexual autonomy and dignity for all people, regardless of housing status.

Decriminalization of Private Sexual Acts

LGBTQ activism has been key to anchoring sexual citizenship to private sexual acts. In 2003, the US Supreme Court ruled on *Lawrence-Garner v. Texas*, the landmark case that deemed anti-sodomy laws—laws criminalizing anal and oral sex, usually only enforced for gay cisgender men—to be unconstitutional. LGBTQ civil rights activists recognized *Lawrence-Garner* as marking an important political moment: one in which legally permissible sexual encounters no longer required penile-vaginal penetration. However, the case also further cemented a legal commitment to sexual privacy. The court upheld the right to same-gender sex on the grounds that the plaintiffs John Lawrence (a white cisgender man) and Tyron Garner (a Black cisgender man) had the right to have sex within the privacy of Lawrence's apartment. Thus, while the case granted LGBTQ people the right to have sex, it simultaneously reinforced the right to sexual freedom as constrained by access to private spaces.

As queer theorists have articulated, *Lawrence-Garner* relied upon a binary of public vs. private space that felt particularly un-queer. Jasbir Puar (2007) argues that the decriminalization of private sodomy engendered an increased surveillance of LGBTQ people in other aspects of intimate life, particularly in intimate public life. She writes:

> . . . the language in *Lawrence-Garner* prescribes the privatization of queer sex, rendering it hidden and submissive to the terrain of the domestic (subjected to insidious forms of surveillance), an affront to the queer public sex cultures that sought to bring the private into the public. (Puar 2007, 118)

By re-allocating queer sex to the "terrain of the domestic," *Lawrence-Garner* bolstered the already firm belief that sex—even, or perhaps especially, queer sex—belongs in private homes.

While the *Lawrence-Garner* decision does indeed have consequences for "queer public sex cultures"—public kink and BDSM groups, LGBTQ people who cruise for sex in public spaces, etc.—these ramifications extend well beyond LGBTQ communities to differently marginalized communities. By confining sex among LGBTQ people to the private domain, *Lawrence-Garner* cements the logics behind the criminalization of public sex. Indeed, Puar notes that "the relegation of decriminalized sodomy to the domestic private realm . . . is tantamount to recriminalizing sodomy and other forms of sexual incarnation outside of the immediacy of one's private home" (2007, 123). At once, this ruling expands rights of access to legal sex to include housed LGBTQ couples and implicitly excludes people experiencing homelessness from legal sex. *Lawrence-Garner*, therefore, provides an example of how rights-based movements may advance the aims of one marginalized group at the expense of others.

Moreover, legal scholars have since shown that Lawrence and Garner were not actually in a relationship or even having sex at the time of the arrest (Carpenter 2013; Eng 2010). Rather, police were responding to a call about a weapons disturbance, in which the caller referred to Garner by a racial slur, and arrested the two men for sodomy after failing to discover weapons in the apartment (Carpenter 2013). The racial violence underpinning the arrest, combined with LGBTQ activists' re-branding of the case as a love story, indicate the rights-based movement's failure to grapple with the co-constitutive nature of race and sexuality (Eng 2010). Rather than appealing to Lawrence and Garner's sexual rights to privacy, a framework of justice reveals the violent social conditions that engender state violence and surveillance against queer and trans people of color and thus informs action that reaches beyond "rights" advocacy, such as abolishing police and prisons.

Legal Recognition for Public Sexual Identities

Efforts to secure sexual citizenship for LGBTQ people have also focused on the right to public recognition of non-heterosexual identities. These efforts have relied upon access to consumption and participation in the formal economy through normative institutions such as marriage and capitalism (Bell and Binnie 2000; Eng 2010; Evans 1993; Richardson 2017), leaving people experiencing homelessness out of consideration. *Obergefell v. Hodges*, which is perhaps the most famous LGBTQ civil rights case in the United States, secured the right to same-sex marriage in 2015. In doing so, LGBTQ activists solidified the public recognition of non-heterosexual identities through appeals to heteronormativity and monogamy. Marriage affords LGBTQ people public validation in conjunction with a constellation of rights, including hospital visits when a spouse is sick, medical insurance through a spouse's employment, and spousal social security benefits. Many marital benefits are tied to the benefits that come with long-term and full-time employment, such as access to medical insurance, family leave, and shared retirement funds (Wells and Baca Zinn 2004). While marriage offers benefits to some people, especially those with middle and upper-class jobs, it risks diminishing benefits for people from certain marginalized groups. For example, scholars have noted how people with disabilities (Waxman Fiduccia 2000) and people who receive certain welfare benefits (Alm et al. 1999)—both groups that are over-represented among people experiencing homelessness—cannot become married without losing state benefits. As such, people experiencing homelessness may be less likely to enter into marriage, gain less advantages from marriage, and even encounter economic disadvantages through marriage. Once again, a movement that focuses on the "right" to marriage makes large gains for some while failing to address the needs of people on the margins.

Sexual citizenship is materially produced through consumption under capitalism (Evans 1993). Thus, attempts to garner LGBTQ civil rights have also focused on the right of people to participate in the formal economy. In the much popularized case, *Masterpiece Cakeshop, Ltd. v. Colorado Rights Commission* (2018), the Supreme Court ruled in favor of a Colorado bakery that refused to create a wedding cake for a gay couple under the purview of religious freedom. This ruling, which has been characterized as a blow to the LGBTQ rights movement, exemplifies the effort to gain sexual rights through participation in consumerism. The link between public recognition of sexual identities and consumption—from corporate-sponsored Pride events to the LGBTQ wedding industry—reinforces efforts to secure sexual citizenship as deeply classed. People experiencing homelessness do not benefit from rights-based movements that recognize marginalized sexual identities through materialism when their participation in consumption is limited, in the same way that they do not benefit from the legalization of queer private sexual acts when their access to privacy is limited.

Within the legal "justice" system, mainstream LGBTQ movements have fought for rights that make substantial advances for some while overlooking the experiences of people at the margins. These efforts attach the rights to sexual behavior and recognition of sexual identities to privacy, marriage, and consumption. By contrast, a framework oriented toward sexual justice foregrounds the validity of queer sexual attraction without conditions. In the following section, we outline how another rights-based sexuality movement, the pro-choice movement, fails to recognize the unique challenges that people who are experiencing homelessness face in having and keeping their children. A justice framework, by contrast, sheds light on the social systems that constrain reproductive freedoms for people on the margins, including people experiencing homelessness.

Homelessness and Reproductive Justice

A justice-oriented understanding of homelessness and sex highlights the intersecting systems of inequality that uphold the state policies which criminalize sex for people without homes. The criminalization of sex for people experiencing homelessness reflects, in part, the consequences of state policy that serves eugenic interests. State policies that "encourage or permit reproduction among individuals who are deemed to have the desirable profile for breeding" have consistently worked to limit the reproduction of racial and ethnic minorities, immigrants, people who are economically marginalized, and people with disabilities in the United States through the coercive implementation of birth control and/or sterilization (Price 2010, 57; Cohen 2017; Roberts 2017). This includes coerced and forced sterilizations at ICE detention centers (Palomo et al. 2021), in healthcare facilities on Native American reservations (Pegoraro 2015), in schools within low-income communities of color (Roberts 2017), and in mental health institutions (Hansen and King 2014).

A lack of sexual citizenship for people experiencing homelessness sustains the tradition of the state restricting reproduction among "undesirable" populations. There are two symbolic and material obstacles that make it difficult for people experiencing homelessness to have children: 1) it is illegal for them to have penile-vaginal sex in public and within shelters, and 2) Child Protective Services oversurveils families with precarious housing and sometimes separates children from parents or caregivers who are racially and economically marginalized (Roberts 2008; 2014), including those who are experiencing homelessness (Dworsky 2014). Of course, people experiencing homelessness have sex and have children, but by criminalizing public sex and increasing state surveillance of families who are experiencing homelessness, the state demonstrates its attempts to reduce their reproductive and caregiving capacities.

While sexual citizenship for people experiencing homelessness is an issue of reproductive freedom, the pro-choice movement—a movement for reproductive rights—has done little to combat state efforts that limit people's capacity to have children. Instead, the pro-choice movement has focused almost exclusively on a person's right to choose to have an abortion. While this fight is undoubtedly important in advocating for health care and self-determination for people experiencing homelessness who wish to end a pregnancy, these efforts fail to recognize how marginalized groups historically and today are denied the ability to have children (Ross 2006; Smith 2005). Furthermore, the reproductive rights movement has been anchored in appeals to privacy. The 1973 Supreme Court case *Roe v. Wade* deemed undue government restriction on abortion unconstitutional on the grounds that it violates the right to privacy under the 14th amendment. The case was heralded by pro-choice feminists for recognizing the body as a space deserving of legal rights to privacy; just as *Lawrence-Garner* did later, the case recognized privacy as the foundation of sexual rights. Indeed, the 2022 repealing of *Roe v. Wade* indicates the limitations of a rights-based framework. Rights are granted by the state, which means that they can also be taken away.

Alternatively, Black feminists in the 1990s developed the concept of "reproductive justice" to combat the reproductive rights movement's limited focus on rights to abortion through appeals to privacy and consequent failure to attend to systems of racism, colonialism, and classism that continually restrict reproductive freedom for people of color. Reproductive justice offers a framework for thinking beyond the right to abortion, fighting against *all* of the systems that restrict people's ability to plan their families as they see fit and raise children in healthy and safe environments (Luna 2020).[4] Thus, sexual citizenship for people experiencing homelessness is an issue that falls firmly within the purview of the reproductive justice framework.

Just as the LGBTQ rights movement has neglected the experiences of people who are unstably housed in efforts to secure sexual citizenship for LGBTQ people, the pro-choice movement has neglected the experiences of low-income women, women of color, trans and nonbinary people, and people who face housing instability to instead secure reproductive rights for middle- and upper-class white cisgender women (Luna 2020; Ross 2006). Time and again, while a rights-based movement can make necessary and important gains for one marginalized group, these gains come at the expense of people who are experiencing homelessness. However, a framework of justice is equipped to contest systems of racism, classism, and neoliberalism, thus tackling issues at the root of sexual citizenship and reproductive freedom for people experiencing homelessness.

Reproductive justice offers a framework for understanding how the criminalization of sex for people experiencing homelessness is inextricably tied to the intersecting systems of white supremacy, patriarchy, heteronormativity, and capitalism, all impact people's abilities to choose whether and how to have children. These efforts prompt us to think beyond safe and accessible spaces for people experiencing homelessness to have sex and towards the systems of inequality that shape the daily lives of people experiencing homelessness. In the next section, we consider intimate justice, which allows us to move beyond only thinking about access to sex to address the stratification of sexual pleasure.

Homelessness and Intimate Justice

A focus exclusively on the right to have sex for people experiencing homelessness obfuscates the more widespread inequalities that permeate sex in the United States. The importance of considering the impact of systems of inequalities on sexual experiences is a point that Sara

McClelland stresses throughout her work on "intimate justice" (2010). While most scholars who study sexual satisfaction do so on an individual level, McClelland argues that such processes are necessarily structural, stating that "intimate justice focuses our attention on how social and political inequities impact intimate experiences, affecting how individuals imagine, behave, and evaluate their intimate lives" (2010, 672). Thus, she theorizes "entitlement and deservingness" to sexual pleasure as fluid categories, contingent upon one's social positioning (McClelland 2010, 665).

Researchers demonstrate how access to sexual pleasure is gendered, with cisgender women in different-gender relationships experiencing fewer orgasms and less entitlement to pleasure than cisgender men (Armstrong, England, and Fogarty 2012). Furthermore, women of color are uniquely subject to racialized eroticization, objectification, and/or exoticization (Collins 2005), each of which likely impacts entitlement to—and experiences of—sexual pleasure. More intersectional research is necessary to understand how access and entitlement to sexual pleasure is gendered, racialized, and classed; however, we do know that gender inequalities shape the landscape of sexual desire and feelings of entitlement (Hirsch and Khan 2021).

While the concept of intimate justice is most frequently associated with studies on sexual pleasure, inequalities also structure experiences of sexual violence. Sexist and heteronormative notions that men are entitled to women's bodies are foundational to sexual violence (Armstrong, Gleckman-Krut, and Johnson 2018; Gavey 2005). Sexual violence occurs across social locations and relationship structures, including in LGBTQ relationships (Ball and Hayes 2010), and women of color are at heightened risk. The controlling images of Black women as innately hypersexual render them particularly vulnerable to sexual violence (Collins 2008). Fear of betraying their community in conjunction with rampant criminalization due to structural racism may also make them less likely to report instances of sexual violence perpetrated by Black men (Collins 2005; Crenshaw 1991). Additionally, language barriers render many immigrant women more vulnerable as they are denied refuge in domestic violence shelters, and those who are undocumented even more so since they may believe that leaving an abusive relationship could result in their deportation (Crenshaw 1991).

Some people (disproportionately women) who do not have access to stable housing have survival sex or engage in sex work as a strategy for obtaining basic necessities. While survival sex may coincide with pleasurable and empowering intimate relationships for people experiencing homelessness (Watson 2011), the structural conditions of homelessness, in conjunction with broader systems of inequality, are conducive to violence. Patriarchy renders it difficult for women to negotiate sex on their own terms, to refuse sex that they do not want, and to seek justice for violence if it occurs (Bay-Cheng and Eliseo-Arras 2008; Martin 2005). These problems are heightened for women engaging in survival sex and/or sex work for survival, women of color, and transgender women because of structural barriers to support (Crenshaw 1991; Deering et al. 2014; Ussher et al. 2020). Thus, even if there were to be a space for people experiencing homelessness to have sex, it may serve as a platform for the reproduction of inequality.

So far, we have argued two seemingly contradictory points: it is a social problem that people experiencing homelessness do not have a space to legally have sex, and sexual experiences are rife with inequality. This echoes conversations of the "sex wars" of the 1970s and 1980s (Duggan and Hunter 2006; Fahs 2014; Ferguson 1984). The sex wars, which came to a head over a different form of public sex—pornography—consisted of two factions: the sex-positive feminists who believed in the right to pornography and the radical feminists who believed that pornography is a form of valorized patriarchy (Fahs 2014; Ferguson 1984). At the heart of this debate is a question about the representation of sex in the public sphere: is it liberatory or is it violence? The debate fractured feminist efforts (Duggan and Hunter 2006; Ferguson 1984). A framework of justice may serve as a reconciliation between these two factions[5] in that it prompts us to consider both the importance of sex and sexual pleasure (for those who desire it) and the ways in which inequality renders sex a site of violence.

Thus, it is not enough to consider sexual citizenship for people experiencing homelessness; rather, it is necessary to consider the social conditions under which enjoyable sex, free from violence, is possible. Such a task means moving beyond a rights-based perspective that people have a "right" to sex—indeed, such language bears an eerie resemblance to harmful discourses that bolster rape culture. It also brings us past an easy solution of creating a space where people experiencing homelessness can have sex. Inequalities in experiences of sexual pleasure, sexual violence, and a lack of access to legal sex are all parts of achieving justice, and to address each of these it is necessary to tackle the undergirding and intersecting systems of race, gender, and class inequity. A framework of intimate justice, therefore, lends itself to policy shifts such as lifting surveilling regulations on people without homes and making housing widely available and accessible for all. It is necessary that people experiencing homelessness have dignity, respect, and autonomy so that housing status does not signal "deservingness," as this would mirror a rights-based perspective. At the same time, it is also necessary for all people to have access to safe and secure housing, regardless of income.

Studying Homelessness and Sex

People experiencing homelessness are denied sexual citizenship, but this does not mean that they are celibate. Instead, the illegality of public sex results in a different set of lived experiences around sex, relationships, and privacy. For example, because public shelters segregate clients by gender, a different-gender couple may have to choose between staying in a shelter and staying together on the street at night. Although able to sleep in the same room, a same-gender couple would likely still be unable to be intimate in a public shelter due to regulations. Another couple might have to choose between spending time together in the evening and making it back to the shelter before curfew at night. Someone else looking to have sex by themselves or with a partner might need to decide between recruiting a friend as a "lookout" or risk getting caught by police. Yet still others might be forced to choose between using their money to rent a motel room for the night and purchasing food for the day.

City-wide bans on public camping that prohibit the use of tents for people experiencing homelessness have further constrained these choices. Tents offer people experiencing homelessness a small measure of privacy through the establishment of an enclosed space that obscures visibility. As housing prices have skyrocketed, communities of tents in urban areas—sometimes referred to as "tent cities"—have also increased. In fact, the National Law Center on Homelessness & Poverty (2017) found a 1,342 percent increase in homeless encampments in the United

States between 2007 and 2017 alone. Many communities have responded to the proliferation of encampments by passing laws that criminalize homelessness in general and public camping more specifically, with city-wide bans on tents in public increasing by 60 percent from 2011 to 2014 (National Law Center on Homelessness & Poverty 2014).

Some cities are particularly strict. In Santa Cruz, California, 83 percent of people experiencing homelessness do not have access to even temporary housing or shelter options (National Law Center on Homelessness & Poverty 2014). Despite the shortage of state-funded housing, the city criminalizes public camping, sleeping in vehicles, and sitting and lying down on public sidewalks (Santa Cruz Chapter 6.36.010). This means that even people who are able to access some measure of privacy through having tents are unable to use them legally. Other cities have made efforts to combat these inequalities, although these efforts are sometimes short-lived. For example, in 2019, lawmakers in Austin, Texas passed an ordinance that legalized public camping for people without homes (Austin Ordinance No. 20191017–029). Then, in 2021, Austin passed a proposition that made it illegal to sit, lie, and camp, punishable by a fine of up to $500 (Austin City Code § 9-4-11). Empirical work is necessary to understand the full impact of such laws on the sexual lives of people experiencing homelessness.

Studying homelessness and sex presents certain methodological challenges. In some ways, studying sex is exceptional. In addition to the difficulty of getting sex research approved by university Institutional Review Boards (Irvine 2012), the topic of sex often makes people in the United States particularly uneasy, which can render talking about sex difficult or uncomfortable. Discussions of sex have the potential to bring up instances of violence, causing distress and harm. These risks may be exacerbated for people experiencing homelessness, since one pathway to homelessness involves fleeing a traumatic home experience, which may include sexual violence (Breton and Bunston 1992; Hamilton, Poza, and Washington 2011). Furthermore, people experiencing homelessness are at increased risk of experiencing violence without the safety of a locked sleeping space, even if they are able to sleep in a tent or on someone's couch. Moreover, it is also often difficult for people experiencing homelessness to access mental health care, so bringing up traumatic instances may bear disproportionate consequences.

Researchers' positionalities impact these consequences. Research is likely to be conducted by people who have access to stable housing and who therefore may be less equipped to recognize participants' nuances in meaning than researchers who are members of the populations they are studying (Winder, this collection). These structural differences may also exacerbate power inequalities between researchers and participants, which may make the discussions even more uncomfortable for people experiencing homelessness. In these cases, the questions that researchers ask and the ways that they make sense of participants' responses may be filtered through a series of classist and racist assumptions vis-à-vis their positionality, resulting in research that does not reflect people experiencing homelessness' lived experiences (Spivak 1988). There also exists the risk that people who write about homelessness and sex will do so in a way that is sensationalizing, fetishizing, otherizing, or dehumanizing to people experiencing homelessness. Thus, we cannot over-stress the importance of taking care in studying homelessness and sex.

In other ways, studying sex and homelessness is not exceptional. Any research topic may be distressing for someone to talk about since we do not know what might trigger memories of trauma for another person. A researcher also may sensationalize, otherize, or dehumanize the people whom they are describing without discussing sex. Finally, power imbalances matter regardless of the research topic. Studying sex and sexuality is necessary in recognizing people's full humanity and understanding people's lives. Because people experiencing homelessness are frequently denied respect or dignity by public policy, it is particularly necessary to study homelessness and sex.

There is a need for further research that explores how people experiencing homelessness navigate their sexual lives in the context of criminalization. How do people experiencing homelessness construct meaning around privacy, sex, sexuality, and relationships? How do they make decisions about when, where, and whether to engage in sexual activity in public? How do policy changes such as camping bans impact that decision-making? This research would further lend itself to understandings of sexuality for other communities that have been historically under-represented in social scientific research, including people of color, LGBTQ people, and people with disabilities, all of whom are disproportionately represented among people experiencing homelessness.

Conclusion

Sexual justice, by recognizing systems of inequality instead of individualized rights, is a movement for those who are on the outskirts. By exploring three different frameworks of justice, we find that individualized movements for rights often come at the expense of sexual citizenship for people experiencing homelessness. By contrast, a sexual justice framework takes a broader perspective on how to achieve safety, dignity, respect, and autonomy for all. This includes access to sexual citizenship for people experiencing homelessness, as well as dismantling systems of oppression that engender homelessness in the first place. Rather than fighting for "the right to sex," this points us towards working for housing for all, and, in the meantime, advocating for decreased surveillance of people experiencing homelessness, ordinances that permit tents and temporary housing structures, and social services that recognize that people's dignity, autonomy, and humanity.

In reviewing the movements for increased sexual rights for LGBTQ people in the US legal "justice" system, we show how LGBTQ sexual citizenship is achieved, in part, through appeals to privacy and consumerism. While these efforts have made large strides for many LGBTQ people, they reinforce a price of entry for citizenship that further marginalizes people experiencing homelessness. In our discussion of reproductive justice, we unpack how a movement for the right to abortion obfuscates state efforts to limit reproduction among "undesirable" populations—a racist and nativist legacy that sets the groundwork for criminalizing sex among people who are experiencing homelessness. Lastly, we consider the concept of intimate justice as it pertains to sexual citizenship, prompting us to think beyond the necessity of attaining sexual rights to envision a world in which social structures render it possible for people to have the kind of sex that they would like and to refuse sex at any time. In each section, we find that a rights-based movement generates quick gains for some at the expense of others. As Sharmila Rudrappa (2015, 166) states in her research on reproductive rights and justice in India: "Rights talk simply juxtaposed one person's rights over another person's rights. If there were winners, there had to be losers." In this case, the losers are consistently people experiencing homelessness. By contrast, a justice-based framework targets intersecting systems of inequality that engender homelessness in the first place.

It might seem that studying sex is frivolous in the face of other struggles that people experiencing homelessness might face, including lack of access to healthcare, vulnerability to extreme weather, and risk of police and civilian violence. Studying sex is often characterized as a distraction from the "real" issues at hand (Rubin 1984; Rodríguez 2014). Yet, sex and sexuality are fundamental aspects of social life and thus central to the study of society. What is at stake is not "just sex," but intimacy in relationships, pleasure, health, self-esteem, well-being, and the recognition of people's humanity (McClelland 2010; Rubin 1984; Rodríguez 2014; Trudel 2000). It is no coincidence that sex is often at the locus of social control, since systems of sexual regulation impact all aspects of life (Foucault 1990). Thus, it is imperative for sociologists who study homelessness to attend to sex and sexuality, and it is equally important for sexuality scholars to consider how economic and housing inequalities shape sexual encounters.

Understanding sexual citizenship from a framework of justice diverts us from any one simple solution. Rather than simply creating spaces for people who are experiencing homelessness to have sex, efforts should work towards a society in which all members can experience consensual sexual pleasure (should they desire) free from violence. At its core, achieving sexual justice means that everyone has access to humanity, respect, and dignity—all of which require the dissolution of gendered and racialized inequalities that engender systemic poverty. This includes working to end the surveillance of people experiencing homelessness and promoting housing for all.

A sexual justice movement cannot make demands for sexual citizenship by asserting membership in hegemonic categories. Like scholars before us and those within this book, we underscore the importance of studying people on the margins to understand the social world and create social change (Bernstein, this collection; Collins 2008; Stone and Compton, this collection; Smith 1987). In particular, we uncover that centering those who are on the margins when envisioning policy change is an important path towards achieving justice. We document how movements for sexual rights have historically relied on housing status, whiteness, claims of "normalcy," and participation in the formal labor force. In doing so, sexual citizenship for people experiencing homelessness was at best overlooked, and at worst denied. Sexual citizenship for people experiencing homelessness cannot be achieved through appeals to normalcy, mental health, monogamy, marriage, ability, workplace participation, whiteness, or veteran status. The time has come for us to conceptualize and care about sexual justice for those who are both without homes in terms of a long-term shelter in the United States and those who are also without a home in prior rights-based movements.

ACKNOWLEDGMENTS

The authors would like to thank Brandon Andrew Robinson, Sharmila Rudrappa, the book's editors, and the anonymous reviewers for their generous feedback on earlier drafts of this chapter.

NOTES

The authors contributed equally to this paper.

1 As is the case with language describing many different marginalized groups, there is no single phrase that is widely agreed upon to describe people experiencing homelessness. Scholars and activists commonly use "person first language" to emphasize people's humanity among groups that face dehumanization (Palmer 2018). Some prefer phrases such as "people without homes" or "people who are unhoused" to avoid the term "homelessness," which has historically been attached to various political projects and sentiments. Others use the phrase "people experiencing homelessness" to emphasize the transient nature of being without a home and to avoid labeling (Martinez 2018). In this chapter, we use the phrase "people experiencing homelessness" with ambivalence. We recognize that terminology is always shifting, that there is often no single "right way" to describe a community, and that community-led language is to be prioritized.

2 We use quotation marks around the work "justice" to indicate that the system is, in fact, deeply unjust.

3 The US Department of Housing and Urban Development collected and recorded ethnicity separately from race. According to the survey, 40 percent of people experiencing homelessness were Black, and 49 percent were white, while 22 percent of all people experiencing homelessness were Hispanic/Latinx. So, it is possible that as little as 27 percent of people experiencing homelessness are white and Non-Hispanic/Latinx, although actual numbers remain unknown. Furthermore, it is important to recognize that this survey, as well as most research on homelessness, does not count a significant population of people who are insecurely housed, such as people who are "couch surfing" or staying with friends and family temporarily, or people who are living in their vehicles. This chapter centers on people

who live on the streets and in shelters, although some concepts and concerns may also hold relevance to people who experience other kinds of homelessness.

4 For more information on the history of reproductive justice in the United States, see SisterSong (https://www.sistersong.net), a women of color reproductive justice collective, as well as the many works of Loretta Ross.

5 For a more detailed discussion of the radical feminists, sex-positive feminists, and a framework of reconciliation, see Fahs 2014.

REFERENCES

Alm, James, Stacy Dickert-Conlin, and Leslie A. Whittington. 1999. "Policy Watch: The Marriage Penalty." *Journal of Economic Perspectives*, 13 (3): 193–204.

Armstrong, Elizabeth A., Paula England, and Alison C. K. Fogarty. 2012. "Accounting for Women's Orgasm and Sexual Enjoyment in College Hookups and Relationships." *American Sociological Review* 77 (May): 435–62.

Armstrong, Elizabeth A., Miriam Gleckman-Krut, and Lanora Johnson. 2018. "Silence, Power, and Inequality: An Intersectional Approach to Sexual Violence." *Annual Review of Sociology* 44 (July): 99–122.

Austin City Code § 9-4-11. Austin Ordinance No. 20191017–029.

Ball, Matthew J. and Sharon L. Hayes. 2010. "Same-Sex Intimate Partner Violence: Exploring the Parameters." *Queering Paradigms*. Oxford: Peter Lang.

Bay-Cheng, Laina Y. and Rebecca K. Eliseo-Arras. 2008. "The Making of Unwanted Sex: Gendered and Neoliberal Norms in College Women's Unwanted Sexual Experiences." *Journal of Sex Research* 45 (4): 386–97.

Bell, David and Jon Binnie. 2000. *The Sexual Citizen: Queer Politics and Beyond*. Cambridge: Polity Press.

Berlant, Lauren and Michael Warner. 1998. "Sex in Public." *Critical Inquiry* 24 (Winter): 547–66.

Breton, Margot and Terry Bunston. 1992. "Physical and Sexual Violence in the Lives of Homeless Women." *Canadian Journal of Community Mental Health* 11 (May): 29–44.

Canaday, Margot. 2011. *The Straight State: Sexuality and Citizenship in Twentieth-Century America*. Princeton: Princeton University Press.

Candid. 2013. "Homelessness, Survival Sex, and Human Trafficking: As Experienced by the Youth of Covenant House New York." https://philanthropynewsdigest.org.

Carpenter, Dale. 2013. *Flagrant Conduct: The Story of Lawrence v. Texas*. New York: W. W. Norton & Company.

Cohen, Adam. 2017. *Imbeciles: The Supreme Court, American Eugenics, and the Sterilization of Carrie Buck*. New York: Penguin.

Cohen, Cathy J. 1997. "Punks, Bulldaggers, and Welfare Queens: The Radical Potential of Queer Politics?" *GLQ: A Journal of Lesbian and Gay Studies* 3 (May): 437–65.

Collins, Patricia Hill. 2005. *Black Sexual Politics: African Americans, Gender, and the New Racism*. New York: Routledge.

Collins, Patricia Hill. 2008. *Black Feminist Thought: Knowledge, Consciousness, and the Politics of Empowerment*. New York: Routledge Classics.

Crenshaw, Kimberlé. 1991. "Mapping the Margins: Intersectionality, Identity Politics, and Violence against Women of Color." *Stanford Law Review* 43 (May): 1241–99.

Deering, Kathleen N., Avni Amin, Jean Shoveller, Ariel Nesbitt, Claudia Garcia-Moreno, Putu Duff, Elena Argento, and Kate Shannon. 2014. "A Systematic Review of the Correlates of Violence against Sex Workers." *American Journal of Public Health* 104 (5): e42–e54.

Duggan, Lisa and Nan D. Hunter. 2006. *Sex Wars: Sexual Dissent and Political Culture*. New York: Routledge.

Durso, Lauren E. and Gary J. Gates. 2012. *Serving Our Youth: Findings from a National Survey of Services Providers Working with Lesbian, Gay, Bisexual and Transgender Youth who are Homeless or at Risk of Becoming Homeless*. Los Angeles: The Williams Institute.

Dworsky, Amy. 2014. "Families at the Nexus of Housing and Child Welfare." State Policy Advocacy and Reform Center. www.childwelfaresparc.org.

Eng, David L. 2010. *The Feeling of Kinship: Queer Liberalism and the Racialization of Intimacy*. Durham, NC: Duke University Press.

Evans, David T. 1993. *Sexual Citizenship: The Material Construction of Sexualities*. New York: Routledge.

Fahs, Breanne. 2014. "'Freedom to' and 'Freedom From': A New Vision for Sex-Positive Politics." *Sexualities* 17 (May): 267–90.

Ferguson, Ann. 1984. "Sex War: The Debate between Radical and Libertarian Feminists." *Signs* 10 (Autumn): 106–12.

Fields, Jessica. 2004. "Same-Sex Marriage, Sodomy Laws, and the Sexual Lives of Young People." *Sexuality Research and Social Policy* 1 (September): 11–23.

Fletcher, Jesse B., Kimberly A. Kisler, and Cathy J. Reback. 2014. "Housing Status and HIV Risk Behaviors among Transgender Women in Los Angeles." *Archives of Sexual Behavior* 43 (November): 1651–61.

Foucault, Michel. 1990. *The History of Sexuality, Vol. 1: An Introduction*. Translated by Robert Hurley. Reissue edition. New York: Vintage.

Gavey, Nicola. 2005. *Just Sex? The Cultural Scaffolding of Rape*. New York: Routledge.

Hamilton, Alison B., Ines Poza, and Donna L. Washington. 2011. "'Homelessness and Trauma Go Hand-in-Hand': Pathways to Homelessness among Women Veterans." *Women's Health Issues* 21 (July): S203–09.

Hansen, Randall and Desmond King. 2013. *Sterilized by the State: Eugenics, Race, and the Population Scare in Twentieth-Century North America*. Cambridge: Cambridge University Press.

Hirsch, Jennifer S. and Shamus Khan. 2021. *Sexual Citizens: Sex, Power, and Assault on Campus*. New York: Norton.

Hoffman, Lisa and Brian Coffey. 2019. "Dignity and Indignation: How People Experiencing Homelessness View Services and Providers." *Social Science Journal* 45 (2): 207–222.

Irvine, Janice M. 2012. "Can't Ask, Can't Tell: How Institutional Review Boards Keep Sex in the Closet." *Contexts* 11 (Spring): 28–33.

Luna, Zakiya. 2020. *Reproductive Rights as Human Rights*. New York: New York University Press.

Liebow, Elliot. 1995. *Tell Them Who I Am: The Lives of Homeless Women*. Reprint edition. London: Penguin Books.

Mann, Emily. 2013. "Regulating Latina Youth Sexualities through Community Health Centers: Discourses and Practices of Sexual Citizenship." *Gender & Society* 27 (July): 681–703.

Martin, Patricia Y. 2005. *Rape Work: Victims, Gender, and Emotions in Organization and Community Context*. New York: Routledge.

Martinez, Sara. 2018. "Homelessness 101: Person-Centered Language—What is It?" Coalition for the Homeless. www.homelesshouston.org.

McClelland, Sara I. 2010. "Intimate Justice: A Critical Analysis of Sexual Satisfaction." *Social and Personality Psychology Compass* 4 (September): 663–80.

National Law Center on Homelessness & Poverty. 2014. *No Safe Place: The Criminalization of Homelessness in U.S. Cities*. Washington, D.C.

National Law Center on Homelessness & Poverty. 2017. *Tent City, USA: The Growth of America's Homeless Encampments and How Communities are Responding*. Washington, D.C.

Ortiz, Jennifer. 2015. "Survival Sex Not a Choice for Many Homeless Youth." Street Sense Media. www.streetsensemedia.org.

Palmer, Geraldine L. 2018. "People Who Are Homeless Are 'People' First: Opportunity for Community Psychologist to Lead Through Language Reframing." *Global Journal of Community Psychology Practice* 9 (November): 1–16.

Palomo, Emily B., Amalie Andersen, and Christina Mikkelsen. 2021. "Forced Sterilization of Immigrant Women in US Detention Center." *Interdisciplinary Journal of International Studies* 11 (June): 52–63.

Pegoraro, Leonardo. 2015. "Second-Rate Victims: The Forced Sterilization of Indigenous Peoples in the USA and Canada." *Settler Colonial Studies* 5 (October): 161–173.

Price, Kimala. 2010. "What Is Reproductive Justice? How Women of Color Activists Are Redefining the Pro-Choice Paradigm." *Meridians* 10 (March): 42–65.

Puar, Jasbir. 2007. *Terrorist Assemblages: Homonationalism in Queer Times*. Durham, NC: Duke University Press.

Ray, Ranita and Korey Tillman. 2018. "Envisioning a Feminist Urban Ethnography: Structure, Culture, and New Directions in Poverty Studies." *Sociology Compass* 13 (December): 1–10.

Rayburn, Rachel L. and Jay Corzine. 2010. "Your Shelter or Mine? Romantic Relationships among the Homeless." *Deviant Behavior* 31 (September): 756–74.

Richardson, Dianne. 2000. "Constructing Sexual Citizenship: Theorizing Sexual Rights." *Critical Social Policy* 20 (February): 105–35.

Richardson, Dianne. 2017. "Rethinking Sexual Citizenship." *Sociology* 51 (November): 208–224.

Roberts, Dorothy. 2008. "The Racial Geography of Child Welfare: Toward a New Research Paradigm." *Child Welfare* 87 (2): 125–150.

Roberts, Dorothy. 2014. "Child Protection as Surveillance of African American Families." *Journal of Social Welfare and Family Law* 36 (4): 426–37.

Roberts, Dorothy. 2017. *Killing the Black Body: Race, Reproduction, and the Meaning of Liberty*. 20th anniversary edition. New York: Vintage.

Robinson, Brandon A. 2020. *Coming Out to the Streets: LGBTQ Youth Experiencing Homelessness*. Berkeley: University of California Press.

Rodríguez, Juana María. 2014. *Sexual Futures, Queer Gestures, and Other Latina Longings*. New York: New York University Press.

Ross, Loretta. 2006. "Understanding Reproductive Justice: Transforming the Pro-Choice Movement." *Off Our Backs* 36: 14–19.

Rubin, Gayle. 1984. "Thinking Sex: Notes for a Radical Theory of the Politics of Sexuality." In *Pleasure and Danger: Exploring Female Sexuality*, edited by Carol S. Vance, 267–319. Boston: Routledge.

Rudrappa, Sharmila. 2015. *Discounted Life: The Price of Global Surrogacy in India*. New York: New York University Press.

Ryan-Flood, Roisin. 2009. *Lesbian Motherhood: Gender, Families and Sexual Citizenship*. Basingstoke: Palgrave Macmillan.

Sabsay, Leticia. 2013. "Citizenship in the Twilight Zone? Sex Work, the Regulation of Belonging and Sexual Democratization in Argentina." In *Beyond Citizenship? Feminism and the Transformation of Belonging*, edited by Sasha Roseneil, 160–83. Basingstoke: Palgrave Macmillan.

Santa Cruz Chapter 6.36.010. Camping prohibited.

Schifter, Jacobo. 2000. *Public Sex in a Latin Society*. Philadelphia: Haworth Hispanic/Latino Press.

Shildrick, Margrit. 2013. "Sexual Citizenship, Governance and Disability: From Foucault to Deleuze." In *Beyond Citizenship? Feminism and the Transformation of Belonging*, edited by Sasha Roseneil, 138–59. Basingstoke: Palgrave Macmillan.

Smith, Andrea. 2005. "Beyond Pro-Choice versus Pro-Life: Women of Color and Reproductive Justice." *American Sociological Review* 17 (Spring): 119–40.

Smith, Dorothy. 1987. *The Everyday World as Problematic: A Feminist Sociology*. Boston: Northeastern University Press.

Spivak, Gayatri C. 1988. "Can the Subaltern Speak?" In *Marxism and the Interpretation of Culture*, edited by Carey Nelson and Lawrence Grossberg, 271–313. Champaign: University of Illinois Press.

Stevenson, Caral. 2013. "A Qualitative Exploration of Relations and Interactions between People Who Are Homeless and Use Drugs and Staff in Homeless Hostel Accommodation." *Journal of Substance Abuse* 19 (1–2): 134–40.

Trudel, Gilles, Lyse Turgeon, and Lyne Piché. 2000. "Marital and Sexual Aspects of Old Age." *Sexual and Relationship Therapy* 15 (August): 381–406.

Tyler, Kimberly A. 2009. "Risk Factors for Trading Sex among Homeless Young Adults." *Archives of Sexual Behavior* 38 (April): 290–97.

The U.S. Department of Housing and Urban Development. 2018. "The 2018 Annual Homelessness Assessment Report (AHAR) to Congress." Washington, D.C. https://files.hudexchange.info.

Ussher, Jane M., Alexandra Hawkey, Janette Perz, Pranee Liamputtong, Jessica Sekar, Brahmaputra Marjadi, Virginia Schmied, Tinashe Dune, and Eloise Brook. 2020. "Crossing Boundaries and Fetishization: Experiences of Sexual Violence for Trans Women of Color." *Journal of Interpersonal Violence* 37 (5–6): NP3552–NP3584.

Walls, Eugene N. and Finn Bell. 2011. "Correlates of Engaging in Survival Sex among Homeless Youth and Young Adults." *Journal of Sex Research* 48 (September): 423–36.

Warner, Michael. 1991. "Introduction: Fear of a Queer Planet." *Social Text* 29: 3–17.

Watson, Juliet. 2011. "Understanding Survival Sex: Young Women, Homelessness and Intimate Relationships." *Journal of Youth Studies* 14 (May): 639–65.

Waxman Fiduccia, Barbara. 2000. "Current Issues in Sexuality and the Disability Movement." *Sexuality and Disability* 18 (3): 167–174.

Wells, Barbara and Maxine Baca Zinn. 2004. "The Benefits of Marriage Reconsidered." *Journal of Sociology and Social Welfare* 31 (4): 59–80.

PART IV

Identities and Relationships

10

"You're Human First"

On Racial and Sexual Identity Prioritization

TERRELL J. A. WINDER

> MALACHI: Gay first. Black second.
>
> AUTHOR: Okay. You said gay first, Black second; what made you say that?
>
> MALACHI: So, in my gay development, I wasn't embraced by the Black community. Girls would bully me; I was bullied a lot in school . . . And I hated Black people in elementary school. I did. I hated them. Because I was tired of getting rocks thrown at me; I fought every day at school. Not really starting the fights but just people would . . . like, why? And I remember asking the teacher, "Why? Why are they bothering me? Leave me alone." And I remember snapping one day . . . HA! And my mom took me out of the school and she put me in a predominantly white school.

The opening quote from Malachi offers insight into one of the ways that Black gay men come to understand the relationship between their racial and sexual identities. In this interview excerpt, Malachi argues that his prioritization of sexuality over race is informed by his childhood experiences with other Black children who ostracized, ridiculed, and physically attacked him for both his darker complexion and suspected sexuality. These childhood experiences with bullying within a Black schooling environment and his mother's subsequent decision to remove him from his predominantly Black school to a predominantly white school influenced and reinforced his decision to argue that he is gay first and Black second. Malachi's narrative, like those of the other young men that I discuss in this chapter, reveals the complex relationships that young Black gay men have with both their individual identities and their racial and sexual communities. Taken together, these reflective narratives illustrate the sociological theoretical potential of studying marginalized groups and illuminate the challenges of investigating traumatized and exploited populations.

This essay uses the case of Black gay men to articulate the importance and methodological insights of in-group positionality in the study of marginalized populations. Between 2012 and 2016, I collected interview data from 50 Black men in Los Angeles who self-identified as gay, bisexual, or pansexual. These interviews covered topics including racial and sexual identity prioritization under stigmatizing conditions and individual perceptions of gay and Black communities. Sociologist Marcus Hunter (2010) conducted a similar study on 50 Black gay men in New York and sought to explain the ways that many perceive non-heterosexual and non-white identities as incompatible. In his work, Hunter identified three primary ways that Black gay men negotiated their racial and sexual identities: *interlocking, up-down,* and *public-private.* Through the analysis of my data with men in Los Angeles, I expand Hunter's (2010) 3-type identity negotiation model to include a fourth identity prioritization, *deemphasized,* and articulate how important individual identity formations are to collective community among Black gay men. The application of these model-types add to our understandings of how similar orientations towards social identities are formed under stigmatizing social conditions and in stigmatizing environments. Through the examination of these identity formations, I highlight the importance of community and its various meanings for Black gay men. As evidenced in their perceptions of "gay community," I articulate how these collective identity communities are racialized, sexualized, and gendered. Ultimately, I use the case of Black gay men to carve out new theoretical and empirical terrain for sociology and sexuality studies.

Studying Folk at the Margins: Inquiry into Black Gay Life

Scholars that have examined Black gay male identity have highlighted the ways in which race, sexuality, religion, and social spaces shape and inform the proclaimed identities of Black gay men (e.g., Crichlow 2004; Hawkeswood 1996; Hunter 2010; Winder 2015). Both Hawkeswood and Hunter describe the varying ways that Black gay men understand their gay identities and emphasize that while many researchers contend that either race or sexuality must dominate as a primary identifier, in many cases Black gay men find these aspects of self inextricable. Crichlow illustrates how Afro-Caribbean and African Canadian same-sex attracted men create lives of "safety and pleasure" (2004, 4) while feeling tenuously positioned within Canadian Black communities. In my prior work, I have illustrated that non-secular spaces can become new religious centers for the negotiation of race and sexuality under the confines of stigmatizing religious messaging (Winder 2015). Even more, Black gay men are often subjected to identity criticisms from Black community members and from white (and sometimes other non-Black) people who cast shame on their social identities simultaneously. This experience of intersectional stigma (Berger 2004) creates unique conditions for the formation of social identities for actors living in contentious environments.

The fear of social backlash that accompanies many young men as they navigate congruent sets of racial and sexual stigma has been long documented in the literature and more recently in the mainstream media. As Cathy Cohen (2009, 12) illustrates, "the ability of patriarchy and sexism, homophobia and heterosexism, as well as classism to define the experiences and concerns of certain group members" can serve to complicate how unified Black people can feel within Black communities. Similarly, work by scholars in performance studies have been critical in elucidating some of the contemporary patterns of behaviors enacted by stigmatized Black gay people. Jeffery McCune's (2014) work on down-low (DL) men offered an in-depth scholarly look into how men avoid stigma associated with gay and queer identities by maintaining discreet sexual lives with other men. Before FX's house/ballroom-centered show, *Pose*, took a prominent spot on American television, work by scholars like Marlon Bailey (2013) revealed the intricate kin relationships and social support networks fashioned by Black and Latinx members of the house ballroom scene. Following in the steps of early documentaries like *Paris Is Burning*, Bailey's foray into ballroom life illustrates how Black queer people have come to create their own communities when they have felt tenuous footing in Black communities and white communities alike. Both of these works offer critical insights into coping and social formation processes in major urban cities of the US—Chicago and Detroit, respectively.

E. Patrick Johnson's (2011) *Sweet Tea: Black Gay Men of the South* is one of the only texts dedicated to life in the South for Black gay people. This oral history, which illuminated the generational insights and intimate knowledge of Black gay life in the South, is canonical literature on the contemporary gay life of southern men. Johnson's centering of particular narratives is a corrective to the stereotypical narratives often spun about the majority of gay life in the US. In capturing the words of these men who are making sense of their current lives and reliving their pasts through memory, we gain insight into the varying ways that stigma, discrimination, and marginalization shape both racial and sexual identities.

Another thread of work on Black gay men has looked into how they negotiate religious beliefs that often disparage their sexualities. Scholars conducting work at the intersection of religion, race, and sexuality have often showed the profound ways that religious dogma influences the proliferation of anti-gay religious stigma. Black gay men and lesbians alike have been studied to better understand their experiences with religion and their relationships with religious communities. These studies collectively have found that Black LGBT persons often maintain their connections with religious communities that may even disparage their sexualities by prioritizing racial connections (Moore 2010) or religious identity (McQueeney 2009), discrediting the speaker but not the text (Pitt 2010), and reinterpreting religious messaging to justify their sexualities (Winder 2015). The strong levels of (predominantly) Christian religiosity among African Americans has unified much of the literature on religious-based stigma. While scholars like Alisha Lola Jones (2020) have shown how Black same-sex relationships or identities in gospel can be an "open-secret" that uses musical talent to obscure sexuality-based judgment, the vast majority of sociological studies have highlighted how Black gay and lesbian Christians continue to struggle with their religious identities. Consistently, this research has found that religious based stigma is thriving and well within communities even as more accepting churches are popping up across the country.

Racial and Sexual Identity Negotiation

Scholars of both racial and sexual identity development have illustrated how life experiences can shift and change one's relationship with and expression of those identities over time. This work similarly identifies a set of ideal types that Black gay, bisexual, and pansexual men use to express their prioritization of their identities. Given their experiences with racism and heterosexism, it is important to consider how these men negotiate and navigate relationships with stigmatized identities. Building on sociologist Marcus Hunter's (2010) conceptions of "interlocking, up-down, and public-private" identities, I illustrate how some young men in Los Angeles embody these categories and others express an apathetic attitude towards prioritizing any aspect of their identities and instead favor a flattened identity response that I term *deemphasized*.

The majority of men that I encountered during my fieldwork expressed an interlocking identity, meaning that they held their racial and sexual identities at equal weight. For these respondents, the inextricability of being Black and being gay (or bisexual or pansexual) simultaneously defined their orientations to community life and identity expression. I classify roughly 50% of these young men into this identity-model group. One such man, whom I call Rahsaan, exemplified this best by his response to a question I posed to him about his sexual orientation:

> AUTHOR: What are some of the messages that you've received about being bisexual?
>
> RAHSAAN: Well, [being] Black and bisexual the first message that I received was that I'm going to hell, it was a sin and it was a choice I made on my own. My parents really didn't approve. Well, they definitely didn't approve of any homosexuality at all. The message I got after that would be that any gay man had HIV and that they were sick or disgusting. That was pretty much the first two messages that I got about that.

From his response, it is clear that Rahsaan cannot separate his experiences of being bisexual from his larger Black experience. The stigmatizing messaging and disapproval from his family are not uncommon across all of the identity model types, and I explore the religious and secular natures of these stigma messages in my prior work (see Winder 2015). Rahsaan's comments also underscore the enduring anti-Black HIV stigma that is associated with Black queer men and often used to enact laws that punish people for choices regarding their sexual health (see Thrasher 2016 and 2019). While these negative messages that Rahsaan (among others) have received are quite revealing, I highlight Rahsaan's reply here for another reason. His immediate revision of my question to include his racial identity underscores how difficult it can be for those in the interlocking group to separate their racial, sexual, and often gendered understandings of these identities.

Another way that young men expressed their identities aligned with Hunter's conception of up-down identities, in other words a "Black-first, gay-second" or "gay-first, Black-second." Like the chapter's opening quote from Malachi, young men who expressed a prioritization of one identity over the other often revealed how past experiences and their relationships with particular communities influenced their expression. While Malachi's past experiences with other Black students in school led him to espouse a gay-first, Black-second identity value presentation, other young men would express Black-first, gay second. For example, one of my respondents, Nicholas, reflected on the importance of history to indicate his feelings towards racial and sexual identity:

> NICHOLAS: I think being Black is more important to me than being gay. Because I feel like being Black has just a deeper history necessary than my sexual identity. But, I'm Black before anything else.
> AUTHOR: So, Black-first, gay-second . . .
> NICHOLAS: Yeah, because I'd say that I'm a Black gay man. Because that's what people see and I also believe that being Black defines so much of me. And I think that gay doesn't necessarily define as much of me. And I also think being at the margin, I'm at the margin because I'm Black first, and then because I'm gay.

Evident in Nicholas's reply is his belief that his racial identity is more important to defining his everyday experiences because it is immediately perceptible and observable by others. His reliance on the "deeper history" of his Black identity underscores how many of my respondents spoke about their racial upbringing. Here, Nicholas gestures to not only a complex legacy of Black exploitation and enslavement in the US, but also to his own personal Black history. That is, for many, recognizing when race became salient was much harder because it was a taken-for-granted fact that was passed from parents, grandparents, and other family to a child. Yet, an awareness of sexuality often developed much later for respondents and, thus, its history was more clearly and neatly defined. Across the 20% of young men that I classified as up-down, more of them identified with a Black-first, gay-second identity prioritization.

Hunter's third type, public-private, where men espoused a public Blackness yet private gayness was much less prevalent among the Los Angeles men that I studied. For a few reasons, I suspect that this is also a reflection of the differing recruitment methods of our studies. Given my fieldsite's emphasis on discussions about racial and sexual identity, it should be unsurprising that these young men were more open about both identities. It is true that to an extent even participating in the group meetings requires a certain level of "outness" around one's sexuality given the public nature of the community organization space. For this reason, I classify less than 5% of my sample into the public-private identity group. Yet, when young men espoused a Black-public and gay-private identity, they used very similar logics to members of the up-down group and focused on the inherent visibility of their Blackness. To illustrate this point, my respondent Donovan discussed how his racial identity is on display at work while his sexuality isn't necessarily visible:

> DONOVAN: At the end of the day, everybody don't know at work, but the ones that do . . . I wanna be respected as me, not as a gay Black male. So, I never wanna be that . . . I have to be Black because they see that, but I don't have to be like "I'm gay."

This response about the way respect is tied to his working experience reveals a complicated relationship between racial and sexual identities for Donovan. His desire to be respected "as me" underlies the importance of narratives beyond race, sexuality, and gender. In highlighting respect, Donovan sought to be treated equally in the workplace without regard to these social identifiers, but rather based on his work performance and personality. Yet, he very much acknowledges that his race is necessarily seen and therefore he "has to be Black." While we might question the private nature of gay sexuality for these young men, Donovan and others go to great lengths to emphasize that this privacy does not equal hiding. I like to consider this point as: *Just because I didn't tell you it doesn't mean I was hiding the information.* Donovan exemplifies this later in our interview by saying:

> DONOVAN: People have to understand, it's not hiding. If you're not being openly gay everywhere you go, it's not . . . You're not hiding your sexuality. You're just you. At the end of the day, you're gonna be you. You don't wanna be, "Okay, you the gay boy, you the Black boy, you the white boy." You don't wanna be like that. You just wanna be you . . .

The emphasis on "just being you" is a clear response from young men who might be attempting to resist being defined simply by their race or sexuality. However, with the looming larger discourse of negative attitudes about closeted and DL men who are preying on heterosexual Black women, my respondents often overemphasized that they were in no way aiming to "hide" an element of themselves. Carlos Decena's (2011) study on Dominican gay immigrants in New York highlighted how gay men believed that their family members tacitly understood their sexualities. As what he terms "tacit subjects," Decena's informants similarly negotiated what it meant to be "both 'in' and 'out' of the closet . . . [and whether to] present their sexual identity in public" (19).

Similar to young men who identified as public-private, a group of my respondents worked to downplay any primary significance of race or sexuality. Adding to Hunter's original 3-type model, I label young men who aim to equalize all elements of their identity as *deemphasized.* This fourth category emerged from young men who resisted placing any emphasis on race or sexuality as primary identifiers. These young men alluded to numerous qualities that they considered equally as important as these two categories. For example, take another respondent, Ricky, who spoke of being raised to be human first:

> Mainly from how I was raised, like typical Black people . . . My dad was Italian and Black, so he was raised differently. He was raised to love ev-

erybody. He was raised to not see color. He was raised to carry yourself a certain way so you're not considered "a Black" or "a nigga." So, I've never really carried myself as a typical Black person . . . So, I've never really, aside from food. Even growing up in high school, I hung around a lot of white people. I went to school where there was a majority of like Samoans and white people. I wouldn't say I'm not Black, but I feel like again, I was raised as a human being . . .

Among my sample, just over 10% of young men were classified as embodying a deemphasized identity expression. Ricky's response highlights two principal aspects of those who fall into this particular category: 1) racial distancing and 2) colorblindness. These men tended to downplay the significance of their sexuality and race as being especially different from other aspects of their identities. Another young man, Courtney, said, *"I'm so much more than that. I don't surround my life around my sexuality and I don't make it a pillar in my life. It's just a small part of who I am. You know what I mean. Yeah, I can be a Black man, I can be 6'5, I happen to do music. You know there are so many aspects of me in my life so it doesn't . . . it's not something that stands out to me."* They argued that there is no true difference that mattered to them; it was simply important to understand everyone's underlying humanity. The distancing work undertaken by Ricky, Courtney, and other deemphasized-identity Black gay men often revealed a commitment to being perceived as not stereotypically Black. We might take this form of response as embodying colorblind ideology, as these respondents overemphasized three major points: 1) love for all people, 2) being a human being first, and 3) not seeing color.

As Hunter originally noted, the three categories, in addition to that of being deemphasized, should be understood not as static unchanging conditions, but rather as potentialities for identity negotiations. As identities and our relationships with them are social constructs, so then are our expressions of those identities. This was most evident in a conversation that I had with one of my respondents who first embodied a public-private identity in interviews and later expressed an up-down orientation during a follow-up interview towards the end of my fieldwork. My initial interview with Julian showed how he was negotiating finally coming out to his family as a teenager at nineteen. He hinted that he didn't care for everyone to know about him and his sexuality but recognized that his race was apparent for others. Almost four years later when I followed up with him about his feelings and if they had changed, he replied:

> JULIAN: I think being Black is more important. Being gay is something that everybody deals with—well, not *every* family, but every race deals with. So, I think that's something familiar. But, Black is something different. You go through a lot more being Black and being gay, especially being in LA in South Central, it's a lot different. So, I think I have more pride in being Black; that's what I care more about—me being Black and my heritage.

Over the span of four years' time, Julian had gone from merely coming out to fully cohabitating with a partner. The progression of his relationship from being public-private to up-down, was evident in this conversation. Yet, I must note that this answer to my question did not stick around for very long. No more than thirty minutes after giving me this response and leaving the community space where I conducted fieldwork, Julian ran back inside to find me and said: *I want to change my answer; I think I care about them both equally.* His revision here moved him to an interlocking expression of racial and sexual identity. When I probed him further on this swift change, he confided that upon leaving the Los Angeles community-based organization UpLiftLA, he realized that much of his life is defined not by simply being Black, but being both Black and gay at the same time.

Julian's shift from a public-private to up-down identity across a four-year span and subsequent change to expressing an interlocking expression underscores the malleability of racial and sexual self-relationships and expression. As such, these model-types are only a small part of the picture in understanding how stigma affects the expression of racial and sexual identities. The consistent and continual experience of stigma moves Black gay men along across these groups and within them as well. That is, even among men who fit the interlocking category, why and how they settled on this expression often varies greatly. In recognizing this continual changing of social identity, research must continually evaluate communities as they navigate identity expression.

Across the four model-types for identity prioritization, my sample was drawn from a community-based organization that focused on the lives of young Black, gay men. While each respondent had varying relationships with a larger Black community or gay community, the organizational space played as a critical intersectional space to address both of their stigmatized identities. As such, when respondents were asked about "community belonging," they often described the importance of spaces like UpLiftLA (community organization) to their building of community. Community in this space, regardless of identity model-type, referred to a Black gay community which acknowledged both their racial and sexual identities simultaneously. As physical communities are made up of networks of homes, UpLiftLA represented home for many respondents. As one young man shared, *It was . . . like home. Strong willed individuals talking about their opinions and expressions and doing it in a respectful, critical manner. You know, it felt good to see diverse people there of different occupations and different backgrounds and different viewpoints come together to eat, laugh, connect in a safe space.* Community spaces thus function as Black gay homes that provide the space, nurturing, and socialization that informed the identity embodiments observed in this project.

Taken together, the four categories of identity negotiation (i.e., interlocking, up-down, public-private, and deemphasized) expand our knowledge about the set of possible ways that young Black gay men elect to express racial and sexual identity under stigmatizing conditions. More revealing is that many of the young men share similar experiences, especially stigmatizing experiences around their racial and sexual identities, but can still have very different ways of prioritizing race and sexuality as individuals. In no way do I think these discourses and prioritizations are exhaustive. Instead, I believe this data from men in Los Angeles (and in conjunction with Hunter's population in New York and Philadelphia) are expressed negotiations in major US cities with sizeable and visible Black and queer populations. Future work on populations at the margins should endeavor to further investigate the discourse around identity negotiations as groups and individuals seek to navigate stigmatizing experiences and create coherent narratives of self-identity. How might these identities differ in predominantly Black cities? How might these negotiations shift in suburban or rural contexts?

Black/Gay Community: Considerations for Access and Method

During my data collection for the larger project from which these data come, it became increasingly evident that my positionality and proximity to my respondents both facilitated and impeded access at varying points. Here, I would like to emphasize the importance of the perceived role of the researcher in the study of the margins. At several points, I was told formally and informally of a fear that Black gay men held about the role of research in their communities. These men felt simultaneously hyper-visible and overlooked by the arms of research they were most frequently exposed to: HIV research. Experiences with researchers that "come to collect our information and leave" was a running narrative against which I was consistently working. How can a researcher assure a population that the care for the individual doesn't cease at the end of data collection? As a scholar who shared numerous identity similarities with my population of interest, the social responsibility of my research felt even more heightened. For the resulting product of my intellectual inquiry was a reflection of my respondents as much as a reflection of my own identity. That is, many of my respondents were very explicit that they expected more from me because we shared a racial identity as Black men.

For example, in one interview, my respondent emphasized that he knew I understood him in a deeper way because of our shared racial and sexual identities. In his discussion of the larger gay community, Darrius confided his viewpoints on how our shared identity aspects affected the interview process:

> People pick up on the little things, your looks, your gestures, your attitude, a Black gay will pick up on that way more than—even just me talking to you right now, if I was talking to a white man, half the body signals and things that I'm doing right now are over his head. Versus you and I coming from the same community, pretty much, you get it.

Darrius's assertion and belief that I was able to better understand his behavior, mannerisms, and gestures given our shared identities underscores how many of my respondents perceived their interactions with researchers. In their view, white researchers were simply missing pieces of their narratives and were incapable of ever truly capturing the full picture. Here, my identity as a Black gay scholar facilitated my access to men who felt that my own social treatment and destiny were intertwined with their own. They expressed a trust in me to share their stories in ways that they would not other white men. Even though they noted we were in some ways different, our racial and sexual affinities helped to close the gap of my insider–outsider status within the community.

Much like the work of Moore (2011), Hunter (2010), and McCune (2010) my ability to traverse an outsider–insider status was critical to community access throughout the project. As someone who did not grow up in Los Angeles and without formal connections to the local community, I had to rely on several gatekeepers who vouched for my character and who assured my participants and respondents that I genuinely cared. As all ethnographers know, entering communities can be a difficult task, but this is even more true of spaces where the people have been exploited and reduced to a fraction of their entire being. Young men like those in my study have often been labeled "hard-to-reach populations"; however, I would argue that they are not so hard to reach if scholars are committed to the continued relationships that are built in the field. Positionality, thus, is an integral component of access to communities that are otherwise simply dissected for scholarly-personal gain. This begs the question: How does our sociological work directly impact the lives of those with whom we study?

Ethnographers who study populations at the margins often take for granted the sorts of access to liminal spaces that our individual positionalities entail. As members of populations, scholars who share identities engage in observing how marginalized groups create space for themselves what Goffman (1959) called "backstage." In order to truly capture this "backstage work" (O'Brien 2011), often it is up to scholars who share identities to foreground their own embeddedness into the life experiences and trajectories of the communities in question. That is, the study of Black gay men by Black gay men is critical to sociological insight into communities that are wary of self-serving research agendas from outsider-scholars. Much like Victor Rios (2011) argued in his work *Punished: Policing the Lives of Black and Latino Boys*, the challenge for insider–outsider researchers is to flip the pejorative ethnographic term "going native" on its head by recognizing our commitment to communities over a superficial commitment to the academy. As a collective, our charge is to bring the plights of marginal communities to light while simultaneously defending them from persecution and from those who might aim to warp the realities of their stigmatized conditions. Often, this means exposing hard truths about populations that may be engaged in behaviors that may be perceived as deviant, immoral, or illegal.

These strategies used at the margins tell us much about mainstream societal behaviors and conditions because often stigmatizing experience is the impetus for many responses that disparaged communities deploy against those deemed deviant. When scholars or researchers ask what is revealed about "white Americans" in my work or whether the strategies found are applicable to majority white populations, I often find that the answer lies in their absence from my work. Work that decenters whiteness and instead investigates the lived realities of sexual and racial minority peoples reveal quite a bit about the material conditions that have been created in a world that benefits cis-hetero white men and women. The community spaces and gathering centers where I locate many underserved Black gay young men are often absent of the physical presence of white men and women, but they are always lingering in the psyche of my respondents. Interactions and social encounters with both heterosexual and queer white folk are the realities of living in a city that is still characterized as a 50% white by the Census; race is an inescapable fact. Thus, many of the struggles and challenges faced by this population stand in stark contrast to the larger white majority of the city. For example, the larger white gay majority have substantially better outcomes on the HIV continuum than do Black gay and bisexual men. Social challenges like HIV, homelessness, poverty, and incarceration are looming realities of difference for Black men in this study.

Revisions from the Margins

This chapter reveals the contested and complex ways that Black gay men come to embody their conflicting social identities. For some it is not simply one or the other, but rather the combination of Black identity and gay identity that offers unique negotiations of self-expression. By applying Hunter's original three types of identity negotiation and incorporating a fourth dimension, we gain greater insight into the lived effects of stigmatizing experiences among Black gay men. For the men in my study, the lifelong accumulation of stigmatizing negative experiences has shaped their subsequent relationships with larger communities both for Los Angeles natives and transplants. As Black communities and queer communities struggle for racial and sexual equality at large, those living in the intersections can find themselves too Black for queer space, and too queer for Black space.

I have endeavored to illustrate the critical ways that marginalizing experiences and stigma shape the social realities of Black gay men. Not only are they maligned within racial communities, but also within queer communities. These simultaneous sets of stigmas have created unique conditions to which Black gay men are forced to respond. Thus, the study of people at the margins may appear at surface to be unique or narrow, but instead these studies reveal the best and worst of the mainstream social world. We at once can see the damage of stigma and perceptions of social deviance while simultaneously witnessing the sheer potentiality for groups to embody resilience in the face of social rejection. Studies that focus on those at the outskirts of our social culture are critical as boundaries of social acceptability shift and transform across generations.

The introduction of this book highlights the tendency of social science in the study of sexualities to focus on what the editors have called "the Great Cities." While this chapter does focus on one of those great cities, I endeavor to show how understanding belonging and the meanings of outskirts can happen even within a major metropolitan space. Black communities in Los Angeles have been experiencing an extended decline over the past fifty years (see Hunter and Winder 2019). In many ways, Black people have become ostracized from their own neighborhoods and communities within the city that only serves to exacerbate existing racial tensions in contemporary times. Through this work, I show how even in the face of a larger displacement, Black gay men are still finding ways to navigate being both on the outskirts of Black communities and white queer communities that dominate major metropolitan areas.

As sociologists continue to study our social world, the study of populations on the fringe offers a great responsibility and moral challenge. We must aspire to conduct ethical work in communities that have been historically maligned and discriminated against. Specifically, work on Black gay men must go beyond HIV and sexually transmitted diseases to better understand the social realities that they face within both queer and Black communities. There is no question why Black gay men are the most impacted by the disease: the confluence of social inequities and social stigma. It is the charge of sociologists not only to record, but to ameliorate the social condition. For this reason, studying racial and sexual identity embodiment at the margins will remain an important domain for sociology.

REFERENCES

Bailey, M. M. 2013. *Butch Queens Up in Pumps: Gender, Performance, and Ballroom Culture in Detroit*. Ann Arbor: University of Michigan Press.

Berger, Michelle. 2004. *Workable Sisterhood*. Princeton, NJ: Princeton University Press.

Cohen, C. J., 2009. *The Boundaries of Blackness: AIDS and the Breakdown of Black Politics*. Chicago: University of Chicago Press.

Crichlow, Wesley Eddison Aylesworth. 2004. *Buller Men and Batty Bwoys: Hidden Men in Toronto and Halifax Black Communities*. Toronto: University of Toronto Press.

Decena, C. U. 2011. *Tacit Subjects: Belonging and Same-Sex Desire among Dominican Immigrant Men*. Durham, NC: Duke University Press.

Goffman, Erving. 1959. *The Presentation of Self in Everyday Life*. Garden City, NY: Anchor.

Hawkeswood, William G. 1996. *One of the Children: Gay Black Men in Harlem*. Berkeley: University of California Press.

Hunter, M. A. 2010. "All the Gays Are White and All the Blacks Are Straight: Black Gay Men, Identity, and Community." *Sexuality Research and Social Policy* 7 (2): 81–92.

Hunter, M. A. and T. J. Winder. 2019. "Visibility Is Survival: The Chocolate Maps of Black Gay Life in Urban Ethnography." In *Urban Ethnography*. Bingley, UK: Emerald Publishing Limited.

Johnson, E. P. 2011. *Sweet Tea: Black Gay Men of the South*. Chapel Hill: University of North Carolina Press.

Jones, A. L. 2020. *Flaming? The Peculiar Theopolitics of Fire and Desire in Black Male Gospel Performance*. Oxford: Oxford University Press.

McCune, Jr., Jeffrey Q. 2014. *Sexual Discretion: Black Masculinity and the Politics of Passing*. Chicago: University of Chicago Press.

McQueeney, K., 2009. "'We Are God's Children, Y'All': Race, Gender, and Sexuality in Lesbian-and Gay-Affirming Congregations." *Social Problems* 56 (1): 151–73.

Moore, M. 2010. "'Black and Gay in L.A.': The Relationships Black Lesbians and Gay Men Have to Their Racial and Religious Communities." In *Black Los Angeles: American Dreams and Racial Realities*, edited by D. Hunt and A. Ramón, 188–212. New York: New York University Press.

Moore, M., 2011. *Invisible Families: Gay Identities, Relationships, and Motherhood among Black Women*. Berkeley: University of California Press.

O'Brien, John. 2011. "Spoiled Group Identities and Backstage Work: A Theory of Stigma Management Rehearsals." *Social Psychology Quarterly* 74 (3): 291–309.

Pitt, R. N., 2010. "'Killing the Messenger': Religious Black Gay Men's Neutralization of Anti-Gay Religious Messages. *Journal for the Scientific Study of Religion*, 49 (1): 56–72.

Rios, V. M. 2011. *Punished: Policing the Lives of Black and Latino Boys*. New York: New York University Press.

Thrasher, S. W. 2016. "Super Slaves: Breeding and Controlling the Modern Black American Male through Sports." *Radical History Review* 125: 168–78.

Thrasher, S. W. 2019. "'Tiger Mandingo,' a Tardily Regretful Prosecutor, and the 'Viral Underclass.'" *Souls* 21 (2–3): 248–52.

Winder, T. J. 2015. "'Shouting It Out': Religion and the Development of Black Gay Identities." *Qualitative Sociology* 38 (4): 375–94.

11

Platonic Couples and the Limits of Queer Theory

The Case of Black Masculinity in Hip-Hop Culture

ANTONIA RANDOLPH

. . . They had a very close relationship, and bizarre relationship to most, that you can't believe that they could have the
kind of relationship without it being sexual; I disagree.
—Tasha Denham, former employee of 7 Grand Records and
mother of Solar's daughter, talking about Solar's relationship
with the late rapper, Guru

Introduction

This chapter explores the separability of intense, consuming emotional
attachment from sexual desire to highlight sexuality research's inatten-
tion to the complex emotional worlds of Black men. In the epigraph,
two Black men of a similar age do everything together, talk adoringly
about each other in public, and profess a special bond. They are close
enough to be lovers and indeed are assumed to be lovers because they
are so close, but they are not lovers. I offer this case of passionate friendships in hip-hop to point to the limits of a queer theory that does not
give sufficient autonomy to emotional attachment when studying sexual
orientation.

Male passionate friendships are just one of several identities that get
overshadowed in conventional accounts of sexual identity, desire, and
behavior. However, unlike asexuality, examined in chapter 12, and bisexuality, examined in chapter 13 of *Outskirts*, male passionate friendships
are not marginalized because of their sexual behavior or desire. Instead,
they are emotional connections that get sexualized because of the way
they scramble the assumed consonance between gender, romance, and

sexual desire. In that sense, men in passionate friendships are more like women who are labeled "crazy cat ladies" because they pour their love into cats instead of male romantic partners (McKeithen 2017). Like crazy cat ladies, passionate friendships frustrate heteronormativity because of what their hearts do, not what their bodies do. As Lauren Berlant argues, even queer theory has conventional ways of thinking about intimacy that need to be constantly questioned (Berlant 1998).

Passionate friendships might fit within recent research on men's sexual fluidity, which shows that putatively straight men's sexual behaviors and desires are more fluid than previously assumed (Savin-Williams 2017; Ward 2015). Yet, the research on male sexual fluidity has focused on white middle-class men. Straight-identified white men have sex with other men while signaling their attachment to white heterosexual culture, such as by engaging in mutual masturbation while watching straight porn (Ward 2008). Other research predominantly with white men finds that male heterosexuality is a continuum, ranging from men with "mostly straight" desires and experiences on (Savin-Williams 2017). Research on a racially diverse sample found that straight-identified men who have had same-sex experiences are more likely to identify as straight when they have conservative sexual and gender attitudes (Silva and Whaley 2018).

This research suggests that modern Western definitions of sexual orientation based on the sex of the person for whom one has sexual desires and/or experiences may not map neatly on to sexual identity (van Anders 2015). Historically, heteronormativity, or the expectation that all people should conform to the norms of patriarchal heterosexual relationships, meant that even one sexual act between straight men would call their straightness into question, but this is less true since the end of the twentieth century (Anderson 2008). Inclusive masculinity theory argues that a decline in homohysteria, or fear of being seen as gay, accounts for men's greater fluidity in showing desire and affection to their male friends and their willingness to engage same-sex sex while identifying as straight (McCormack and Anderson 2014).

While the work on male sexual fluidity has challenged some aspects of how social scientists categorize sexual orientation, some assumptions remain underexamined. For instance, social scientists continue to characterize Black men as especially homophobic and socially conservative and thus resistant to the progressive changes that are transforming white middle-class masculinity, which obscures the focus on white men in sexual fluidity research (Bridges and Pascoe 2014). Indeed, scholars have pathologized the disjuncture between the sexual identity and sexual behaviors of Black and Latino men by labeling them on the "down low," rather than questioning dominant sexual categorizations (McCune 2014; Ward 2015).

Moreover, sexuality research continues to overlook the emotional aspect of sexual orientation in favor of emphasizing sexual behavior and desires. Sexual orientation is thought to reflect emotional lives as well as sexual lives, such that people partner emotionally with those they sexually desire (Diamond 2003). Yet, sex of emotional attachment can vary from sex of sexual attraction, just as sexual identity can. In the past, scholars called intense, exclusive, openly affectionate emotional attachments between two people of the same-sex romantic friendships (Faderman 1981). Today, research on passionate friendships, the current term for romantic friendships, finds that women are more likely to have them than men. This gender difference is tied to the fact that close, openly affectionate friendships are consistent with heterosexual norms for women, but not men (Diamond 2003). Still, more research is needed on how passionate friendships relate to sexual orientation and sexual identity, especially for men.

This chapter examines passionate friendships among Black men using a close friendship between two hip-hop artists, Guru and Solar, as an example. Guru, the late rapper best known as the MC for the quintessential 1990s East Coast hip-hop duo, Gang Starr, collaborated and founded a record label with producer Solar after Gang Starr disbanded (Kot 2010). Rap fans went from bewildered to outraged as Solar, heretofore unknown in the music industry, displaced DJ Premier, Gang Starr's beloved producer, first by prohibiting Guru from talking about him in interviews then by barring Premier from any rights to Gang Starr's music in a disputed letter supposedly written by Guru on his deathbed (Rula 2013).

More than a salacious story, this music industry intrigue shows how hip-hop culture normalizes emotionally intense and openly affectionate bonds between men that challenge fans' categorization of sexual orientation (Randolph, Swan, and Rowe 2017). Guru and Solar's relationship is an example of what I call "illegible intimacy" or relationships that confound norms within both dominant and Black culture about how Black men interact. Illegible intimacy extends Neal's (2013) work on illegible masculinities by making relationships, not individuals, the object of analysis. Both Guru and Solar identified as straight, but the intensity and exclusivity of their friendship, Guru's compliance with Solar's bizarre demands, as well as Guru's staying partners with Solar despite his abuse, caused many fans to suspect that they had a sexual relationship (Paine 2010). Through analyzing media accounts about Guru and Solar's relationship, before and after Guru's death in 2010, I show that research on male sexual fluidity must be intersectional and must expand to include an examination of men's emotional attachments.

I call the type of well-known, highly visible, and relatively stable passionate friendship that Guru and Solar had a "platonic couple." Platonic couples challenge the way sociology collapses the boundaries between sexual desire, sexual identity, and emotional attachment. The sex of one's sexual attraction, the basis of contemporary sexual orientation, can be separated from the sex of one's emotional attachment. Dominant Western sociology of sexuality proceeds from the assumption that sexual orientation organizes other facets of an individual's emotional and social life, such as with whom one spends time and seeks emotional support.

Yet, as work on sexual discretion shows, sociology's sexual categories may not map on to people's experiences or identities very well (McCune 2014). In the case of sexual discretion, sociologists categorize Black men who sleep with men with the sexual category of their behavior, that is, as gay or bisexual men, rather than honoring the men's own sexual identities (McCune 2014). With platonic couples, sociology might rewrite Guru and Solar's sexual orientation as gay due to their atypical emotional closeness or overlook the non-normativity of their relationship because they are not gay. Platonic couples show that sociology needs more nuanced language to describe the variability of how emotional attachment and sexual attraction are related in people's lives. As the chapter will show, the rigidity of how sociology categorizes sexuality centers the experience of white middle-class people. The rigidity also shows how conventional ideas about masculinity creep into sexual categorization. By centering the experience of Black men, this chapters offers a conceptualization of sexuality that gives autonomy to emotional attachment. Future work on sexuality should also examine the specific resources and challenges that shape Black sexuality due to how white supremacy constructs Black gender and sexuality as inherently deviant (Cohen 1997; Ferguson 2003). Platonic couples show that the Black community has unique challenges, but also a unique cultural toolkit for remaking gender and sexual norms (Swidler 1986).

From Sexually Fluid to Homo-Nurturant: Expanding the Bounds of Sexual Categorization

Queer theorists trace the emergence of sexual orientation, or the relatively stable and defining selection of the sex to whom one is sexually attracted, to the Enlightenment's fever for scientific categorization of human behavior (Foucault 1980). The advent of sexual science congealed the prejudices about "natural" sexual differences into a body of scientific knowledge about categories of sexual beings. The new categories of heterosexual and homosexual gave the veneer of science to the West's belief that real men "naturally" desired women and vice versa (Foucault 1980). Homosexuality emerged as a variation from this norm that marked a deviant combination of gender expression and sexual desire. Later, Kinsey (1998) and his colleagues examined people's actual sexual behaviors to show that sexuality is a continuum rather than a binary.

Sexual orientation based on sex of object is not the only way to categorize sexuality, however. Sexual configuration theory (SCT) conceptualizes sexuality in a way that decenters sexual orientation. SCT captures the variety of partnered sexual orientations without reifying the gay/straight binary or privileging monogamy (van Anders 2015). Moreover, SCT provides language outside of sexual fluidity to describe when people's sexual behaviors and desires differ from their sexual identity. Sexual fluidity still retains the idea that individuals flow between binary poles of sexual orientation, rather than recognizing the relative autonomy between sexual behavior, desire, and identity. Instead, SCT categorizes people based on factors like number of partner(s) (e.g., uni- or multi-partnered), branch of their behavior (e.g., kinky or vanilla), sex of their sexual object choice, and sex of emotional attachment (e.g., hetero- or homo-nurturant) (van Anders 2015).

This last category, sex of emotional attachment, is the focus of the chapter. While sexual orientation assumes that heterosexual people have opposite-sex emotional partnerships, SCT allows sex of object choice and sex of emotional attachment to vary. Thus, Guru and Solar would be heterosexual in sexual categorization terms, but homo-nurturant in terms of their emotional attachment (van Anders 2015). Guru and Solar had an intense same-sex emotional bond that would likely be thought to be sexual if we follow the dominant model for categorizing sexual orientation. SCT gives language to describe different facets of an individual's sexual and emotional life, rather than conflating the sexual and the emotional.

Race-ing Passionate Friendships

Research on passionate friendship challenges the conflation of emotional attachment with sexual orientation. Historically, women were more likely to have passionate friendships than men due to a combination of sexism and heteronormativity (Diamond 2003). Heteronormativity brands men's closeness to other men as feminizing and thus a sign of homosexuality that straight men should avoid (Diamond 2003).

Since the 1980s, though, the norms on straight men's intimacy with each other has loosened (McCormack and Anderson 2014). The decline in straight white men's fear of being seen as homosexual allowed them to be physically affectionate with their friends (Anderson and McCormack 2014). Straight male homosociality has shifted to include more expressions of vulnerability and support between men. A key change is that men now seek equality, rather than dominance, in intimate relationships (Hammarén and Johansson 2014). As a result, young men are now likely to express desire for male friendships that provide social support and that are safe for self-disclosure (Way 2013). Women still outnumber men in terms of passionate friendships, but many men have passionate friendships, including a significant minority of straight men who have passionate friendships with men (Peterson 2010).

The literature's focus on white men fuels a belief that Black and brown men do not seek intimate bonds with each other (Way 2013). Niobe Way's (2013) work breaks this trend by focusing on the emotional worlds of poor and working-class young men of color. She found that 85% of American boys across race, ethnicity, and class treasured their close friendships with other boys and saw them as vital to their emotional well-being. They especially valued their ability to self-disclose in close male friendships (Way 2013). However, by the time they are high school seniors, boys claim not to have time for male friendships, though they still desire them. Their perceptions that adult men cannot have close male friends without seeming gay, childish, and/or feminine stop them from seeking friendship (Way 2013).

Hip-Hop as a Space for Queer Intimacy

While the preceding literature review examined everyday life, much of the contemporary research on male passionate friendships examines popular culture, especially the portrayal of "bromances" in the media. Critics coined the term "bromance" to describe a spate of movies in the early 2000s featuring dyadic friendships between men that rivaled romantic partnerships with women (Chen 2012). Yet, the bromances portrayed in film and TV feature white middle-class men, creating a gap in our knowledge of representations of Black bromances in popular culture.

Hip-hop is an ideal space to study male intimacy because of its focus on male homosocial bonds (Oware 2011). Like many genres of popular music, hip-hop is a male dominated space (Rose 1994). However, rap music is distinct in its thematic focus on men's relationships with each other. Rap music's self-conscious focus on Black masculinity distinguishes it from other popular forms of Black music (Cheney 2005).

Hip-hop's notoriety for homophobia and misogyny seems at odds with it being a welcoming space for non-normative intimacy. Yet, hip-hop culture has expanded the norms of masculinity enough to view two gangsta rappers (Lil Wayne and Birdman) kissing as an "unconventional," but legitimate, expression of their platonic bond (Randolph, Swan, and Rowe 2017, 627). Indeed, stories about men's bonds with other men are a hallmark of gangsta rap, a subgenre focused on the illegal economy that has become synonymous with misogyny (Oware 2011). Still, the illegal economy is what legitimates the close bonds between men in hip-hop. Tales of "thug life," or hustling with one's friends to survive on the streets, leads to a valorization of "thug love," or close bonds between male friends (Jeffries 2011). This is not to say rap fans treat passionate male friendships as normative, since most fans labeled the kissing gangsta rappers as gay and un-masculine due to their kiss. Rather, the thug life-thug love narrative gives rap fans a cultural toolkit with which to interpret passionate male friendships as masculine and heterosexual (Randolph, Swan, and Rowe 2017; Swidler 1986).

Yet, Guru and Solar are not gangsta rappers, which raises questions about how rap fans would perceive their passionate friendship. Rap music is rife with what I call "platonic couples" or well-known and relatively stable dyadic bonds between men in hip-hop. Other famous platonic couples in hip-hop include the Notorious B.I.G. and Diddy or Jay-Z and Kanye West (Tietjen 2015). Guru and Solar's bond tests the limits of what hip-hop culture can reconcile as being consistent with heteronormativity. Rap fans' skepticism about the basis of their bond shows that passionate friendships still frustrate dominant understandings of sexual categorization.

Platonic Couples as Passionate Friends

The remainder of the chapter shows the singularity of passionate friendships by describing exceptional moments of Guru and Solar's relationship and reactions to them within hip-hop culture. It analyzes media about their relationship before and after Guru's death from cancer in 2010 to study how hip-hop culture interpreted their platonic bond. Interviewers noted the uniqueness of their bond, characterizing them as having a "bizarre relationship" (Paine 2010), and saying that outsiders questioned "the peculiar nature of the Solar-Guru tandem" (Faraone 2014). While an unusual case, Guru and Solar's passionate friendship shows how sexual categorization fails to capture the range of emotional attachments men can have with each other.

Guru (Keith Elam) is best known as the emcee for the standard-bearing East Coast hip-hop duo, Gang Starr, along with producer DJ Premier (Christopher Martin). Fans viewed Gang Starr as the perfect musical marriage between Guru's monotone voice and Premier's choice jazz samples and crisp scratching (Kot 2010). Though critically acclaimed, Gang Starr was never very commercially successful. Still, the group was beloved by underground hip-hop fans and remain influential long after their disbanding in 2004 (Kot 2010).

Fans were heartbroken when Guru began recording with his next producer, Solar (John Mosher), mourning the musical divorce of a favorite duo. Rap fans imbued Guru and Premier with a fairytale-like sense of destiny, arguing that though Premier produced other people and Guru had his solo project, nothing matched the perfection of Gang Starr (Rhodes and Wong 2019). Fans treated Solar like an interloper who broke up the marriage of their favorite band. Guru aided fans' sense of betrayal by downplaying Premier's contribution to Gang Starr, while touting Solar's prowess as a producer (Rula 2013).

Yet, fans' belief in the simpatico between Guru and Premier belied reality. Interpersonal strife lurked beneath Gang Starr's ideal musical marriage. Guru and Premier often fought due to Guru's drinking and Guru threatened to break up the group on nearly every tour (Faraone 2014). They unofficially broke up after their first gold record in 1998, *Moment of Truth*, and only got back together for their last album of new material, *The Ownerz*, in 2003 (Faraone 2014). For Guru's part, he believed that Premier cheated him out of money and gave his best beats to other MCs (Rodriguez 2010). Moreover, Solar encouraged Guru to believe that Premier had arranged Guru's robbery and beating in 1999 (Allah 2013; Reiss 1999).

Guru maintained that he and Premier were only bandmates, never friends (Faraone 2014). Frustrated about being asked again about his Gang Starr days, Guru told an interviewer:

> People ask me about my ex-DJ and all that. We were never that close. We hooked up in the studio and did great music, but we were never hanging and all that cool. Solar and I, we got tight before we even started doing music. (Rula 2013)

Fans mistook Gang Starr's musical compatibility for emotional intimacy. They were not even "love at first sight" as musical partners, since they were put together by their label (Faraone 2014).

In contrast, Solar affirms that friendship was the basis of his musical partnership with Guru, saying, "I was already a producer, but we didn't come together as an artist and producer. We came together as friends" (R. Schwartz n.d.). They couched the development of their business relationship in the language of friendship, care, and intimacy. Solar said that he encouraged Guru to leave his previous record label and start his own because he knew Guru was unhappy saying, "No wants to see there

[sic] friend miserable" (R. Schwartz n.d.). Eventually, Solar and Guru founded 7 Grand Records in 2004 to release Guru's post-Gang Starr albums ("Guru & Solar Interview" 2006). While Solar did not know that Guru wanted him to co-found the label, Guru insisted that he did not want to start the label without him. He told Solar, "'I want you to get involved WITH me.' Because even when we first met, I just knew he was a VISIONARY" (Lewis 2010). Indeed, Guru believed that he and Solar would be "the perfect match—like a Dynamic Duo sorta thing" (Lewis 2010).

Guru praised Solar for a kind of intimacy that is unique to musicians, understanding how to record his voice. He told an interviewer, "It's like Solar has read my mind and had the sound that I was looking for" (R. Schwartz n.d.). In another interview, Guru said that he "used to get frustrated" with Premier recording his voice so low on songs that he could not hear his vocals. Solar agreed, saying that he was able to make Guru's voice sound "more harmonic," because he had "taken a while to study how to record him" (FaceCulture 2010). Their comments suggest that they had a musical intimacy born of mutual understanding that Guru lacked with Premier. Guru enjoyed the kind of resonance from being known that band members often experience (Grønnerød 2007). He said, "The way that Solar analyzes my vocal ability, he's very intense with the way he does that," continuing, "He gets very involved in producing me and that to me is a pleasure" ("Guru & Solar Interview" 2006). In contrast, while Premier excelled at sampling and using the drum machine, he never got to know Guru's voice well enough to make music that complimented it ("Guru & Solar Interview" 2006).

Solar's musical "chemistry" with Guru is what made Guru stay in touch with him after they met through a mutual musical industry friend (Rodriguez 2010). Guru told an interviewer, "Solar and I are developing chemistry which is beyond compare" that would cause each of their albums to be more successful than the last one ("Guru & Solar Interview" 2006). The word "chemistry" can be used to describe a spark between any two people, but it is associated with romantic couples. Thus, romantic couples dominate our conception of dyadic intimacy such that the singularity of platonic couples lacks its own language.

Guru uses emotionally intense language to describe Solar that is consistent with passionate friendships. Feeling seen and understood was the basis of his music with Solar, rather than technical skill, as was the case with Premier. Guru says of Solar that, "It was like he'd read my mind, spontaneous combustion, and I felt creatively rejuvenated" (B. Schwartz 2007). He felt the intersubjectivity of passionate friendships, where Solar implicitly understood his musical needs (Redman et al. 2002). Yet, the emotional closeness did not seem mutual. Solar was quick to praise Guru, but he did not reciprocate the feelings of being understood and known that Guru expressed.

Intimate Partner Violence without Intimate Partners

Nevertheless, Guru and Solar's friendship alone would not have been enough to cause people to question their sexuality. Critics were disturbed by the exclusivity of their bond and further alarmed when Guru made decisions before dying that gave Solar undue power over Gang Starr's catalog and money (Faraone 2014). When Guru was hospitalized with cancer in 2010, Solar prevented friends and family from visiting him until Guru's nephew complained about it on social media. More controversially, Solar released a letter allegedly written by Guru before dying granting Solar complete control over Gang Starr's recordings and likeness and barring Premier from any proceeds from their catalog (*Toronto Star* 2010). Further, the letter named Solar as the guardian of Guru's young son (*Toronto Star* 2010). These developments, especially how the will excluded Premier from Gang Starr's legacy, angered fans and caused them to wonder if Solar's hold on Guru was sexual, not just platonic. In other words, rap fans re-coded their bond as sexual because they doubted that mere friendship could explain Guru's decisions.

After Guru's death, the press aired their frustrations with how Guru insisted that Solar be included in every interview and how he prevented them from talking about Premier's contributions to Gang Starr. A journalist complained that Guru demanded that Solar be included in an interview about the twentieth anniversary of Gang Starr's first album. He said the interview "left Gang Starr's legacy on a sour note" because of how Guru "constantly threw DJ Premier under the bus by referring to him as his 'Ex DJ'" rather than by name (Rula 2013). Tasha Denham, a former employee of 7 Grand Records and Solar's former romantic partner, confirmed that Guru refused to be interviewed without Solar, at Solar's request (Paine 2010). Solar did not want the press to ask about Gang Starr or Premier because he resented fans preference for the old band. Because of this, Guru would suppress questions about Gang Starr to avoid fighting with Solar (Paine 2010).

Thus, while exclusivity is a hallmark of passionate friendships, Solar's controlling behavior seemed to prompt Guru's exclusive attachment to him. Not only did Solar prevent Guru from talking about his old DJ and band, he isolated him from his former musical collaborators (Faraone 2014; Paine 2010). The Gang Starr Foundation was a loose crew of musicians that recorded together. It included friends, like Big Shug, who encouraged Guru to make a career in music when he was a college student (Faraone 2014). Solar allegedly isolated Guru from the Gang Starr Foundation and other industry friends, telling him that they meant him harm (Paine 2010). Guru never saw Big Shug or Premier again after he left the Gang Starr tour (Faraone 2014).

Solar even ran off members of Guru's touring band, mistreating their deejay, Doo Wop, and trumpeter, Brownman, until they both left (Faraone 2014). According to Denham, Solar forbade Doo Wop from talking to Guru after he quit, even though Doo Wop had known Guru for nearly fifteen years and had performed with him for five years (Paine 2010). Solar exiled Denham in 2008, but she secretly stayed in contact with Guru. Guru told her that Solar was checking his email, taking his phone away, and taking away his asthma inhaler, saying that "it was a crutch" (Paine 2010). Solar also kept Guru away from his family and his ex-girlfriend (Paine 2010). Brownman corroborated this in a separate interview, saying that Solar helped estrange Guru from his sister by telling him not to attend a family funeral. Solar's goal was to make Guru believe that he was the only one he could depend on (Faraone 2010). From what Denham observed, Guru was either alone, with his son, or with Solar (Paine 2010).

Here the story veers into more troubling territory. Bandmates and employees witnessed Solar emotionally and physically abuse Guru (Faraone 2010; 2014; Paine 2010). Guru confided to Denham that Solar only became controlling once they went into business together (Paine 2010). He belittled Guru in public and private (Paine 2010). Solar used the fact he and Guru were part of The Five Percent Nation, an African American offshoot of Islam, against Guru, saying that the group would be ashamed of him and that he "doesn't live up to their teachings" (Paine 2010). Emotional abuse led to physical abuse. Denham witnessed Solar beating Guru over a dispute about religious teachings. He would not stop even after Guru began hyper-ventilating because he needed his inhaler (Paine 2010). In fact, she saw Solar hit Guru several times, giving him a black eye and knocking out a tooth (Paine 2010). Trumpeter Brownman also saw Solar abuse Guru. He saw Solar punch Guru in the head and face in an alleyway while on a European tour. Tellingly, Solar avoided Guru's body, because he knew he had cancer (Faraone 2014).

Guru and Solar's bond looks different due to these reports. Once news of Solar's abuse of Guru came out, fans accused Solar of sexually seducing Guru. They believed that Solar turned Guru gay in order to exploit him (Paine 2010). For instance, hip-hop media personality Sway asked Solar on MTV if rumors that he and Guru were lovers were true (Paine 2010). The categorization of Guru's bond as sexual highlights the limits of our conception of emotional attachment. Solar and Guru's relationship fits the model of intimate partner violence, yet there was no indication that they were romantic partners (McClennen 2005). Still, platonic couples are not socially intelligible the way romantic couples are. A man allowing a friend of equal status to abuse and exploit him exceeds normative conceptions of friendship. Instead, rap fans turned to the more recognizable formulation that Guru and Solar were gay. Their form of intimacy was illegible to dominant modes of understanding sexual orientation and emotional attachment.

Consequently, Guru's former bandmates and friends tried to prove his straightness and distance him from gay rumors. They used the discourse of sexual orientation to refute the accusations; yet their bond was homo-nurturant, not homosexual. One strategy was to provide proof of Guru and Solar's sexual and romantic attachments to women. Brownman vouches for Guru's heterosexuality, saying that "Guru loved women. I've seen that smooth talking brother roll up on a lot girls" (Faraone 2010). He calls the gay rumors a "lack of understanding," saying "I guess it's easier to think of someone as iconic as Guru as gay rather than controlled." He continues that he "was a victim, not a punk. . . . You don't fault an abused and battered wife for what they endured? Let's not fault G" (Faraone 2010).

Likewise, Denham inoculated Guru against gay rumors by affirming that homosexuality was bad and thus not befitting of someone like him. She was "disgusted" by the online speculation that Guru and Solar were romantically involved. She suggests that the gay rumors could harm their kids and damage their legacy (Paine 2010). Guru's son should be able to cherish and respect the memory of his dad, Denham said, not deal with "rumors and speculation" about his sexuality (Paine 2010). She doubts they had a sexual relationship based on the extensive time she spent with Guru and Solar. She said, "I never saw any type of affection in that way" (Paine 2010). Yet, she also said her child with Solar did not mean he was not gay, playing into the trope of the down low Black man (McCune 2014).

In this way, defenses of male passionate friendships can re-inscribe the gay/straight binary and perpetuate homophobia. Rather than expanding the bounds of male intimacy, friends responded to the illegibility of Guru and Solar's relationship by redrawing the boundaries around normative straight masculinity. For instance, Denham treats homosexuality itself as a source of stigma and "disgust" rather than simply asserting that Guru and Solar were not gay. Similarly, Brownman figures Guru as a "ladies' man" to dispel the rumors that he was gay and re-inscribes the heteronormative notion that "real men" should have many sexual partners. Finally, Denham traffics in down low discourse to suggest that while Solar may have been gay, Guru was not.

Yet, Brownman and Denham also sought to distinguish Guru's and Solar's platonic bond from a romantic bond and to identify the non-sexual, non-romantic hold that friends can have on each other. Brownman affirms the toxicity of Solar and Guru's relationship without casting it as homosexual. He says that "less intelligent men mistakenly thought that they were gay" because they were inseparable: ". . . They would go EVERYWHERE together . . . even to the bathroom. They sat together on planes, cars, vans, trains . . . would go to the gym together" (Faraone 2010). Still, Brownman believed their inseparability was an outgrowth of Solar's desire to control and isolate Guru, not a sign that they were lovers (Faraone 2010). Solar isolated Guru, not "cuz they're gay," but so that Solar could "continue his quiet indoctrination" of him (Faraone 2010). Brownman thought Guru was vulnerable to being controlled by Solar because he needed a new addiction after getting sober from alcohol.

Also, he needed guidance after leaving his old label (Faraone 2010). He explains Guru's compliance in terms of emotional vulnerabilities that can characterize any relationship, not just romantic ones.

Denham also explains their attachment as based on emotional, not sexual connection. Echoing Brownman, she attributes Guru and Solar's closeness to Solar's desire to "control" and be invaluable to Guru (Paine 2010). Solar's strategy was to isolate Guru and always be around him: "You're their man day in and day out, the first person you talk to in the morning, the last person you talk to before you go to bed" (Paine 2010). Hip-hop culture creates a slippage where "my man" could refer either to a close friend or a romantic partner. Yet, Denham clearly states that while Solar made Guru dependent on him, his control was not based on a sexual bond.

Like Brownman, Denham believed that Guru's emotional vulnerabilities, especially in the wake of going solo, made him susceptible to Solar's exploitation. When asked by the interviewer about his compliance, she said that Guru did not fight back because of his fear, insecurities, and loyalty (Paine 2010). Guru credited Solar with helping him stop drinking, such as when Solar let Guru stay with him when his house burned down while he was trying to get sober. In short, Solar exploited Guru's most vulnerable moments to place him in his emotional debt. He established a lopsided emotional relationship with Guru instead of the interdependence and mutuality that is supposed to characterize passionate friendships. Echoing Brownman, Denham thought that Guru was afraid that he would feel lost and directionless without Solar guiding him. He isolated Guru so that he could feed his insecurities instead of lessening them (Paine 2010).

Conclusion: Bringing Emotional Attachment Back In

Fans scrutinized the intimacy between Guru and Solar because their relationship violated norms of heterosexual masculinity. The exclusivity of their bond, such that mention of Guru's former DJ was verboten, perplexed fans who romantically believed that Guru and Premier were the perfect musical partners. When Solar isolated Guru from friends and family and claimed control of his assets, fans' frustration turned into accusations that something was amiss in their relationship. Their friendship went from unusual to illegible, especially after Solar's physical and emotional abuse of Guru was revealed. As a result, the hip-hop community categorized their bond as sexual to make sense of an attachment that they could not otherwise explain.

Yet, as Denham and Brownman's accounts show, platonic couples can be the site of the type of abuse that we associate with romantic partners. Guru's former friends outline what a proper accounting of male passionate friendships might entail. Solar violated the mutuality and trust of passionate friendship. This violation is especially devastating for male passionate friendships, since society tells men not to confide in and seek help from other people. Guru sought support from Solar in arenas where he did not feel confident, such as starting a new record label and getting sober. Solar exploited the self-revelation that is the basis of passionate friendships, rather than supporting Guru or matching his vulnerability.

Thus, we can specify the dynamics of emotional attachment in relationships and analyze them separately from sexual orientation. Guru and Solar self-identified as straight and evidence of their sexual behavior and desire support that claim. Yet, the musicians' sexual orientation was beside the point, since their conflict was rooted in their emotional relationship. Mainstream sexuality scholarship does not offer us language to think through their homo-nurturant, not homosexual, relationship. Still, those fields cannot afford to ignore the kind of relationship that Guru and Solar had, since fans and friends mobilized the logics of heteronormativity and sexual categorization to understand it.

While exceptional even among platonic couples in hip-hop culture, Guru and Solar's case suggests an agenda for studying sexuality that is not based on the logic of sexual orientation. Instead, sexuality scholars should adapt the more expansive view of sexual identity offered by SCT or by other models that take emotional attachment seriously (van Anders 2015). Moreover, Guru and Solar's relationship shows the importance of using intersectionality to examine sexual subcultures. The nature of their intimacy baffled hip-hop culture, even though hip-hop has provided some space for men to expand the norms of legitimate intimacy (Randolph, Swan, and Rowe 2017). Future research should explore how sexual and gender norms evolve within specific racial and ethnic communities. Inclusive masculinity research, which studies sexual fluidity mostly among white men, cannot explain hip-hop's acceptance of platonic couples, nor can it explain when the expansion of boundaries hit their limits. Greater attention to the intersection of race, gender, and sexual norms within specific communities would help better account for variations in sexual and emotional attachments in contemporary society.

Platonic couples offer insights into the contemporary Black family and to the study of emotions. Guru and Solar put their bond with each other above heterosexual romance and their family of origin. For instance, Solar put his bond with Guru before his romantic relationship with Tasha Denham, firing her from 7 Grand Records when he sensed that she was sabotaging his relationship with Guru. Guru and Solar were each other's family of choice, not because their family of origin abandoned them, but because they felt a connection that they could not get elsewhere. This elective family of choice differs from research that finds LGBT friends forming families with each other due to rejection from their families of origin (Bailey 2013; Weston 1997).

In this way, hip-hop's valorization of platonic couples responds to unique circumstances within the Black community. Platonic couples show how Black culture has begun challenging the myth that the Black nuclear family can save the Black community. Hip-hop is typical of the post–Civil Rights era in that regard, since contemporary R&B has also questioned the idea that heterosexual marriage is the solution to the Black community's problems (Patterson 2019). Still, hip-hop, in its focus on men, picks up on challenges to the Black family that distinguishes it from R&B of the same era.

Hip-hop's ambivalence towards the centrality of the Black family is rooted in gender and class dynamics. Hip-hop is oriented to poor and working-class Black men, especially those involved in the illegal economy (McLaren 1999). Socioeconomic transformations, such as deindustrialization and the dominance of service work, combined with mass incarceration meant that the economic worlds of Black men growing up in the 1980s were radically different from their parents' generation. Simply put, working-class Black men could not hope to follow their fathers into factories once work disappeared (Wilson 1997). Many Black men cycled through the criminal justice system as they turned to the illegal economy to make up for the absence of legal work in their communities (Jones 2018). In this radically different context, where generations of Black men struggle to find legal work and are taken from their communities through incarceration, the Black family becomes a less central space for the socialization of young Black men. Instead, communities of men, particularly the ones men hustle with on the street, become more important (Randolph 2018).

The rise of platonic couples as a valorized relationship in hip-hop culture reflects these socioeconomic transformations. The fathers of Black men growing up in the hip-hop generation could not teach them how to survive on the streets, nor could they prepare them to join the deindustrialized work force. Similarly, Black mothers, who got jobs more easily in the service economy, could not help their sons overcome employers' racist and sexist beliefs that Black men lacked the "soft skills" needed to succeed in the service economy (Newman 2000). This chapter only hints at these transformations, but a fuller study of how hip-hop captures changes in the Black family in the post-Civil Rights era remains to be done.

Finally, the chapter contributes to our understanding of the emotional world of Black men. Black men have a distinct set of feeling rules shaped by race, class, and gender (Jackson and Harvey Wingfield 2013; Wingfield 2010). Much of the extant research on intra-racial Black male friendships are set in formal institutions, like college, and formal organizations, such as fraternities and rites of passage programs (Jackson 2012; McClure 2013). In contrast, this chapter shows Black men choosing openly affectionate, intense emotional relationships with each other that are not a survival mechanism to cope with predominantly white institutions, at least not in the immediate sense.

Platonic couples are born from Black men's interpretation of the emotional support systems available to them within the post-Civil Rights era. As stated above, changes in the socioeconomic landscape shaped Black men's view of intimate bonds such that friends seemed like the appropriate source of emotional and social support. In this way, platonic couples differ from the bromances found among white middle-class men, where white men are freed from the fear of seeming gay that suppressed straight male friendships in the past (Robinson, White, and Anderson 2017). In contrast, platonic couples are a solution to the emotional landscape that the hip-hop generation perceives, where Black men's need for safe harbor from a hostile and uncomprehending world allows them to rewrite gender and sexual norms. Black men's intimacy is rooted in a redefinition of legitimate masculinity, rather than a decline in homohysteria. Sociology should seek to describe the specific social contexts tied to the emergence of emotional closeness between men and resist universalizing accounts of men's emotional worlds.

REFERENCES

Allah, Sha Be. 2013. "The Source EXCLUSIVE: Solar Speaks Out Three Years after the Death of Guru (Part 2)." *Source* (blog). April 20, 2013. http://thesource.com.

Anderson, Eric. 2008. "'Being Masculine Is Not about Who You Sleep With . . .': Heterosexual Athletes Contesting Masculinity and the One-Time Rule of Homosexuality." *Sex Roles* 58 (1–2): 104–15. https://doi.org/10.1007/s11199-007-9337-7.

Anderson, Eric and Mark McCormack. 2014. "Cuddling and Spooning: Heteromasculinity and Homosocial Tactility among Student-Athletes." *Men and Masculinities*, March. https://doi.org/10.1177/1097184X14523433.

Bailey, Marlon M. 2013. *Butch Queens Up in Pumps: Gender, Performance, and Ballroom Culture in Detroit*. Ann Arbor: University of Michigan Press.

Berlant, Lauren. 1998. "Intimacy: A Special Issue." *Critical Inquiry* 24 (2): 281–88.

Bridges, Tristan and C. J. Pascoe. 2014. "Hybrid Masculinities: New Directions in the Sociology of Men and Masculinities." *Sociology Compass* 8 (3): 246–58. https://doi.org/10.1111/soc4.12134.

Chen, Elizabeth J. 2012. "Caught in a Bad Bromance." *Texas Journal of Women, Gender, and the Law* 21 (2): 241.

Cheney, Charise. 2005. *Brothers Gonna Work It Out: Sexual Politics in the Golden Age of Rap Nationalism*. New York: New York University Press.

Cohen, Cathy J. 1997. "Punks, Bulldaggers, and Welfare Queens: The Radical Potential of Queer Politics?" *GLQ: A Journal of Lesbian and Gay Studies* 3 (4): 437–65. https://doi.org/10.1215/10642684-3-4-437.

Diamond, Lisa M. 2003. "What Does Sexual Orientation Orient? A Biobehavioral Model Distinguishing Romantic Love and Sexual Desire." *Psychological Review* 110 (1): 173–92. https://doi.org/10.1037/0033-295X.110.1.173.

FaceCulture, dir. 2010. *Interview Guru and Solar—2007—Part 2*. https://www.youtube.com/watch?v=NPhFcVERJWw.

Faderman, Lillian. 1981. *Surpassing the Love of Men: Romantic Friendship and Love between Women from the Renaissance to the Present*. New York: Morrow.

Faraone, Chris. 2010, September. "Finally . . . The Interview Everybody Has Been Waiting For . . . The FULL Brownman Interview!" (Www.Fucksolar.Com). https://web.archive.org.

Faraone, Chris. 2014. "GURU's Guru." *Subterranean Thump* (blog). April 19, 2014. https://medium.com.

Ferguson, Roderick A. 2003. *Aberrations in Black: Toward a Queer of Color Critique*. Minneapolis: University of Minnesota Press.

Foucault, Michel. 1980. *The History of Sexuality*. New York: Vintage.

Grønnerød, Jarna. 2007. "The Power of Relationships: Idealization, Validation and Mutuality between Young Men." In *Young People at the Crossroads. Proceedings of the 5th International Conference on Youth Research: 1–5 September 2006*, edited by Martti Muukkonen and Tiina Sotkasiira, 93–102. Petrozavodsk, Russia: University of Joensuu, Publications of the Karelian Research Institute.

"Guru & Solar Interview: Talkin' All That Jazz." 2006, February. *RiotSound* (blog). https://riotsound.com.

Hammarén, Nils, and Thomas Johansson. 2014. "Homosociality: In between Power and Intimacy." *SAGE Open* 4 (1). https://doi.org/10.1177/2158244013518057.

Jackson, Brandon A. 2012. "Bonds of Brotherhood: Emotional and Social Support among College Black Men." *Annals of the American Academy of Political and Social Science* 642 (1): 61–71. http://o-dx.doi.org.read.cnu.edu/10.1177/0002716212438204.

Jackson, Brandon A. and Adia Harvey Wingfield. 2013. "Getting Angry to Get Ahead: Black College Men, Emotional Performance, and Encouraging Respectable Masculinity." *Symbolic Interaction* 36 (3): 275–92. https://doi.org/10.1002/symb.63.

Jeffries, Michael P. 2011. *Thug Life: Race, Gender, and the Meaning of Hip-Hop*. Chicago: University of Chicago Press.

Jones, Nikki. 2018. *The Chosen Ones: Black Men and the Politics of Redemption*. Oakland: University of California Press.

Kinsey, Alfred C. 1998. *Sexual Behavior in the Human Male*. Reprint edition. Bloomington: Indiana University Press.

Kot, Greg. 2010, April 21. "KEITH 'GURU' ELAM: 1966–2010: Gifted MC Fused Jazz, Hip-Hop in Gang Starr." *Chicago Tribune*.

Lewis, Pete. 2010, April 6. "Guru & Solar: Team Talk." Blues & Soul. www.bluesandsoul.com.

McClennen, Joan C. 2005. "Domestic Violence between Same-Gender Partners: Recent Findings and Future Research." *Journal of Interpersonal Violence* 20 (2): 149–54. https://doi.org/10.1177/0886260504268762.

McClure, Stephanie M. 2013. "Improvising Masculinity: African American Fraternity Membership in the Construction of a Black Masculinity." *Journal of African American Studies* 10 (1): 57–73. https://doi.org/10.1007/s12111-006-1013-4.

McCormack, Mark and Eric Anderson. 2014. "Homohysteria: Definitions, Context and Intersectionality." *Sex Roles* 71 (3–4): 152–58. http://o-dx.doi.org.read.cnu.edu/10.1007/s11199-014-0401-9.

McCune, Jeffrey Q. 2014. *Sexual Discretion: Black Masculinity and the Politics of Passing*. Chicago: University of Chicago Press.

McKeithen, Will. 2017. "Queer Ecologies of Home: Heteronormativity, Speciesism, and the Strange Intimacies of Crazy Cat Ladies." *Gender, Place & Culture* 24 (1): 122–34. https://doi.org/10.1080/0966369X.2016.1276888.

McLaren, Peter. 1999. "Gangsta Pedagogy and Ghettocentricity: The Hip-Hop Nation as Counterpublic Sphere." *Counterpoints* 96: 19–64.

Neal, Mark Anthony. 2013. *Looking for Leroy: Illegible Black Masculinities*. New York: New York University Press.

Newman, Katherine S. 2000. *No Shame in My Game: The Working Poor in the Inner City*. New York: Vintage.

Oware, Matthew. 2011. "Brotherly Love: Homosociality and Black Masculinity in Gangsta Rap Music." *Journal of African American Studies* 15 (1): 21–39.

Paine, Jake. 2010, April 27. "Tasha Denham: 'Just to Get a Rep?'" HipHopDX. http://hiphopdx.com.

Patterson, Robert J. 2019. *Destructive Desires: Rhythm and Blues Culture and the Politics of Racial Equality*. New Brunswick, NJ: Rutgers University Press.

Peterson, Katherine. 2010. "Bosom Buddies: Factors Associated with Experiences of Passionate Friendship among Men and Women." PhD dissertation, Utah State University.

Randolph, Antonia. 2018. "When Men Give Birth to Intimacy: The Case of Jay-Z's '4:44.'" *Journal of African American Studies* 22 (4): 393–406. https://doi.org/10.1007/s12111-018-9418-4.

Randolph, Antonia, Holly Swan, and Kristin Denise Rowe. 2017. "'That $hit Ain't Gangsta': Symbolic Boundary Making in an Online Urban Gossip Community." *Journal of Contemporary Ethnography* 47 (5): 609–39. https://doi.org/10.1177/0891241617716744.

Redman, Peter, Debbie Epstein, Mary Jane Kehily, and Mairtin Mac An Ghaill. 2002. "Boys Bonding: Same-Sex Friendship, the Unconscious and Heterosexual Discourse." *Discourse: Studies in the Cultural Politics of Education* 23 (2): 179–91. https://doi.org/10.1080/0159630022000000769.

Reiss, Randy. 1999, January 11. "Gang Starr's Guru Beaten, Robbed Outside Studio." MTV. www.mtv.com.

Rhodes, Morgan and Oliver Wong, dirs. 2019. "Vikki Tobak and Joseph Patel on Gang Starr's 'Hard to Earn' (1994) | Maximum Fun." Heat Rocks. www.maximumfun.org.

Robinson, Stefan, Adam White, and Eric Anderson. 2017. "Privileging the Bromance: A Critical Appraisal of Romantic and Bromantic Relationships." *Men and Masculinities*, October, 1097184X17730386. https://doi.org/10.1177/1097184X17730386.

Rodriguez, Jayson. 2010. "Guru Associate Black Jesus Recalls Introducing Late MC to Solar." MTV News. April 27, 2010. www.mtv.com.

Rose, Tricia. 1994. *Black Noise: Rap Music and Black Culture in Contemporary America*. Hanover, NH: Wesleyan University Press.

Rula, Vic Da. 2013, January 9. "Guru's Last Interview with Allhiphop.Com." Da Shelter (blog). https://escobar300.wordpress.com.

Savin-Williams, Ritch C. 2017. *Mostly Straight: Sexual Fluidity among Men*. Cambridge, MA: Harvard University Press.

Schwartz, Barry. 2007. "Gang Starr's Guru: Solar Power." JazzTimes. https://jazztimes.com.

Schwartz, Rob. n.d. "Guru and Solar." Who?Mag (blog). Accessed May 19, 2018. www.whomagvideovision.com.

Silva, Tony J. and Rachel Bridges Whaley. 2018. "Bud-Sex, Dude-Sex, and Heteroflexible Men: The Relationship between Straight Identification and Social

Attitudes in a Nationally Representative Sample of Men with Same-Sex Attractions or Sexual Practices." *Sociological Perspectives* 61 (3): 426–43. https://doi.org/10.1177/0731121417745024.

Swidler, Ann. 1986. "Culture in Action: Symbols and Strategies." *American Sociological Review* 51 (2): 273–86.

The Toronto Star. 2010, May 5. "A Hip-Hop Soap Opera: Guru's Life and Death an Arguable Legacy; Toronto Bandmate Left to Answer the Questions about His Rap Hero."

Tietjen, Alexa. 2015, March 13. "Hip Hop Besties: 9 Pairs of Rappers Who Are Best Friends." VH1 News. www.vh1.com.

van Anders, Sari M. 2015. "Beyond Sexual Orientation: Integrating Gender/Sex and Diverse Sexualities via Sexual Configurations Theory." *Archives of Sexual Behavior* 44 (5): 1177–1213. https://doi.org/10.1007/s10508-015-0490-8.

Ward, Jane. 2008. "Dude-Sex: White Masculinities and 'Authentic' Heterosexuality among Dudes Who Have Sex with Dudes." *Sexualities* 11 (4): 414–34. https://doi.org/10.1177/1363460708091742.

Ward, Jane. 2015. *Not Gay: Sex between Straight White Men.* New York: New York University Press.

Way, Niobe. 2013. "Boys' Friendships during Adolescence: Intimacy, Desire, and Loss." *Journal of Research on Adolescence* 23 (2): 201–13. https://doi.org/10.1111/jora.12047.

Weston, Kath. 1997. *Families We Choose: Lesbians, Gays, Kinship.* New York: Columbia University Press.

Wilson, William Julius. 1997. *When Work Disappears: The World of the New Urban Poor.* New York: Vintage.

Wingfield, Adia Harvey. 2010. "Are Some Emotions Marked 'Whites Only'? Racialized Feeling Rules in Professional Workplaces." *Social Problems* 57 (2): 251–68.

12

What Does Asexuality Offer Sociology?

Insights from the Asexual Community Survey

MEGAN CARROLL

In August 2018, the ASA Section on the Sociology of Sexualities hosted a preconference before the annual meeting of the American Sociological Association to gather insights and showcase the work of top contributors in the field. Outstanding work from across the discipline was featured in panels, workshops, and roundtables across the two days of conferencing. While this preconference served to advance the discipline's efforts toward generating knowledge and healing social divides, it also symbolized the range of American sociology's contributions to interdisciplinary knowledge on sexuality. Missing from the work presented at the preconference was any mention of asexualities.

An asexual identity movement has grown exponentially in the twenty-first century, adopted by those who experience little to no sexual attraction (AVEN Livestreams 2021), yet sociological insights on asexuality have been very limited. While some sociologists have devoted attention toward asexualities in their work (e.g., Carrigan 2011; Cuthbert 2017; Dawson, Scott, and McDonnell 2018; Poston and Baumle 2010; Scherrer 2008, 2010a, 2010b; Scherrer and Pfeffer 2017; Simula, Sumerau, and Miller 2019; Sumerau et al. 2018; Troia 2018; Vares 2018; Yang 2021), the field more often contributes to the invisibility of asexuality than sheds light on it. Much of the current knowledge of asexuality comes from psychology and the humanities, and the work of these scholars is rarely integrated into our sociology journals or classrooms. The resultant gaps in the literature represent theoretical and empirical opportunities to explore new frontiers in the range of human sexuality, creative family arrangements, and the impact that intersecting systems of oppression have on sexual minorities.

What an Understanding of Asexuality Contributes to Sociology

The sociology of sexualities has historically embraced empirical approaches to human sexuality that shine light on otherwise invisible and marginalized populations. It has foreseen a more fluid and complex landscape of identity formation among younger generations, including the proliferation of new and more specific terms that describe gender and sexual diversity (Garrison, this collection; Robertson 2019; Savin-Williams 2001). Asexuality embodies these trends. Asexual communities have developed new vocabularies to describe a range of asexual dispositions. These new vocabularies challenge the traditional definitions and instruments used to measure sexuality, complicating our methodological choices and paradigms of sexual orientation (Cerankowski and Milks 2010; Chasin 2019; Poston and Baumle 2010). By centering asexuality from the outskirts of LGBTQ+ studies, we gain a deeper understanding of how sexual attractions and sexual relationships organize social life.

Asexuality is not only a worthy topic of the sociology of sexualities, as a subfield; it also offers important contributions to sociology as a whole. Asexuality speaks to sociological theories of postmodernism and feminism. It queers dominant norms of love, marriage, gender, and sex. It challenges what it means to be human. Key social institutions and social constructs like medicine, family, gender, race/ethnicity, sexuality, disability, technology, media, religion, education, and the body all interact with asexualities. Each has a stake in whether one experiences sexual attraction. An understanding of asexualities thus advances sociological theories across multiple subfields that pertain to the precarious relationship between social institutions and marginalized populations.

This chapter is divided into four sections designed to answer the question, *what does asexuality offer sociology?* First, an understanding of asexuality helps sociologists adapt to a postmodern, fluid landscape of sexuality. In this section I review new vocabularies of asexualities and their implications for sexual identity. Second, asexuality helps sociologists of sexuality develop theories of consent and sexual boundaries. In this section, I examine the sexual and relationship histories of asexual people, whose experiences can serve as models of communication and violence prevention. Third, asexualities can shine light on how sexuality intersects with gender, race, and class, among other social dimensions.

The demographics of the online asexual community reveal a unique gender composition, and emerging work on race and asexuality offers a new paradigm for understanding white supremacy and racialized sexual subjectivities. Finally, asexuality can also shine light on how boundaries within the LGBTQ community are made and remade as gender and sexual orders change to accommodate relationships and identities beyond the gay/straight and male/female binary.

In each section, I review the existing knowledge on asexualities, much of which originates from the fields of psychology and gender studies, and I supplement this information with characteristics of the online asexual community from the 2020 Asexual Community Survey. In the discussion, I synthesize this information into sociological questions that can push the field forward. My goal is to demonstrate the potential theoretical contributions that research on asexualities can offer to the sociology of sexualities, gender, social movements, and related fields in light of contemporary shifts in the global landscape of sexual identities, spaces, and concepts.

Measuring Asexuality

Asexuality exposes many of the assumptions embedded in our measurement systems for sexual orientation, necessitating new quantitative strategies. Early social science approaches to sexual orientation, such as those developed by Masters and Johnson, tended to conflate asexual and bisexual respondents, and many asexual-spectrum people today have histories of identifying as bisexual/pansexual before they had access to asexual terminology (Storms 1980; Winer et al. 2022). Furthermore, asexual communities regularly differentiate their romantic and sexual attractions (Sennkestra 2020), yet surveys rarely ask about romantic orientation and assume that romantic and sexual orientations will align for respondents. Data indicates that some people on the asexual spectrum may use their romantic orientation as their primary identifier, and some do not see sexual orientation categories as mutually exclusive (Winer et al. 2022). These insights, uncovered by qualitative research on asexual communities, have yet to be broadly adopted by our quantitative systems, a situation that in turn makes generating new knowledge about asexuality challenging.

Conventional instruments of measuring sexuality that rely on identity, attraction, and/or behavior do not translate well to asexualities (Poston and Baumle 2010). Behavioral metrics potentially conflate asexuality (a sexual orientation) and celibacy (a choice) (Cerankowski and Milks 2010; Poston and Baumle 2010), whereas asexual-spectrum respondents' sexual behavior tends to vary (Aicken, Mercer, and Cassell 2013; Van Houdenhove et al. 2015a). Collecting data on asexuality using metrics of identity is also complicated by the fact that few people are familiar with the definition of "asexual" (MacInnis and Hodson 2012). Surveys of random samples that have included asexuality as an option (particularly when identity options are listed in alphabetical order) have led to poor reliability as most populations are unfamiliar with asexual terminology (Mary Hoban, American College Health Association, email to the author, June 19, 2018). Due in part to the potential for error caused by asexuality's place at the outskirts of sexual identity, asexuality is often excluded from surveys or subsumed within the category of "other," further reinforcing its place at the epistemic margins of sociology and creating barriers to empirical analysis (Compton, Meadow, and Schilt 2018).

Popular instruments of sexual attraction are also unreliable as they tend to measure responses to gendered object of desire (Poston and Baumle 2010). For example, the National Survey of Family Growth (NSFG), widely considered to be the most robust and inclusive national survey for measurements of sexuality, asks respondents to decide whether they are (a) only attracted to the opposite sex, (b) mostly attracted to the opposite sex, (c) equally attracted to the opposite sex and the same sex, (d) mostly attracted to the same sex, (e) only attracted to the same sex, or (f) not sure. No option exists for those who are attracted to no one. By excluding the possibility that respondents are not attracted to anyone, surveys like the NSFG fail to account for asexual respondents, as well as others whose attractions are not defined in reference to binary gender systems (Callis 2014; Poston and Baumle 2010).

In this chapter, I use data from the 2020 Asexual Community Survey (ACS), a volunteer-run organization led by members of the asexual community that has gathered survey data annually since 2014 for the purpose of providing information on the asexual community to researchers. The 2020 ACS consisted of about 120 questions that cover respondents' demographics and histories of relationships, sex, health, violence, and community interactions. Convenience sampling and snowballing techniques were utilized by distributing the survey online through major asexual websites and asexuality-themed groups on social networking platforms.

Sample Description

A total of 6,568 respondents between the ages of 18 and 73 were included in the analysis. The mean age was 25.4, indicating a relatively young sample. Respondents included in the analysis indicated their nationality as either the United States (76%), the United Kingdom (15%), or Canada (10%). For consistency, respondents who did not identify within the asexual spectrum, including some who identified as aromantic, were excluded from the present analysis. Insights drawing from aromanticism, as distinct from asexuality, would be valuable to scholars theorizing from the outskirts of identity but were beyond the scope of the present analysis.

The 2020 Asexual Community Survey was distributed online through popular asexual forums. The online asexual community, like all minority community spaces, is governed by a specific set of norms and is likely to be frequented by those who are relatively comfortable with their identity and frame their identity as appearing on the asexual spectrum. As a large, robust sample of the asexual community, this dataset offers a grand and rare opportunity to explore characteristics and complexities of asexual communities.

Postmodern Landscape of Sexuality

Research has shown that younger generations are embracing fluid and complex models of sexuality, developing new vocabularies to include more specific terms that describe their sexual orientations (Robertson 2019; Savin-Williams 2001). The rise of asexualities is part of this pattern. Asexuality has generally referred to those who do not experience sexual attraction, a definition which originated with the Asexual Visibility and Education Network (AVEN) and appears in much of the literature (Brotto et al. 2010; Jones, Hayter, and Jomeen 2017; Van Houdenhove et al. 2015a). Although there are competing definitions of asexuality that refer to individuals' sexual desire or sexual behavior (Aicken, Mercer, and Cassell 2013; Brotto et al. 2010; Prause and Graham 2007), Van Houdenhove and colleagues (2015a) studied the interaction between identity, attraction, and behavior among 566 asexual survey respondents aged 18 to 72 and concluded that "lack of sexual attraction" was the most appropriate and commonly shared definition. AVEN announced in 2021 that they would be changing the definition of asexual on their webpage to refer to those who experience "little to no" sexual attraction, in recognition that asexuality is a spectrum (AVEN Livestreams 2021; Copulsky and Hammack 2021).

Among the 6,568 asexual-spectrum respondents included for analysis in the 2020 Ace Community Survey, the majority (69%) identified themselves as simply "asexual," whereas 12% identified as gray-ace, which generally means they experience sexual attraction rarely or under specific circumstances. Ten percent identified as demisexual, meaning they experience sexual attraction only after an emotional bond has formed (Copulsky and Hammack 2021; Decker 2014). Another 6% of respondents identified on the asexual spectrum but were questioning or unsure of their specific sexual orientation label.

Complex Identity Models

Attitudes toward romance vary significantly among asexual individuals, and the emerging discourse within asexual communities regularly differentiates sexual and romantic attraction (Carrigan 2011; Jones, Hayter, and Jomeen 2017; Sennkestra 2020). The discourse of differentiated attraction, sometimes referred to as the "Split Attraction Model," serves to explain that one can be romantically interested in another person and not desire to have sex with them (Sennkestra 2020). The language emerging within the asexual community regarding differentiated attraction exposes nuance and potential within sociological concepts of identity and attraction that have been under-utilized by the discipline.

Just as sexual attraction falls across a spectrum, romantic attraction also occurs along a spectrum. Many people who experience sexual attraction do not experience romantic attraction (Przybylo 2019). But just as not all aromantic people are asexual, not all asexual people are aromantic. Many asexual-spectrum individuals experience romantic attraction and/or strongly desire romantic relationships in their lives (Brotto et al. 2010; Decker 2014; Van Houdenhove et al. 2015b). When asked if they consider themselves to be on the aromantic spectrum, 41% of 2020 ACS respondents said yes, with another 21% who were questioning or unsure. The remaining 38% of respondents on the asexual spectrum indicated that they did not consider themselves to be on the aromantic spectrum, meaning they experience romantic attraction.

Within the asexual community, the specific terms for asexual individuals' sexual orientations are regularly paired with terms that describe the individual's romantic orientation (Carrigan 2011). This phenomenon is not necessarily limited to asexual individuals. Troia (2018), in her analysis of millennials' sexual identities, found that multi-term identities, non-binary identities, and "asterisk identities" were common patterns among young respondents situated within a postmodern era of sexual fluidity. In other words, millennials would qualify the subjective meanings of their identity labels to communicate a more specific understanding of their sexuality. Consistent with Troia's argument, most asexual-spectrum respondents of the 2020 ACS (56%) identified with multiple romantic orientations, and 23% were questioning their romantic orientation. The most common romantic orientation among asexual-spectrum respondents were biromantic or panromantic (34%), followed by aromantic (29%), grayromantic or demiromantic (28%), heteroromantic (19%), and homoromantic (8%). Only 5% of 2020 ACS respondents said that they preferred not to use a/romantic terminology—a segment of the asexual-spectrum population who needs more representation in research. By using multi-term identities that describe both sexual and romantic attractions, many social actors in asexual communities are constructing themselves as straddling multiple categories that are not captured by our current sociological concepts of "sexual orientation" (Chasin 2019). Centering asexual dispositions and their use of differentiated attraction can therefore contribute greater nuance and deeper understandings of sexual and romantic identities within sociology.

Sexual Desire and Activity

Compulsory sexuality (i.e., the idea that all human beings are sexual) represents a marginalizing social force for asexual people (Gupta 2015;

Przybylo 2019). The nuances with which asexual individuals navigate compulsory sexuality offers sociologists insights into the meaning-making processes underlying specific sexual practices. For example, people who identify as asexual appear in many places along the continuum of experiencing sexual desire (i.e., libido), which suggests meaning systems that disaggregate sexual desire and sexual attraction (Bogaert 2004; Brotto et al. 2010). The 2020 ACS survey asked respondents to rate their sex drive/libido on a scale of 0 ("nonexistent") to 4 ("very strong"). About one-fifth of respondents (19%) rated their sex drive as "0," 39% rated their sex drive as "1," 26% rated their sex drive as "2," 12% said "3," and 4% said "4." In other words, there was considerable variety in the self-ratings of asexual-spectrum respondents' libidos, with the average being about 1.41. ACS respondents who identified as demisexual, gray-ace, or questioning were more likely to report slightly higher sex drives than those who identified only as asexual (see also Copulsky and Hammack 2021).

Sexual activity also varied among asexual-spectrum respondents. Thirty-six percent of 2020 ACS respondents on the asexual spectrum reported that they have had consensual sex in their lifetime, and 22% reported that they had consensual sex in the past year. When asked about their relationship to kink, BDSM, or fetish practices, whether sexual or non-sexual, 17% said they had participated and want to have more of such experiences, and another 13% said that they did not have experience with kink, BDSM, or fetish activities but were interested in participating.

Intimate relationships and constructions of family among asexual people is one area that is particularly understudied in sociology, with many questions remaining. For example, how do asexual individuals negotiate physical and emotional boundaries with their allosexual (i.e., non-asexual) partners? How does the concept of "chosen family" map onto queerplatonic relationships (i.e., intimate relationships that queer norms of friendship and romance) within asexual communities (Chasin 2015; Sennkestra 2019)? What meanings do asexual individuals assign to masturbation, pornography, and sexual fantasies? Do they construct these activities as sexual, and under what circumstances do they view them as compatible with their identity status? How does compulsory sexuality facilitate sexual violence, and what models of consent help asexual individuals resist? Each of these research questions inform sociological understandings of how the meanings assigned to family, relationships, sex, and identity have changed within a postmodern landscape, thus creating a dialogue between asexualities and key questions within sociology.

Intersections

The data also shows that asexualities intersect with race, class, and gender in meaningful ways. Research regarding gender and asexualities, for example, has consistently found that cisgender women make up a large portion of asexual communities online, and that the asexual community includes a disproportionately high number of people under the transgender umbrella. The gender composition of asexual communities has become a subject of curiosity and exploration for some scholars. Chasin (2011) speculated that gender diversity in asexuality communities could be the result of freedom from gendered performances that are tied to attracting a sexual partner, but Cuthbert (2019) makes a less liberatory argument, finding that agender, asexual people felt a strong disconnection and alienation from gender, especially those who were assigned female at birth and were distressed by the sexualization of their bodies. The intersection of masculinity and compulsory sexuality has also been a growing area of scholarship. In interviews with three asexual men, Przybylo (2014) highlights specific discourses of sexuality that asexual men adopt to make sense of their gendered subjectivities and society's expectations of sexual aggression from men. Gupta (2019) argues that hegemonic masculinity is in conflict with asexuality for white, middle-class men, whereas some asexual women found social acceptance by blending in with gendered expectations of sexual disinterest. Vares's (2018, 2019) study of asexual people's dating experiences similarly found that asexual men were unintelligible to others due to conflicting meanings of masculinity and asexuality, whereas asexual women's dating experiences were structured by stereotypes of sexual passivity and feelings of guilt for "leading" men on. Given the close relationship between the social construction of gender and sexuality, interrogating how gender is performed within asexual frameworks can expand major theories of social inequality and is sure to be an area of growth in future sociological studies.

Questions of race and class remain especially understudied in asexualities research. The empirical data indicates that most members of the online asexual community are well-educated and do not identify as racial or ethnic minorities. Scholarship on the intersections of race and asexuality has been emerging in recent years, highlighting how compulsory sexuality and racism are co-constituted. For example, Owen (2014, 2018) has written about the asexual Mammy and the hypersexual Jezebel as tools of oppression that deny Black women's sexual agency in service of white supremacy. Smith (2020) advocates for a Black Ace politic that rejects capitalist commodification of Black bodies, and Miles (2019) theorizes a Conscious Black Asexual politic that recognizes intersections of race and sexuality and interrogates racialized sexual scripts. Thematic in this body of literature is the erasure of Black asexuality from mainstream asexual spaces and the restoration of sexual agency to Black folks. Kenney (2020) has also written about how asexuality can expand our thinking of the platonic relationalities that structure Filipinx diasporic communities, building on sociological research about Filipinx fictive kin (Ocampo 2016; Parreñas 2001) and theorizing how compulsory sexuality is intertwined with colonialism.

Finally, research on the points of connection and disruption between asexuality and the larger LGBTQ+ community allows sociologists to trace changes in the culture, boundaries, and identity discourses of postmodern sexualities. Prior research describes isolation and rejection that asexual individuals have encountered from within the LGBTQ+ community (Mollet and Lackman 2018). The 2020 ACS data indicates that 73% of asexual-spectrum respondents have participated in either online or offline LGBTQ+ communities. However, 59% report having some negative experience in online LGBTQ+ community spaces, and 38% report having some negative experience in offline LGBTQ+ spaces. More research is needed to examine why—or in what contexts—some individuals on the asexual spectrum encounter symbolic boundaries in LGBTQ+ spaces. In what circumstances have asexual individuals found understanding and acceptance versus exclusion in LGBTQ+ spaces? Do shared experiences of institutional and cultural exclusion in the form of medicalization, rejection, and harassment create opportunities for cohesion between asexual individuals and the larger LGBTQ+ community (see Bernstein, this collection)? Or are boundaries being drawn within

LGBTQ+ spaces that exclude experiences unique to asexual-spectrum individuals? Our measurement instruments of sexuality create major inhibitions to answer these questions, so how do we adjust our methodologies to capture more complex combinations of romantic and sexual identities?

Learning from Asexualities

Generational changes in sexuality and new technologies have allowed asexualities to flourish and become more visible. Complex discourses of sex, romance, gender, and family have emerged, undermining binary and essentialist ideals in favor of a more fluid reality. As sociologists, an increased awareness and understanding of asexualities helps us adapt to this new landscape and push the field forward in new theoretical directions.

As a liminal sexual orientation on the outskirts of LGBTQ studies, asexuality presents sociologists with a unique lens through which they can examine the relationship between sexual attraction, sexual desire, sexual practices, and dominant institutions and social constructs like medicine, family, gender, race/ethnicity, the body, technology, and community. Its emergence as a sexual orientation category was enabled by the postmodernist decoupling of love, marriage, sex, and romance, as well as access to new technologies and generational shifts in discourses of sexuality. Asexual people represent a heterogenous population with diverse romantic and sexual dispositions, yet shared experiences within the asexual community of medicalization and isolation resonate with existing patterns of marginalization for those who exist outside the charmed circle of heterosexuality (Rubin 1998). Moving asexuality from the outskirts of sociology to the center—without losing sight of the emphasis on pleasure, in all its forms—can encourage sociologists to explore more inclusive models of intimacies and challenge the boundaries between the "sexual" and "non-sexual" (Jones 2019).

REFERENCES

Aicken, Catherine R. H., Catherine H. Mercer, and Jackie A. Cassell. 2013. "Who Reports Absence of Sexual Attraction in Britain? Evidence from National Probability Surveys." *Psychology & Sexuality* 4: 121–35. doi:10.1080/19419899.2013.774161.

AVEN Livestreams. 2021. "Updating the Definition on the AVEN Homepage." You-Tube. https://youtu.be/EouWUIU5FnM.

Bauer, Caroline, Tristan Miller, Mary Ginoza, Yue Guo, Kristin Youngblom, Ai Baba, Phil Penten, Max Meinhold, Varshini Ramaraj, Theresa Trieu, Jacci Ziebert, and Mel Adroit. 2018. "The 2016 Asexual Community Survey Summary Report." The Asexual Community Survey Team. https://asexualcensus.files.wordpress.com.

Bogaert, Anthony F. 2004. "Asexuality: Prevalence and Associated Factors in a National Probability Sample." *Journal of Sex Research* 41 (3): 279–87. doi:10.1080/00224490409552235.

Brotto, Lori A., Gail Knudson, Jess Inskip, Katherine Rhodes, and Yvonne Erskine. 2010. "Asexuality: A Mixed-Methods Approach." *Archives of Sexual Behavior* 39: 599–618. doi:10.1007/s10508-008-9434-x.

Callis, April Scarlette. 2014. "Bisexual, Pansexual, Queer: Non-Binary Identities and the Sexual Borderlands." *Sexualities* 17 (1–2): 63–80. doi:10.1177/1363460713511094.

Carrigan, Mark. 2011. "There's More to Life than Sex? Difference and Commonality within the Asexual Community." *Sexualities* 14 (4): 462–78. doi:10.1177/1363460711406462.

Carroll, Megan. 2020. "Asexuality and Its Implications for LGBTQ-Parent Families." In *LGBTQ-Parent Families: Innovations in Research and Implications for Practice*, second edition, edited by Abbie E. Goldberg and Katherine R. Allen, 185–98. New York: Springer.

Cerankowski, Karli June and Megan Milks. 2010. "New Orientations: Asexuality and Its Implications for Theory and Practice." *Feminist Studies* 36 (3): 650–64.

Chasin, C. J. DeLuzio. 2011. "Theoretical Issues in the Study of Asexuality." *Archives of Sexual Behavior* 40 (4): 713–23. doi:10.1007/s10508-011-9757-x.

Chasin, C. J. 2015. "Making Sense in and of the Asexual Community: Navigating Relationships and Identities in a Context of Resistance." *Journal of Community & Applied Social Psychology* 25: 167–80. doi:10.1002/casp.2203.

Chasin, C. J. 2019. "Asexuality and the Re/Construction of Sexual Orientation." In *Expanding the Rainbow: Exploring the Relationships of Bi+, Polyamorous, Kinky, Ace, Intersex, and Trans People*, edited by Brandy L. Simula, J. E. Sumerau, and Andrea Miller, 209–220. Leiden, The Netherlands: Brill | Sense.

Compton, D'Lane R., Tey Meadow, and Kristen Schilt. 2018. "Introduction: Queer Work in a Straight Discipline." In *Other, Please Specify: Queer Methods in Sociology*, edited by D'Lane R. Compton, Tey Meadow, and Kristen Schilt, 1–34. Oakland: University of California Press.

Copulsky, Daniel and Phillip L. Hammack. 2021. "Asexuality, Graysexuality, and Demisexuality: Distinctions in Desire, Behavior, and Identity." *Journal of Sex Research* (Online First). doi:10.1080/00224499.2021.2012113.

Cuthbert, Karen. 2017. "You Have to Be Normal to Be Abnormal: An Empirically Grounded Exploration of the Intersection of Asexuality and Disability." *Sociology* 51 (2): 241–57. doi:10.1177/0038038515587639.

Cuthbert, Karen. 2019. "'When We Talk about Gender We Talk about Sex': (A)Sexuality and (A)Gendered Subjectivities." *Gender & Society* 33 (6): 841–64. https://doi.org/10.1177/0891243219867916.

Dawson, Matt, Susie Scott, and Liz McDonnell. 2018. "'Asexual' Isn't Who I Am': The Politics of Asexuality." *Sociological Research Online* 23: 374–91. doi:10.1177/1360780418757540.

Decker, Julie Sondra. 2014. *The Invisible Orientation: An Introduction to Asexuality.* New York: Skyhorse Publishing.

Gazzola, Stephanie B., and Melanie A. Morrison. 2012. "Asexuality: An Emergent Sexual Orientation." In *Sexual Minority Research in the New Millennium*, edited by Todd G. Morrison, Melanie A. Morrison, Mark A. Carrigan, and Daragh T. McDermott, 21–44. New York: Nova Science Publishers.

Gupta, Kristina. 2015. "Compulsory Sexuality: Evaluating an Emerging Concept." *Signs: Journal of Women in Culture and Society* 41 (1): 131–54. doi:10.1086/681774.

Gupta, Kristina. 2019. "Gendering Asexuality and Asexualizing Gender: A Qualitative Study Exploring the Intersections between Gender and Asexuality." *Sexualities* 22 (7–8): 1197–1216. doi:10.1177/1363460718790890.

Jones, Angela. 2019. "Sex Is Not a Problem: The Erasure of Pleasure in Sexual Science Research." *Sexualities* 22 (4): 643–68.

Jones, Catriona, Mark Hayter, and Julie Jomeen. 2017. "Understanding Asexual Identity as a Means to Facilitate Culturally Competent Care: A Systematic Literature Review." *Journal of Clinical Nursing* 26 (23–24): 3811–3831. doi:10.1111/jocn.13862.

Kenney, Theresa N. 2020. "Thinking Asexually: Sapin-Sapin, Asexual Assemblages, and the Queer Possibilities of Platonic Relationalities." *Feminist Formations* 32 (3): 1–23. doi:10.1353/ff.2020.0038.

MacInnis, Cara C. and Gordon Hodson. 2012. "Intergroup Bias toward 'Group X': Evidence of Prejudice, Dehumanization, Avoidance, and Discrimination against Asexuals." *Group Processes & Intergroup Relations* 15 (6): 725–43. doi:10.1177/1368430212442419.

Miles, Brittney. 2019. "Theorizing Conscious Black Asexuality through Claire Kann's *Let's Talk about Love*." *Humanities* 8 (4): 165. https://doi.org/10.3390/h8040165

Mollet, Amanda L. and Brian R. Lackman. 2018. "Asexual Borderlands: Asexual Collegians' Reflections on Inclusion under the LGBTQ Umbrella." *Journal of College Student Development* 59 (5): 623–28. doi:10.1353/csd.2018.0058.

Ocampo, Anthony Christian. 2016. *The Latinos of Asia: How Filipino Americans Break the Rules of Race*. Stanford, CA: Stanford University Press.

Owen, Ianna Hawkins. 2014. "On the Racialization of Asexuality." In *Asexualities: Feminist and Queer Perspectives*, edited by Karli June Cerankowski and Megan Milks, 119–135. New York: Routledge.

Owen, Ianna Hawkins. 2018. "Still, Nothing: Mammy and Black Asexual Possibility." *Feminist Review* 120: 70–84. doi:10.1057/s41305-018-0140-9.

Parreñas, Rhacel Salazar. 2001. *Servants of Globalization: Women, Migration and Domestic Work*. Stanford, CA: Stanford University Press.

Poston, Dudley L. and Amanda K. Baumle. 2010. "Patterns of Asexuality in the United States." *Demographic Research* 23: 509–530. doi:10.4054/DemRes.2010.23.18.

Prause, Nicole, and Cynthia A. Graham. 2007. "Asexuality: Classification and Characterization." *Archives of Sexual Behavior* 36: 341–56. doi:10.1007/s10508-006-9142-3.

Przybylo, Ela. 2011. "Crisis and Safety: The Asexual in Sexusociety." *Sexualities* 14 (4): 444–61. doi:10.1177/1363460711406461.

Przybylo, Ela. 2014. "Masculine Doubt and Sexual Wonder: Asexually-Identified Men Talk about Their (A)Sexualities." In *Asexualities: Feminist and Queer Perspectives*, edited by Karli June Cerankowski and Megan Milks, 225–47. New York: Routledge.

Przybylo, Ela. 2019. *Asexual Erotics: Intimate Readings of Compulsory Sexuality*. Columbus: The Ohio State University Press.

Robertson, Mary. 2019. *Growing Up Queer: Kids and the Remaking of LGBTQ Identity*. New York: New York University Press.

Rubin, Gayle. 1998. "Thinking Sex: Notes for a Radical Theory of the Politics of Sexuality." In *Social Perspectives in Lesbian and Gay Studies: A Reader*, edited by Peter M. Nardi and Beth E. Schneider, 100–133. New York: Routledge.

Savin-Williams, Ritch C. 2001. "A Critique of Research on Sexual-Minority Youths." *Journal of Adolescence* 24 (1): 5–13. doi:10.1006/jado.2000.0369.

Scherrer, Kristin S. 2008. "Coming to an Asexual Identity: Negotiating Identity, Negotiating Desire." *Sexualities* 11 (5): 621–41. doi:10.1177/1363460708094269.

Scherrer, Kristin S. 2010a. "What Asexuality Contributes to the Same-Sex Marriage Discussion." *Journal of Gay and Lesbian Social Services* 22 (1–2): 56–73. doi:10.1080/10538720903332255.

Scherrer, Kristin S. 2010b. "Asexual Relationships: What Does Asexuality Have to Do with Polyamory?" In *Understanding Non-Monogamies*, edited by Meg Barker and Darren Langdridge, 154–59. London, England: Routledge.

Scherrer, Kristin S. and Carla A. Pfeffer. 2017. "None of the Above: Toward Identity and Community-Based Understandings of (A)Sexualities." *Archives of Sexual Behavior* 46 (3): 643–46. https://doi.org/10.1007/s10508-016-0900-6.

Sennkestra. 2020. "Differentiating Attraction/Orientations (Or, the 'Split Attraction Model' by Any Other Name Is So Much Sweeter)." Blog Post. Next Step: Cake. https://nextstepcake.wordpress.com.

Simula, Brandy L., J. E. Sumerau, and Andrea Miller, eds. 2019. *Expanding the Rainbow: Exploring the Relationships of Bi+, Polyamorous, Kinky, Ace, Intersex, and Trans People*. Leiden, The Netherlands: Brill | Sense.

Smith, Justin. 2020. "'[T]he Happiest, Well-Feddest Wolf in Harlem': Asexuality as Resistance to Social Reproduction in Claude McKay's *Home to Harlem*." *Feminist Formations* 32 (3): 51–74. doi:10.1353/ff.2020.0040.

Storms, Michael D. 1980. "Theories of Sexual Orientation." *Journal of Personality and Social Psychology* 38: 783–92.

Sumerau, J. E., Harry Barbee, Lain A. B. Mathers, and Victoria Eaton. 2018. "Exploring the Experiences of Heterosexual and Asexual Transgender People." *Social Sciences* 7: 162–78. doi:10.3390/socsci7090162.

Troia, Bailey. 2018. "'You're the One That Put Me in a Box': Integration, Cultural Con-straints, and Fluid LGBTQ+ Millennial Identities." In *113th Annual Meeting of the American Sociological Association*. Philadelphia, PA.

Van Houdenhove, Ellen, Luk Gijs, Guy T'Sjoen, and Paul Enzlin. 2015a. "Asexuality: A Multidimensional Approach." *Journal of Sex Research* 52 (6): 669–78. doi:10.1080/0 0224499.2014.898015.

Van Houdenhove, Ellen, Luk Gijs, Guy T'Sjoen, and Paul Enzlin. 2015b. "Stories about Asexuality: A Qualitative Study on Asexual Women." *Journal of Sex & Marital Therapy* 41: 262–81. https://doi.org/10.1080/0092623X.2014.889053.

Vares, Tiina. 2018. "'My [Asexuality] Is Playing Hell with My Dating Life': Roman-tic Identified Asexuals Negotiate the Dating Game." *Sexualities* 21 (4): 520–36. doi:10.1177/1363460717716400.

Vares, Tiina. 2019. "Asexualities, Intimacies, and Relationality." In *Expanding the Rainbow: Exploring the Relationships of Bi+, Polyamorous, Kinky, Ace, Intersex, and Trans People*, edited by Brandy L. Simula, J. E. Sumerau, and Andrea Miller, 189–98. Leiden, The Netherlands: Brill | Sense.

Winer, Canton, Megan Carroll, Yuchen Yang, Katherine Linder, and Brittney Miles. 2022. "'I Didn't Know Ace Was a Thing': Bisexuality and Pansexuality as Identity Pathways in Asexual Identity Formation." *Sexualities* (Online First). doi:10.1177/13634607221085485.

Yang, Yuchen. 2021. "Gender Uncoupled: Asexual People Making Sense of High School Sex Talk." *Sexualities* (Online First). doi:10.1177/13634607211033865.

PART V

Centering the Disciplinary Outskirts

13

"All the Way in the Back of the Room"

Being/Studying Bisexual(ity) in Sociology

LAIN A. B. MATHERS AND J. E. SUMERAU

I (Lain) was a second-year graduate student the first time a fellow sociologist explained to me that bisexuality did not exist. As someone who identified as bisexual and had already become experienced in the marginalization of bi people in gay and straight monosexual spaces, this was not an unusual experience.[1] What was interesting, however, was that this was the first time I encountered this biphobic trope from a fellow sociologist and self-identified queer scholar. It would not be the last. Rather, the years since have consistently brought me into contact with many sociologists who, regardless of their intentions or awareness, believe and espouse this and other types of monosexism[2] in their personal and professional endeavors. In each case, I am reminded of my grandfather, J's birth father, and other gay/lesbian elders who were once told they did not exist in the worldviews of many heterosexuals the same way—and often with the same phrases—as I apparently do not exist in the worldview of many lesbian, gay, and straight (LGS) monosexuals.

When Lain called me (J) following the interaction above to express their frustration and otherwise process the experience, I found myself occupying two distinct yet interrelated spaces at once. As a mentor and friend for Lain and other bi and trans people seeking to navigate contemporary sociology, I sought to listen to their experiences, comfort them as best I could, and provide whatever encouragement possible to aid their ongoing navigation of the monosexism within and beyond sociology. As a fellow bi+ person and scholar myself, however, I also flashed back to my own experiences with monosexual researchers unwilling or unable to step outside their own binary sexual norms enough to recognize or understand bi+ existence in the discipline or world.[3] I recalled my own phone calls to bi+ mentors following similar incidents until I got used to this aspect of normative sociological and sociology of sexualities cultures. As one of my mentors put it when I began graduate study,[4] "You can pretend to be just gay and find community, or you can pretend to be straight and be treated better overall, but to my knowledge, there still isn't any room for bi people in the sociological imagination."

These experiences with monosexism are prevalent in our personal and professional lives. As bi+ people who study bi+ issues we routinely navigate obstacles, not unlike the bi+ people we interview, in arguing that bi+ experience is valid and important to sociological understandings of sexuality. Below, we will expand on some of these issues while also providing examples of how these patterns show up in our research through the words of our respondents. In so doing, we argue that, as was the case when sociology lacked systematic study of gay/lesbian experience,[5] our conceptualizations of sexualities are fundamentally flawed and incomplete without systematic attention to bi+ experience and the operations of monosexism in society.[6]

Monosexism in Research and the Discipline

When we decided to contribute to this book, we both felt a pang of excitement paralleled by anxiety and discomfort. As people who have navigated monosexism in multiple settings, both personally and in our work as sociologists, we were skeptical that the field would welcome an analysis rooted both in our lived experiences as bi+ people as well as our research findings on bi+ issues. Before agreeing to contribute, we had a conversation where we discussed our uncertainties about contributing the chapter. Namely, we recalled the myriad instances of sociologists, even those studying sexualities, suggesting that a bi+ perspective might be deemed "too queer" or "too radical" for a sociology of sexualities volume at present.[7] While such arguments vary from implicit (e.g., not publishing work on bi+ experience because it is deemed "niche" or not offering a significant enough contribution to the field) or explicit (like Lain's colleague mentioned above), we both have numerous experiences of running up against the wall of monosexism in our work. Such experiences represent a pattern within sociology: the minimization of research that emphasizes bi+ experience, critiques monosexism, or otherwise focuses on sexualities outside of LGS experience. Considering that bi+ people comprise the largest sexual minority group in the US (Gates 2011), sociology's current inability to speak to the complexity of bi+ existence is a significant shortcoming of our discipline. Were sexualities research to exist proportionally to how many bi+ people are estimated to exist in the US and beyond, studies like ours would be the majority, not the minority of research about sexual minorities in sociology. The dearth of such research is significant. As we discuss here, a shift toward bisexualities as a primary focus of sexualities scholarship could lead to deeper and more complex understandings of not only bi+ experience, but also the way we understand sexualities, power, and inequality more broadly.

The irony of this, as J's research below will reveal, is that contemporary sociologists sound like non-sociologist monosexual people who minimize and demean the existence of bi+ people in our social world. Were social groups, political organizations, and community spaces to exist in proportion to those they serve, bi+ organizations would far outnumber those for lesbian and gay people. Furthermore, as bi+ sociologists, we expressed a shared skepticism of broader monosexist patterns as the bi+ respondent's in Lain's research when they discuss their frustration with monosexual people. Like our respondents, we must navigate monosexism in the form of LGS others minimizing the relevancy and contributions of bi+ people to the world.

The minimization of bi+ experience is connected to another broader pattern of monosexism, both within and beyond sociology: bi+ erasure. If one were to conduct a cursory search of the literature, they would be hard pressed to find more than a handful of contemporary studies focusing on bi+ people and experiences. As I (Lain) considered how to develop this chapter, I was in the thick of working on my dissertation, which focused on the ways bi+ people make sense of identity, community, and social change in the years after same-sex marriage legalization in the US. I initially became interested in this topic because I am a bisexual person and I noticed that on my reading list for my preliminary exams in sexualities, there was only one book chapter about bisexualities, and it was published in the 1990s. I thought to myself, "there must be more sociological literature out there on bi+ experiences." I quickly learned, however, that this was not the case. Sociologists, like others in the social sciences (Monro et al. 2017), have paid little attention to bisexualities and monosexism to date.[8] When bisexuality does come up in sociological research, it is frequently in the context of an obligatory explanation of the LGBTQ acronym without significant attention to bi+ experiences specifically. In the wake of being both surprised (and not at all surprised at the same time) by this glaring omission in the sociological literature, the foundation of my dissertation was laid, and I began to explore literatures from other fields to supplement my analysis.

Again, our experiences as bi+ sociologists doing bi+ work mirrored those of our respondents. As I (Lain) discuss elsewhere (Mathers 2019), bi+ people are hungry for representation of themselves in media and popular culture. This hunger emerges from a desire to understand their experiences, which don't fit neatly into either/or hetero/homosexual frameworks. Similarly, we as bi+ researchers are at a disadvantage when doing our sociological work. There are countless studies that analyze the experiences of lesbian, gay, and heterosexual people in families (Garcia 2012; Lareau 2003), religion (Avishai 2008; Yip 1997), relationships (Buggs 2019; Wolkomir 2009), the workplace (Martin 2005; Prokos and Padavic 2002), medical institutions (Link and Phelan 1995; Quadagno 2005), and more. Thus, those scholars who focus on monosexual people in their work start with a significant advantage, namely that their research is deemed "acceptable" by those who will evaluate it for publication, for funding, for presentation at professional meetings, on the job market, and in other professional settings. In this way, sociology as a field is reflective of the world in which it exists; bi+ research is deemed unimportant and irrelevant, and thus monosexist boundaries around what counts as legitimate research into sexual inequalities are maintained (just like monosexist boundaries are maintained around what counts as a "real" type of sexuality).

In this chapter, this type of illustration—that contemporary sociology adheres to similar monosexist understandings of the world as those outside of our field—is our goal. Although the paragraphs above only offer a few examples from our sociological careers, they also illustrate societal patterns of monosexism active and constant within and beyond sociology and the sociological study of sexualities.[9] As such, here we utilize our own experiences navigating sociology as openly bi people alongside two separate research studies to demonstrate the importance of interrogating monosexism in society and incorporating bi+ experiences into the sociology of sexualities. In the first case, we draw on forty interviews Lain conducted with bi+ people to illustrate how they experience monosexism in society. Then, we draw on thirty interviews J conducted with monosexual people (lesbian, gay, and straight) to illustrate how monosexual people frame bisexuality in ways that facilitate monosexism in society. In the discussion of our data analyses, we extend our critiques to highlight what can be gained from centering bi+ experience in future sociological study, and a few suggestions of how future scholars could begin this work.

Bi+ Experiences and the Monosexual Imaginary

As I (Lain) note above, my dissertation grew out of a noticeable lack of bi+ representation in the sociological literature. For my research, I conducted interviews with forty bi+ people in the Chicago area to gain a better understanding of how they encounter, identify, and navigate monosexism. Research from public health, demography, and psychology suggests that not only are bi+ people the largest sexual minority population in the US (Gates 2011), but also that they experience inequality differently, and sometimes more severely, than LGS people (Badgett et al. 2013; Gorman et al. 2015). Considering this information, I saw an important opportunity to dig deeper into the ways bi+ people make sense of their place in the social world. To this end, I wanted to understand how self-identified bi+ people made sense of their experiences and (in)visibility in contemporary US social-sexual relations.

While my dissertation focuses on the topics of identity, community, and politics, the overarching themes in my work point to the ways in which, currently, much conversation among bi+ people ultimately comes back to dynamics of visibility and erasure. To highlight the broader implications of the erasure bi+ people experience, I developed the term *the monosexual imaginary* (Mathers 2019). The monosexual imaginary refers to existing social scripts and meanings that eradicate the possibility of bi+ existence and, in so doing, render both bi+ people and monosexist inequalities unintelligible. Furthermore, the monosexual imaginary obfuscates the ways in which monosexism is deeply tied to, and underpins, other forms of sexual and broader inequalities.

Drawing on Ingraham's (1994) formulation of a heterosexual imaginary, this understanding of bi+ life demonstrates the ways in which our understanding of sexualities and inequality are profoundly lacking without more attention to bi+ people and monosexism as a social structure.

In this chapter, I want to move away from my specific dissertation findings and highlight some of the key ways respondents talked about visibility, and how such conversations mirror what we, as bi+ scholars, communicate to our peers in sociology. Specifically, respondents highlighted the ways they felt left behind, secondary, and unimportant in comparison to other LGBTQ concerns. For instance, one twenty-one-year-old white bisexual queer cisgender man noted:

> And I feel the same is true for activism where bisexuality is kind of ignored. Or, it's there, but it's there in an acronym kind of way, where it's like you're the audience, you're in the group but the people who are the center stage are mostly the gay groups, and again, mostly it's the most privileged gay men. And then everyone else takes a back row. And I feel like bisexuals are like all the way in the back of the room.

Echoing the pattern in sociological literature to date (see Sumerau, Mathers, Moon 2019 for review), this interviewee highlights the fact that bi+ issues and concerns are often placed on a backburner in comparison to lesbian and gay issues. As Stone (2009) noted in relation to transgender politics, respondents like this point out that only adding a letter does nothing to bring forth any concrete community or recognition (see also Sumerau and Mathers 2019). Some respondents, like the twenty-five-year-old white queer transgender woman quoted next, specifically illustrated this pattern: "I'm just thinking about like how a lot of people morbidly joke about how LGBT is really just the L and the G and then like the B and the T get left behind." As we note above, this is a fair summary of sociological literature on sex, gender, and sexualities today as well.

Quotes like these are pervasive in my interviews. Bi+ respondents were keenly aware of the ways they were considered less important, and sometimes nonexistent in broader conversations about sexuality within and beyond their immediate networks. Often, they talked about experiencing pushback when they tried to center bi+ issues in conversations within their networks. For example, a twenty-six-year-old white bisexual queer cisgender man noted:

> Where I'll see it [bi erasure] most often now is more and more studies coming out about how bi people—one, there's more of them in the LGBT community than is given credit for, two, bi people are less likely to be out, and have higher rates of anxiety and depression and mental issues and in general it seems to be now more and more the case that it's a more difficult space to occupy, and people struggle with it more (*L: bisexuality?*) Yep . . . as a result of that, there's been a bit of a push lately sort of within the queer community to address issues of biphobia and bi erasure within the community. And it's in response to *that* that I've see the most gross pushback . . . so yeah, it's usually you see it in response to calls for increased awareness and increased visibility. (*emphasis original*)

A twenty-eight-year-old multiracial queer fluid cisgender woman further echoes these points when she explains an important component of visibility: "I think just to see that you don't have to be boxed into certain categories, too, that you can be queer or bi and be secure in that. Um, but then I think, too, the awareness for people who are not bi or queer [is important], including the gay community." Like these respondents, scholars like J and myself have encountered pushback, denial, and other forms of monosexist erasure when we try to raise similar questions, or center bi+ experiences, in conversations with other sociologists, including those who focus on sexualities. Such experiences mirror the respondents above who encounter monosexism in LG and/or LGS spaces. Such a connection between the lives of respondents and the current state of sociological work in sexualities illustrates the monosexual imaginary at work: we bi+ people, those of us within and beyond the academy, are rarely given the space to interrogate and challenge monosexism when we see it. Instead, such conversations are pushed to the side, seen as minimally relevant to the field or broader issues of sexual politics. These dynamics persist while studies that *could* highlight the relevance and importance of monosexism (but ultimately fail to do so) garner significant attention, praise, and awards within and beyond sociology even if they are used against LGBTQ people outside the academy (see, Silva 2018, Ward 2015 for examples; and see Sumerau and Mathers 2019; Sumerau, Mathers, and Moon 2019 for discussions of such work).

The fact that sociologists are (mostly) unwilling to engage in serious conversations about monosexism to date is startling when we consider the fact that bi+ people, based on the best information available to us, experience different and sometimes worse forms of inequality than LG people. This lack of sociological engagement is also significant given that bi+ people are more likely to be people of color (Movement Advancement Project 2016). Women of color, Black women in particular, are the main force behind increased numbers or people identifying as bi+ and LGBT overall (Compton and Bridges 2019). Bi+ people, like LGBTQ people more broadly in the US, are more likely to live in the Southeast, commonly referred to as the Bible Belt, yet no studies focus *specifically* on how religion and monosexism may be intertwined in the experiences of southern bi+ people.[10] Additionally, little research exists on the specificity of bi+ experiences in rural areas, or the ways in which bi+ people form community beyond major LGBTQ+ centers. As others in this book note, attending to physical space and place is a critical component of sexualities scholarship (Abelson's, Compton's, Mattson's, Ota's, and Stone's contributions to this collection); this is true for the study of bisexualities as well.

At the same time, transgender people, particularly women, are more likely to identify as bi+ than other groups (Movement Advancement Project 2017), and yet very few works look at the experiences of bi+ transgender people and the overlap between cissexism and monosexism (but see, Ghabrial 2019; Sumerau 2019; Sumerau and Mathers 2019; Sumerau, Mathers, and Lampe 2019; Sumerau, Mathers, and Moon 2019).[11] Thus, when scholars look at me and say, without hesitation, that questions about monosexism aren't important to sociologists, or are too niche or minimal to warrant larger conversations in the field, I can't help but wonder if they recognize that they are part of the very same patterns my respondents detail when they discuss bi+ erasure. I also wonder if this response—a desire to avoid facing the existence of bi+ people in society—is part of the lesser representation of southern cultures (Stone 2018), trans people and especially trans women (Sumerau and Mathers 2019), people of color (Buggs 2017), and religion (Avishai,

Jafar, and Rinaldo 2015) in existing sex, gender, and sexualities journals and sociology literatures more broadly.

In fact, the unwillingness of sociologists to at least consider how monosexism may influence one's experience with heterosexism, racism, cissexism, classism, patriarchy, religio-normativity, and other structures of inequality, is reflective of the same patterns where men, white people, cisgender people, and middle- and upper-class people in sociology perceived their experiences to be normal, worthy of examination, and the "proper object" (Butler 1994) of sociological analysis (for critiques of these historical patterns in sociology, see Collins 2000; Rich 1980; Smith 1987; Sumerau and Cragun 2018; Sumerau and Grollman 2018; Sumerau and Mathers 2019). Put simply, as one twenty-six-year-old Latinx bisexual queer cisgender woman said:

> I guess to me it [bi visibility] would look like support and understanding and inclusion. Not just centering monosexuality constantly and valuing monosexuality above all. That's kind of how it feels now. It would be pervasive in a way . . . Meaning it would touch a lot of people's lives. I guess that would mean acceptance. I don't like that word, acceptance, this expectation of assimilating. I think it's just like acknowledging people for who they are and supporting that and not being shitty about it.

Here, we argue that if sociology wants to push past a monosexual imaginary, we can do it; we can rethink the "proper object" (Butler 1994) of sexualities research. However, it will need to involve, like the respondent above suggests, recognizing the ways that monosexism is important to understand the lives of bi+ people and the shape of sexual politics and inequalities throughout our contemporary social world and sociology itself (Sumerau, Mathers, Moon 2019). It will also require, as we note in the next section, taking seriously the ways LGS monosexuals create and enforce monosexism through their interpretations of sexual fluidity in society.

Monosexualizing Reality

When Lain asked me to work on this chapter with them, I (J) was completing data collection on an interview project seeking to understand how monogamous monosexual people constructed bi+ and poly others. This project arose when some sociologists responded to earlier work of mine on the ways heterosexual people denigrated bisexualities and polyamory (Mathers, Sumerau, and Cragun 2018; Sumerau and Cragun 2018; Sumerau, Grollman, and Cragun 2018) by vehemently arguing that such findings only applied to heterosexual people. In short, these sociologists claimed that a focus on mononormativity was not sociological.[12] Especially having personally experienced similar behavior patterns from lesbian/gay people within and beyond sociology,[13] I was not convinced. As a result, I sought to explore this question instead of drawing on my own experience or trusting others' opinions for an answer. To this end, I interviewed thirty people who identified as monogamous LGS monosexuals about their thoughts on bisexualities and polyamory.

In this chapter, I complement Lain's data above by sharing some of the responses of my interviewees for the first time in print. For the purposes of this chapter, however, I only focus on the responses to bisexualities here even though there are both similarities and differences in the ways that monogamous LGS people respond to both topics. Overall, my respondents engaged in a process of meaning making I refer to elsewhere as "monosexualizing reality" (Sumerau 2019) wherein lesbian/gay/straight monosexual people work to limit their own world and the people they encounter to only monosexual options (i.e., everyone must only be gay/lesbian/homosexual or straight/heterosexual) through denigrating, denying, and otherwise erasing the possibility of sexual fluidity in their ongoing daily accomplishment of social life.

As co-authors and I have noted in other studies cited above, heterosexual people often talked about bisexualities as a magical or mystical thing that did not really exist. Specifically, as illustrated by a twenty-four-year-old, white, upper-class, cisgender, heterosexual woman, they defined bisexualities as, in fact, imaginary rather than an actual part of the world they inhabit:

> The thing about the bi, pan, queer whatever stuff is that we all know that's just something you do in college, right, I mean, okay maybe not just in college, but like, it's not something real, it's more like a hangover, you know, it's something that happens when you're out drinking that you don't really tell anyone about because everyone knows, like, you have to

choose a side, that's just the way it is in the real world, you have to pick a team, you can't just be like anything you want, I mean, that's what the gay people say, and they would know right, so yeah, I think it's more like a hobby you have for a while and then you, I don't know, you grow up and go out into the real world.

Like the rest of the heterosexual respondents in my interview data set (n = 10) and those in prior studies noted above, this respondent echoes two important patterns in the monosexualizing of reality. First, bisexualities are not something real or grown-up, but rather some kind of other thing people do while they are figuring out who they really are before starting their real, adult life. Second, heterosexual respondents often cite gay/lesbian people as the ones who taught them that bisexuality is not real and use these monosexual others to justify their own belief that everyone is and must become only homo/heterosexual in the real world.

The same two patterns noted above often show up in the responses of gay/lesbian people. As the following excerpt from a twenty-two-year-old, Hispanic, middle-class, cisgender gay man illustrates, gay/lesbian respondents (n = 20; 10 gay and 10 lesbian) often noted that bisexualities were a "rest stop" rather than a destination, and often said they learned this from other gay/lesbian people in their lives:

> It was one of the first lessons when I came out, because I thought I was bisexual and I still sometimes feel attracted to girls and trans people, but that's not the main attraction for me so it's not the real, or I guess, right one, but yeah, see, the way my lesbian friend explained it was that it was like a highway, bi stuff is like the rest stop, because it's hard to come out, but everyone who doesn't give up will reach where they're really trying to go, that has stuck with me. I was really on my way to gay, and I think the bi people are just, yeah, they are just stuck at the rest stop. Does that make sense? I hope they figure it out like I did.

Like other gay/lesbian respondents, this example defines bisexuality as something that should not be taken seriously, but rather as a phase that one goes through on the way to a "real" (i.e., monosexual) sexual identity. Echoing studies of bi+ people's experiences with gay/lesbian communities and coming out more broadly (Gamson 1995; Mathers

2019; McLean 2007; Rust 1993; Sumerau, Mathers, and Moon 2019), such responses erased or "foreclosed" the possibility of fluidity as a real, lasting, and potentially positive thing for anyone.

Interestingly, reading statements like this from my respondents in 2019 reminded me of my birth father talking about his early twenties when he arrived in New York in the 1980s. He explained to me many times how he was encouraged by other gay men not to mention his prior fluidity because, as he put it, "The gay men I met then only accepted you if you conformed. You had to have no choice to be really gay; bisexuality was seen as kind of a threat." Echoing my birth father's recollection of the decade I (J) was born, my respondents—like the twenty-three-year-old, white, middle-class, cisgender lesbian woman quoted next—learned the same lesson:

> Look, I get it, I thought I was bi too, but then I grew out of that, so I began to really fit in with the lesbians I know, and realize how bi stuff is kind of like a threat because like people think that if you could be with a man, of course you would choose a man over a woman, right? I wouldn't, but I don't want to have to explain or worry about that kind of thing when I just wanna be with my girlfriend, you know, like have a real lesbian relationship so that's kind of, I think, why the bi stuff is just so weird for people.

Especially alongside marketing campaigns and highly touted surveys announcing how things have changed, it got better, and we are post gay, respondents demonstrate that not much has changed in the messages about bi+ people LGS people receive(ed) and disseminate(d) now and in my birth father's generation (see also, Mathers, Sumerau, and Cragun 2018). The same way that mine and Lain's experiences of sociology as openly bi+ people eerily fit with the experiences my mentor shared with me, sociology—as well as the society more broadly of which it is a part—remains mostly a monosexual reality predicated upon a monosexual-only sociological *imagination*.

Discussion and Future Considerations

As we have written elsewhere with other colleagues (Mathers, Sumerau and Cragun 2018; Moon, Tobin, and Sumerau 2019; Sumerau, Mathers, and Moon 2019), contemporary sociology, society, and sociological studies of sex, gender, and sexualities are almost entirely limited to monosexual (and cisgender) beliefs, expectations, norms, and traditions. As we have noted here and in prior studies, this pattern relies upon both (1) bi+ people experiencing monosexist and biphobic erasure and other marginalization within society (Mathers 2019), and (2) the efforts, intentionally or otherwise, of monosexual people to promote and police societal and academic knowledge limited only to monosexuality. In this chapter, we have summarized and expanded this line of work to demonstrate how we experience such patterns as openly bi+ people in sociology, and sociologists daring to study, talk about, and center bi+ social life in our work.

In closing, we thus ask what it says about our field when sociologies of sex, gender, and sexualities (as well as the discipline more broadly) mirror the experiences with monosexism shared by bi+ respondents beyond the academy? Likewise, what does it say about our field that we encounter the same monosexual norms and narratives from colleagues within the academy as we hear from monosexual respondents beyond the academy? Intentionally or otherwise, it seems sociologists are perpetuating the monosexual imaginary (Mathers 2019) and monosexualizing reality (Sumerau 2019) through their work (see also Sumerau, Mathers, Moon 2019), and in so doing missing crucial information about the ways sexual inequalities shape our social world and our discipline itself. Put simply, what might the sociology of sexualities look like if it expanded beyond its current shape as a sociology of almost entirely only monosexuality?

Such questions are critical to the future of our field. As we note above, failing to adequately address the largest sexual minority group in the US (Gates 2011) in our research means that our work in the realm of sexualities may not actually represent the reality it suggests it does. One of the primary ways that sociologists can start to move bi+ research to the center of our analyses starts with a relatively simple thing: *say* and actually *approach* monosexism as a real structure of sexual inequality. Avoid the pitfalls of research that discusses sexual fluidity without being rooted in the concrete ramifications of structural monosexism (see Silva 2018; Ward 2015 for examples of research that falls into this trap).

Challenging the existing monosexual imaginary (Mathers 2019) in sociological research and centering questions of monosexism in future studies of sexuality could substantially impact for how we think about power and inequality in society. For instance, in what ways may sexual inequalities persist that don't fit existing understandings of what "anti-queer" discrimination or abuse looks like? What might it mean to forge community as bi+ people in the context of a monosexist society? In what ways do space and place shape how monosexism operates as a social structure? What are the deep and intricate ways that monosexism is fundamentally connected to racial, gender, class, and other sexual inequalities? Monosexism has material impacts on the lives of bi+ people (see, Eisner 2013 for a review). What can *starting* our theorizations of queer life and norms at the outskirts—specifically with questions of monosexism and bisexualities—tell us about other sexual identities and experiences? These questions are not only empirically interesting, but also could lead to crucial insights into challenging the persistence of monosexism in our social world.

As Shiri Eisner (2013) argues, monosexism is a structure of inequality like sexism, heterosexism, racism, and classism. To date, sociologists have failed to meaningfully acknowledge and analyze patterns and processes of monosexism *as a structure.* Though some scholars might suggest there isn't evidence that monosexism constitutes a structure in its own right, we would argue that, in fact, that is part of the problem; what little evidence of structural monosexism exists comes from disparate fields and is not routinely in conversation with one another. Coalescing this focus in future sociological research would be a strong jumping-off point to avoid power-neutral analyses of sexualities that implicitly perpetuate patterns of monosexism in our field. Without analyses that focus on the power of monosexism, sociology will continue to exist within a monosexual imaginary (Mathers 2019).

One way to answer this call to bring bisexualities and monosexism from margin to center involves analyzing processes of "monosexualizing reality" in various realms of social life. For example, what might the monosexualization of the workplace, schools, public policy, and healthcare look like? How do processes of monosexualizing reality intersect with racial, gender, class, citizenship, and other structures of inequality? Interrogating these processes would be a strong first step in moving contemporary sociology toward a more accurate analyses of the complexity of sexual inequalities in our social world. Such questions would also push our field out of a monosexual imaginary and into a realm where our work reflects important questions not only about the experiences of bi+ people, but also how monosexism is deeply connected to other forms of structural inequality (see, for example, Steele, Collier, and Sumerau 2018). Even if one were to just focus on sexualities, one could investigate how processes of monosexualizing reality are tied to the perpetuation of monosexism and heteronormativity. How does the persistence of homonormative politics rely not only on LGBTQ approximations of heterosexuality, but also on continuing to subscribe to narrow, monosexist ideals? These questions represent only a fraction of the questions we don't yet have answers to because of the continual marginalization of bi+ studies in sociology (Barringer, Gay, and Sumerau 2017; Mathers 2019).

These observations and questions may seem odd or surprising to scholars who have had the privilege of ignoring monosexism at work. Our hope is that future sociologies of sexualities will embrace these questions to present a more empirical understanding of sexuality and the ways we can challenge societal patterns of inequality. Finally, while our argument in this chapter stems from our experiences as bi+ people doing research on bisexualities and monosexism, these questions should be of concern to all sexualities and inequalities scholars. Such a revise-and-resubmit of sexualities scholarship could shift interrogations of monosexism, bi+ people, and bi+ issues—including the nuances such studies may reveal—away from being "all the way in the back of the room" (as one of Lain's respondents stated) and toward the center of understandings of our social world.

NOTES

1 For detailed reviews, see Eisner 2013; Mathers 2015, 2019; Rust 1993; Sumerau 2019; Sumerau, Mathers, and Moon 2019.
2 Monosexism is a structure of inequality that privileges the experiences of monosexual people over those of bi+ people. See Eisner 2013 for further information.
3 See Sumerau 2015a and 2015b, 2019 for more writing on these experiences.

4 This is a direct quote J wrote in her journal after she received it from her under-graduate mentor as part of preparing her to go to graduate school in sociology in 2008.

5 See Rich 1980; Sedgwick 1990; Warner 1999.

6 See also Eisner 2013; Mathers 2019.

7 While sociologists have begun noting the tension and stress gay/lesbian people face when interacting professionally with heterosexual people and the same with transgender people interacting with cisgender people; bi+ people experience this same tension and stress when interacting with gay/lesbian/straight or monosexual people in much the same way (see Eisner 2013; Mathers 2017; Sumerau 2019 for examples).

8 But see Moss 2012; Simula 2012 for examples of sociologists publishing on bi+ communities in other fields.

9 See Mathers 2019; Monro et al. 2017; Sumerau 2019; Sumerau, Mathers, and Moon 2019.

10 Amy Stone (2019) summarizes the general lack of attention to the South in socio-logical studies of LGBTQ people.

11 In line with our observations in note 10, we would like to point out that none of these works were published in sociologies of sex, gender, sexualities journals (though one was rejected from one of these).

12 These reactions occurred prior to publication at conferences when I was discuss-ing such work but have disappeared (at least so far) following peer-reviewed publications of this work.

13 See also Cragun and Sumerau 2015; 2017 for survey results to this effect, i.e., where LGS people share similar attitudes toward bi+ and poly people.

REFERENCES

Avishai, Orit. 2008. "'Doing Religion' in a Secular World: Women in Conservative Religions and the Question of Agency." *Gender & Society* 22 (August): 409–33.

Avishai, Orit, Afshan Jafar, and Rachel Rinaldo. 2015. "A Gender Lens on Religion." *Gender & Society* 29 (February): 5–25.

Badgett, M. V. Lee, Laura E. Durso, and Alyssa Schneebaum. 2013. *New Patterns of Poverty in the Lesbian, Gay, and Bisexual Community.* Los Angeles: The Williams Institute.

Barringer, M. N., J. E. Sumerau, and David A. Gay. 2017. "Examining Differences in Identity Disclosure between Monosexuals and Bisexuals." *Sociological Spectrum* 37: 319–33.

Buggs, Shantel Gabrieal. 2017. "Dating in the Time of #BlackLivesMatter: Explor-ing Mixed-Race Women's Discourses of Race and Racism." *Sociology of Race and Ethnicity* 3 (October): 538–51.

Buggs, Shantel Gabrieal. 2019. "Color, Culture, or Cousin? Multiracial Americans Framing Boundaries in Interracial Relationships." *Journal of Marriage and Family* 81 (October): 1221–236.

Butler, Judith. 1994. "Against Proper Objects." *Differences: A Journal of Cultural Studies* 6: 1–26.

Collins, Patricia Hill. 2000. *Black Feminist Thought*. 2nd edition. Routledge: New York.

Compton, D'Lane R. and Tristan Bridges. 2019. "The Bisexual Boom." Retrieved May 6, 2019 (https://thesocietypages.org).

Compton, D'Lane R., Tey Meadow, and Kristen Schilt, eds. 2018. *Other, Please Specify: Queer Methods in Sociology*. Oakland: University of California Press.

Cragun, Ryan T. and J. E. Sumerau. 2015. "The Last Bastion of Sexual and Gender Prejudice? Sexualities, Race, Gender, Religiosity, and Spirituality in the Examination of Prejudice toward Sexual and Gender Minorities." *Journal of Sex Research*, 52: 821–34.

Cragun, Ryan T. and J. E. Sumerau. 2017. "No One Expects a Transgender Jew: Religious, Sexual and Gendered Intersections of the Evaluation of Religious and Nonreligious Others." *Secularism and Nonreligion* 6: 1–16.

Eisner, Shiri. 2013. *Bi: Notes for a Bisexual Revolution*. Berkeley, CA: Seal Press.

Gamson, Joshua. 1995. "Must Identity Movements Self-Destruct? A Queer Dilemma." *Social Problems* 42 (August): 390–407.

Garcia, Lorena. *Respect Yourself, Protect Yourself: Latina Girls and Sexual Identity*. New York: New York University Press, 2012.

Gates, Gary J. 2011. "How Many People Are Lesbian, Gay, Bisexual, and Transgender?" Los Angeles: The Williams Institute.

Ghabrial, Monica A. 2019. "'We Can Shapeshift and Build Bridges': Bisexual Women and Gender Diverse People of Color on Invisibility and Embracing the Borderlands." *Journal of Bisexuality* 19: 169–97.

Gorman, Bridget K, Justin T. Denney, Hillary Dowdy, and Rose Anne Medeiros. 2015. "A New Piece of the Puzzle: Sexual Orientation, Gender, and Physical Health Status." *Demography* 52: 1357–382.

Ingraham, Chrys. 1994. "The Heterosexual Imaginary: Feminist Sociology and Theories of Gender." *Sociological Theory* 12 (July): 203–219.

Laureau, Annette. 2003. *Unequal Childhoods: Class, Race, and Family Life*. Berkeley: University of California Press.

Link, Bruce G. and Jo Phelan. 1995. "Social Conditions as Fundamental Causes of Disease." *Journal of Health and Social Behavior*: 80–94.

Martin, Patricia Yancey. 2005. *Rape Work: Victims, Gender, and Emotions in Organization and Community Context*. New York: Routledge.

Mathers, Lain A. B. 2015. "What 'Team'? Some Thoughts on Navigating Monosexism." *Write Where It Hurts*. Retrieved June 28, 2019 (https://writewhereithurts.net).

Mathers, Lain A. B. 2017. "Navigating Genderqueer Existence within and beyond the Academy." In *Negotiating the Emotional Challenges of Conducting Deeply Personal Research in Health*, edited by Alexandra "Xan" C. H. Nowakowski and J. E. Sumerau, 125–34. New York: Routledge.

Mathers, Lain A. B. 2018. "The Truth in Fiction (Or, when Your Friend Starts Writing Bi Novels)." *Bi Women Quarterly* 36 (4): 9–10. Retrieved June 28, 2019 (http://biwomenboston.org).

Mathers, Lain A. B. 2019. "Bi+ People's Experiences in the Post Gay Era." PhD diss., University of Illinois at Chicago.

Mathers, Lain A. B., J. E. Sumerau, and Ryan T. Cragun. 2018. "The Limits of Homonormativity: Constructions of Bisexual and Transgender People in the Post-Gay Era." *Sociological Perspectives* 61 (December): 934–52.

McLean, Kirsten. 2007. "Hiding in the Closet? Bisexuals, Coming Out and the Disclosure Imperative." *Journal of Sociology* 43 (June):151–66.

Monro, Surya, Sally Hines, and Antony Osborne. 2017. "Is Bisexuality Invisible? A Review of Sexualities Scholarship 1970–2015." *Sociological Review* 65 (November): 663–81.

Moon, Dawne, Theresa W. Tobin, and J. E. Sumerau. 2019. "Alpha, Omega, and the Letters in Between: LGBTQI Conservative Christians Undoing Gender." *Gender & Society* 33 (August): 583–606.

Moss, Alison R. 2012. "Alternative Families, Alternative Lives: Married Women *Doing* Bisexuality." *Journal of GLBT Family Studies* 8: 405–427.

Movement Advancement Project. 2016. "Invisible Majority: The Disparities Facing Bisexual People and How to Remedy Them." Accessed May 29, 2019 (www.lgbtmap.org).

Movement Advancement Project. 2017. "A Closer Look: Bisexual Transgender People." Accessed May 25, 2019 (www.lgbtmap.org).

Prokos, Anastasia and Irene Padavic. 2002. "'There Oughtta Be a Law against Bitches': Masculinity Lessons in Police Academy Training." *Gender, Work, & Organization* 9 (August): 439–59.

Quadagno, Jill. 2005. *One Nation Uninsured: Why the U.S. Has No National Health Insurance.* New York: Oxford University Press.

Rich, Adrienne. 1980. "Compulsory Heterosexuality and Lesbian Existence." *Signs: Journal of Women in Culture and Society* 5 (Summer): 631–60.

Rust, Paula C. 1993. "Neutralizing the Political Threat of the Marginal Woman: Lesbians' Beliefs about Bisexual Women." *Journal of Sex Research* 30 (August): 214–228.

Sedgwick, Eve. 1990. *Epistemology of the Closet.* Berkeley: University of California Press.

Silva, Tony J. 2018. "'Helpin' a Buddy Out': Perceptions of Identity and Behavior among Rural Straight Men that Have Sex with Each Other." *Sexualities* 21 (February): 68–89.

Simula, Brandy. 2012. "Does Bisexuality 'Undo' Gender? Gender, Sexuality, and Bisexual Behavior among BDSM Participants." *Journal of Bisexuality* 12: 484–506.

Steele, Sarah M., Megan Collier, and J. E. Sumerau. 2018. "Lesbian, Gay, and Bisexual Contact with Police in Chicago: Disparities across Sexuality, Race, and Socioeconomic Status." *Social Currents* 5 (August): 328–49.

Stone, Amy L. 2009. "More than Adding a T: American Lesbian and Gay Activists' Attitudes towards Transgender Inclusion." *Sexualities* 12 (June): 334–54.

Stone, Amy L. 2018. "The Geography of Research on LGBTQ Life: Why Sociologists Should Study the South, Rural Queers, and Ordinary Cities." *Sociology Compass* 12: e12638.

Sumerau, J. E. 2015a. "Academic or Actual Bisexuality, Part I." *Conditionally Accepted*. Retrieved June 28, 2019 (https://conditionallyaccepted.com).

Sumerau, J. E. 2015b. "Academic versus Actual Definitions of Bisexuality, Part II." *Conditionally Accepted*. Retrieved June 28, 2019 (https://conditionallyaccepted.com).

Sumerau, J. E. 2019. "Embodying Nonexistence: Experiencing Cis and Mono Normativities in Everyday Life." In *Body Battlegrounds: Transgressions, Tensions, and Transformations*, edited by Samantha Kwan and Christina Bobel. Nashville: Vanderbilt University Press.

Sumerau, J. E. and Ryan T. Cragun. 2018. *Christianity and the Limits of Minority Acceptance in America: God Loves (Almost) Everyone*. Lanham, MD: Lexington Books.

Sumerau, J. E., Eric Anthony Grollman, and Ryan T. Cragun. 2018. "'Oh My God, I Sound Like a Horrible Person': Generic Processes in the Conditional Acceptance of Sexual and Gender Diversity." *Symbolic Interaction* 41 (February): 62–82.

Sumerau, J. E. and Lain A. B. Mathers. 2019. *America through Transgender Eyes*. Lanham, MD: Rowman & Littlefield.

Sumerau, J. E., Lain A. B. Mathers, and Nik Lampe. 2019. "Learning from the Religious Experiences of Bi+ Trans People." *Symbolic Interaction* 42 (May): 179–201.

Sumerau, J. E., Lain A. B. Mathers, and Dawne Moon. 2019. "Foreclosing Fluidity at the Intersection of Gender and Sexual Normativities." *Symbolic Interaction* 43 (2): 205–234. DOI: 10.1002/symb.431.

Ward, Jane. 2015. *Not Gay: Sex between Straight White Men*. New York: New York University Press.

Warner, Michael. 1999. *The Trouble with Normal: Sex, Politics, and the Ethics of Queer Life*. Cambridge, MA: Harvard University Press.

Wolkomir, Michelle. 2009. "Making Heteronormative Reconciliations: The Story of Romantic Love, Sexuality, and Gender in Mixed-Orientation Marriages." *Gender & Society* 23 (August): 494–519.

Yip, Andrew K. 1997. "Gay Male Christian Couples and Sexual Exclusivity." *Sociology* 31 (May): 289–306.

14

Queer Students, Queer Hookups, Queer Cultures

The Potential for Critical Contributions to Theories of Sexuality

LISA WADE AND JANELLE M. PHAM

Most US residential college campuses today host "hookup cultures" (Bogle 2008; Allison and Risman, 2017; Wilkins and Dalessandro 2013; Wade 2017a). These are sexual cultures organized around the facilitation of "hookups," presumed one-time sexual encounters with no acknowledged romantic intent. While hooking up on college campuses is nothing new (Horowitz 1987), collegiate hookup *culture* is new. This is an environment in which hookups are institutionalized, routinized, and ideologically hegemonic (Wade 2017b). Students living on such campuses may choose to "opt out" of hooking up, but they must still contend with hookup culture.

Over a decade of research on hookup cultures has led to a robust literature (for reviews, see Garcia et al. 2012; Heldman and Wade 2010; Padgett and Wade 2019; Wood and Perlman 2016). This research, however, has largely focused on the experiences of men seeking women and women seeking men (Pham 2017; Watson, Snapp, and Wang 2017). This, despite the fact that 20 percent of today's students describe themselves as non-heterosexual (American College Health Association 2019).

Calls to correct this shortcoming in the literature have produced a growing number of studies. These have focused on students who identify as LGBTQ+ as well as students of all sexual orientations who participate in same-gender hookups (e.g., Anderson, Ripley, and McCormack 2018; Esterline and Muehlenhard 2017; Hamilton 2007; Knox, Beaver, and Kriskute 2011; Kuperberg and Walker 2018; Pham 2019a; Rupp 2019; Rupp, Taylor, and Pham 2019). A handful of scholars have also explored whether and how students form alternative queer hookup cultures (Lamont, Roach, and Kahn 2018; Pham 2019c; Rupp et al. 2014).

Research on queer students, queer experiences, and queer hookup cultures is important for understanding how students who experience same-gender desire or engage in same-gender sexual behavior navigate college life. However, we argue that it is also essential for theorizing hookup cultures and sexual culture more generally. To make this case, we offer examples of how this burgeoning literature can help scholars build theory.

As a loose framework, we employ sexual field theory. We fold a review of the literature on queer students, queer experiences, and queer collegiate hookup cultures into four avenues of theoretical inquiry promoted by sexual field theorists. These concern the relationship between sexual cultures and student desires, sexual districts and circuits, the relationship between organizations and the cultures they host, and the mechanisms by which sexual cultures exert their reach. We pose related questions and offer empirically grounded observations without attempting to provide definitive answers. Instead, we hope that this discussion testifies to the theoretical value of studying queer sexualities, and sparks further research in this direction.

Sexual Field Theory

Building on Bourdieu (1977, 1990), sexual field theory is a meso-level approach to thinking about sexual negotiations among individuals in a defined space (Green 2014; Martin and George 2006). That space, or the "sexual field," is characterized by a distinctive sexuality termed the "structure of desire." Clues as to a field's structure of desire can be found in a location's name (and other linguistic signs), its décor (and other indications of taste), the nature of its participants (and their presentations), and so on. Accordingly, different sexual fields—say, a strip club in Las Vegas, an adult furry convention in San Francisco, and a party beach on the Jersey Shore—will all host different flavors of sexuality.

Structures of desire interact with individuals' characteristics to determine their "sexual capital," or the erotic value they bring to negotiations in the sexual field (Martin and George 2006). Sexual capital may be more or less important than other forms of capital in any given sexual field. The fungibility of sexual capital with cultural, economic, social, or symbolic capital varies by sexual field, too. A youthful appearance may be more important at the Jersey Shore, for example, than it is at the furry convention. The right costume (an objectified cultural capital) may be the most important form of capital at the furry convention, whereas economic capital may hold more sway at the strip club.

If sexual fields are bounded sites with distinct structures of desire, then fields can aggregate into a "sexual district," an arena in which several sexual fields coexist (Green 2014c). Urban areas that host an active nightlife, for example, may include several bars and clubs, each signifying, rewarding, and eliciting a different flavor of sexuality. A lively "gayborhood" might have a Western-themed bar, a "leather" bar, and a bar that primarily serves men who identify as "bears" and "cubs" (Green 2008b).

Sexual fields in the same district may attract different or overlapping sets of patrons. Adam et al. (2008) describe patterns of patronage by groups of individuals who routinely occupy the same space or spaces as "sexual circuits" (see also Adam and Green 2014). Understanding a sexual district, then, requires knowing not just what structures of desire are represented by various sexual fields, but who circulates within which ones.

To these districts, field participants bring a pre-formed "erotic habitus" to sexual fields. This is an embodied set of erotic habits, dispositions, and skills that reflects a person's lifetime of experience. The erotic habitus may influence which sexual fields individuals find appealing and which sexual circuits they take up. Individuals also, though, encounter the logics of sexual fields and experience shifts in their habitus (Hammers 2008; Hennen 2008; 2014). The habitus is both a driver of individuals' experiences and a consequence of them.

These are but a few of the concepts that scholars are using to build sexual field theory. In developing them, sexual field theorists are attempting not merely to describe, but to theorize sexual subcultures. To that end, they aim for these concepts to be portable; that is, to describe generic processes that are at play across all or most sexual fields. This is helpful for drawing analysts' attention to interesting and productive questions that will help us understand sexual cultures writ large. It is to such questions that we now turn.

Queer Avenues of Inquiry

Sexual Cultures and Student Desires

Structures of desire are not merely the aggregated desires of their participants (Green 2014c). Instead, they reflect distinct sexualities that need not—and likely will not—perfectly reflect the sexualities of the people who find themselves within them. The degree to which structures of desire can deviate from the aggregated desires of a field's participants, however, is unknown, as is the dynamics of fields with different degrees and types of deviation. Hence, an active area of inquiry in sexual field theory involves mapping the possible relationships between sexual cultures and the desires of a culture's inhabitants.

On most campuses, hookup culture's structure of desire manifests most vividly at high-energy, hypersexualized, heterocentrist and sometimes homophobic parties at which hooking up is a central activity (Allison and Risman 2014; Armstrong and Hamilton 2013; Armstrong, Hamilton, and Sweeney 2006; Bogle 2008; Hamilton and Armstrong 2009; Hollowell 2010; Kuperberg and Padgett 2015; Paul and Hayes 2002; Pham 2018; Rupp et al. 2014; Vander Ven 2011; Wade 2017a). Parties are usually explicitly heterosexualized. For example, they often have themes and activities that posit gendered pairs (as in "pimp and ho" or "CEOs and office hoes"). Visible sexual activity is also restricted largely to couples composed of a single man and a single woman (with important exceptions discussed below) (Ronen 2010; Russett 2008). These dynamics are present even in so-called "queer-friendly" schools (Pham 2018).

Heterosexuality, in other words, is an organizing force in most campus hookup cultures. When the dominant sexual fields on college campuses are heterocentrist, they fail to reflect the desires of those who identify as other than heterosexual. The presence of sexual minorities on campus, and their experiences in heteronormative hookup cultures, present an opportunity to explore the relationship between structures of desire and students' desires.

More interesting than the mere fact of a mismatch is how same-gender sexual behaviors and sexual minority identities are simultaneously erased by and incorporated into overtly heterocentrist hookup cultures. Though these environs often stigmatize non-heterosexual identities, for instance, they also actively elicit some forms of same-gender sexual behavior. The most well-documented is that of "straight girls kissing," or ostensibly heterosexual women who kiss each other at college parties (Esterline and Muehlenhard 2017; Hamilton 2007; Knox, Beaver and Kriskute 2011; Kuperberg and Walker 2018; Pham 2019a; Rupp and Taylor 2010; Rupp et al. 2014; Yost and McCarthy 2012). A smaller subset of studies examines same-gender kissing between ostensibly heterosexual college men (Anderson, Ripley, and McCormack 2018; Scoats, Joseph, and Anderson 2018; Ward 2015).

These parallel behaviors are interpreted in gendered ways by many of the students who engage in or observe them. When women kiss other women, the behavior is often framed as a form of heterosexual seduction, engaged in for the enticement of men onlookers in mixed-gender settings (Esterline and Muehlenhard 2017; Hamilton 2007; Pham 2019a; Rupp and Taylor 2010). Men's same-gender kisses are framed as a form of male bonding, used to strengthen men's friendships, and typically performed in all-men settings such as fraternity initiations (Scoats, Joseph, and Anderson 2018; Ward 2015). In both cases, heterosexual men are the presumed audience.

Divergent interpretations of men's and women's same-gender kissing reflects the contrasting expectations they face in heteronormative hookup cultures. Women's sexual capital is highly dependent on physical attractiveness, while men's is more strongly shaped by their social and economic capital (Wade 2017a). Women's same-gender kissing, then, is interpreted as an effort to raise their *sexual* capital, while men's is interpreted as an effort to raise their *social* capital.

Ironically, compared to other men, men who kiss men have an especially high likelihood of belonging to homophobic organizations such as fraternities and sports teams (Anderson, Ripley, and McCormack 2018; Tillapaugh 2013). Likewise, women who engage in same-gender kissing at college parties have been found to express higher levels of homophobia than women who do not engage in such behaviors (Hamilton 2007). Scholars theorize that this is because the activity is premised on the assumption that same-gender sexual desire is pretend. It's only a heterosexual activity, in other words, if all students involved are heterosexual. Heightened homophobia among people who participate in heterosexuality frames same-gender kissing, then, functioning to protect the frame students have for the activity. Ostensibly heterosexual students must exclude potentially queer ones because the presence of people who actually experience same-gender sexual desire threatens to break the frame, thus making the kisses queer.

Yet, multiple studies find that same-gender desire does motivate at least some women's engagement in these encounters (Knox, Beaver, and Kriskute 2011; Kuperberg and Walker 2018; Yost and McCarthy 2012). It is reasonable to suspect that the same is true for at least some men. Thus, these heteronormative settings serve as unwitting "opportunity structures" for students who wish to act on same-gender desire, but only if they remain closeted and sufficiently conform to gender norms to pass as heterosexual (Rupp et al. 2014). Some queer students are willing to "give in" to this environment in exchange for hookup opportunities, especially in light of the difficulty of finding a same-gender hookup beyond these sites.

The same-gender sexual behavior engaged in by ostensibly heterosexual students, then, does not translate into an opportunity for queer-identifying students to be open about their desires. Some also report feeling exploited by women who use them to arouse men and men who are aroused by them (Pham 2019c; Rupp, Taylor, and Pham 2019). Rupp (2019) refers to this as a "queer dilemma of desire," a set of conflicts uniquely experienced by queer students in hookup culture.

In other instances, heterosexual students may engage in same-gender kissing only to discover that hookup culture, by heterosexualizing or desexualizing same-gender sexual activity, shifts their erotic habitus in ways they did not anticipate. In the first author's research (Wade 2017a, 181–2), a student had just this experience. When Brooke arrived on campus as a first-year student, she identified as heterosexual and was unsure that bisexuality was real. "I am so skeptical when people identify as bisexual," she wrote. "I usually assume it's to fulfill an image [as a radical], or to cover up their homosexuality" (full quote from original data). Brooke "intensely" enjoyed kissing her girlfriends when drunk, however. By the end of the year, she identified as bisexual herself. Undoubtedly, she is not the only student who has discovered same-gender desire in the process of engaging in heterosexually framed same-gender encounters.

In sum, queer, queer-curious, and not-yet-queer students are members of heteronormative and homophobic hookup cultures that, counterintuitively, elicit some forms of same-gender sexual behavior even as they erase or suppress queer sexual identities. Ironically, this both allows same-gender sexual desire to hide in plain sight and potentially elicits such desires in students who have yet to recognize them in themselves. These observations make for provocative hypotheses regarding the possible relationships between sexual cultures and the desires of students within them. In this case, the heteronormative context of hookup culture is a powerful interpretive lens, making it so that queer behavior is often read as heterosexual. This means that some forms of sexual behavior that are incongruent with the dominant structure of desire are not banished, but interpreted in ways consistent with the sexual field. Men kissing men is desexualized, while women kissing women is heterosexualized. Ironically, this makes some college parties relatively safe spaces in which women—and perhaps men, too—can rather safely engage in same-gender sexual behavior. In this way, heteronormative hookup culture simultaneously erases queer identities, facilitates queer behavior, and potentially ignites queer desires.

Sexual Districts and Circuits

Queer students on campus may offer sexuality scholars the opportunity to theorize both sexual districts (arenas in which several sexual fields coexist) and sexual circuits (groups of individuals who patronize the same set of sexual fields). The second author, for example, compared and contrasted the sexual cultures at an Ivy League and a state school (Pham 2018). On both campuses, she found alternative sexual fields: ones serving queer students and ones serving students of color. Several observations can be derived from her and others' observations.

First, the presence of alternative queer sexual cultures on campus can teach us something about how sexual fields emerge. Pham argued that alternative cultures exist precisely because the wider collegiate culture is so unwelcoming and unsupportive. This suggests that, when conditions for their existence are present (e.g., a critical mass of students and physical or virtual spaces to gather), sexual fields that meet specific unserved needs may emerge. This is consistent with Hennen (2014), who argued that gay "bear" culture was partly a response to gay leather culture, signifying resistance to a military masculinity in favor of a softer one. Men whose bodies were judged unsexy, and whose desire for connection was judged as uncool, articulated and ultimately shared an alternative set of desires that congealed into gay bear culture.

Second, queer cultures on campus can illuminate how sexual cultures can influence one another. When sexual cultures are formed in response to exclusion and stigma, they may correspond to communities offering mutual support. Indeed, this is exactly what Pham (2018) discovered. The queer sexual cultures she studied operated "first and foremost as spaces of support" and only secondarily as a source of sex and romance (148). As a result, parties were smaller with less drinking, fewer strangers, greater female control, and less pressure to hook up (see also Wamboldt et al. 2019). The cultivation of these social spaces reduced the risk of sexual violence and enhanced interpersonal accountability. Hookup cultures that serve marginalized communities may translate into more positive outcomes than those serving centered ones (see also Hall et al. 2017; Lamont, Roach, and Kahn 2018). Specifically, because the dominant sexual field in the sexual district is unwelcoming, alternative cultures may be relatively kinder and safer.

The hostility of the dominant culture, however, may also press members of alternative ones to enforce rules of their own more harshly than they would otherwise. Pham (2019c) found that, in an effort to distinguish themselves from the mainstream heteronormative cultures, queer subcultures tend to police the nature of queerness. To fit in to the alternative scenes, a student has to be queer "enough" and queer in the "right" way. Orne (2017) documented similar pressures in his ethnography of Chicago's Boystown, coining the term "queernormativity." Queer and queer-curious students have to "prove" their membership in queer campus spaces to be fully accepted within them. In response, some queer women describe feeling intimidated or uncomfortable in queer campus spaces (Pham 2018, 2019c; Waling and Roffee 2017). In this way, queer capital is defined in relationship to what it seeks to reject—heteronormativity.

Finally, studying queer, queer-curious, and queer-friendly students may reveal how individuals encounter and navigate multiple sexual fields. Some fields within a sexual district will be more visible and accessible than others, making entry into those fields more dependent on networks (Pham 2018). Even when students encounter them, in other words, they can still be intimidating to enter. While the women in Pham's study were exposed to clear evidence of queer spaces on campus (e.g., Queer Student Unions, advertising for queer parties), the ability to acquire the queer capital needed to comfortably access these spaces rendered some women hesitant to engage in these alternative fields. Women who were sufficiently intimidated to engage these alternative sexual fields described "settling" for heterocentrist ones, viewing the opportunities for same-gender sexual contact with women to be worth the downsides (i.e., experiencing men's ogling or acknowledging that these women were not interested in them).

The study of queer students can also extend our understanding of sexual circuits inasmuch as universities with prominent hookup cultures compel students to "drop in, move through or try out several circuits to discover their own affinities and achieve the connections . . . they seek" (Adam and Green 2014, 130). Queer students may opt into certain campus spaces from which they anticipate possibilities for sexual engagements, circuits may introduce new desires, or both (Rupp et al. 2014).

And what other features of a campus may drive students to take up certain circuits? That is, once they are aware of them, how do students decide which sexual fields in a district they will patronize? Pham's (2019a) study of predictors of sexual encounters between college women, for instance, found women's participation in team-based athletics to strongly predict a history of genital sexual contact with other women, while participation in individual-based sports did not. The presence or absence of such conduits into same-gender sexual behavior may influence the degree to which students enter alternative sexual fields and take up opportunities for such contact. These conduits may or may not coexist with a shift in an individual's habitus, as described in the previous section.

In sum, acknowledging and incorporating queer hookup cultures into the literature promises to open up new avenues of inquiry about how separate fields of sexuality interact and whether and how people navigate competing sexual cultures. This could include work on how sexual fields emerge, how they influence one another, how individuals navigate multiple fields, and how subgroups develop unique circuits.

Organizations and the Cultures They Host

Colleges and universities are bounded spaces with distinctive geographies, histories, reputations, and relationships to surrounding communities. They vary tremendously in size, situatedness, culture, and more. Yet, scholars often do not find statistically significant or qualitatively substantial differences across collegiate hookup cultures, even when they are hosted by very different sorts of institutions of higher education (Bogle 2008; Lovejoy 2012; 2015; Pham 2018). Across institutions, some scholars find no noteworthy differences in who hooks up, how much, and with what motivation and consequence. These include colleges and universities of various sizes, locations, and exclusivity, as well as those that are religiously affiliated.

Other scholarship does find some differences. There may be somewhat more hooking up at large colleges and ones with high gender ratios, less at campuses with heavy top-down sexual control (such as evangelical campuses), and no hookup culture at all at commuter campuses (Adkins et al. 2015; Allison and Ralston 2018; Allison and Risman 2017; Malone 2018). Pham (2019b) is the first to make a case for a qualitative difference. Her study of an elite college and a large state school found women attending the elite school were more likely to argue that hookup culture protects their career ambitions (consistent with the academic pressures of their institution), while women at the state school were proportionately more likely to argue that it allows them to have fun (consistent with the institution's party-heavy reputation).

The existing literature has little to say about why we might see different sorts of hookup cultures, however. Allison and Risman (2017) offer evidence that the proportions of men and women on college campuses matters. Hamilton and Armstrong (2009) and Wade (2017a) note privileged men's disproportionate control over the sexual scene on some campuses. Clearly, this does not go far enough. We need more research on differences and similarities across hookup cultures and how institutional features prompt convergences and divergences.

Research on queer hookup cultures may help scholars build this literature. Because queer cultures are less subject to an overbearing media narrative, queer students have to do more work to build, structure, and make meaning from their alternative cultures. These efforts might make queer hookup cultures more sensitive to organizational features. And, because campuses can be sampled, studies across institutions could conceivably allow researchers to draw conclusions about how these features correlate with cultural dynamics.

For example, queer hookup cultures emerge in part in response to heteronormativity and homophobia in the wider sexual cultures on campus. We might expect the presence of alternative scenes to vary, then, according to how aggressively queer students are pushed out. Theoretically, a campus's hookup culture could be wholly inclusive, making no distinction between different-gender and same-gender sexual activity. In this case, there would less need for an alternative or fewer students who felt inclined to seek it out. In overtly homophobic campus environments, queer hookup cultures may not develop. Or, if they do, they may be more secretive and difficult to discover and access.

The level of heteronormativity and homophobia might change the nature of the alternative culture, as well as its development. If the wider campus environment is inclusive, queer students might feel less need to come together for mutual support. In which case, alternative queer hookup cultures could develop that were as centered on sex as heteronormative hookup cultures are now, to the exclusion of the enhanced kindness and safety that is prompted by the need for shared social support. Such alternative cultures might have the same risk of sexual violence and lack of interpersonal accountability that we now see in heteronormative hookup cultures.

If the wider campus is overtly homophobic, queer students might cling together for social support even more tightly. But they might be even more suspicious and fearful of outsiders, incentivizing them to police their borders and maintain their secrecy even more aggressively. Ironically, on especially hostile campuses some queer or queer-curious students might struggle to discover or access the culture that develops to protect them.

In sum, features of organizations certainly shape the nature of the sexual districts they host. In this case, the force of the dominant sexual field's homophobia may influence whether alternative queer fields exist and the degree to which they police their own members. Other features may shape heteronormative and queer sexual cultures and the influence they have on one another, too. The presence and power of Greek life, the size of institutions, their level of isolation, and the relationships they have with nearby colleges and universities may be relevant features as well.

Fields and Their Edges

One of the most pressing theoretical lacunae in sexual field theory is in regard to the very concept of sexual field. Abstractly, Green (2015, 27) defines a sexual field as "a configuration of social spaces, anchored to physical and virtual *sites*, that are inhabited by actors who strive to obtain the rewards of the field" (emphasis in original). Concretely, though, what are the possible reaches and bounds of these so-called "sites"?

The literature provides conflicting answers. In one chapter of his anthology, Green (2014b) argues that sexual fields are differentiated by geography and patronage, or a physical location and regular clientele. Indeed, much of the research is tightly focused on individual bars or clubs (e.g., Green 2008a; 2008b; Hammers 2008; 2010; Hennen 2008; Weinberg and Williams 2010). This suggests that sexual fields operate in quite small or otherwise clearly bounded physical spaces.

Green, however, also includes virtual sites and other scholars describe apps or websites as discernible sexual fields. Scheim et al. (2019, 577), for instance, identify Craigslist personals as "a [sexual] field unto itself" and Robinson (2013) does the same with the dating site Adam4Adam.com. Many such apps and websites are location-sensitive or geo-located, which may satisfy the geography and patronage requirement. In other instances, scholars make a case for even larger and more diffuse sexual fields. Farrer (2010) and Farrer and Dale (2014) theorize Shanghai nightlife as a single sexual field and Inglis (1997) describes an Irish sexual field that encompasses the whole of the country.

This raises many questions. How far can a sexual field exert its influence? How many individuals can it include? What mechanisms of interaction can it involve? If it has a social media dimension, how far can it extend through networks? Can it be a primarily media-driven phenomenon, with independent outposts gravitationally influencing each other through mass communication? In other words, if a sexual field is a field of force and struggle, then field participants must be able to interact with some regularity in some way, but how regularly and in what ways?

Queer campus hookup cultures are especially useful sites with which to explore these questions. Queer students are more likely than strictly heterosexual students to be underserved by their campus cultures. They are also a statistical minority. For both of these reasons, they face greater challenges in building a coherent sexual field.

Queer students have faced these challenges by extending their sexual fields off-campus and enhancing them virtually. Students seeking same-gender sexual contact are more likely than ones seeking different-gender contact to turn to virtual spaces to meet partners, especially when the queer community is smaller or less visible (Kuperberg and Padgett 2015; 2017; Lamont, Roach, and Kahn 2018; Lundquist and Curington 2019). Queer students are also more likely than heterosexual ones to go to gay-friendly neighborhoods and bars off-campus (Pham 2018).

Whether these virtual and off-campus spaces are extensions of the on-campus cultures queer students have built for themselves is an empirical question for which we have mixed evidence. On the one hand, Pham (2019c) finds off-campus environments—both online and in-person—are used not only as sources of same-gender sexual partners, but also as spaces in which some students learn "how to be queer." Students study these environments and learn and practice the performance of queerness to bolster their queer social capital on-campus. In other words, the experiences they have *off* campus helps make entering queer spaces *on* campus less intimidating. If students can acquire relevant cultural capital off campus, it suggests that the on- and off-campus sites share a structure of desire and, thus, perhaps a contiguous sexual field.

On the other hand, Pham (2018) also finds that some queer women go off-campus in order to secure anonymity. Some gay bars, for example, are not only geographically distinct from campus spaces, but attract a different clientele. This allows some women to explore same-gender sexual attraction at a geographic and interpersonal distance from their campus life. This suggests that there are queer sexual fields off-campus that are not contiguous with the ones on campus. This also raises questions as to what differentiates off-campus fields that do and do not overlap with on-campus ones, and what relationships those fields have to one another and to the overlapping circuits that may be built within or across them.

Online communities are especially curious from a sexual fields perspective. In the case of a particularly hostile campus environment, queer and queer-curious students might be forced to explore their sexuality almost exclusively online. Can a purely virtual space be a sexual field, with all its relevant components: structure of desires, tiers of desirability, erotic habitus, and so forth? Can virtual sexual fields spawn or support full-fledged sexual fields that involve in-person interaction? Because queer students have more precarious sexual lives, studying their sexual fields are more likely to offer answers to these questions.

In sum, studying queer and queer-curious students and their choices has the potential to help us better theorize the potential reach and bounds of sexual fields. It may help us consider the extent to which a virtual site can be a field unto itself or merge with sexual fields that are based in geography and in-person interaction. It may also help us think through how sexual fields do or do not cross socially constructed borders, like the one between the campus and the community. And it may help us think through how sexual fields preserve boundaries, so as to offer students anonymity when they leave campus.

Conclusion

Most of the research supporting sexual field theory involves the study of queer communities, so much so that the first author has argued elsewhere that it must expand its scope to reach its true potential, using hookup culture as a case in point (Wade 2020). This chapter further elaborates that argument, exploring how queer students' navigation of heterocentrist and often homophobic space shapes their identities, experiences, and cultures. We used sexual field theory to offer several avenues of potential inquiry, arguing that scholars could exploit queer individuals, behaviors, and scenes to better understand the possible relationships between sexual cultures and the desires of students who participate in them, how sexual districts emerge and produce sexual circuits, the role of organizational features in shaping sexual cultures, and the potential for sexual fields to extend across virtual and real borders, as well as the limits of their reach.

We hope to have shown that the extant literature on queer student understanding of and engagement with heteronormative hookup cultures reveals more about these sexual fields than a singular focus on its heterosexual participants would. Centering the LGBTQ+ student experience in the study of campus sexual fields asks us to question those features of campus sexual fields that may seem patently obvious (e.g., is the phenomenon of "straight girls kissing" purely to entice men?), while also providing insights about the genesis of new fields in response to the limited structures of desire within the dominant heteronormative campus hookup culture. It is hoped that future research will expand these lines of inquiry to consider how other identities intersect with sexuality in the development and experience of sexual fields within or beyond organizational settings. These are but a few insights revealing how studying the outskirts will enhance our understanding of hookup culture on college campuses and the full range of human sexuality around the world.

REFERENCES

Adam, Barry, and Adam Isaiah Green. 2014. "Circuits and the Social Organization of Sexual Fields." In *Sexual Fields: Toward a Sociology of Collective Sexual Life*, edited by Adam Isaiah Green, 123–42. Chicago: The University of Chicago Press.

Adam, Barry, Winston Husbands, James Murray, and John Maxwell. 2008. "Circuits, Networks, and HIV Risk Management." *AIDS Education and Prevention* 20 (5): 420–53.

Adkins, Timothy, Paula England, Barbara Risman, and Jessie Ford. 2015. "Student Bodies: Does the Sex Ratio Matter for Hooking Up and Having Sex at College?" *Social Currents* 2: 144–62.

Allison, Rachel and Margaret Ralston. 2018. "Opportune Romance: How College Campuses Shape Students' Hookups, Dates, and Relationships." *Sociological Quarterly* 59 (3): 495–518.

Allison, Rachel and Barbara J. Risman. 2014. "'It Goes Hand in Hand with the Parties': Race, Class, and Residence in College Student Negotiations of Hooking Up." *Sociological Perspectives* 57 (1): 102–23.

Allison, Rachel and Barbara J. Risman. 2017. "Marriage Delay, Time to Play? Marital Horizons and Hooking Up in College." *Sociological Inquiry* 87 (3): 472–500.

American College Health Association. 2019. *National College Health Assessment Reference Group Data Report*. www.acha.org.

Anderson, Eric, Matthew Ripley, and Mark McCormack. 2018. "A Mixed-Method Study of Same-Sex Kissing among College-Attending Heterosexual Men in the U.S." *Sexuality and Culture* 23 (1): 26–44.

Armstrong, Elizabeth A. and Laura T. Hamilton. 2013. *Paying for the Party: How College Maintains Inequality*. Cambridge, MA: Harvard University Press.

Armstrong, Elizabeth A., Laura Hamilton, and Brian Sweeney. 2006. "Sexual Assault on Campus: A Multilevel, Integrative Approach to Party Rape." *Social Problems* 53 (4): 483–99.

Bogle, Kathleen A. 2008. *Hooking Up: Sex, Dating, and Relationships on Campus*. New York: New York University Press.

Bourdieu, Pierre. 1977. *Outline of a Theory of Practice*. Cambridge: Cambridge University Press.

Bourdieu, Pierre. 1990. *The Logic of Practice*. Stanford: Stanford University Press.

Esterline, Kate M. and Charlene L. Muehlenhard. 2017. "Wanting to Be Seen: Young People's Experiences of Performative Making Out." *Journal of Sex Research* 54: 1051–63.

Farrer, James. 2010. "A Foreign Adventurer's Paradise? Interracial Sexuality and Alien Sexual Capital in Reform Era Shanghai." *Sexualities* 13 (1): 69–95.

Farrer, James and Sonja Dale. 2014. "Sexless in Shanghai: Gendered Mobility Strategies in a Transnational Sexual Field." In *Sexual Fields: Toward a Sociology of Collective Sexual Life*, edited by Adam Isaiah Green, 143–70. Chicago: The University of Chicago Press.

Garcia, Justin R., Chris Reiber, Sean G. Massey, and Ann M. Merriwether. 2012. "Sexual Hookup Culture: A Review." *Review of General Psychology* 16 (2): 161–76.

Green, Adam Isaiah, ed. 2014. *Sexual Fields: Toward a Sociology of Collective Sexual Life*. Chicago: The University of Chicago Press.

Green, Adam Isaiah. 2015. "Sexual Fields." In *Handbook of the Sociology of Sexualities*, edited by John DeLamater and Rebecca Plante, 23–39. Cham, Switzerland: Springer International Publishing.

Green, Adam Isaiah. 2008a. "Erotic Habitus: Toward a Sociology of Desire." *Theoretical Sociology* 37 (6): 597–626.

Green, Adam Isaiah. 2008b. "The Social Organization of Desire: The Sexual Fields Approach." *Sociological Theory* 26 (1): 25–50.

Hall, Scott, David Knox, and Kelsey Shapiro. 2017. "'I Have,' 'I Would,' 'I Won't': Hooking Up among Sexually Diverse Groups of College Students." *Psychology of Sexual Orientation and Gender Diversity* 4 (2): 233–40.

Hamilton, Laura. 2007. "Trading on Heterosexuality: College Women's Gender Strategies and Homophobia." *Gender and Society* 21 (2): 145–72.

Hamilton, Laura, and Elizabeth Armstrong. 2009. "Gendered Sexuality in Young Adulthood: Double Binds and Flawed Options." *Gender and Society* 23 (5): 589–616.

Hammers, Corie. 2008. "Making Space for an Agentic Sexuality? The Examination of a Lesbian/Queer Bathhouse." *Sexualities* 11 (5): 547–72.

Hammers, Corie. 2010. "Corporeal Silences and Bodies that Speak: The Promises and Limitations of Queer in Lesbian/Queer Sexual Spaces." In *Transgender Identities: Toward a Social Analysis of Gender Diversity*, edited by Sally Hines and Tam Sanger, 224–41. New York: Routledge.

Heldman, Caroline, and Lisa Wade. 2010. "Hook-Up Culture: Setting a New Research Agenda." *Sexuality Research and Social Policy* 7: 323–33.

Hennen, Peter. 2014. "Sexual Field Theory: Some Theoretical Questions and Empirical Complications." In *Sexual Fields: Toward a Sociology of Collective Sexual Life*, edited by Adam Isaiah Green, 71–100. Chicago: The University of Chicago Press.

Hennen, Peter. 2008. *Faeries, Bears, and Leathermen: Gay Men in Community Queering the Masculine.* Chicago: University of Chicago Press.

Hollowell, Clare. 2010. "The Subject of Fun: Young Women, Freedom, and Feminism." Ph.D. diss, Lancaster University.

Horowitz, Helen Lefkowitz. 1987. *Campus Life: Undergraduate Cultures from the End of the Eighteenth Century to the Present.* New York: Alfred A. Knopf.

Inglis, Tom. 1997. "Foucault, Bourdieu, and the Field of Irish Sexuality." *Irish Journal of Sociology* 7: 5–28.

Knox, David, Tiffany Beaver, and Vaiva Kriskute. 2011. "'I Kissed a Girl': Heterosexual Women Who Report Same-Sex Kissing (and More)." *Journal of GLBT Family Studies* 7 (3): 217–25.

Kuperberg, Arielle and Alicia M. Walker. 2018. "Heterosexual College Students Who Hookup with Same-Sex Partners." *Archives of Sexual Behavior* 47: 1387–1403.

Kuperberg, Arielle and Joseph Padgett. 2015. "Dating and Hooking Up in College: Meeting Contexts, Sex, and Variation by Gender, Partner's Gender, and Class Standing." *Journal of Sex Research* 52 (5): 517–31.

Kuperberg, Arielle and Joseph Padgett. 2017. "Partner Meeting Contexts and Risky Behavior in College Students' Different-Gender and Same-Sex Hookups." *Journal of Sex Research* 54 (1): 55–72.

Lamont, Ellen, Teresa Roach, and Sope Kahn. 2018. "Navigating Campus Hookup Culture: LGBTQ Students and College Hookups." *Sociological Forum* 33 (4): 1000–22.

Lovejoy, Meg. 2012. "Is Hooking Up Empowering for College Women? A Feminist Gramscian Perspective." PhD diss., Brandeis University.

Lovejoy, Meg. 2015. "Hooking Up as an Individualistic Practice: A Double-Edged Sword for College Women." *Sexuality and Culture* 19 (3): 464–92.

Lundquist, Jennifer Hickes and Celeste Vaughan Curington. 2019. "Love Me Tinder, Love Me Sweet: Reshaping the College Hookup Culture." *Contexts* 18 (4): 22–7.

Malone, Dana. 2018. *From Single to Serious: Relationships, Gender, and Sexuality on American Evangelical Campuses.* Newark: Rutgers University Press.

Martin, John Levi and Matt George. 2006. "Theories of Sexual Stratification: Toward an Analysis of the Sexual Field and a Theory of Sexual Capital." *Sociological Theory* 24 (2): 107–32.

Orne, Jay. 2017. *Boystown: Sex and Community in Chicago.* Chicago: University of Chicago Press.

Padgett, Joseph and Lisa Wade. 2019. "Hookup Culture and Higher Education." *Handbook of Contemporary Feminism*, edited by Andrea Press and Tasha Oren. New York: Routledge.

Paul, Elizabeth and Kristen Hayes. 2002. "The Casualties of 'Casual' Sex: A Qualitative Exploration of the Phenomenology of College Students' Hookups." *Journal of Social and Personal Relationships* 19 (5): 639–61.

Pham, Janelle M. 2017. "Beyond Hook-up Culture: Current Trends in the Study of College Student Sex, and Where to Next." *Sociology Compass* 11 (8): e12499.

Pham, Janelle M. 2018. "The Sexual Organization of the University: Women's Experiences of Sex and Relationships on Two American College Campuses." PhD diss., University of California, Santa Barbara.

Pham, Janelle M. 2019a. "Institutional, Subcultural and Individual Determinants of Same-Sex Sexual Contact among College Women." *Journal of Sex Research* 56 (8): 1031–44.

Pham, Janelle M. 2019b. "Campus Sex in Context: Organizational Cultures and Women's Engagement in Sexual Relationships on Two American College Campuses." *Sociological Forum* 34 (1): 138–57.

Pham, Janelle M. 2019c. "Queer Space and Alternate Queer Geographies: LBQ Women and the Search for Sexual Partners at Two LGBTQ-Friendly U.S. Universities." *Journal of Lesbian Studies* 24 (3), 227–39.

Robinson, Brandon. 2013. "The 'Gay Facebook': Friendship, Desirability, and HIV in the Lives of the Gay Internet Generation." PhD diss., University of Texas at Austin.

Ronen, Shelly. 2010. "Grinding on the Dance Floor: Gendered Scripts and Sexualized Dancing at College Parties." *Gender and Society* 24 (3): 355–77.

Rupp, Leila. 2019. "Queer Dilemmas of Desire." *Feminist Studies* 45 (1): 67–93.

Rupp, Leila and Verta Taylor. 2010. "Straight Girls Kissing." *Contexts* 9: 28–32.

Rupp, Leila, Verta Taylor, and Janelle M. Pham. 2019. "Straight Girls Kissing: Heteroflexibility in the College Party Scene." In *The Routledge International Handbook of Heterosexualities Studies*, edited by James Joseph Dean and Nancy L. Fischer. New York: Routledge.

Rupp, Leila, Verta Taylor, Shiri Regev-Messalem, Alison Fogarty, and Paula England. 2014. "Queer Women in the Hookup Scene: Beyond the Closet?" *Gender and Society* 28 (2): 212–35.

Russett, Jill. 2008. *Women's Perceptions of High-Risk Deinking: Understanding Binge Drinking in a Gender Biased Setting.* PhD diss., The College of William and Mary.

Scheim, Ayden, Barry Adam, and Zack Marshall. 2019. "Gay, Bisexual, and Queer Trans Men Navigating Sexual Fields." *Sexualities* 22 (4): 556–86.

Scoats, Ryan, Lauren J. Joseph, and Eric Anderson. 2018. "'I Don't Mind Watching Him Cum': Heterosexual Men, Threesomes, and the Erosion of the One-Time Rule of Homosexuality." *Sexualities* 21 (1/2): 30–48.

Tillapaugh, Daniel. 2013. "Breaking Down the 'Walls of a Façade': The Influence of Compartmentalization on Gay College Males' Meaning-Making." *Culture, Society and Masculinities* 5 (2): 127–46.

Wade, Lisa. 2017a. *American Hookup: The New Culture of Sex on Campus.* New York: W. W. Norton and Company.

Wade, Lisa. 2017b. "What's So Cultural about Hookup Culture?" *Contexts* 16 (1): 66–68.

Wade, Lisa. 2020. "In Pursuit of the Potential of Sexual Field Theory: A Research Agenda." *Sexualities* 25 (3): 284–300.

Waling, Andrea and James Roffee. 2017. "Knowing, Performing and Holding Queerness: LGBTIQ+ Student Experiences in Australian Tertiary Education." *Sex Education* 17 (3): 302–18.

Wamboldt, Alexander, Shamus Khan, Claude Mellins, Melanie Wall, Leigh Reardon, and Jennifer Hirsch. 2019. "Wine Night, 'Bro-dinners,' and Jungle Juice: Disaggregating Practices of Underage Binge Drinking." *Journal of Drug Issues* 49 (4): 643–67.

Ward, Jane. 2015. *Not Gay: Sex between Straight White Men.* New York: New York University Press.

Watson, Ryan J., Shannon Snapp, and Skyler Wang. 2017. "What We Know and Where We Go from Here: A Review of Lesbian, Gay, and Bisexual Youth Hookup Literature." *Sex Roles* 77: 801–11.

Weinberg, Martin and Colin Williams. 2010. "Men Sexually Interested in Transwomen (MSTW): Gendered Embodiment and the Construction of Sexual Desire." *Journal of Sex Research* 47 (4): 374–83.

Wilkins, Amy C. and Cristen Dalessandro. 2013. "Monogamy Lite: Cheating, College, and Women." *Gender and Society* 27 (5): 728–51.

Wood, C. and Perlman, D. 2016. "Hooking Up in the United States." In *The Wiley Blackwell Encyclopedia of Family Studies.* Edited by Constance Shehan. Hoboken, NJ: Wiley.

Yost, Megan R. and Lauren McCarthy. 2012. "Girls Gone Wild? Heterosexual Women's Same-Sex Encounters at College Parties." *Psychology of Women Quarterly* 36 (1): 7–24.

15

Truth Regimes, the Charmed Circle, and Multi-Institutional Politics

A Theory of Sexualities and Social Change

MARY BERNSTEIN

The question that I was asked to address for this chapter is why studying liminal sexualities or sexualities at the margins shapes the field of sexualities and informs larger sociological questions. To answer these questions, we need to first ask what we mean by "liminal" and "margins." As a sociologist, the answer is easy. These terms are socially constructed and the boundaries shift. These terms are also context-specific, and context is related to culture, institutional configurations, and power.

Gayle Rubin (1984) was among the first to clearly articulate "marginalizing" or "liminalizing" sexualities through her concept of the "charmed circle." She presented a radical critique of the moral panics, essentialist thinking, and undue importance attributed to various sexualities as stand-ins for larger social cleavages, what she called "the fallacy of misplaced scale" (1984, 278). These moral crusades resulted in the exclusion and condemnation of some sexualities enforced through societal norms, laws, and policies. As sexualities gain acceptance, they enter what Rubin termed "the charmed circle," while others remain at the margins. Rubin proposed replacing a narrow-minded sexual morality that serves dominant groups with "[a] democratic morality [that] should judge sexual acts by the ways partners treat one another, the level of mutual consideration, the presence or absence of coercion, and the quantity and quality of the pleasures they provide" (283). In other words, Rubin wanted to alter the terms of admission to the charmed circle. I argue that, as sociologists, it is our task to analyze the process by which admission takes place, who is admitted, and under what conditions. We should consider whether everyone wants to be admitted or if some may gain pleasure from their outlaw status and if so in what ways. We should clearly and empirically analyze the ways in which struggles for social change affect groups across and within the margins. As a social movements and sexualities scholar, my interests have always centered on the nexus of understanding processes of social change and the role of social movements in facilitating change.

Foucault (1978) conceptualized truth regimes as sets of discourses that make certain configurations of sexualities and gender culturally intelligible and thus "normal" and others unintelligible, resulting in their marginalization. Both Rubin and Foucault want to understand which sexualities are considered normal, charmed, intelligible, and accepted in contrast to those that are condemned. However, Foucault theorized a way to understand power that could in part explain the processes of marginalization and exclusion. According to Foucault, the production of discourse is an exercise of power that produces understandings of what is "normal" and what is not. Thus, discourse is itself a source of power. One can never escape truth regimes (or the charmed circle), but as sociologists, we can examine and uncover the power that shapes these regimes, how they might be altered, the role of ordinary people, activists, the state, and various institutions in the processes of change.

In this chapter, I argue that a "multi-institutional politics" (MIP) approach to understanding social movements and social change (Armstrong and Bernstein 2008; Bernstein 2011; see Kane 2013, Steinman 2012 for examples of applications of the MIP model) provides the tools needed to understand these sociological processes of marginalization, activism, and social change. The MIP approach builds on the concept of truth regimes, viewing discourse as integral to the production, maintenance, and transformation of cultural norms. And, the MIP model views discourse as constitutive of social structures, institutions, and practices. Power and domination are organized around multiple sources of power that are simultaneously cultural and material. The importance of any given institution relative to other institutions varies across issues and over time and space. "Culture itself is constitutive of institutions, and social movements may target the state and various institutions to change culture; create new policies, benefits, and forms of inclusion (or exclusion); and alter the rules that structure particular institutions or fields" (Bernstein 2018, 3). By studying society as a set of institutions that are

constituted by culture, that are multiple, overlapping, and often contradictory, we can understand the shifting nature of domination. Sociologists can bring these conceptual tools to bear on the study of sexualities,
which will also advance the discipline as a whole. By excavating processes that explain the shifting boundaries of liminality and marginalization of various sexualities and gender identities, we can uncover the
more general processes and mechanisms in which power and discourse
are challenged and can be applied to understanding social change more
generally. In short, studying liminal sexualities and social movements
helps to answer broader sociological questions related to understanding
inequality and social change. In what follows, I begin with my personal
journey that intersects with profound institutional change and shifts in
heteronormative truth regimes. I then use the MIP model to elucidate
broader processes of social change.

"Do You Want to Get a Job or Study That?"

During my high school years (I graduated in 1981) when I was wrestling
with my sexual orientation, there were virtually no images of LGBTQ
people on television or in the movies. Sometime in high school, I happened to see a movie on television about a lesbian couple where one of
the women had a child from her past marriage to a man. The lesbian
lost custody of her daughter. I have a vague recollection of a gay-themed
episode of *Barney Miller*, but it certainly did not make me want to throw
open the proverbial closet doors. The internet did not exist. No one had
ever said the words "lesbian" or "gay" in my presence, let alone the words
bisexual or transgender. I was stranded in the suburbs of New York City
far away from gay meccas such as Greenwich Village, Provincetown, or
San Francisco, which, to be honest, I did not even know existed *as* gay
meccas. My mother used the term "queer" on occasion as a synonym
for "odd" or "peculiar." I had no idea that the word referenced an entire
group of people and would one day come to form the core of a theoretical perspective and politics. In short, I was isolated, lonely, and had
no idea that I had "people" or that "my people" might be somewhere
out there (so to speak). Although the Stonewall riots took place in 1969
and Anita Bryant had already waged her "Save Our Children Crusade"
against lesbian and gay people (Bernstein 2002), such political events

had not penetrated my adolescent, suburban, pre-internet life. Silence and erasure are themselves exercises in power (Sullivan 2001).

College was not much better. I attended Middlebury College, which provided an amazing education, but had almost nothing available for lesbian and gay people at the time. I became friends with some gay male students (yes, they were involved in theater) and discovered "Gay People at Middlebury" (GPM) a small group that turned out to be all men. I came out for the first time to a friend of mine, walking into his dorm room which was across the hallway from mine, bursting into tears, and stating, "We have more in common than you think." He looked at me appraisingly and said, "You don't mean you're Black, do you?" That made me smile through my tears and I felt better. At least I had a confidant. Then he advised me not to bother with GPM since, as I had already gleaned, it was all men.

But there were glimmers of hope. Somehow I discovered the publication *Lesbian Connection*, which assured privacy, and ordered it. The "magazine" arrived as series of photocopied papers, folded in half, with staples all around the perimeter, which probably took me half an hour to open and destroyed several fingernails in the process of prying the staples off. Then, as today, the word "lesbian" does not appear on the outside. *Lesbian Connection* probably saved my life or at least my sanity. There were people like me out there (however far away they might be) who were isolated and struggling, just as I was. But not only that, some were joyous and triumphant and political. In my undergraduate Sociology of Women course (what it was called back then), we read an excerpt from Mary Daly, who talked about lesbianism. After class, I made a beeline to the library to check out everything she had written. I was on to something. I wrote my term paper that semester, a response to the question (I paraphrase), "what would have to change in society to indicate that gender equality had been achieved?" My essay proclaimed (albeit perhaps naively) that the acceptance of lesbianism would mean that gender equity had been achieved. Women loving women, fully accepted, not needing men to protect them or support them financially or in any other way, would mean that women had achieved equality and the patriarchy was no more. And no, I had not yet read Adrienne Rich.

During my senior year at Middlebury, an esteemed history professor whom I had previously admired made homophobic, racist, and sexist remarks in the school newspaper. In brief, he stated that unlike Blacks or women who cannot change their race or sex, gay people have a choice. The insinuation that being gay or lesbian was a bad choice was clear. I couldn't let that go, so I wrote a letter to the school paper documenting my experiences of isolation at Middlebury and stating that being a lesbian was not a choice for me (I don't experience my being a lesbian as a choice, though I have great respect for those who do and today would have added that regardless of whether or not it is a "choice," lesbian and gay people deserve equal rights and respect) (see also Jakobsen and Pellegrini 2003). I pointed out that this professor's remarks implied that people of color and women would change their race or gender if they could, which I found offensive. I signed my letter to the editor, "Anonymous." Once published, my letter was the talk of the campus and, since I hadn't signed my name, people discussed it openly in front of me. Subsequently, my letter enabled me to come out to a few other friends that year, by telling them simply, "I'm Anonymous." Looking back, the racism, sexism, and homophobia that congealed in the professor's remarks comprised a set of interlocking discourses irrevocably linked to structural racism, sexism, and homophobia. These discourses reflect what Alexander (2004) termed meaning systems, which continue to exert power and shore up those structures of inequality that disadvantage a range of people including BIPOC, women, and queer people.

After college, I moved to New York City, and worked for a women's rights organization for one year where my colleagues included several out lesbians. I also discovered (what was then called) the Lesbian and Gay Community Center, which changed my life. I then taught high school math in New York City for two years. This was when you could be fired for being a lesbian teacher in New York City, so I only came out to a few select people at work, though by then, I was out in my private life. The furor over *Heather Has Two Mommies* was yet to erupt. In 1986, the US Supreme Court issued the *Bowers v. Hardwick* decision that found no constitutional right to what they termed homosexual sodomy and thus paved the way for ongoing legal discrimination against lesbians and gay men (Bernstein 2002, 2011). I went to DC the following year to protest the decision. The AIDS crisis was worsening and ACT UP had just formed (e.g., Gould 2009). If my adolescence was marked by discursive erasure and the psychic annihilation it produced, homophobia ensconced in institutional practices and discourses was quite literally killing people in the 1980s as Reagan refused to even say the word AIDS, let alone allocate funding for research and treatment.

Amidst the AIDS crisis and its backlash, in the wake of *Hardwick*, I started graduate school at New York University. NYU's graduate program in sociology was a mostly welcoming place. On my first day, I walked into the department, looked down the hall, and saw another graduate student whom I clearly identified as a lesbian. I practically ran down the hall and introduced myself and we have been friends ever since. Worlds away from high school and college. While the LGBTQ community was experiencing its most devastating crisis, political activism had never been stronger. It was the courage of activists and ordinary people who had suffered tremendously that began to shift both discourse and institutions. This is what I wanted to write about in graduate school.

Yet social change is always uneven and incomplete. When I went to form a committee, one professor whom I had previously respected, informed me that I could either write about the LGBTQ movement or I could choose another dissertation topic and get a job. I decided that there was a third option. I could form a dissertation committee without this person on it. And I am forever grateful to Edwin Amenta, David Greenberg, James Jasper, and the late Jo Dixon for their unwavering and unquestioning support of my research. My dissertation and job talk analyzed social movements, identity, and change in laws banning discrimination against LGBTQ people and in anti-sodomy statutes. But the biggest lesson I learned, which is the focus of this book, is to link the study of sexualities to broader questions within the discipline.

Lessons Learned and Debates Challenged by the Study of Liminal Sexualities

Perhaps my biggest pet peeve in debates over LGBTQ politics and social movements is the debate about whether same-sex marriage and the movement for marriage equality is assimilationist or transformationist (for my numerous critiques of how this debate is framed and my efforts to pose more complex questions that can be answered empirically, see Bernstein and Taylor 2013; Bernstein 2015, 2018; Bernstein, Naples and Harvey 2016; Bernstein, Harvey, and Naples 2018). I suggest that the assimilation/transformation debate is a theoretical dead end that fails to understand processes of social change because it lacks an adequate theory of power. A question such as, "Is the movement for same-sex marriage assimilationist?" that can be answered "yes" or "no" is probably not a productive research question, as any first-year graduate student in sociology should know. Assimilationist according to whom? Transforming what? Many would answer, "heteronormativity." But even a cursory look should suffice to show that the contours of heteronormativity as a truth regime, what is a part of the charmed circle, is shifting and varies according to context and over time. The more interesting questions are how, why, and with what consequences.

In order to answer the how/why/with-what-consequences questions, we need a theory of power and social change. By studying the LGBTQ movement for many years, Elizabeth Armstrong and I (2008) developed a multi-institutional politics (MIP) model of social movements and social change. By studying liminal movements, it became clear to us that the theoretical approaches that dominated the social movements literature—namely political process, political opportunity, and contentious politics theories—could not adequately account for the LGBTQ movement. Traditional social movement theory relied on a narrow neo-Marxist or materialist view of power as concentrated in the hands of political and economic elites and understood activism as targeting the state. Such perspectives ignored culture or relegated it to a secondary status. The MIP model, by contrast, argues that one cannot understand social change without understanding the ways in which power is dispersed across institutions and is simultaneously material and cultural.

Homophile activists from the 1950s and 1960s knew that it was not only the state that oppressed them, but the trifecta of psychology, religion, *and* the state (Bernstein 2002). Older models of social movements and social change could not explain protest aimed, for example, at the American Psychiatric Association designed to challenge the designation of homosexuality as a mental disorder. How could coming out be understood as political? How could strategies that would alienate lawmakers such as showing up to New York City hearings on antidiscrimination ordinances in full drag be understood (Bernstein 1997)? How could the erasure of LGBTQ experiences from the media be understood as an exercise in power and psychic violence? Such questions were incomprehensible from within existing frameworks. Drawing on insights from organizational theory, the sociology of culture, new social movement theory, Foucault, and political process theory, which was still useful for understanding the state, we argued that power is best understood as dispersed across a variety of institutions that are simultaneously cultural and material. Rather than understanding culture as epiphenomenal or secondary to the "real" politics of the state, we argued that the significance of the state was an empirical question, not a given, and that other institutions exercised power as well that could not be understood apart from culture. We suggested cultural norms, values, and discourses constituted forms of power that are embedded in institutional logics. Institutional power could include claims to what is normal and what is not, as Foucault (1978) so eloquently theorized. Furthermore, social movements could use the logic of certain institutions to foster change in other institutions.

The MIP model can help to explain activism directed at institutions such as psychiatry. For example, as LGBTQ activists in the 1960s and early 1970s well knew, the state relied on the APA diagnosis of homosexuality as a mental disorder. Activists marshaled the logic of science to ultimately shift political logics. Activists demanded that psychiatrists conduct controlled studies of non-institutionalized populations of straight and gay people (rather than relying on homophobic assumptions about gay people) which found the groups indistinguishable from each other in blinded controlled studies. This, along with protest designed to pressure the APA to move beyond stereotypes, challenged the cultural logic and categories of an institution with great power to regulate and discipline LGBTQ people. As a result, the APA eliminated its diagnosis of homosexuality as a mental disorder in 1973, curing tens of thousands of people with the stroke of a pen, and giving activists a strong tool they could bring to bear on the state when demanding changes in laws and policies. However, the APA diagnosed trans people with gender dysphoria, and they are now undergoing a similar struggle, as are people who are intersexed (Spade 2006; Davis 2015). For example, Meadow (2018) notes that in 2013, the APA changed the diagnostic criteria for gender dysphoria to include only those experiencing "'clinically significant distress'" (3–4).

LGBTQ activists became expert at leveraging the logic of some institutions to produce change in others by exploiting contradictions across those institutions. For example, co-parent adoption is a process that allows a parent to become a second parent to a child who is the biological and/or legal dependent of the partner. Although "best interest of the child" standards facilitated these cases (Richman 2008), part of what constituted "best interest" was based on a neoliberal capitalist logic. This logic is apparent in arguments stating that should something happen to the original legal parent, the child could not only have continued care needed for the child's psychological and emotional development, but that parent would be financially obligated to take care of the child. These arguments emphasized privatized care and the child not becoming a ward of the state as justifications for co-parent adoption. To be sure, neoliberalism was not the only logic at force here. Academics had produced volumes of research documenting that same-sex parents did not damage their children and in fact might even benefit them (Stacey and Biblarz 2001; Cheng and Powell 2015). The LGBTQ movement, both activists and ordinary LGBTQ people living their lives, had changed social norms. Together, these forces created co-parent adoption and eventually helped to achieve same-sex marriage. We have moved far beyond the 1995 Florida court case, *Ward v. Ward*, where a lesbian lost custody of her child to her ex-husband who had been convicted of murdering his first wife. Denying that it was about homophobia, the judge said, "I believe that this child should be given the opportunity to live in a non-lesbian world" (Gabrielle 2012). What a sad world that would be. This is not by any means to say that families headed by same-sex couples are now secure from legal and social threats.

Lawyers who specialize in protecting LGBTQ families advise same-sex couples who marry to pursue co-parent adoption as an extra safety precaution should the right of same-sex couples to marry disappear (Baumle and Compton 2015). The case *Obergefell v. Hodges* that allowed same-sex marriage in the states that had not yet legalized it, followed a line of precedent rooted in a constitutional right to privacy, due process, and equal protection, and the case that legalized abortion, *Roe v. Wade*, was critical in that line of jurisprudence. The overturning of *Roe* in *Dobbs v. Jackson Women's Health Organization* in 2022 placed same-sex marriage at risk. Justice Clarence Thomas, in his concurring opinion in *Dobbs*, called for the Court to reconsider its decisions on access to contraception, same-sex sexual relations, and same-sex marriage. In response to the perceived threat to same-sex marriage, the US Congress in 2022 passed the *Respect for Marriage Act (RFMA)* which, should *Obergefell* be overturned, mandates that both interracial marriage and same-sex marriage are protected by statute and recognized by the federal government. While the RFMA does not mandate that every state license same-sex marriages, it would require states to recognize same-sex marriages that were valid where they were issued. So a same-sex couple might have to travel to a different state to marry, but their home state would be required to recognize their marriage (Stern 2022). This example demonstrates the impact of massive shifts in public opinion in favor of same-sex marriage in the US since 1996 when Congress overwhelmingly passed the so-called Defense of Marriage Act, barring states from having to recognize same-sex marriages performed in other states and banning federal recognition of such marriages.

The media landscape has shifted almost completely from when I was growing up. While I never saw any positive images of LGBTQ people in movies or on television when I was a child, today such images abound (see Walters 2001 and 2014 for a summary and critique of how these images have changed over time). Of course, these images do not completely represent the range of LGBTQ people in term of race, ethnicity, gender identity, geographic location (e.g., Crawley, this collection) and so on, as Walters so aptly demonstrates, and many representations are problematic. But the difference from when I was growing up is undeniable. As was the case with co-parent adoption, these changes in media representation were motivated by the hard work of activists demanding change, dating back to early gay liberation activists and LGBTQ media groups such as the Gay and Lesbian Alliance Against Defamation (GLAAD) that organized, protested, and worked to challenge negative and harmful media images of LGBTQ people while promoting more positive images.

Here again, activists latched onto the logic of capitalism to make change. LGBTQ people had to change social norms and discourse—that is, they had to reshape dominant truth regimes—in order to make the production of positive images financially viable. These shifts in truth regimes that facilitate the production of better images of LGBTQ lives in turn reshape cultural norms about LGBTQ people as they demand entry into the charmed circle. So those kids who are living in the more conservative pockets of the US can still watch *Modern Family*, *The Fosters*,

Laverne Cox as Sophia in *Orange is the New Black*, and *Pose* and perhaps not feel so alone. Not only that; these images spark conversations that can be transforming. For several years I have taught a summer class for high school students. My students tell me that images of Caitlin Jenner and Laverne Cox have enabled them to have conversations with their parents *and their grandparents* about gender identity. I'm not endorsing either Jenner or Cox as role models and am sympathetic to the many critiques of Jenner in particular, but I want to stress that this is one important way that change happens. One could make a similar argument about how the right of same-sex couples to marry throughout the US helps to facilitate cultural change, however bumpy, uneven, and filled with backlash it may be (e.g., Stone 2012), which brings me to my next point.

Change is uneven, incomplete, and nearly always threatened. Recently, my kids and I watched an old episode of *Glee*, where a gay football player attempts suicide. The episode was sad and moving, a good reminder that the struggle continues and that there are disproportionately high rates of suicide among LGBTQ youth and that a disproportionately high percentage of homeless youth are LGBTQ, runaways and throwaways from disapproving families. The most marginalized from within LGBTQ communities face discrimination on multiple levels. Transgender people are particularly vulnerable with so-called bathroom bills that require people to use the bathrooms that match the gender they were assigned at birth, as well as everyday violence, especially against trans people of color. As I put the finishing touches on this chapter, the governor of Texas issued an executive order declaring that gender-affirming care for minors constitutes child abuse and directed social service agencies to commence investigations. After several investigations had started, a Texas state court issued an injunction halting those inquiries, at least for now (Goodman 2022). Families in Texas are terrified and their trans children are traumatized. Many states have now passed bans on the provision of gender-affirming care, and several have been blocked by the courts. This battle is far from over. Recently, Florida passed what opponents call a "don't say gay" bill that bans the discussion of sexual orientation and gender identity in Florida's primary schools. *Heather Has Two Mommies* redux.

This is where understanding the relationship between institutional and cultural change as in the MIP approach is so critical. Membership in the charmed circle is always threatened and, as we learn from Gayle Rubin (1984), current controversies are stand-ins for greater cleavages and attempts by a minority to retain their power by seizing on issues related to sexual orientation and gender identity. Whose interests are served and who is harmed by these attempts to extinguish the existence of LGBTQ people? I believe that we have reached a point where we cannot *pretend the gay (or trans) away*. The cultural and institutional changes with regard to LGBTQ people are too profound and too ensconced in other institutions. Trans people are not there yet; however, my hope is that with increased visibility and changes in institutions, including psychiatry, child welfare, the media, that cultural opprobrium will be launched not at LGBTQ people but at the homophobic and transphobic proposals. Professional medical groups and health experts have spoken out against halting gender-affirming care for transgender teenagers (Goodman and Morris 2022) and young people have launched protests against the onslaught of anti-LGBTQ bills. The opposition to these bills by various institutions and youth protest speaks to the importance of shifts in cultural meaning systems. Regardless of whether legislation such as the Florida and Texas bills and policies stem from homophobia or transphobia or they are merely the product of cold political calculations designed to foster fear and maintain power on the part of Republicans (e.g., Goodman and Morris 2022), we see a battle between cultural meaning systems rooted in various institutions and in the material power of the state. Which logic will prevail remains to be seen; however, the power of cultural changes regarding sexual orientation and gender identity is profound and LGBTQ people are not alone; they have allies in powerful institutions and in changes in public opinion (e.g., Powell et al. 2012).

But make no mistake about it. These proposals and policies are harming real people right now. Several chapters in this book note the relatively clandestine organizing that takes place in many "red" states and the open hostility to LGBTQ people expressed in recent anti-LGBTQ measures will place LGBTQ people at even greater risk of harm. And it touches all of us whose admission into the charmed circle is provisional at best as the criteria expands and shrinks. My teenage daughter told me about her rage at the Florida bill as she imagined not being able to talk about her family of two moms when she was in elementary school.

She also expressed fear for her best friend who is transgender. LGBTQ people must always remain vigilant and never be complacent.

Conclusion

A multi-institutional power approach to social change helps us to understand the ways in which change is uneven and incomplete. Power is simultaneously cultural and material, ensconced in our social norms, values, discourses, ideologies, interactional routines, as well as material, rooted in institutions and institutional practices. Power produces a matrix of domination (Collins 1990) that can only be understood intersectionally. Whereas white, middle-class, cis gay men may be "normal" *but for* being gay, queer people of color must contend with discourse that may condemn them not only for being gay, lesbian, bisexual, or trans but also based on racialized controlling images as well (Collins 1990). As Schilt (2010, 67) quotes and describes the experiences of a Black transgender man: "'As a man, if I get mad, it is like, 'Oh no, crazy black man in there!' He felt that he had no choice but to adopt a strong, silent persona—worlds away from his self-described 'loud black woman' behavior—to protect himself." This example illustrates how discourse and stereotypes about Black male criminality are part of background structures of cultural meaning (Braunstein 2015; Bernstein, McMillan, and Charash 2019) that shape the experiences of Black transgender men in ways that their white transgender counterparts do not have to contend with.

To understand the process by which the place of LGBTQ people in society changes over time, we need a robust understanding of power. Cultural meaning systems, institutions, and political power reinforce, produce, and perpetuate inequality. State policies may protect LGBTQ people or place them in emotional, financial, and physical jeopardy, or protect some segments of LGBTQ communities more than or at the expense of others (Misra and Bernstein 2019). By understanding the ways in which power is cultural, anchored in meaning systems or truth regimes, and material, embedded in institutions and institutional logics that are multiple and contradictory, a multi-institutional politics approach can make sense of how and why access to the charmed circle shifts over time and across place.

ACKNOWLEDGMENT
I would like to thank Kathleen Ragon, Jordan McMillan, and Davida Schiffer for comments on earlier drafts of this paper.

REFERENCES

Alexander, Jeffrey C. 2004. "Cultural Pragmatics: Social Performance between Ritual and Strategy." *Sociological Theory* 22 (4): 527–73.

Armstrong, Elizabeth A. and Mary Bernstein. 2008. "Culture, Power, and Institutions: A Multi-Institutional Politics Approach to Social Movements." *Sociological Theory* 26 (1):74–99.

Baumle, Amanda K. and D'Lane R. Compton. 2015. *Legalizing LGBT Families: How the Law Shapes Parenthood.* New York: New York University Press.

Bernstein, Mary. 1997. "Celebration and Suppression: The Strategic Uses of Identity by the Lesbian and Gay Movement." *American Journal of Sociology* 103 (3): 531–65.

Bernstein, Mary. 2002. "Identities and Politics: Toward a Historical Understanding of the Lesbian and Gay Movement." *Social Science History* 26 (3): 531–81.

Bernstein, Mary. 2011. "United States: Multi-Institutional Politics, Social Movements and the State." In *The Lesbian and Gay Movement and the State: Comparative Insights into a Transformed Relationship*, edited by Manon Tremblay, David Paternotte, and Carol Johnson, 197–211. Surrey, England: Ashgate Publishing Ltd.

Bernstein, Mary. 2015. "Same-Sex Marriage and the Future of the LGBT Movement." *Gender & Society* 29 (3): 321–37.

Bernstein, Mary. 2018. "Same-Sex Marriage and the Assimilationist Dilemma: A Research Agenda on Marriage Equality and the Future of LGBTQ Activism, Politics, Communities, and Identities." *Journal of Homosexuality* 65 (14): 1941–1956.

Bernstein, Mary, Jordan McMillan, and Elizabeth Charash. 2019. "Once in Parkland, a Year in Hartford, a Weekend in Chicago: Race and Resistance in the Gun Violence Prevention Movement." *Sociological Forum* 34 (1): 1153–173.

Bernstein, Mary, Nancy A. Naples, and Brenna Harvey. 2016. "The Meaning of Marriage to Same-Sex Families: Formal Partnership, Gender, and the Welfare State in International Perspective." *Social Politics* 23 (1): 3–39.

Bernstein, Mary, Brenna Harvey, and Nancy A. Naples. 2018. "The Final Frontier? Same-Sex Marriage and the Future of the LGBT Movement." *Sociological Forum* 33 (1): 30–52.

Bernstein, Mary and Verta Taylor, eds. 2013. *The Marrying Kind: Debating Same-Sex Marriage within the Lesbian and Gay Movement.* Minneapolis: University of Minnesota Press.

Braunstein, Ruth. 2015. "The Tea Party Goes to Washington: Mass Demonstrations as Performative and Interactional Processes." *Qualitative Sociology* 38: 353–74.

Cheng, Simon and Brian Powell. 2015. "Measurement, Methods, and Divergent Patterns: Reassessing the Effects of Same-Sex Parents." *Social Science Research* 52: 615–26.

Collins, Patricia Hill. 1990. *Black Feminist Thought: Knowledge, Consciousness, and the Politics of Empowerment*. New York: Routledge.

Davis, Georgiann. 2015. *Contesting Intersex: The Dubious Diagnosis*. New York: New York University Press.

Foucault, Michel. 1978. *The History of Sexuality: An Introduction* (volume I). New York: Vintage Books.

Gabrielle. 2012. "Watch and Walk Away Angry: Ward v. Ward, A Documentary on Lesbian's Custody Battle." www.autostraddle.com.

Goodman, J. David. 2022. "Texas Court Halts Abuse Inquiries into Parents of Transgender Children." *New York Times*, March 11. www.nytimes.com.

Goodman, J. David and Amanda Morris. 2022. "Texas Investigates Parents Over Care for Transgender Youth, Suit Says." *New York Times*, March 1. www.nytimes.com.

Gould, Deborah B. 2009. *Moving Politics: Emotion and ACT UP's Fight against AIDS*. Chicago: University of Chicago Press.

Jakobsen, Janet R. and Ann Pellegrini. 2003. *Love the Sin: Sexual Regulation and the Limits of Religious Tolerance*. New York: New York University Press.

Kane, Melinda D. 2013. "LGBT Religious Activism: Predicting State Variations in the Number of Metropolitan Community Churches, 1974–2000." *Sociological Forum* 28 (1): 135–58.

Lavietes, Matt. 2022. "Florida Students Stage School Walkouts over 'Don't Say Gay' Bill." NBC News, March 3. www.nbcnews.com.

Meadow, Tey. 2018. *Trans Kids: Being Gendered in the Twenty-First Century*. Oakland: University of California Press.

Misra, Joya and Mary Bernstein. 2019. "Sexuality, Gender, & Social Policy." In *The New Handbook of Political Sociology*, edited by Thomas Janoski, Cedric de Leon, Joya Misra, and Isaac William Martin, 1375–444. Cambridge: Cambridge University Press.

Powell, Brian, Catherine Bolzendahl, Claudia Geist, and Lala Carr Steelman. 2012. *Counted Out: Same-Sex Relations and Americans' Definitions of Family*. New York: Russell Sage Foundation.

Richman, Kimberly D. 2008. *Courting Change: Queer Parents, Judges, and the Transformation of American Family Law*. New York: New York University Press.

Rubin, Gayle. 1984. "Thinking Sex: Notes for a Radical Theory of the Politics of Sexuality." In *Pleasure and Danger: Exploring Female Sexuality*, edited by Carol Vance, 267–319. London: Pandora Press.

Schilt, Kristen. 2010. *Just One of the Guys? Transgender Men and the Persistence of Gender Inequality*. Chicago: University of Chicago Press.

Spade, Dean. 2006. "Mutilating Gender." In *The Transgender Studies Reader*, edited by Susan Stryker and Stephen Whittle, 435–41. New York: Routledge.

Stacey, Judith and Timothy J. Biblarz. 2001. "(How) Does the Sexual Orientation of Parents Matter?" *American Sociological Review* 66 (2): 159–83.

Steinman, Erich. 2012. "Settler Colonial Power and the American Indian Sovereignty Movement: Forms of Domination, Strategies of Transformation." *American Journal of Sociology* 117 (4): 1073–1130.

Stern, Mark Joseph. 2022. "Progressive Critics Are Wrong about the Senate's Landmark Marriage Equality Bill." *Slate.* November 15. https://slate.com.

Stone, Amy. 2012. *Gay Rights at the Ballot Box.* Minneapolis: University of Minnesota Press.

Sullivan, Maureen. 2001. "Alma Mater: Family 'Outings' and the Making of the Modern Other Mother (MOM)." In *Queer Families, Queer Politics: Challenging Culture and the State,* edited by Mary Bernstein and Renate Reimann, 231–53. New York: Columbia University Press.

Walters, Suzanna Danuta. 2001. *All the Rage: The Story of Gay Visibility in America.* Chicago: University of Chicago Press.

Walters, Suzanna Danuta. 2014. *The Tolerance Trap: How God, Genes, and Good Intentions are Sabotaging Gay Equality.* New York: New York University Press.

ACKNOWLEDGMENTS

The initial idea of *Outskirts* began as a bumper sticker that read, "queers and steers, only in Texas." Compton thinks it was a University of Oklahoma (football) battle cry against that school in Austin. There were other variations, such as, "steers and queers, only in Austin" and so forth, that they saw all throughout their childhood in Texas. Compton was so literal and earnest, they never read it as a negative—more as a demographic fact. These stickers existed through the 2000s and during grad school while they were doing their demographic work, and they just couldn't let go of the idea of reclaiming them. They imagined a book that celebrated how queer Texas was. One that countered stereotypes and drew on empiricism. They imagined a book cover of the back of their truck with the sticker on it, along with some other queer/gay pride stickers. Their heart broke a little when they saw Mary Gray's book come out their first year in a tenure-track position. At the same time, they were also stoked to learn of this work and similar perceptions of queer life. Over time, however, this notion later transformed—beyond Texas and beyond demography.

First and foremost, Compton would like to thank to all those who collaborated and contributed to this project. In particular, special thanks to the support of Vern Baxter and Susan Mann for seeing the potential and encouraging me to go after this project dream circa 2009. Especially Susan Mann, who continually inquired about how this work was coming along. Clearly, I was shy about it in many ways—maybe because it meant so much to me. It is during this time that Compton met Amy Stone and discovered their shared passion on the topic of vibrant queer life beyond the big queer cities. Compton is most thankful they undertook this project with me. It is with them this project became a reality and its focus and framing was solidified. Further, special thanks to Lisa Wade for walking and talking through so many big ideas with Compton and to S. L. Crawley for always being willing to read our work. Compton would also like to thank Lauren Berlant for insights on post-tenure life and producing the work that was important to them.

For Stone, the origins of this book came from conversations that happened all over the South—from their back porch in Austin during the pandemic to coffee breaks at conferences to a Mardi Gras ball on New Year's Eve in Mobile, Alabama. Stone would like to thank Compton, who year after year insisted that it was time to put this together. Their persistence is admirable. However, our timing was not impeccable, as the editing of this collection stretched through a global pandemic, along with multiple breakups, health tribulations, moves, and promotions.

Both Compton and Stone are appreciative of Ilene Kalish, who expressed enthusiasm in this project from the start. And Compton is most grateful for your patience and kid gloves in dealing with their concerns for cover art—always. Further, this book would not have come together without the supportive network of sexualities colleagues far and wide. Yes, the Sexualities reception at the American Sociological Association annual meeting will always be Stone's favorite part of the conference. And Stone has always been moved by the way our section respects differences in institutions, mentors junior scholars, and embraces queer culture. They would not be who they are as a scholar without you all.

This is the first book Stone has written with children, and they can't imagine life without their two teens—Maggie and Sierra—along with their bonus teens of Emily, Sophia, AB, Ben, Hailey, and Selena and babies of Stella, Josiah, and Zeke. Who knew life would involve so many hot chips, car rides, and trips to Target! Here's to many years of seeing you all grow up into the best and brightest version of yourselves. Shout out to Stone's queer single parent-ish network, including Holly, Carol, Dee, Colleen, Niki, Hex, Mack, and Lee. Firefly and Grin warm their heart, which makes their brain work on the daily. And most of all, this book would not have been completed without the canine support of Cleo, Penny, and Lady.

ABOUT THE CONTRIBUTORS

MIRIAM J. ABELSON is Associate Professor of Women, Gender, and Sexuality Studies at Portland State University. Her research focuses on race, sexuality, and gender in rural and urban spaces, masculinities, and queer and transgender studies. Her ongoing projects examine how LGBTQ and other marginalized peoples inhabit and move through rural and urban landscapes. She is the author of *Men in Place: Trans Masculinity, Race, and Sexuality in America*.

MARY BERNSTEIN is Professor of Sociology and Associate Dean of The Graduate School at the University of Connecticut. Her research encompasses a wide range of issues concerning social movements, race, politics, gender, and law with a particular focus on LGBTQ social movements and on gun violence prevention. She is the author of over fifty articles and book chapters and co-editor of three books: *Queer Families, Queer Politics*; *Queer Mobilizations: LGBT Activists Confront the Law*; and *The Marrying Kind? Debating Same-Sex Marriage Within the Lesbian and Gay Movement*. Her publications appear in a wide variety of disciplinary outlets that include the humanities, social sciences, sociology, sexualities, women's studies, political science, law, history, health, and public policy. She has received several national awards for her work, most notably the Simon & Gagnon Lifetime Achievement Award from the American Sociological Association's Section on Sexuality (2016) and the Outstanding Article Award from the *American Sociological Association Section on Collective Behavior and Social Movements*. She is winner of the 2022 Provost's Distinguished Scholar Research Award for Excellence in Community Engaged Scholarship at UConn. She is currently president of the *Society for the Study of Social Problems* (SSSP) and past president of *Sociologists for Women in Society*.

MEGAN CARROLL is Assistant Professor of Sociology at California State University, San Bernardino, specializing in gender, family, sexualities, and social movements. Her research on gay fatherhood has been published in the *Journal of Family Issues* and *Family Relations*. Her latest research is a mixed-methods, community-engaged study of asexualities.

S. L. CRAWLEY is Associate Professor of Sociology and affiliated faculty in Women's and Gender Studies at the University of South Florida. Crawley has published in such journals as *Sociological Theory*, *Symbolic Interaction*, *Gender and Society*, *Sexualities*, *Journal of Lesbian Studies*, *The American Sociologist*, *Journal of Contemporary Ethnography*, *The Sociological Quarterly*, and *Hypatia*, and co-authored the book *Gendering Bodies*. Crawley's current interests involve comparative epistemological approaches within social science, American pragmatism, and feminist and queer interventions to traditional methods. Some of Crawley's work has been translated into Russian and Ukrainian.

TEHQUIN D. FORBES is an administrative faculty member of the University of Florida Honors Program. At UF, he takes point on the recruitment of new students to the honors program as well as honors alumni relations. He also teaches professional development and enrichment courses and advises honors students and student organizations. His research has focused on heterosexism and racism in intimate relationships, social movements, and higher education, and his published work has appeared in outlets such as *Social Problems*, *Journal of LGBT Youth*, and *The Journal of Sex Research*. Connect with Dr. Forbes on Twitter @Soc_Forbes.

SPENCER GARRISON is a recent PhD graduate in Sociology from the University of Michigan.

CAYDEN GOLDSTEIN-KRAL is a PhD candidate and Urban Ethnography Lab Fellow in the Sociology Department at the University of Texas at Austin. Their research interests focus on the sociology of gender, sexuality, and intimate relationships. Their dissertation, "Power within Polyamory: Women's Experiences of Decision-making, Labor, and Violence in Polyamorous Relationships," examines the relationship between institutionalized monogamy and gendered and racialized inequalities.

LAIN A. B. MATHERS is Assistant Professor of Sociology and Affiliated Faculty in Gender Studies in the Department of Multidisciplinary Studies at Indiana State University. Zir work focuses on gender, sexualities, and religion, with a focus on bi+ and transgender experiences. They are the co-author of the book *America through Transgender Eyes*, along with J. E. Sumerau.

GREGGOR MATTSON is Professor and Chair of Sociology and Gender, Sexuality, and Feminist Studies at Oberlin College and Conservatory, where he is also the Mellon Mays Undergraduate Fellowship Faculty Coordinator. He is the author of *Who Needs Gay Bars? Bar-Hopping through America's Endangered LGBTQ+ Places* and *The Cultural Politics of European Prostitution Reform: Governing Loose Women*. His work can be found at http://greggormattson.com or @greggormattson.

KENDALL OTA is a PhD candidate in the Department of Sociology at the University of California, Santa Barbara, whose research interests lie at the intersection of sexuality, space, and race. His work is primarily concerned with how same-sex seeking men make decisions regarding their sexual behavior.

JAMIE O'QUINN is Assistant Professor in the Department of Sociology at California State University, San Bernardino. Her research examines how sexual inequalities are reproduced through social institutions. Her current project investigates US child marriage (marriage including individuals under eighteen years old), tracing the social processes that facilitate child marriage and centering the voices of women who were married as minors.

JANELLE M. PHAM is Assistant Professor of Sociology at Oglethorpe University in Atlanta. Her research examines how organizational history and change informs the development of sexual cultures, with a current focus on the gender integration of the United States military's combat arms. Her published work has appeared in *Sociological Forum*,

The Journal of Sex Research, The Sociological Quarterly, and *Journal of Lesbian Studies.*

ANTONIA RANDOLPH is Assistant Professor of American Studies at University of North Carolina-Chapel Hill. Her interests include diversity discourse in education, affect theory, Black feminist thought, non-normative Black masculinity and sexuality, and the production of misogyny in hip-hop culture. Her book *The Wrong Kind of Different: Challenging the Meaning of Diversity in American Classrooms* examined the hierarchies elementary school teachers constructed among students of color. She has also published in *QED, Journal of African American Studies, Journal of Popular Music Studies, Sociology of Race and Ethnicity, Journal of Contemporary Ethnography,* and *The Feminist Wire.* Her current book project, *That's My Heart: Queering Intimacy in Hip-Hop Culture,* which is forthcoming from University of California Press, examines portrayals of Black men's intimate relationships in hip-hop culture.

BRANDON ANDREW ROBINSON is Chair and Associate Professor of Gender and Sexuality Studies at the University of California, Riverside. They arc the author of *Coming Out to the Streets: LGBTQ Youth Experiencing Homelessness* and the co-author of *Race and Sexuality.*

J. E. SUMERAU (she/they) is a writer and scholar focused on the intersection of sexualities, gender, health, violence, and religion in social life. They are the author of seven novels and five nonfiction research monographs, including the 2021 George Garrett Prize in Fiction winner *Transmission* and an exploration of masculinities entitled *Violent Manhood.* She is also the Director of Applied Sociology at the University of Tampa, and the author of over 100 short fictional and nonfictional works published in varied literary, medical, and social scientific journals and edited volumes. For more information, please visit www.jsumerau.com.

LISA WADE is Associate Professor at Tulane University with appointments in Sociology, the Gender and Sexuality Studies Program, and the Newcomb Institute. She is the author of *American Hookup: The New*

Culture of Sex on Campus; an introduction to sociology titled *Terrible Magnificent Sociology*; a sociology of gender textbook, *Gender: Ideas, Interactions, Institutions*, with Myra Marx Ferree; and numerous other research publications. Her newest project documents undergraduate social life during the pre-vaccine pandemic. As a public-facing scholar, Lisa works to make her and others' scholarship engaging to a public audience. You can find her online at lisa-wade.com.

TERRELL J. A. WINDER is Assistant Professor of Sociology at the University of California, Santa Barbara. His research interests are racial and sexual stigma, sexual health, and identity development. In previous projects, he has assessed the role of mobile technology for the prevention and treatment of HIV, the impact of community organizations in religious and racial identity development, and the barriers to PrEP use among Black men who have sex with men. Winder's current book project investigates the impacts that chosen family, community organizations, and visual media have on the gender expression, racial identification, sexual identity, and life trajectories of young Black gay men.

ABOUT THE EDITORS

D'LANE R. COMPTON is a Full Professor of Sociology at the University of New Orleans. Their two major research interests are social psychology and the demography of sexual orientation and gender identity. Their research uses both approaches to examine sexual, gender, and family inequalities. They are the co-author of *Same-Sex Partners: The Social Demography of Sexual Orientation* and *Legalizing LGBT Parents: How the Law Shapes Parenthood*, and co-editor of *Other, Please Specify: Queer Methods in Sociology*.

AMY L. STONE (they/them) is Professor of Sociology and Anthropology at Trinity University. They study LGBTQ life in the United States with a focus on the urban South and Southwest. They are the author of *Queer Carnival, Gay Rights at the Ballot Box*, and *Cornyation: San Antonio's Outrageous Fiesta Tradition*, and co-editor of *Out of the Closet, Into the Archives*. They are co-director of the community-based research project Strengthening Colors of Pride and a longitudinal study of LGBTQ youth and housing instability, Family Housing and Me.

INDEX